ActionScript 3.0 Design Patterns

Other resources from O'Reilly

Related titles   Essential ActionScript 3.0   Learning JavaScript
                      Dynamic HTML: The   Programming Atlas
                        Definitive Reference   Head Rush Ajax
                      Ajax on Java   Rails Cookbook
                      Ajax on Rails

oreilly.com   *oreilly.com* is more than a complete catalog of O'Reilly books. You'll also find links to news, events, articles, weblogs, sample chapters, and code examples.

oreillynet.com is the essential portal for developers interested in open and emerging technologies, including new platforms, programming languages, and operating systems.

Conferences   O'Reilly brings diverse innovators together to nurture the ideas that spark revolutionary industries. We specialize in documenting the latest tools and systems, translating the innovator's knowledge into useful skills for those in the trenches. Visit *conferences.oreilly.com* for our upcoming events.

Safari Bookshelf (*safari.oreilly.com*) is the premier online reference library for programmers and IT professionals. Conduct searches across more than 1,000 books. Subscribers can zero in on answers to time-critical questions in a matter of seconds. Read the books on your Bookshelf from cover to cover or simply flip to the page you need. Try it today for free.

ActionScript 3.0 Design Patterns

William B. Sanders and
Chandima Cumaranatunge

O'REILLY®

Beijing · Cambridge · Farnham · Köln · Paris · Sebastopol · Taipei · Tokyo

ActionScript 3.0 Design Patterns
by William B. Sanders and Chandima Cumaranatunge

Published by O'Reilly Media, Inc., 1005 Gravenstein Highway North, Sebastopol, CA 95472.

O'Reilly books may be purchased for educational, business, or sales promotional use. Online editions are also available for most titles (*safari.oreilly.com*). For more information, contact our corporate/institutional sales department: (800) 998-9938 or *corporate@oreilly.com*.

Editor: Steve Weiss
Developmental Editor: Robyn G. Thomas
Production Editor: Philip Dangler
Copyeditor: Sohaila Abdulali

Indexer: John Bickelhaupt
Cover Designer: Karen Montgomery
Interior Designer: David Futato
Illustrators: Robert Romano and Jessamyn Read

Printing History:

July 2007:   First Edition.

 This book uses RepKover™, a durable and flexible lay-flat binding.

ISBN-10: 0-596-52846-9
ISBN-13: 978-0-59652846-1
[M]

Bill would like to dedicate this to the new kids on the block, Ricky and Olivia.

Chandima would like to dedicate this book to his parents, Gaya and Lakshmie.

Table of Contents

Part III. Structural Patterns

Part V.   Multiple Patterns

Preface

As ActionScript has evolved from a few statements in Flash to a full-fledged Internet programming language in the latest release of Flash and Flex, we have the ability to implement sophisticated designs developed for languages using object-oriented programming (OOP). ActionScript 3.0 heralds a new era in Flash and Flex programming because it implements the ECMAScript standard for Internet languages. Many features found in languages such as C++ and Java™ are now available in Action-Script 3.0.

Along with more sophisticated features in ActionScript 3.0 come more sophisticated ways of programming and *thinking* about programming. Most readers of this book will be familiar with OOP to some degree, and like the step from sequential or procedural programming to OOP, the step to design pattern programming is a step up for OOP programmers. We felt that because ActionScript 3.0 had arrived at a point where more complex and challenging programming structures can be developed, Flash and Flex programmers needed to understand programming techniques to cope with these structures.

By understanding design pattern programming, you will be able to write better OOP code, and reuse that code in other programs. The better paying positions in the programming field favor those developers who can work with team development, and the sophisticated structures that design patterns and OOP were developed to handle. At the same time that you gain proficiency in programming more complex applications, design patterns actually make programming easier. In large and complex applications, programmers have the most difficulty with poor planning and awkward design structures. Design patterns not only provide solutions for common challenges, but also focus on maintenance and change. The vocabulary of design patterns is equally important because with it, you can become part of the developer community that communicates clearly in the language of design patterns.

Who This Book Is For

We wanted to develop a book for intermediate to advanced ActionScript 3.0 users. Unlike some languages, such as Java, where the readers are likely to have computer science or computer engineering degrees, most ActionScript 3.0 users are likely to have learned ActionScript in developmental stages using Flash. As a result, their backgrounds are far more varied, and the programming base less definite. We're sure that a number of ActionScript programmers have computer science or related backgrounds, and much of the introductory materials in the first chapter will be redundant. Likewise, we're certain that some readers on the lower end of the intermediate level are learning object-oriented programming at the same time that they're trying to pick up design patterns; they may have little or no formal training in programming.

Given the range of ActionScript programming backgrounds, we're bound to be too difficult for some and too simplistic for others. However, this book's overall goal is to explain how to use different design patterns. We targeted whom we considered intermediate level ActionScript developers. We've provided everything the intermediate level developer will need to move to the advanced level. For the advanced user, we provide explanations and examples of how to use design patterns with ActionScript 3.0.

How This Book Is Organized

The book's organization reflects the topic organization found in *Design Patterns Elements of Reusable Object-Oriented Software* by Erich Gamma, Richard Helm, Ralph Johnson, and John Vlissides (Addison-Wesley, 1995).

The first part contains Chapter 1, which is an introduction to design patterns. We added an introductory section for readers with minimal object-oriented programming experience. More advanced users may want to skip the review of OOP, but go over the materials on design patterns.

Part I, *Constant Change*

    Chapter 1, *Object-Oriented Programming, Design Patterns, and ActionScript 3.0*

Parts II, III and, IV are the three major parts of the book. They examine fundamental design patterns, and organize the patterns into *creational*, *structural* and *behavioral* categories. Representative design patterns are included in each part, but we didn't include every single design pattern from the book by Gamma and his associates.

Part II, *Creational Patterns*

    Chapter 2, *Factory Method Pattern*

    Chapter 3, *Singleton Pattern*

Part III, *Structural Patterns*

Part IV, *Behavioral Patterns*

Part V contains two chapters on using multiple design patterns in application development. The Model-View-Controller and Symmetric Proxy designs incorporate more than a single design pattern. They're organized like the other chapters on design patterns as far as explaining how the multiple patterns work. However, the multiple designs rely more on object diagrams than class diagrams.

Part V, *Multiple Patterns*

Each chapter on design patterns is organized to optimize and clarify understanding the purpose of a design pattern and how to use it. The following sections, although not necessarily in this order, can be found in each of the chapters on design patterns:

- What is the pattern?
- Key features of the pattern
- The formal model of the pattern including a class diagram
- Key OOP concepts found in the pattern
- Minimalist abstract example
- Applied examples

We organized the book in this manner to provide a well-rounded picture of each design pattern. By explaining the pattern and its key features, we focus on the pattern's function and structure. The formal model and class diagram gives a wider overview, so you can see the structure and the interconnected classes and interface. We also included certain key OOP concepts for the different patterns. We did this for two reasons. First, the intermediate user will be better able to understand the OOP concept at work, and so understand OOP better. Second, we hoped that advanced users could see the concepts as shorthand to quickly determine how the design pattern is structured.

What You Need to Use This Book

You will need either Flash CS3 or Flex 2 to work with the program examples in this book. All the applications were developed in the Flash IDE, so Flex 2 developers will need to make modifications, especially where certain features were developed using Flash drawing tools and components.

A few examples use Flash Media Server 2 (FMS2). The examples using FMS2 can be created using the Developer's version of FMS2 and can be freely downloaded at *http://www.adobe.com/downloads/*. You will need either a Windows or Linux OS to run Flash Media Server 2. If you have a "MacTel" Macintosh, you can use the Window OS to run FMS, but if you have an older Macintosh running on the Motorola CPU, you'll need to have a LAN or Internet access to a Windows or Linux platform running FMS2. Alternatively, you can skip the examples with FMS2.

Say It Again, Sam

One thing we can guarantee is redundancy. We know that people have different styles of learning. Some are conceptual learners, some experiential, and some metaphorical or any combinations of those, plus others we haven't heard about yet. So you will see that we use several different ways to say the same thing with the idea that if you don't get it one way, you'll get it another.

At the same time, we feel that by discussing the same idea or concept in different ways and in different contexts, the *specific* sense of that concept is better shaped. In looking over reference materials published in books, articles, and online regarding Design Patterns, we found that some materials were not quite accurate in depicting some features. We worked very hard not to make mistakes, and so by providing numerous contexts, we can help filter out what we specifically mean, and, equally important, what we don't mean. The ultimate authority is always *Design Patterns: Elements of Reusable Object-Oriented Software,* and if you have any questions about exactly what we mean, you can always check it out at the original source.

Over the years, a number of articles, books, dissertations and other treatises have appeared offering suggestions for improving the original design patterns. Some of these documents are quite useful, and even have the endorsement of members of the Gang of Four (GoF)—Erich Gamma, Richard Helm, Ralph Johnson, and John Vlissides. Others are not too useful, especially for learning design patterns, and tend to complicate an already complex subject. As a result, we have not strayed from the path laid down in the original text by GoF.

User's Guide

This book, at its core, is an introduction to a relatively advanced topic for writing reusable OOP code for ActionScript 3.0. Like "jumbo shrimp," an "elementary introduction to an advanced topic" is an oxymoron. Advanced developers may want less of the elementary and less senior developers may demand more preparatory materials.

Because we cannot measure any reader's level, we urge you to go through the Table of Contents and flip through the chapters to find what you want. Find your level and use the book at that level. For some, it will be an exercise of reading from cover to cover, while for others it will be a reference work for looking up how ActionScript 3.0 works with different features of design patterns. After all, it's your book, and you should use it to best suit your needs.

Flex 2 developers

We developed all the examples for this book using Flash CS3. So, if you're looking to use these examples for Flex 2, you'll need to make the appropriate Flex adjustments. In some cases, examples were developed using user-created movie clip classes in the Flash CS3 IDE and stored in the Library panel. These cannot be employed directly using Flex 2. So, if you're using Flex 2, plan on some workarounds.

Flash Media Server 2 developers

We have a few examples that use Flash Media Server 2 (FMS2). The examples don't require anything more than the Developers Version of FMS2. The Developers Version can be freely downloaded from the Adobe site at *http://www.adobe.com/devnet/flashmediaserver/*. Alternatively, you can skip the examples, or substitute some other open socket technology.

Companion Tools You'll Want

In an ideal world, those reading this book would have a solid background in object oriented programming and ActionScript 3.0. However, ActionScript 3.0 was released in a non-beta format in Flex 2 only about six months before this book, and in Flash at about the same time this book was published. So, you may not be familiar with ActionScript 3.0, and this book is not a tutorial in ActionScript 3.0. At a minimum, you will want to keep the *ActionScript 3.0 Reference Guide* handy along with any other ActionScript 3.0 documentation that comes with Flash CS3.

We strongly urge you to get a copy of *Design Patterns: Elements of Reusable Object-Oriented Software* sooner or later. At a minimum, check it out of your library. Another book we found to be invaluable is the wonderfully fun and enlightening book, *Head First Design Patterns* by Eric and Elisabeth Freeman (O'Reilly, 2004). All the examples are in Java, but even so, you'll learn a great deal about design patterns and OOP. (Working out how to convert the Java examples to ActionScript 3.0 will teach you a lot about ActionScript 3.0 as well—however, before tackling the Java translations, be sure to go over the design pattern examples in this book.)

If you don't have a good ActionScript 3.0 book yet, get one. We can recommend *ActionScript 3.0 Cookbook* by Joey Lott, Darron Schall, and Keith Peters (O'Reilly, 2006) and *Essential ActionScript 3.0* by Colin Moock (O'Reilly, 2007). For a very brief introduction to ActionScript 3.0, take a look at the Short Cut publication, *ActionScript 3.0 Programming: Overview, Getting Started, and Examples of New Concepts* by Bill Sanders (O'Reilly, 2007). Also, you'll want an ActionScript 3.0 book on object-oriented programming. We've included an introduction to OOP in Chapter 1 that will suffice for now, and both the Moock and Lott books have some great OOP materials as well. However, a book dedicated to OOP concepts should be part of your library if you plan to write programs on the level of design patterns.

Conventions Used in This Book

The following typographical conventions are used in this book:

Plain text
> Indicates menu titles, menu options, menu buttons, and keyboard accelerators (such as Alt and Ctrl).

Bold
> Indicates text that should be entered by the user.

Italic
> Indicates new terms, URLs, email addresses, filenames, file extensions, pathnames, directories, and Unix utilities.

`Constant width`
> Indicates commands, options, switches, variables, attributes, keys, functions, types, classes, namespaces, methods, modules, properties, parameters, values, objects, events, event handlers, XML tags, HTML tags, or the output from commands.

`Constant width bold`
> Shows commands that should be typed literally by the user.

`Constant width italic`
> Shows text that should be replaced with user-supplied values.

> This icon signifies a tip, suggestion, or general note.

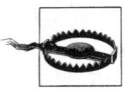
> This icon indicates a warning or caution.

Using Code Examples

This book will help you get your job done. In general, you may use the code in this book in your programs and documentation. You do not need to contact us for permission unless you're reproducing a significant portion of the code. For example, writing a program that uses several chunks of code from this book does not require permission. Selling or distributing a CD-ROM of examples from O'Reilly books *does* require permission. Answering a question by citing this book and quoting example code does not require permission. Incorporating a significant amount of example code from this book into your product's documentation *does* require permission.

We appreciate, but do not require, attribution. An attribution usually includes the title, author, publisher, and ISBN. For example: "*ActionScript 3.0 Design Patterns,* by Bill Sanders and Chandima Cumaranatunge. Copyright 2007 O'Reilly Media, Inc., ISBN 978-0-596-52846-1."

If you feel your use of code examples falls outside fair use or the permission given, feel free to contact us at *permissions@oreilly.com*.

How to Contact Us

Please address comments and questions concerning this book to the publisher:

O'Reilly Media, Inc.
1005 Gravenstein Highway North
Sebastopol, CA 95472
800-998-9938 (in the United States or Canada)
707-829-0515 (international or local)
707-829-0104 (fax)

We have a web page for this book, where we list errata, examples, and any additional information. You can access this page at:

http://www.oreilly.com/catalog/9780596528461

To comment or ask technical questions about this book, send email to:

bookquestions@oreilly.com

For more information about our books, conferences, Resource Centers, and the O'Reilly Network, see our web site at:

http://www.oreilly.com

Safari® Enabled

 When you see a Safari® Enabled icon on the cover of your favorite technology book, it means the book is available online through the O'Reilly Network Safari Bookshelf.

Safari offers a solution that's better than e-books. It's a virtual library that lets you easily search thousands of top technology books, cut and paste code samples, download chapters, and find quick answers when you need the most accurate, current information. Try it for free at *http://safari.oreilly.com.*

Acknowledgments

Since being introduced to design patterns by aYo Binitie, these programming structures have been a topic of close interest. Like a lot of ActionScript developers, we are grateful to Colin Moock for breaching the topic of ActionScript's use with design patterns, in *Essential ActionScript 2.0.* We are also grateful to Eric Freeman and Elisabeth Freeman for their fabulous *Head First Design Patterns*—even struggling through the Java code, we found it possible to appreciate how design patterns could be used in ActionScript 3.0. At the root of design patterns, we must acknowledge the venerable Gang of Four who produced *Design Patterns: Elements of Reusable Object-Oriented Software*, Erich Gamma, Richard Helm, Ralph Johnson and John Vlissides. We have spent endless hours poring over this tome.

Several people at Adobe were very generous with their time in helping out with the ActionScript 3.0 and some insights into design patterns. They include Chris Nuuja, Erica Norton, Geoffrey Williams, Grant Skinner, Jeffrey Mott, Mike Downey, Nivesh Rajbhandari, Peter DeHaan, Robert Penner, Gary Grossman, Ali Mills, Francis Cheng, David Mendels, Gordon Smith, Roger Gonzalez, Sho Kuwamoto, Francis Chen, Emmy Huang, Werner Sharp, Joan Tan, Phil Costa, Mally Gardiner, Asa Whillock, Chris Hock, Tareq Aljaber, San Khong, and Peter von dem Hagen.

In the Flash community, several Flash developers added further insight to both design patterns and ActionScript 3.0. They include Peter Hall, Aral Balkan, Robert Penner, Beau Ambur, Stefan Richter, Joey Lott, Guy Watson, Keith Peters, Will Law, and Brian Lesser. Jonathan Kaye, who brought state machines to ActionScript, was a huge help by going over a state design pattern that served as a model for what was developed for the book.

We're also very grateful to Margot Maley Hutchison at Waterside Productions for helping to make the arrangements with O'Reilly Publishers. As always, Margot smoothed a complex process.

We are grateful to Professor John Gray, chair of the Multimedia Web Design and Development program at the University of Hartford. His encouragement and support in all matters pertaining to Internet and Web development, research and learning provide us with a rich atmosphere and wonderful resources to keep on track with the ever expanding universe of the technology we use.

Technical Reviewers

The technical reviewers had their job cut out for them. Some of the reviewers were experts on design patterns with C# and Java backgrounds, but were unfamiliar with ActionScript. Fortunately, ActionScript 3.0 is looking and acting like other OOP languages, and so they were able to give us a great deal of help. Chief among this group was Adrienne Decker who is a Lecturer in the Department of Computer Science and Engineering at SUNY Buffalo. After sharing a session with Adrienne at the 2006 Object-Oriented Programming, Systems, Languages and Applications (OOPSLA) Conference in Portland, Oregon, it became clear that Adrienne not only was wise in the ways of design patterns, she was also very interested in how to best communicate the inner workings of design patterns. She was an immense help. Two other academics recruited to this project were Dr. James Heilotis and Dr. Axel Schreiner, both of the Rochester Institute of Technology, Department of Computer Science. Professor Schreiner had presented a design pattern named the Symmetric Proxy Pattern at the 2006 OOPSLA conference. Based on a paper, *A Pattern for Distributing Turn-Based Games*, by Heilotis and Schreiner, this new pattern seemed to be an excellent tool for gaming over the Internet using Flash and Flash Media Server 2. We believed that given the newness and creativity of the Symmetric Proxy Pattern, we would be well-advised to ask them for a technical review of our implementation and explanation of their pattern. They were very helpful in seeing to it that we were able to communicate their ideas, and we are most grateful to them both.

We were most fortunate to get the services of Todd Anderson. Todd is a bright light in the ActionScript 3.0 and design pattern mix. He helped us immensely and we are most grateful to Todd's sharp eye and spot-on comments. Darren Richardson was our technical reviewer from the outset. He also brought an international perspective in case we got a bit too ethnocentric.

We also had the unique opportunity of working with The City's Flash Coders New York (FCNY) group led by Jean-Charles Carelli. With considerable talent to spare, members of this group worked on (and over) our manuscript as technical reviewers. Their comments were quite helpful, and reflected an excellent cross-section of savvy ActionScript developers. Chief among those who aided in this process were Tyler Larson, Jim Kremens, Dominic Tancredi, Shari Halter, James O'Reilly, Andrew Hunt, Brian Weisenthal, Oscar Trelles, Seth Hillinger, Lisa Larson, and Edward Skrypa.

Editors

Our development editor, Robyn Thomas, had to make sense out of a highly technical corpus of work in addition to guiding us through The King's English to insure what we said was what we meant. She also kept an array of technical editors supplied with chapters, updated where all the pieces were (and where they should be), and generally made the writing experience one of the nicest possible. Steve Weiss is an incredibly supportive publisher—getting everything organized and on track. Steve is also open to new perspectives and all things creative; most likely because he is so creative himself.

Authors

Bill Sanders, PhD, and Chandima Cumaranatunge, PhD, are both professors in the Multimedia Web Design and Development (MWD²) program at the University of Hartford. Bill teaches courses in Flash, ActionScript, Flash Media Server 2, PHP, C#, SQL, CSS and XHTML among other Internet languages. He has published 44 computer and computer-related books, written software ranging from Basic to Flash Media Server ActionScript, and served as a consultant for different computer software companies. Chandima teaches an introduction to the MWDD major, covering Flash and some ActionScript, a gaming course using Flash and ActionScript, as well as educational technology courses in the Education, Nursing, and Health Professions College. Recently he received a grant to teach an experimental course in robotics.

Bill Sanders

Bill would like to thank his co-author Chandima for a great writing experience and someone to really talk with about design patterns. Bill would also like to thank his wife Delia for her forbearance while she completed her doctorate and our two offices sang the song of two fully employed word processors. Our obsessive-compulsive Greater Swiss Mountain Dog, WillDe, added a measure of reality to both of our efforts. He always knew what was really important—going for a walk.

Chandima Cumaranatunge

Chandima considers himself very lucky, not only to have Bill as a writing partner, but as a professional mentor and friend. He is also eternally grateful to his wife Reshmaal for being totally supportive and putting up with his long writing stints away from the family. Finally, Chandima's daughter Sayuri, the two-year-old "little lily" in "the ocean" (based on the meaning of her name in Japanese and Sinhalese) kept him sane by reminding him every day about the important things in life.

PART I

Constant Change

You must be the change you wish to see in the world.
—Mohandas Gandhi

They must often change, who would be constant in happiness or wisdom.
—Confucius

Without change, something sleeps inside us, and seldom awakens. The sleeper must awaken.
—Frank Herbert

Life belongs to the living, and he who lives must be prepared for changes.
—Johann Wolfgang von Goethe

If we had to summarize design patterns in a single sentence, we'd say that they're *tools for coping with constant change* in software design and development. When you look at the different design patterns in this book, they're optimized to allow the programmer to make changes and reuse most of the software developed. The key concepts are change and flexibility. That same theme will be repeated throughout the book. This Part I provides a general guide for understanding and using this book.

To work with design patterns, you need to know basic object-oriented programming (OOP) principles. If you're not familiar with these concepts, spend some quality time with Chapter 1. The latter part of Chapter 1 gets into some of the design pattern principles, and understanding these concepts will help you better understand the chapters covering the individual design patterns.

If you use and understand the basic OOP concepts such as abstraction, encapsulation, inheritance and polymorphism, you won't necessarily be a good OOP designer. As a professional designer and developer, you need to design software that's easy to maintain and flexible enough to accept change. In other words, you need to develop software that reflects the real world. Any tool you use on the Web today must have the capacity to easily change, be updated, and be reused. Otherwise, the software lacks the capacity to adapt to real world usage.

Design patterns provide object-oriented designs that can cope with change using different OOP tools. If you think about using OOP designs with an eye to how those designs can deal with change, how they can be reused, and how to build in flexibility; then you're beginning to think like a design pattern programmer.

Chapter 1, *Object-Oriented Programming, Design Patterns, and ActionScript 3.0*

Object-Oriented Programming, Design Patterns, and ActionScript 3.0

Let it be your constant method to look into the design of people's actions, and see what they would be at, as often as it is practicable; and to make this custom the more significant, practice it first upon yourself.

—Marcus Aurelius

The life history of the individual is first and foremost an accommodation to the patterns and standards traditionally handed down in his community.

—Ruth Benedict

At the lowest cognitive level, they are processes of experiencing, or, to speak more generally, processes of intuiting that grasp the object in the original.

—Edmund Husserl

The Pleasure of Doing Something Well

The idea of design patterns is to take a set of patterns and solve recurrent problems. At the same time (even in the same breath), the patterns reflect good object-oriented programming (OOP) practices. So, we cannot separate OOP from design patterns, nor would we want to do so.

In answering the question of why bother with design patterns, we are really dealing with the question of why bother with OOP. The standard response to both design patterns and OOP often points to working with a team of programmers and speaking the same language. Further, it's easier to deal with the complexities involved with programming tasks requiring a division of labor for a large project using an object metaphor and practices.

In addition to coordinating large projects, programmers use both OOP and design patterns to deal with change. One key, important element, of design patterns is that they make changing a program much easier. The bigger a program and the more time you've spent developing it, the greater the consequences in making a change to that program. Like pulling a string in a sweater that unravels it, changing code in a program can have the same unraveling consequences. Design patterns and good OOP ease the task of making changes in complex programs, and reduce the changes or global problems.

Team coordination and application update and maintenance are reasons enough to learn design patterns. However, this is not the case if most programs you write are relatively short, you don't work with teams, and you don't worry about change. Then rewriting the short program is neither time-consuming nor difficult. What possible reason would you then have for learning design patterns?

Beside the fact that ActionScript 3.0 is based on ECMAScript and is not likely to have major changes with each new release of Flash or Flex as in the past, you have a far more personal reason for learning design patterns. Alexander Nakhimovsky and Tom Myers, in writing about using OOP with JavaScript (Wrox, 1998), point out the value in the pleasure derived from doing something well. Like any endeavor, whether it be skateboarding or building a house, people can find pleasure in doing a task well. By "doing something well," we do not mean an obsessive perfectionism—especially since perfectionism often leads to task paralysis. Rather, like any task that one can see an outcome and experience a process of accomplishment, when it's done right, you experience the craftsman's pleasure of the creative process and results.

Sequential and Procedural Programming

If you've never heard of *sequential programming*, that's the kind of programming you've most likely been doing. Most amateur programmers just write one statement after another, and any program that has the correct sequence of statements works just fine. However, as programs became more complex, programmers ran into an unruly jumble of code often called *spaghetti programs*. To remedy the jumble effect of sequential programming, programmers began organizing programs into a set of procedures and set of rules, and *procedural programming* was born. Instead of willy-nilly GOTO statements jumping all over a program, subroutines modularly defined program flow with appropriate GOSUB/RETURN procedures to keep everything tidy.

 The RETURN statements back then were different from what they are today. A RETURN meant to return to the position in a sequence of code where the GOSUB had originated. In ActionScript, a return statement means that an operation sends back information generated in the operation [the method or procedure].

Also, from procedural programming came the concept of *scope* so that variables in functions and subroutines could be reused and one procedure would not contaminate another.

The great majority of programming languages today are considered procedural in that they have the concepts and syntax that support it. The different versions of BASIC are procedural, as are languages like ColdFusion, PHP and Perl. However, C++ is a procedural language, as is ECMAScript (ActionScript 3.0) and Ada, languages many consider object-oriented. Languages like Java are considered true OOP languages. Without going into a lot of detail, the reason Java is considered a true OOP language and the others are not is because the only kind of procedure in Java is a class method. Its structure forces procedures to be class methods, and doesn't allow other procedures to operate outside the class structure.

 You might be surprised at how heated a discussion can get when it comes to a language being an OOP language or not. Two versions of OOP criteria exist. One is fairly inclusive and allows any language with certain features that can generate OOP code to be considered OOP. (ActionScript 3.0 is among those.) The other version has a restrictive criterion that includes those languages that *only* allow methods as procedures to be admitted to the exclusive club of OOP languages. Both versions have valid points. However, we will sidestep the issue by not taking a position, but note that both sides agree that you can create good OOP code with a procedural language.

To make a long story short, this does not mean that the other languages are unable to generate true OOP programs. Well before Java was even available, developers were creating OOP programs. Some languages, especially those with the ability to use class structures and override methods, such as ActionScript 3.0, are more OOP friendly than others. As ActionScript has matured from a few statements to a true ECMAScript language, it has become more OOP friendly.

Transition to OOP

Changing from sequential or procedural programming to OOP programming is more than picking up a language that gives you little choice in the matter, as is the case with Java. However, certain changes in a language can make it more amenable to OOP, even if it's not considered a true OOP language by some criterion. In the following sections, some new features in Flash CS3 provide a summary of relevant changes to the way ActionScript is used.

MovieClip and Button scripts

For the ActionScript veterans whose introduction to programming was writing little sequential scripts or procedures using the on statements associated with MovieClip or Button objects, you're probably aware that the latest version of Flash doesn't allow script embedded in either.

 Built-in State Machines: while most programmers welcomed the demise of movie clip and button embedded scripts, one astute programmer observed that Flash used to have built-in state machines. Jonathan Kaye, PhD, co-author of *Flash MX for Interactive Simulation: How to Construct and Use Device Simulations* (Delmar Learning, 2002), noted that the button and movie clip scripts often served to create state machines. Each button or movie clip could serve as an encapsulated, context-sensitive trigger for changing state. (See how design patterns deal with State Machines in Chapter 10.)

In general, the demise of movie clip and button scripts is seen as a boon to better programming, especially OOP programming. Keeping track of the isolated button and movie clip codes could be a headache, even with relatively small applications. For structuring larger programs, where OOP and Design Patterns are most useful, having movie clips and buttons floating around with their own code moves the problem from the realm of headache to nightmare. So, for learning design patterns, be glad you don't even have to think about little scripts isolated in movie clips and buttons.

Timeline scripts

Another kind of scripting you'll be seeing less of in Flash are those embedded in your Timeline. For the most part, placing scripts in the Timeline probably left a lot to be desired in the first place, but worked out to be a convenient location. In Action-Script 2.0, you were able to place a script in a class and call it from a script embedded in the Timeline, and so all that the Timeline code was really used for was to call a class that would launch a script in an ActionScript file (*.as*). That being the case, the Flash CS3 *.fla* file has a little window where you can add the name of the class to call. (See the next section.) So, if all you want to do is to call a program and compile it into an SWF file, you no longer need to use the Timeline for your code at all.

However, Flash CS3 doesn't do away with code in the Timeline. You can still use it, but in this book, we use it selectively only with movie clips that are called from a class outside the movie clip or button class. (See the section "Movie clip and button classes.")

Document class

You won't be placing much, if any, code in the Timeline using ActionScript 3.0. Rather than using an object with a Timeline script, you can now compile your *.as* files by entering the name of the class name you want to launch your application. Figure 1-1 shows how to use the Document class window in the Properties panel to enter the name of the class you want to launch:

You can still use the Timeline, but unless there's a good reason to do so, there's no need. Most of the examples in this book use the Sprite object instead of the

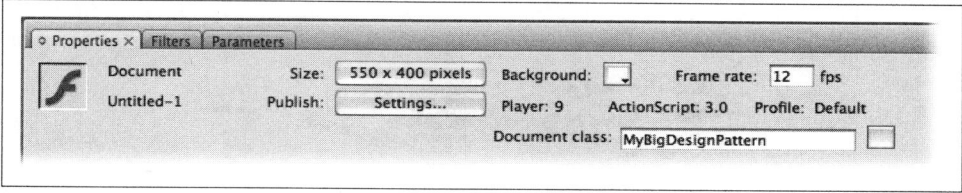

Figure 1-1. Document class window

`MovieClip` class. A `Sprite` object has no Timeline, but a `MovieClip` class does. So using `Sprite` objects save a bit of extra weight that the Timeline has.

Movie clip and button classes

In Flash CS3, MovieClip and Button objects you create using the Symbol dialog box and store in the Library can be made available to work with ActionScript 3.0. Unlike ActionScript 2.0 where MovieClip and Button symbols could be associated with a class, with Flash CS3, *they can be made into classes themselves.* The object's name entered into the Name window when the symbols are created becomes the class name for the object. (In past versions, references to a movie clip are made through an *instance name.* You can still make those references, but in a different context.)

The advantage of this new procedure is that the symbol objects can be instantiated just like any other class through the code, as long as the symbols are in the Library. You don't have to place them on the stage. They can be dynamically instantiated and placed into a display array just like a dynamically generated object. Further, objects contained within the MovieClip or Button can be addressed as a property just like any other class.

While this book is in no way an introduction to Flash CS3, walking through one example of this new way of creating a class with movie clips and buttons may be useful to those new to Flash and experienced users alike. The following steps walk you through this new feature:

1. Open a new Flash document and save it as *rocket.fla.*

2. Select Insert → New Symbol from the menu bar to open the Create New Symbol Dialog box. Enter **Rocket** in the Name window, and Click OK to enter the Symbol Edit Mode.

3. In the Symbol Edit Mode, draw a rocket on the stage with the dimensions W=89, H=14, as shown in Figure 1-2. Once finished, position the drawing at X=0, Y=0. Click the Scene 1 icon to exit the Symbol Edit Mode.

Figure 1-2. Rocket drawing

4. Select Insert → New Symbol from the menu bar to open the Convert to Symbol Dialog box. Enter **FireRocket** in the Name window, select Movie clip as Type, and click the Export for ActionScript checkbox. Once you've clicked the checkbox, Figure 1-3 shows what the dialog box looks like. Notice that the Base class is flash.display.MovieClip. The base class is the reference to the package required for ActionScript to display a MovieClip object. Click OK to enter the Symbol Edit Mode.

Convert to Symbol		
Name: FireRocket		OK
Type: ● Movie clip Registration: ▦		Cancel
○ Button		
○ Graphic		Basic
Linkage		
Identifier:		
Class: FireRocket		☐ ☐
Base class: flash.display.MovieClip		☐ ☐
Linkage: ☑ Export for ActionScript		
☐ Export for runtime sharing		
☑ Export in first frame		
☐ Import for runtime sharing		
URL:		

Figure 1-3. Setting a MovieClip class

5. Drag a copy of the Rocket movie clip from the Library to the center of the stage. Move the center point of the movie clip to the rear of the rocket and position it at X=0, Y=0.

6. Click on Frame 40 of the Timeline and press F5 to create 40 frames. Click Frame 40 again and press F6 to insert a keyframe. Click on the keyframe in Frame 40 and move the rocket to X=400, Y=0.

7. Click on the first keyframe, and, in the tween drop-down menu in the Properties inspector, select Motion. You should now see a blue arrow in the Timeline. Move the playhead from left to right to make sure that the motion tween is working right. Figure 1-4 shows what you should see.

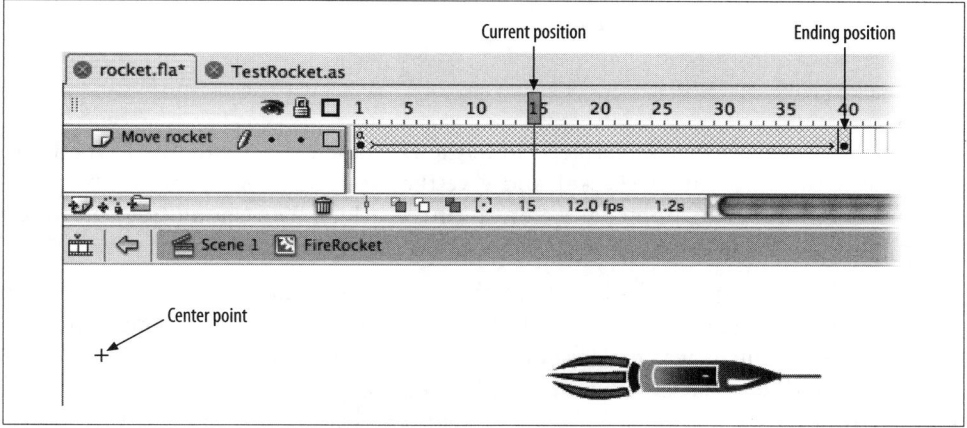

Figure 1-4. Rocket in motion tween

8. Open the Actions panel. Click on a blank area of the stage to make sure you don't have any objects selected, and then click on Frame 1. In the Actions panel, type in the **stop()** statement. Save the *Rocket.fla* file.

9. Open a new ActionScript file and save it as TestRocket.as in the same folder as the *Rocket.fla* file. Enter the script in Example 1-1 in the *TestRocket.as* file, and save the file once again:

Example 1-1. TestRocket.as

```
package
{
    import flash.display.Sprite;

    public class TestRocket extends Sprite
    {
        private var fireRocket:FireRocket;
        public function TestRocket()
        {
            fireRocket=new FireRocket();
            fireRocket.x=50;
            fireRocket.y=100;
            addChild(fireRocket);
            fireRocket.gotoAndPlay(2);
        }
    }
}
```

10. Finally, open the *Rocket.fla* file, and in the Document class window in the Properties panel, type in **TestRocket** and save the file. Then test the movie by pressing Ctrl + Enter (Command + Return on the Mac). You should see the rocket move from left to right across the screen and then return to its original position.

Using Flash in a more or less traditional manner to create movie clips is still an important part of using ActionScript, but it has changed. You can no longer attach a class to a movie clip as was the case in previous versions. However, in creating applications using design patterns, you can still integrate different aspects created in the Flash IDE. So while ActionScript 3.0 has made the leap to a true ECMAScript language, it has not abandoned its roots in animated graphics.

OOP Basics

If you're familiar with OOP and have been practicing good OOP for some time now, you might want to skip this section or just skim over it to see if we've added anything new, or if there's something new as far as ActionScript is concerned. Later in this chapter, we introduce good practices in OOP on which design patterns are based. These more advanced concepts depend on understanding these basics. However, this short discussion is no substitute for a more in-depth understanding of OOP. If this is your first exposure to OOP, you will definitely want to supplement your understanding of OOP with an introductory book dedicated to OOP.

Throughout the book, you will find references to how a design pattern employs different basic and design pattern OOP principles. Each chapter includes a section on key OOP concepts, and so what you read in this introductory chapter is only the first of many times an OOP concept will be described. This is intentional. By looking at an OOP concept from different angles, we believe you will have a better understanding of OOP's many nuances. We ourselves were surprised at how different design patterns brought out different perspectives on the same OOP concept and helped further clarify it.

To get started, we'll review the four basic OOP concepts:

- Abstraction
- Encapsulation
- Inheritance
- Polymorphism

Each of these concepts needs reflection, and if you're new to OOP, don't worry about getting it right the first time. We go over these concepts time and again in the design pattern chapters.

Abstraction

In general, an abstraction is a model or ideal. You don't have all of the details, but you have the general parameters that can be filled in with details. Further, an abstraction is clear enough for you to tell one abstraction from another. Take, for example, two jobs your company is trying to fill. One's for a Web designer and the other's for a programmer. To advertise for the position, you would not describe the person as a specific person but instead in terms of the characteristics you want for the position. You might have the two abstractions representing the two different positions:

Two Positions Open:

- Programmer
  - Experienced with multi-programmer projects
  - Experienced with middleware and database programming
  - ECMAScript programming background
  - OOP and Design Pattern programming skills
- Web designer
  - Experienced with creating Web graphics
  - Familiar with animation graphics
  - Can work with vector graphics
  - Client-centered approach

You can tell the difference between the two positions and their general requirements (properties), but the details are left fairly open. A programmer is unlikely to apply for the Web designer position and a designer is just as unlikely to apply for the programmer position. However, a pool of applicants could have a wide range of skills that would provide the concrete details for each position. For example, one programmer may have PHP middleware skills and/or MySQL database skills, while another may be experienced in using ASP.NET, C# and MS SQL. The abstraction is in the job description and the details are provided by the applicants' unique sets of skills and experience.

In *Object-Oriented Design with Applications* (Benjamin/Cummings), Grady Booch, one of the design pattern pioneers, provides the following definition of an abstraction that is both clear and succinct:

> An abstraction denotes the essential characteristics of an object that distinguish it from all other kinds of object and thus provide crisply defined conceptual boundaries, relative to the perspective of the viewer.

Booch's definition pretty well describes the two job descriptions. The descriptions provide the essential characteristics of the position and they distinguish one from the other.

Abstractions in ActionScript 3.0

Turning now to abstractions in ActionScript programming, we'll take a simple video player for an example. This player will be made of certain elements that we need; so we start by listing them as abstractions:

- A Net connection
- A video screen
- A stream
- An FLV file to play

If we put these together just right, we'll be able to play a video. However, instead of starting with an abstraction, we want to start with something concrete that works for us right away. Enter the code in Example 1-2 saving the file using the name in the caption:

 Throughout the book, with a few exceptions, caption names represent the name used for the file.

Example 1-2. PlayVideo.as

```
package
{
    import flash.net.NetConnection;
    import flash.net.NetStream;
    import flash.media.Video;
    import flash.display.Sprite;

    public class PlayVideo extends Sprite
```

Example 1-2. PlayVideo.as (continued)

```
    {
        public function PlayVideo( )
        {
            var nc:NetConnection=new NetConnection( );
            nc.connect(null);
            var ns:NetStream = new NetStream(nc);
            var vid:Video=new Video( );
            vid.attachNetStream(ns);
            ns.play("adp.flv");
            addChild(vid);
            vid.x=100;
            vid.y=50;
        }
    }
}
```

You'll need an FLV file named *adp.flv*—any FLV file with that name will work. Open a new Flash document file, enter **PlayVideo** in the Document class window, and test it.

To change this to an abstract file, take out all specific references to any values with the exception of the null value in the NetConnection.connect( ) method. (We could pass that value as a string, but we're leaving it to keep things simple.) Example 1-3 shows essentially the same application abstracted to a "description" of what it requires to work.

Example 1-3. PlayVideoAbstract.as

```
package
{
    import flash.net.NetConnection;
    import flash.net.NetStream;
    import flash.media.Video;
    import flash.display.Sprite;

    public class PlayVideoAbstract extends Sprite
    {
     public function PlayVideoAbstract(nc:NetConnection,
        ns:NetStream,vid:Video,flick:String,xpos:uint,ypos:uint)
        {
            nc=new NetConnection( );
            nc.connect(null);
            ns= new NetStream(nc);
            vid=new Video( );
            vid.attachNetStream(ns);
            ns.play(flick);
            vid.x=xpos;
            vid.y=ypos;
            addChild(vid);
        }
```

Example 1-3. PlayVideoAbstract.as (continued)

```
        }
}
```

All the values for the different elements (with the exception of null) have been abstracted to *describe* the object. However, like a job description that abstracts requirements, so too does the PlayVideoAbstract class. All the particulars have been placed into one long set of parameters:

```
PlayVideoAbstract(nc:NetConnection,ns:NetStream,vid:Video,flick:String,
    xpos:uint,ypos:uint)
```

The abstract parameters in the constructor function let us add any concrete elements we want, including the specific name of a video we want to play. Example 1-4 shows how concrete instances are implemented from an abstract class.

Example 1-4. PlayAbstract.as

```
package
{
    import flash.display.Sprite
    import flash.net.NetConnection;
    import flash.net.NetStream;
    import flash.media.Video;

    public class PlayAbstract extends Sprite
    {
        private var conn:NetConnection;
        private var stream:NetStream;
        private var vid:Video;
        private var flick:String="adp.flv";

        public function PlayAbstract()
        {
var playIt:PlayVideoAbstract=new PlayVideoAbstract(conn,stream,vid,
    flick,100,50);
            addChild(playIt);
        }
    }
}
```

All the entire class does is to create a single instance of the PlayVideoAbstract class and place it on the stage. Private variables serve to provide most of the concrete values for the required parameters. Literals provide the data for both the horizontal (x) and vertical (y) positions of the video. To test it, just change the Document class name in the Flash document (FLA) file to PlayAbstract.

Why Abstractions Are Important

We can see two key reasons that abstractions are important for both OOP and Design Patterns. Rather than being dogged by minutiae of the problem, abstraction helps to focus on what parts, independent of their details, are required to solve the problem. Does this mean that you ignore the details? Not at all. Rather, the details are handled by adding them just when they're needed. For instance, in the example in the previous section, the exact video file is unimportant. All that's important is that some video name (a detail) be provided when we're ready to play it. We don't need to build a theater around a single movie. Likewise, we don't need to build a class around a single video file.

The second advantage of abstraction is flexibility. If you're thinking that in the previous section the Example 1-2 was easier and took less code and classes, you're right. However, suppose you want to place four videos on the stage. Then, all you would need to do is to create four instances using the abstract class instead of re-writing three more classes. In other words, the second method using abstraction is more flexible. In addition to adding more videos instances, we can easily change the video file we choose to play.

Encapsulation

Encapsulation is what makes a code object an object. If you have a tail, four legs, a cold nose and a bark, you do not have a dog. You just have a collection of parts that make up a dog. When you bring all of the doggy parts together, you know that each part is a part but collectively, you do not think of parts but a reality *sui generis*. That is, a dog is an object unto itself and not doggy parts that happen to hang together. Encapsulation has a similar effect on a collection of operations and properties.

Encapsulation has been used synonymously with other terms such as *component* and *module*. In the context of OOP, encapsulation is often called *a black box*, meaning you can see it do certain things but you cannot see the inner workings. Actually, a lot of things we deal with all the time are black boxes, such as our dog. We can see the dog do a lot of different things, and we can interact with the dog. However, we really don't know (or usually care) about how the physiology of the dog works—dogs are not transparent. They're black boxes.

The good thing about the concept of a black box is that we don't have to worry about the inner workings or parts. We just have to know how we can deal with it, secure in the knowledge that whatever makes the black box work is fine as long as it works as we think it should.

Hiding Your Data from Bad Consequences

To see why you might want to encapsulate your data, we'll take a look at two programs. One is not encapsulated, leading to unwanted consequences, and the other is encapsulated, preventing strange results.

If you make a dog object, you may want to include an operation that includes the way a dog communicates. For purposes of illustration, we'll include a method called dogTalk that will let the dog make different sounds. The dog's communication will include the following:

- Woof
- Whine
- Howl
- Grrrr

We'll start off with *bad* OOP to illustrate how you may end up with something you don't want in your dog's vocabulary. Example 1-5 is not encapsulated and will potentially embarrass your dog object.

Example 1-5. NoEncap.as

```
package
{
    //This is BAD OOP -- No encapsulation
    import flash.text.TextField;
    import flash.display.Sprite;

    public class NoEncap extends Sprite
    {
        public var dogTalk:String="Woof, woof!";
        public var textFld:TextField=new TextField( );

        public function NoEncap( )
        {
            addChild(textFld);
            textFld.x=100;
            textFld.y=100;
        }
        function showDogTalk( )
        {
            textFld.text=dogTalk;
        }
    }
}
```

As a black box, you *should not* be able to change the internal workings of a class, but this class is wide open, as you will see. You can interact with an encapsulated object through its interface, but you should not allow an implementation to make any changes it wants. Example 1-6 breaks into the object and changes it in ways you don't want.

Example 1-6. TestNoEncap.as

```
package
{
    import flash.display.Sprite;

    public class TestNoEncap extends Sprite
    {
        public var noEncap:NoEncap;
        public function TestNoEncap()
        {
            noEncap=new NoEncap();
            noEncap.dogTalk="Meow";
            noEncap.showDogTalk();
            addChild(noEncap);
        }
    }
}
```

Open a new Flash document file, and, in the Document class window, type in **TestNoEncap**. When you test the file, you'll see "Meow" appear on the screen. Such a response from your dog object is all wrong. Dogs don't meow and cats don't bark. However, that's what can happen when you don't encapsulate your class. When you multiply that by every un-encapsulated class you use, you can imagine the mess you might have. So let's find a fix for this.

Private variables

The easiest way to insure encapsulation is to use private variables. The private statement in ActionScript 3.0, whether it's used with variables, constants or methods (functions) makes sure that only the class that defines or declares it can use it. This not only shuts out implementations that attempt to assign any value they want, but it also excludes subclasses. (This is a difference from ActionScript 2.0; so watch out for it if you're converting an application from ActionScript 2.0 to ActionScript 3.0.)

To see how the private statement will change how the application works, Example 1-7 changes the NoEncap class by adding the private statement to the variables.

Example 1-7. Encap.as

```
package
{
    //This is GOOD OOP -- It has encapsulation
    import flash.text.TextField;
    import flash.display.Sprite;

    public class Encap extends Sprite
    {
        private var dogTalk:String="Woof, woof!";
        private var textFld:TextField=new TextField();
```

Example 1-7. Encap.as (continued)

```
      public function Encap( )
      {
          addChild(textFld);
          textFld.x=100;
          textFld.y=100;
      }
      function showDogTalk( )
      {
          textFld.text=dogTalk;
      }
  }
}
```

Also, minor changes have to be made to the test file. The supertype implemented must be changed. Example 1-8 shows the new test class, TestEncap , for the Encap class.

Example 1-8. TestEncap.as

```
package
{
    import flash.display.Sprite;

    public class TestEncap extends Sprite
    {
        public var encap:Encap
        public function TestEncap( )
        {
            encap=new Encap( );
            encap.dogTalk="Meow";
            encap.showDogTalk( );
            addChild(encap);
        }
    }
}
```

Go ahead and test it by changing the Document class name to TestEncap. This time, though, you'll get the following error in the Complier Errors panel:

```
Line 11: 1178: Attempted access of inaccessible property dogTalk through a reference
with static type Encap.
Source: encap.dogTalk="Meow";
```

It shows the source of the error to be the line:

```
encap.dogTalk="Meow";
```

That error reflects the fact that it attempted to access a private variable outside the class. To fix the script, comment out the offending line:

```
//encap.dogTalk="Meow";
```

Try testing it again. This second time, everything works fine, except, you don't get the dog object expressing "Meow." You see "Woof, woof."

You may be thinking that private variables really limit what you can do. Suppose you want the dog object to howl, growl or whimper? How do you make the changes dynamically? Preventing an encapsulated object from doing something wrong is one thing, but how can an object be set up to accept variables?

The many meanings of interface

In this book, you will find the term *interface* used in different contexts, and each context gives the term a slightly different meaning. (Thanks a lot!) Up to this point, you're probably familiar with terms like UI (user interface) or GUI (graphic user interface). These terms refer to different tools you use to interact with a program. For example, a button is a common UI in Flash. When you click a button, something predictable happens. You may not know how it happens (or care), but you know that if you press the button, the video will play, a different page will appear, or an animation will start. So if you understand the basic concept of a UI, you should be able to understand how an interface works with an object.

With a UI, the black box is the application you're using, whether it's shopping at eBay or using a word processor. If you follow certain rules and use the different UIs in the appropriate manner, you get what you want. In the same way, an encapsulated object is a black box, and the interface describes the ways you can interact with it programmatically. It's the UI for the object.

Design Patterns: Elements of Reusable Object-Oriented Software (page 13) nicely clarifies object interfaces and their signatures. An object's *signature* is its operation name, parameters, and return datatype. Figure 1-5 graphically shows the makeup of a typical object's signature.

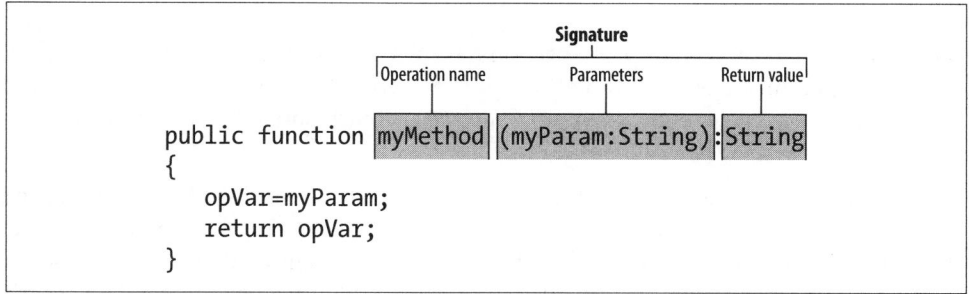

Figure 1-5. Object's signature

All of an object's signatures defined by its operations is the interface. In this context then, *the interface for the object constitutes the rules for access, list of services, and controls for it.*

 Wait! There's more! Later in this chapter you will find an `interface` statement as part of ActionScript 3.0's lexicon, which is a whole different use of the term, *interface*. You will also find the term used synonymously with *supertype* elsewhere in this book. All the different uses of *interface* will be explained in time.

Before getting bogged down in contextual definitions, it's time to move on to see what an encapsulated object's interface looks like. The following section does just that.

Getters and setters

The most common way to enforce encapsulation but to give implementations access to an object is with getter and setter interfaces. The object controls both access to it and what is allowed. Keeping our example of a dog object, we know that the dog has a limited vocabulary, and it's not one that includes "Meow." So, we'll just make a setter that allows only the dog's limited vocabulary.

A setter method includes parameter variables of some kind, and an algorithm that allows certain things and excludes others. However, most setters just assign the parameter value to a private member regardless of its value. The algorithm and everything else in the function that makes up the method is invisible to the implementation, and if the wrong parameter or wrong datatype is entered, either an error message appears or the value will not be passed. The following shows the general structure of a setter:

```
function setterMethod(parameter)
{
    if(parameter=="OK")
    {
        private variable = parameter;
    }
}
```

So the trick is to have the implementation pass any data to the object as a parameter, and if the parameter is acceptable, the private variable is assigned the parameter's value. This is a very general overview of the setter, but it shows the essentials of how it works.

Compared to setters, getter methods are pretty straightforward. In Example 1-7, the `showDogTalk( )` method is the getter function. The getter method's job is to provide data for the implementation. Thus, while the original example doesn't have a setter method, it does have a getter. The setter makes sure that the client gets only what it's supposed to get.

In Example 1-9, the private variable, `dogTalk`, is not assigned a default value. However, the variable is still used in both the setter and getter methods. As you will see when you test the new class, `EncapSet`, the implementation has access to the private variable through the setter's interface.

Example 1-9. EncapSet.as

```
package
{
    //This is BETTER OOP -- It's got encapsulation
    //plus a decent interface for an object

    import flash.text.TextField;
    import flash.display.Sprite;

    public class EncapSet extends Sprite
    {
        private var dogTalk:String;
        private var textFld:TextField=new TextField( );

        public function EncapSet( )
        {
            addChild(textFld);
            textFld.x=100;
            textFld.y=100;
        }

        //Setter
        function setDogTalk(bowWow:String)
        {
            switch (bowWow)
            {
                case "Woof" :
                    dogTalk=bowWow;
                    break;

                case "Whine" :
                    dogTalk=bowWow;
                    break;

                case "Grrrr" :
                    dogTalk=bowWow;
                    break;

                case "Howl" :
                    dogTalk=bowWow;
                    break;

                default :
                    dogTalk="Not dog talk!";
            }
        }

        //Rendering value
        function showDogTalk( )
        {
            textFld.text=dogTalk;
        }
    }
}
```

As you can see in Example 1-9, the setter method allows only the four expressions we had listed for a dog. Anything else (including "Meow") is not allowed. Next, Example 1-10 shows how to interface with the encapsulated dog object:

Example 1-10. TestEncapSet.as

```
package
{
    import flash.display.Sprite;

    public class TestEncapSet extends Sprite
    {
        private var encapSet:EncapSet
        public function TestEncapSet( )
        {
            encapSet=new EncapSet( );
            encapSet.setDogTalk("Howl");
            encapSet.showDogTalk( );
            addChild(encapSet);
        }
    }
}
```

Enter **TestEncapSet** in the Document class of the FLA file and test it. As you will see, the string "Howl" is perfectly acceptable. Now, test it again using "Meow." This time, you will see that the object rejected the kitty cat sound as "Not dog talk." This arrangement represents the best of both worlds; encapsulation and a way to execute operations within an encapsulated object.

The get and set methods

Another way to maintain encapsulation and hide the information in your objects is to use the ActionScript 3.0 get and set methods. Some programmers find it awkward to create their own getter and setter methods as we did in the previous section, preferring the simplicity of the get *accessor* and set *mutator*.

> Accessors and mutators versus Frankenstein: they sound like something from a horror flick, but the terms *accessor* and *mutator* are used to describe getters and setters. The accessor (getter) does access or *get* information, and that's perfectly reasonable. But mutators? Well, if we think about it, a mutation does refer to a change, and when we set information, we do indeed change it. It too makes perfect sense. So if you're happily reading an article on design patterns and you see the terms *accessor* or *mutator*, don't let it creep you out.

In looking at how get and set are used, a key feature is the absence of parentheses. Changes (setting) are not accomplished by adding values. Rather, the getters and setters are treated like properties where values are assigned or retrieved through assignment.

Example 1-11 and Example 1-12 show how you can lock up your encapsulated objects using getters and setters with the get and set methods.

Example 1-11. FlowerShop.as

```
package
{
    public class FlowerShop
    {
        private var buds:String;

        public function FlowerShop( ):void {}

        //Getter function
        public function get flowers( ):String
        {
            return buds;
        }

        //Setter function
        public function set flowers(floral:String):void
        {
            buds=floral;
        }
    }
}
```

In Example 1-12, keep in mind that flowers is a method, and not a property. However, setting and getting values using the flowers( ) method looks exactly like setting and getting a property value.

Example 1-12. Send Flowers.as

```
package
{
    import flash.display.Sprite;

    public class SendFlowers extends Sprite
    {
        public function SendFlowers( )
        {
            var trueLove:FlowerShop = new FlowerShop( );
            //Set values
            trueLove.flowers="A dozen roses";
            //Get values
            trace(trueLove.flowers);
            //Set different values
            trueLove.flowers="And a dozen more....";
            //Get the changed values
            trace(trueLove.flowers);
        }
    }
}
```

Using Encapsulation and Design Patterns

This section on encapsulation has been fairly long. The reason for the attention to encapsulation is because of its importance to good OOP; it's a crucial element in design patterns. Of the 24 original design patterns, only 4 have a class scope and the remaining 20 have an object scope. Rather than relying on inheritance (which is discussed in the next section), the great majority of design patterns rely on composition.

Later in this chapter, in the section, "Favor Composition," you will see how design patterns are made up of several different objects. For the design patterns to work the way they are intended, object encapsulation is essential.

Inheritance

The third key concept in good OOP is *inheritance*. Inheritance refers to the way one class inherits the properties, methods, and events of another class. If Class A has Methods X, Y, and Z, and Class B is a subclass (extends) Class A; it too will have Methods X, Y and Z. This saves a lot of time and adds functionality to your programming projects. If you've done virtually any programming using ActionScript 3.0, you've probably extended the Sprite class as we've done in Example 1-1 through Example 1-10. Because of inheritance, the new classes (subclasses) derived from the Sprite class have all the functionality of the Sprite class, in addition to anything you add to the subclass.

Looking at the Ancestors

The best place to start looking at how inheritance works is with ActionScript 3.0. Open your online *ActionScript 3.0 Language Reference*. In the Packages window, click flash.display. In the main window that opens the Package flash.display information, click MovieClip in the Classes table. At the very top of the Class MovieClip page, you will see the Inheritance path:

```
MovieClip → Sprite → DisplayObjectContainer → InteractiveObject →
    DisplayObject → EventDispatcher → Object
```

That means that the MovieClip class inherited all the characteristics from the root class, Object, all the way to Sprite object and everything in between.

Scroll down to the Public Properties section. You will see nine properties. Click the Show Inherited Public Properties link. Now you should see 43 additional properties! So of the 52 properties in the MovieClip class, you can see that only 9 are unique to MovieClip class. The rest are all inherited. Likewise, the methods and properties we added are unique to the class—the rest are inherited from Sprite.

To see the effect of inheritance and the effect of using one class or another, change the two references to Sprite to MovieClip in Example 1-9. Because the MovieClip class inherits everything in the Sprite class, the application should still work. As you will see, it works just fine. The reason that Sprite is used instead of MovieClip is that we did not want to have any unnecessary baggage—just the minimum we needed. If you change Sprite to the next class it inherits from, DisplayObjectContainer, you will see that the application fails. This means that the application requires one of the Sprite class properties that is *not* inherited.

 One byte over the line: in Example 1-9, if you substitute the MovieClip for Sprite classes for the parent class, you will find that your SWF file is larger than when you tested it with Sprite (708 bytes versus 679 bytes). The 29 byte difference probably won't bloat your program significantly, but with added classes in design pattern applications, an unnecessary byte here and one there might add up. (When you win a contract because your application was 1 byte less than the competition's, you'll be glad we had this little chat.)

In addition to seeing what is inherited in ActionScript 3.0 in the *Language Reference*, you might also want to note what's in the packages you import. If you import flash.display.* you can bring in everything in the display package. That's why importing just what you need, e.g., flash.display.Sprite or flash.display.Shape, is far more frugal and less cluttering.

Writing Classes for Inheritance

As can be seen from looking at the inheritance structure of ActionScript 3.0, a well-planned application benefits greatly from a well-organized plan of inheritance. To see how inheritance works from the inside, the next example provides a simple inheritance model for our four-legged friends. Even with this simple example, you can see what is inherited and what is unique to an application.

Example 1-13 through Example 1-16 make up the application illustrating inheritance. The first class, QuadPets, is the parent or superclass with a constructor that indicates when an instance of the class is instantiated using a trace statement. Any class that inherits the QuadPets class gets all of its methods and interfaces.

Example 1-13. QuadPets.as

```
package
{
    public class QuadPets
    {
        public function QuadPets():void
        {
            trace("QuadPets is instantiated");
        }
        public function makeSound():void
        {
```

Example 1-13. QuadPets.as (continued)

```
            trace("Superclass:Pet Sound");
        }
    }
}
```

Any class that uses the extends statement to declare a class inherits the class characteristics it extends. The class that's extended is the *superclass* (or parent). The class
that extends another class is the *subclass*. Both the Dog and Cat classes are subclasses
of the QuadPets class. They inherit all the superclass' functionality. To see how that
happens, we'll have to first create the two subclasses.

Example 1-14. Dog.as

```
package
{
    public class Dog extends QuadPets
    {
        public function Dog( ):void
        {
        }
        public function bark( ):void
        {
            trace("Dog class: Bow wow");
        }
    }
}
```

Example 1-15. Cat.as

```
package
{
    public class Cat extends QuadPets
    {
        public function Cat( ):void
        {
        }
        public function meow( ):void
        {
            trace("Cat class: Meow");
        }
    }
}
```

To see how the Dog and Cat classes inherit the operations of the superclass, the
TestPets class simply invokes the single method (makeSound) from the superclass. As
you can see from the Dog and Cat classes, no such method can be seen in their construction, and so you can see that it must have originated in the QuadPets class.

Example 1-16. TestPets.as

```
package
{
    import flash.display.Sprite;

    public class TestPets extends Sprite
    {
        public function TestPets():void
        {
            var dog:Dog=new Dog();
            dog.makeSound();
            dog.bark();
            var cat:Cat=new Cat();
            cat.makeSound();
            cat.meow();
        }
    }
}
```

In addition to invoking the makeSound() method, the Dog and Cat instances invoke their own methods, bark() and meow(). Also, when you test the application, you will see:

```
QuadPets is instantiated
```

That output is caused by the line:

```
trace("QuadPets is instantiated");
```

placed in the constructor function of the QuadPets class. It fires whenever an instance of the class is invoked. So in addition to having the capacity to use methods from the superclass, subclasses inherit any actions in the constructor function of the superclass.

Open a Flash document, and type **TestPets** in the Document class window. When you test it, you should see the following in the Output window:

```
QuadPets is instantiated
Superclass:Pet Sound
Dog class: Bow wow
QuadPets is instantiated
Superclass:Pet Sound
Cat class: Meow
```

Looking at the output, both the dog and cat instances display two superclass messages (QuadPets is instantiated, Superclass:Pet Sound) and one message unique to the respective subclasses (Dog class: Bow wow, Cat class: Meow.) These examples show how inheritance works, but in practical applications, and in design patterns, inheritance is planned so that they cut down on redundancy and help build a program to achieve an overall goal.

Using Interfaces and Abstract Classes in ActionScript 3.0

Inheritance can also be linked to two other structures; *interfaces* and *abstract classes*. However, the connection between the `interface` structure (a statement in Action-Script 3.0) or the abstract class and inheritance is a bit different from the one with the `class` structure we've examined thus far.

Interface constructs

First of all, in this context, `interface` refers to an ActionScript 3.0 statement and not the object interface discussed in the "Encapsulation and Design Patterns" section. While a class can be said to be an abstraction of an object, an `interface` is an abstraction of methods. They are widely used in design patterns. Beginning in Chapter 5 with the adapter pattern, you will see interfaces at work in several of the other design patterns.

To begin to see what an interface does, a simple example illustrates the use of one. However, once you start seeing how they're used in design patterns, you will better see their utility. Example 1-17 shows how a typical interface is created. The application is made up of Example 1-17 to Example 1-20.

The first thing we'll do is to make our interface. As you can see in Example 1-17, the single function is quite simple and devoid of content. It does have a name, parameter, and return type, but note that the function is only a single line.

Example 1-17. BandFace.as

```
package
{
    //Interface
    public interface BandFace
    {
        function playInstrument(strum:String):void;
    }
}
```

Each implementation of the interface must have exactly the same structure in all of the methods in the interface, and if anything is not the same, you'll get an error message. As long as the signature for the methods is the same, everything should work fine. Example 1-18 is the first implementation of the of the BandFace interface.

Example 1-18. Guitar.as

```
package
{
    public class Guitar implements BandFace
    {
        public function Guitar() {}
```

Example 1-18. Guitar.as (continued)

```
    public function playInstrument(strum:String):void
    {
        trace("Playing my air "+ strum);
    }
  }
}
```

Looking at Example 1-19 and the Bongo class, at first you may think that the method is built incorrectly. It's wholly different from the Guitar class in its details, but the method's signature is identical.

Example 1-19. Bongo.as

```
package
{
    import flash.media.Sound;
    import flash.media.SoundChannel;
    import flash.net.URLRequest;

    public class Bongo implements BandFace
    {

        public function Bongo( ){}

        private var sound:Sound;
        private var playNow:SoundChannel;
        private var doPlay:URLRequest;

        public function playInstrument(strum:String):void
        {
            sound=new Sound( );

            doPlay=new URLRequest(strum);
            sound.load(doPlay);
            playNow=sound.play( );
        }
    }
}
```

Remember, when working with interfaces, the number of methods in an interface can be many or few, but as long as each implementation of the interface includes every method in the interface and maintains the structure, everything works fine.

You may be wondering where the inheritance is. Given the fact that you must build all the interface's methods, it looks more like a customization than an inheritance. However, the BandFace subclasses all inherit its interfaces. So essentially, the subclasses inherit the interface but not the implementation.

Finally, to test the application, the MakeSound class, listed in Example 1-20, tests both classes and their very different constructions of the single method from the BandFace interface. You'll need an MP3 file named *bongo.mp3* (use any handy MP3 file) saved in the same folder as the *MakeSound.as* file.

Example 1-20. MakeSound.as

```
package
{
    import flash.display.Sprite;
    public class MakeSound extends Sprite
    {
        private var guitar:BandFace;
        private var bongo:BandFace;

        public function MakeSound( ):void
        {
            guitar=new Guitar( );
            guitar.playInstrument("Gibson");

            bongo=new Bongo( );
            bongo.playInstrument("bongo.mp3");
        }
    }
}
```

Note that both instances, guitar and bongo, are typed to the supertype, BandFace, and not to either the Guitar or the Bongo classes. This practice follows the first principle of reusable object-oriented design: *Program to an interface, not an implementation.*

The purpose of doing so is to maintain flexibility and reusability. This principle will be fully explored elsewhere in this chapter and in Chapter 8, but for now, just note that fact.

A word about the interface and abstract class naming conventions used in this book: with the focal point of this book on object-oriented programming and design patterns, we use naming conventions that best reflect and clarify the structure of the different design patterns. As a result, we don't always follow some of the naming conventions. One convention is to name interfaces beginning with a capital I. So following that convention, the BandFace interface would have been named IBandFace. Where using the I does not interfere with clarifying a design pattern structure, we use it, but where we have several interfaces in a design pattern, often we forego that convention. Another convention is to name abstract classes using Abstract+ Something. So, AbstractHorses would be a name for a class you'd otherwise name Horses. Again, our focus on revealing structure supersedes using these conventions. We differentiate abstract from concrete classes using comments in the code. Throughout the book, however, we attempt to be as clear as possible in naming the different classes. You may want to adopt some of these more common conventions, once you better understand them, to aid in keeping your code clear.

Abstract classes and overriding inheritance

As you become familiar with design patterns, you'll see more and more use of interfaces and its close cousin the *abstract class*. In ActionScript 3.0 the abstract class is a little problematic because no class can be actually defined as abstract. While you can use the public statement to make a class public, ActionScript 3.0 (and ECMAScript) chose not to include abstract classes in the language, as does Java.

However, you can create an abstract class in ActionScript 3.0. All you have to do is create a regular class and treat it as an abstract class. Like interfaces, abstract classes can have abstract methods that are not directly implemented. Rather, abstract classes are subclassed and any abstract methods are overridden and implemented very much like methods are in using interfaces. However, abstract classes can have implemented methods as well; so when you need both abstract and implemented methods, abstract classes are key to such design patterns as the Factory Method (Chapter 2), Decorator (Chapter 4), and the Composite (Chapter 6), as well as others.

You know from inheritance that when one class subclasses another, the subclass inherits the methods of the superclass. With an abstract class, you do not implement the class but instead subclass it, and then implement the subclass and its methods. Because of the abstract nature of at least some of the methods in the abstract class, you must *override* them. Using the override statement, an overridden class maintains its signature but can have its own unique details. You must be sure that the name, number, type of parameters, and the return type are the same. In other words, when you override a method from an abstract class, you treat the method exactly the same as an interface method.

Example 1-21 through Example 1-23 make up an application that illustrates how an abstract class works. The abstract class has two methods; a concrete one and an abstract one.

Example 1-21. AbstractClass.as

```
package
{
    //Abstract class
    public class AbstractClass
    {
        function abstractMethod():void {}
        function concreteMethod():void
        {
            trace("I'm a concrete method from an abstract class")
        }
    }
}
```

The subclass inherits the methods and interface from the abstract class, and it provides details for the abstract method by overriding it. However, the subclass leaves the concrete class as is and does not attempt to instantiate the superclass.

Example 1-22. Subclass.as

```
package
{
    //Subclass of Abstract class
    public class Subclass extends AbstractClass
    {
        override function abstractMethod( ):void
        {
            trace("This is the overidden abstract method");
        }
    }
}
```

When the application finally implements the methods originating in the abstract class, it does so by programming to the interface (AbstractClass) but instantiates through the subclass (Subclass). So the instance, doDemo, is typed as AbstractClass but instantiated as Subclass.

Example 1-23. ImplementSub.as

```
package
{
    //Implement Subclass of Abstract class
    import flash.display.Sprite;

    public class ImplementSub extends Sprite
    {
        private var doDemo:AbstractClass;

        public function ImplementSub( )
        {
            doDemo=new Subclass( );
            doDemo.abstractMethod( );
            doDemo.concreteMethod( );
        }
    }
}
```

The following shows what appears in the Output window when you test the program:

```
This is the overidden abstract method
I'm a concrete method from an abstract class
```

At this point you may be scratching your head wondering why you should go through this kind of convolution to do what you could do with a non-abstract class. Instead of subclassing the abstract class, overriding one of the methods, and then implementing the subclass, we could have just written both methods the way we wanted them in the first place and not have to override anything. The next section attempts to answer that question.

Why use interfaces and abstract classes?

To understand why to use interfaces and abstract classes, we need to consider the whole purpose of design patterns. It's the *ability to reuse object-oriented software*. We've been using fairly simple examples to help clarify the concepts. However, typical software is usually far more complex, and the algorithms more sophisticated. Once you complete a project, you're likely to have to make a change. The larger and more complex the project, the more difficult it is to reuse the assets you've developed, maintain the interconnections and generally make any kind of change without unraveling the whole thing or introducing code that may make future change impossible.

To illustrate what this means, consider the application in Examples 1-21 to 1-23 in the previous section. Multiply the complexity of the class `AbstractClass` by a factor of 10. Do the same to the number of subclasses. Now you're dealing with some serious complexity. Next, consider that you need to maintain the functionality of the class, `Subclass`, and yet change the abstract method in the `AbstractClass` for a new functionality. Also, you have to maintain all of the interfaces and connections you've built.

Because you used an abstract class, you can create a new subclass that overrides the abstract function and uses it in a different way. To see how this all works, we'll make a new subclass of the `AbstractClass` and change the abstract method. We're not changing anything else in the entire application, so we don't have to worry about everything working together because we can separate our new subclass and method and only implement them where needed. Other subclasses of the `AbstractClass` are unaffected. Examples 1-24 and 1-25 show the two new classes created to make the change.

Example 1-24. SubclassChange.as

```
package
{
    //A New Subclass of Abstract class with a change
    public class SubclassChange extends AbstractClass
    {
        override function abstractMethod( ):void
        {
            trace("This is the new abstractMethod!!")
            trace("Made just one little important change.");
            trace("But this still works just fine!");
        }
    }
}
```

Note that instead of having a single `trace` statement, Example 1-24 uses three. This modification simulates a more complex change. However, Example 1-25, which implements the application, is identical to Example 1-23.

Example 1-25. ImplementSubChange.as

```
package
{
    //ImplementSubChange of Abstract class
    import flash.display.Sprite;

    public class ImplementSubChange extends Sprite
    {
        private var doDemo:AbstractClass;

        public function ImplementSubChange()
        {
            doDemo=new SubclassChange();
            doDemo.abstractMethod();
            doDemo.concreteMethod();
        }
    }
}
```

All the changes are revealed in the line,

```
doDemo.abstractMethod();
```

Even though the line is the same as Example 1-23, the output window reveals that a good deal has changed:

```
This is the new abstractMethod!!
Made just one little important change.
But this still works just fine!
I'm a concrete method from an abstract class
```

What's important is *not* that it made the changes. The point that you need to consider carefully is the fact that such changes can be made without disrupting the other elements in your application that you have reused. So without having to rewrite the entire application, you can keep its functionality while making necessary changes.

Polymorphism

The root of polymorphism is a word that could easily replace it to describe the process— *metamorphosis*. The term is from the Greek *metamorphoun*, meaning to transform. One definition describes metamorphosis as a magic-like transformation—something a sorcerer would do. If you like, think of polymorphism as giving the programmer the power of a sorcerer.

Generating Polymorphism Using an Abstract Class

Another definition of polymorphism is that it allows for *many* (poly) *forms* (morph). In Example 1-21 through Example 1-25, you saw how the `abstractMethod` had more than a single form. That's polymorphism. To see it in a more practical application, consider people's taste in music and emerging forms of music. Suppose you create a class with a method set up to show a person's musical tastes, and then build your application using that method for the different genres. Example 1-26 through Example 1-31 provide a simple example of such an application. The root abstract class is named `Polymorphism` in honor of the concept it illustrates.

Example 1-26. Polymorphism.as

```
package
{
    //Abstract class
    public class Polymorphism
    {
        public function myMusic( ):void
        {
            //Reserve details for subclasses
        }
    }
}
```

Example 1-27. Rock.as

```
package
{
    public class Rock extends Polymorphism
    {
        override public function myMusic( ):void
        {
            trace("Play Jimmie");
        }
    }
}
```

Example 1-28. Classic.as

```
package
{
    public class Classic extends Polymorphism
    {
        override public function myMusic( ):void
        {
            trace("Play Mozart");
        }
    }
}
```

Example 1-29. Country.as

```
package
{
    public class Country extends Polymorphism
    {
        override public function myMusic( ):void
        {
```

Example 1-29. Country.as (continued)

```
        trace("Play Willie");
      }
    }
}
```

Example 1-30. Jazz.as

```
package
{
    public class Jazz extends Polymorphism
    {
        override public function myMusic():void
        {
            trace("Play Coltrane");
        }
    }
}
```

Example 1-31. PlayMusic.as

```
package
{
    import flash.display.Sprite;
    public class PlayMusic extends Sprite
    {
        var rock:Polymorphism;
        var classic:Polymorphism;
        var country:Polymorphism;
        var jazz:Polymorphism;

        public function PlayMusic():void
        {
            rock=new Rock();
            rock.myMusic();
            classic=new Classic();
            classic.myMusic();
            country=new Country();
            country.myMusic();
            jazz=new Jazz();
            jazz.myMusic();
        }
    }
}
```

When you test the program, you'll see the following:

```
Play Jimmie
Play Mozart
Play Willie
Play Coltrane
```

As you can see, it's not rocket science and hardly cloaked in mystery. It's just poly-morphism. All instances were typed to the abstract class Polymorphism. Then they were

---

instantiated using the subclasses, and each launched the same method, `myMusic( )`. However, with each usage, even though all shared the same datatype (or supertype), `Polymorphism`, each instance's use of the method generates a unique outcome.

Looking at the program and your MP3 library, you may be thinking, "That's not nearly enough music categories." What about *R&B*, *Country*, *Alternative, Hip-Hop*, and *Cowboy* music? (*Cowboy?*) We couldn't agree more. Go ahead and create new subclasses using polymorphism to add all the categories you want. (This is not one of those exercises where the answer is at the end of the chapter or the back of the book. You're on your own. Programmers don't get polymorphism right without writing their own code. See if you've got the right stuff.) By the way, notice that you can make all the changes you want with polymorphism without having to change any of the other classes. That's the whole point of polymorphism.

Implementing Polymorphism with Interfaces

The ActionScript 3.0 `interface` statement and structure is the other powerful tool for polymorphism in both object-oriented programming and design patterns. Suppose you're building an e-business site. You have no idea how many new products the site will have, but you know the site will have many different products that change regularly. You're going to need something that will handle a wide variety of products, and a way of displaying them.

You know that you'll need the following operations, but you're not sure about the details:

* Description
* Price
* Product display

One way to set up an e-business site would be to create a class that has methods for all three operations. However, suppose you find out that the client wants different kinds of displays for the different products. She wants dynamically loaded video for video products (e.g. TV sets), sound for sound products (e.g. MP3 players) and graphic images for all other products. The operations for both description and price methods are pretty standard, but the display method is going to have to be very flexible. That's where polymorphism comes in. We could use an abstract class, but to provide ever more flexibility just in case other unanticipated requirements crop up, we'll use an interface.

Example 1-32 through Example 1-36 make up the e-business application. The interface, `IBiz`, contains the primary operations with unique signatures but not any details. This will allow us to create the unique details we need as long as we keep all the signatures the same.

Example 1-32. IBiz.as

```
package
{
    public interface IBiz
    {
        function productDescribe( ):String;
        function productPrice(price:Number):String;
        function productDisplay(product:String):void;
    }
}
```

Example 1-33 introduces something new. The Plasma class extends one class, Sprite, and implements another, IBiz. Placing a video on the stage requires a Sprite object, but we still need the IBiz interface methods; so using both the extends and implements statements, we're able to have the best of both worlds.

Example 1-33. Plasma.as

```
package
{
    import flash.net.NetConnection;
    import flash.net.NetStream;
    import flash.media.Video;
    import flash.display.Sprite;

    public class Plasma extends Sprite implements IBiz
    {

        private var ns:NetStream;
        private var vid:Video;
        private var priceNow:Number;


        public function productDescribe( ):String
        {
            return "42 inch TV with Plasma screen";
        }

        public function productPrice(price:Number):String
        {
            priceNow=price;
            return "$" + priceNow + "\n";
        }

        public function productDisplay(flv:String):void
        {
            var nc:NetConnection=new NetConnection( );
            nc.connect(null);
            ns=new NetStream(nc);
            ns.play(flv);
            vid=new Video( );
            vid.attachNetStream(ns);
            addChild(vid);
```

Example 1-33. Plasma.as (continued)

```
        }
    }
}
```

In comparing Example 1-33 with Example 1-34, both the `productDescribe( )` and `productPrice( )` methods look pretty much the same other than the literal used in the return statement in the `productDescribe( )`. In fact, by adding a string parameter to the `productDescribe( )` method, we could make them identical. However, the point of this application is to demonstrate polymorphism, and so creating different forms of the methods is intentional.

You can see the practicality of polymorphism by comparing the `productDisplay( )` methods in the two examples. Example 1-33 is set up to play a video and Example 1-34 a sound. However, note that the identical signatures are maintained in both examples.

Example 1-34. MP3Player.as

```
package
{
    import flash.media.Sound;
    import flash.media.SoundChannel;
    import flash.net.URLRequest;

    public class MP3Player implements IBiz
    {
        private var sound:Sound;
        private var playChannel:SoundChannel;
        private var doPlay:URLRequest;
        private var MP3Price:Number;

        public function productDescribe( ):String
        {
            return "MP3Player with 1 Terabyte of Memory";
        }

        public function productPrice(price:Number):String
        {
            MP3Price=price;
            return "$" + MP3Price + "\n";
        }

        public function productDisplay(song:String):void
        {
            sound=new Sound( );
            playChannel=new SoundChannel( );
            doPlay=new URLRequest(song);
            sound.load(doPlay);
            playChannel=sound.play( );
        }
    }
}
```

Example 1-35 has further differences in its productDisplay( ) details. Instead of either video or sound operations, it contains operations for loading files. Yet, like the other two, the signature and interfaces are still the same.

Example 1-35. Computers.as

```
package
{
    import flash.display.Loader;
    import flash.net.URLRequest;
    import flash.display.Sprite;

    public class Computers extends Sprite implements IBiz
    {
        private var hotz:Number;
        private var loadPix:Loader;
        private var namePix:URLRequest;

        public function productDescribe( ):String
        {
            return "New 10 gHz processor, 30 gigabyte RAM, includes
                32 inch screen";
        }

        public function productPrice(price:Number):String
        {
            hotz=price;
            return "$" + hotz + "\n";
        }

        public function productDisplay(computer:String):void
        {
            loadPix=new Loader( );
            namePix=new URLRequest(computer);
            loadPix.load(namePix);
            addChild(loadPix);
        }
    }
}
```

Now that all the classes and the interface are complete, all that's left is a class to test the application. As you've seen, good OOP and preparation for working with design patterns suggests programming to the interface and not the implementation as we've been doing. However, in looking at Example 1-36, all the typing (setting the datatype) is to the Plasma, MP3Player, and Computers implementations and not the IBiz interface. This is because each of the implementations extended the Sprite class. So we're dealing with two supertypes, IBiz and Sprite. To test the application, the instances are typed as one of the specific implementations instead of the interface. In the section "Program to Interfaces over Implementations" later in this chapter, you'll see how to construct your interface and implementation so that you can still type to the interface when there's more than a single type in the implementation. (In Example 1-20 you can see how an interface structure is programmed to the interface instead of an implementation.)

Example 1-36. DoBusiness.as

```
package
{
    import flash.display.Sprite;

    public class DoBusiness extends Sprite
    {
        public function DoBusiness()
        {
            //TV
            var tv:Plasma=new Plasma();
            trace(tv.productDescribe());
            trace(tv.productPrice(855));
            tv.productDisplay("plasma.flv");
            tv.x=160;
            tv.y=110;
            addChild(tv);

            //MP3
            var mp3:MP3Player=new MP3Player();
            trace(mp3.productDescribe());
            trace(mp3.productPrice(245));
            mp3.productDisplay("bongo.mp3");

            //Computers
            var computers:Computers=new Computers();
            trace(computers.productDescribe());
            trace(computers.productPrice(1200));
            computers.productDisplay("whizbang.gif");
            addChild(computers);
        }
    }
}
```

You will need an FLV file, an MP3 file, and a GIF file for this application. Name the FLV file *plasma.flv*, the MP3 file *bongo.mp3*, and the GIF file *whizbang.gif*. The contents are unimportant but the names and file types are important.

Open a new Flash document, save it in the same folder with the rest of the application, and type in **DoBusiness** in the Document class window. When you test it, the Output window shows the following:

```
42 inch TV with Plasma screen
$855

MP3Player with 1 Terabyte of Memory
$245

New 10 gHz processor, 30 gigabyte RAM, includes 32 inch flat screen monitor
$1200
```

In addition to messages in the Output window, you should see something like Figure 1-6 on the stage.

Figure 1-6. Graphic file and video appear on the stage

In addition to the visible graphics, you should also hear the sound played by the MP3 file. (This multimedia experience has been brought to you by polymorphism and the letter P.)

Principles of Design Pattern Development

The founding principles of design patterns are laid down in the Gang of Four's (GoF) canon, *Design Patterns: Elements of Reusable Object-Oriented Software*. The two essential principles are:

- Program to an interface, not an implementation
- Favor object composition over class inheritance

If you skipped the section on the four basic OOP principles because you already know them, the first principle of Design Pattern OOP was introduced, but only briefly. Not to worry, we'll go over it in detail.

Before going further, we need to clarify some basic terms. While these terms are fairly simple, they can trip you up if you don't understand how they're used in context. The subsequent chapters use these terms a good deal, and a misunderstanding at the outset can lead to confusion now and later.

Implementation

For the most part, the term *implementation* is a noun referring to the details—the actual code—in a program. So when referring to an implementation, the reference is to the actual program as it is coded. Implementation is the internal details of a program, but is often used to refer to a method or class itself.

You may run into some confusion when the keyword `implements` refers to contracting with an `interface` structure. For example, the line:

```
class MyClass implements IMyInterface
```

has the effect of passing the *interface* of `IMyInterface` to `MyClass`. To say that `MyClass` *implements* `IMyInterface` really means that `MyClass` promises to use all the signatures of `IMyInterface` and add the coding details to them. So the phrase `MyClass` implemented `IMyInterface` means that `MyClass` took all the methods in `IMyInterface` and added the code necessary to make them do something while preserving their signatures.

One of the two main principles of design pattern programming is *program to an interface, not an implementation*. However, you must remember that *implementation* is employed in different contexts, and its specific meaning depends on these contexts. Throughout this book, you will see references to implementation used again and again with different design patterns, and you need to consider the other elements being discussed where the term is used.

State

The term *state* is not part of the ActionScript 3.0 lexicon (like `implements` is), but the term is used in discussing design patterns. Essentially, state is used to refer to an object's current condition. For the most part you will see state used to convey the value of a key variable. Imagine a class with a single method with a Boolean value set in the method. The Boolean can either be `true` or `false`. So its state is either `true` or `false`—which could represent on/off, allow/disallow, or any number of binary conditions. The exact meaning of `true` or `false` depends on the position of the class in the rest of the design pattern. A more specific example would be an object that plays and stops an MP3 file. If the MP3 is playing, it's in a play state, while if it's not playing, it's in a stop state.

One use of state is in the context of a state machine and the State design pattern you will be seeing in Chapter 10. A *state engine* is a data structure made up of a state network where changes in state affect the entire application. The State design pattern is centered on an object's behavior changing when its internal state changes. The term state here is a bit more contextually rich because it is the key concept around which the design pattern has been built.

In general, though, when you see *state* used, it's just referring to the current value of an object's variables.

Client and Request

In this age of the Internet and Web, the term *client* is used to differentiate the requesting source from the *server* from which a request is being made. We think of client/server pairs. Moreover, the term *request* is used to indicate that a Web page has been called from the server.

In the context of design patterns, instead of a client/server pair, think of a *client/ object* pair. A request is what the client sends to the object to get it to perform an operation—launch a method. In this context, a *request is the only way to get an object to execute a method's operations*. The request is the only way to launch an operation since the object's internal state cannot be accessed directly because of encapsulation.

 Don't forget Flash Media Server clients and servers! If you work with Flash Media Server 2, you're aware of client-side and server-side programs. You can launch a server-side method with a request from a client-side object. However, you can launch a client-side operation with a client-side request as well and a server-side method with a server-side request. So if you're using Flash Media Server 2, you're just going to have to keep the concepts separate.

In a nutshell, the *client* is the source of a *request* to an object's method. A quick example shows exactly what this looks like. Example 1-37 and Example 1-38 make up an application that does nothing except show a client making a request to an object.

Example 1-37. MyObject.as

```
package
{
    public class MyObject
    {
        private var fire:String;

        public function MyObject():void {}
        public function worksForRequest():void
        {
            fire="This was requested by a client";
            trace(fire);
        }
    }
}
```

The `MyObject` class's sole method is `worksForRequest( )`. The method is encapsulated, so it should have only a single way to launch its operations. Fortunately, all we need to do is create an instance of the class, and add the method to the instance to make it work, as Example 1-38 shows.

Example 1-38. MyClient.as

```
package
{
    import flash.display.Sprite;

    public class MyClient extends Sprite
    {
        var myClient:MyObject;
        public function MyClient( ):void
        {
            myClient=new MyObject( );
            myClient.worksForRequest( );
        }
    }
}
```

The output tells the whole story:

```
This was requested by a client
```

The client in this case is simply an instance of the object whose method it requests. The client/object relationship is through the request. Often the client adds specific details through a parameter, but the concept of a request is usually nothing more than invoking the method with an instance of the object that owns the method.

Program to Interfaces over Implementations

To understand why the authors of design patterns encourage programming to interfaces over implementations, you need to first understand the general goal of flexibility and reusability. Second, you need to appreciate the problem of managing dependency in large programs.

As we have noted in this chapter, the overall goal of design patterns is to create reusable code. In order to meet this overall goal, the code must be flexible. This does *not* mean that your application runs better or compiles faster. All it does is help you create code that you can reuse in other projects. The more time and effort you spend, the larger the team engaged in working with the code, the more important this overall goal.

Managing Dependency

The need for software flexibility leads to the need to manage dependency. When your code depends on a specific implementation, and the implementation changes, your client dependency leads to unexpected results or fails to run altogether. By depending on interfaces, your code is decoupled from the implementation, allowing variation in the implementation. This does not mean you get rid of dependency, but instead you just manage it more flexibly. A key element of this approach is to separate the design from the implementation. By doing so, you separate the client from the implementation as well.

As we have seen, you can use the ActionScript 3.0 interface structure or an abstract class to set up this kind of flexible dependence. However, when you use either, you must be aware of the way in which to manage the dependency. If you use an interface structure, any change in the interface will cause failure in all the clients that use the interface. For example, suppose you have five methods in an interface. You decide that you need two more. As soon as you add the two new methods to your interface, your client is broken. So, if you use the interface structure, you must treat the interface as set in stone. If you want to add new functionality, simply create a new interface.

The alternative to using the interface structure is to use abstract classes. While the abstract class structure is not supported in ActionScript 3.0 as interfaces are, you can easily create a class to do everything an abstract class does. As we saw in several examples in this chapter beginning with Example 1-3, creating and using an abstract class is simply adhering to the rules that abstract classes follow anyway. For example, abstract classes are never directly implemented.

The advantage of an abstract class over an interface is that you won't destroy a client when you add methods to the base class. All the abstract function must be overridden to be used in a unique manner, but if your client has no use for a new method, by doing nothing, the method is inherited but not employed or changed. On the other hand, every single method in an interface structure must be implemented.

A further advantage of an abstract class is that you can add default behaviors and even set up concrete methods inherited by all subclasses. Of course the downside of default behaviors and concrete methods is that a subclass may not want or need the default or concrete methods, and a client may end up doing something unwanted and unexpected if any concrete changes are introduced. Whatever the case, though, management of dependency is easier with the flexibility offered by interfaces and abstract classes over concrete classes and methods.

So the decision of whether to use an interface or abstract class depends on what you want your design to do. If the ability to add more behaviors easily is most important, then abstract classes are a better choice. Alternatively, if you want independence from the base class, then choose an interface structure. No matter what you do, though, you need to think ahead beyond the first version of your application. If your application is built with an eye to future versions and possible ways that it can expand or change, you can better judge what design pattern would best achieve your goals.

Using Complex Interfaces

As you saw in Example 1-36, the program typed the instances to the implementation and not the interfaces as was done in Example 1-20. This was caused by the key methods being part of classes that implemented an interface and extended a class. Because of the way in which the different display objects need to be employed, this dilemma will be a common one in using Flash and ActionScript 3.0. Fortunately, a solution is at hand. (The solution may be considered a *workaround* instead of the correct usage of the different structures in ActionScript 3.0. However, with it, you can create methods that require some DisplayObject structure and program to the interface instead of the implementation.)

If the interface includes a method to include a DisplayObject type, it can be an integral part of the interface. Because Sprite is a subclass of the DisplayObject, its inclusion in the interface lets you type to the interface when the class you instantiate is a subclass of Sprite (or some other subclass of the DisplayObject, such as MovieClip.)

To see how this works, the application made up of Example 1-39 and Example 1-40 creates a simple video player. The VidPlayer class builds the structural details of the video playing operations. To do so requires that it subclass the Sprite class. By placing a getter method with a DisplayObject type in the IVid interface, the application sets up a way that the client can program to the interface.

Example 1-39. IVid.as

```
package
{
    import flash.display.DisplayObject;

    public interface IVid
    {
        function playVid(flv:String):void;
        function get displayObject():DisplayObject;
    }
}
```

The implementation of the IVid interface includes a key element. The displayObject() function is implemented to the DisplayObject class in building the VidPlayer class.

Example 1-40. VidPlayer.as

```
package
{
    import flash.net.NetConnection;
    import flash.net.NetStream;
    import flash.media.Video;
    import flash.display.Sprite;
    import flash.display.DisplayObject;
```

Example 1-40. VidPlayer.as (continued)

```
public class VidPlayer extends Sprite implements IVid
{

    private var ns:NetStream;
    private var vid:Video;
    private var nc:NetConnection;

    public function get displayObject():DisplayObject
    {
        return this;
    }

    public function playVid(flv:String):void
    {
        nc=new NetConnection();
        nc.connect(null);
        ns=new NetStream(nc);
        ns.play(flv);
        vid=new Video();
        vid.attachNetStream(ns);
        addChild(vid);
    }
}
}
```

Keep in mind that a getter method, using the get keyword, looks like a property, and is treated like one. Any reference to displayObject is actually a method request. The trick is to add the instance to the display list, and at the same time call the method that establishes the instance as a DisplayObject. Example 1-41 does just that.

Example 1-41. DoVid.as

```
package
{
    import flash.display.Sprite;

    public class DoVid extends Sprite
    {
        //Type as Interface
        private var showTime:IVid;

        public function DoVid()
        {
            //Play the video
            showTime=new VidPlayer();
            showTime.playVid("iVid.flv");
            //Include DisplayObject instance
            addChild(showTime.displayObject);
            showTime.displayObject.x=100;
            showTime.displayObject.y=50;
        }
    }
}
```

In reviewing how the process works, first, the showTime instance is typed to the interface, IVid. Next, showTime instantiates the VidPlayer class that has all the details for playing the video. By doing so, it inherits the Sprite class as well as the IVid interface. Then the showTime client plays the video using the playVid( ) method. Finally, when the showTime instance is added to the display list with the addChild statement, it is added as both the child of the VidPlayer class and the DisplayObject class by using the displayObject getter. Because the getter, displayObject, is included in the display list, you will *not* get the following error:

```
1067: Implicit coercion of a value of type IVid to an unrelated type
    flash.display:DisplayObject.
```

IVid appears in the error because the instance was typed to the interface instead of the implementation. By slipping in the DisplayObject typed getter method, we avoid the error.

Favor Composition

Throughout this chapter, we have discussed the principle of programming to the interface instead of the implementation. The second principle of object-oriented design posited by Gamma, Helm, Johnson and Vlissdes (GoF) is: *Favor object composition over class inheritance.*

To understand this second key principle, we need to understand exactly what *composition* means, and its advantages over inheritance. After all, the principle is essentially stating that your programs will be better using composition than inheritance.

Does this mean to abandon inheritance? After all, inheritance is one key concept in object-oriented programming. Actually, what GoF discuss is that most programmers rely too heavily on inheritance, and need to use it more in conjunction with composition. Most programmers create new objects from old objects using inheritance, and, through composition, the old and new objects can be used together.

The best way to understand composition is to see it in the context of its use. In this book, both the State and Strategy patterns are built using composition, and they depend on delegation. In the State design pattern, an object delegates requests to an object representing the current state in an application. In the Strategy design pattern, specific requests are delegated to objects representing strategies (algorithms) for solving problems. The great advantage of both these design patterns is that they are flexible and not bogged down in inflexible dependencies.

Doing Composition

To understand composition, we will start with a simple example. In the next sample application you'll see that both inheritance and composition are used together. Each example will show one of the following relationships:

- "Is a" relationship: object inherited
- "Has a" relationship: object composition
- "Uses a" relationship: one object used by another object (instantiated without inheritance or composition.)

In the next section on delegation, we'll look at these relationships. For now, though, each of the classes in the application made up of Examples 1-42 through 1-44 show each of these relationships. The comments in the examples identify the type of relationship. First, we establish a base class to be the delegate.

Example 1-42. BaseClass.as

```
package
{
    public class BaseClass
    {
        public function homeBase()
        {
            trace("This is from the Base Class");
        }
    }
}
```

Composition includes a reference to another class in a class definition. Example 1-43 shows how a class is set up to use composition. The line

```
    private var baseClass:BaseClass;
```

keeps the reference to BaseClass in its class definition. That line is the basis of composition. The HasBase class now *Has a* BaseClass. In this particular implementation, the HasBase class creates an instance of BaseClass in its constructor. Finally, a public function, doBase( ), delegates the work back to BaseClass.

Example 1-43. HasBase .as

```
package
{
    //Composition
    public class HasBase
    {
        private var baseClass:BaseClass;

        public function HasBase()
        {
            baseClass=new BaseClass();
```

Example 1-43. HasBase .as (continued)

```
        }
        public function doBase( )
        {
            baseClass.homeBase( );
        }
    }
}
```

Now, in Example 1-44, the HasBase class is used to delegate an operation back to BaseClass. All this is done without having to inherit any of BaseClass' properties, but HasBase does have a BaseClass. However, HasBase is not a BaseClass.

Example 1-44. DoHasBase.as

```
package
{
    //Executes the HasBase Composition class
    import flash.display.Sprite

    public class DoHasBase extends Sprite
    {
        private var hasBase:HasBase;
        public function DoHasBase( )
        {
            hasBase=new HasBase( );
            hasBase.doBase( );
        }
    }
}
```

The advantages of using composition over inheritance are difficult to see in such a small example. Later in the book, when examining the different design patterns, the advantages will become clearer. However, when composition is used with a large project, especially with a design pattern, its advantages begin to make even more sense. You'll really see why composition is preferred over inheritance when you have to make changes to a large, complex program working with several other co-developers.

Using Delegation

Delegation is one of the most important concepts in working with design patterns because by using it, composition can have the same power of reusability as inheritance, with far greater flexibility. Because delegation typically works with inheritance, any examination should *not* be one where inheritance and delegation are treated as mutually exclusive. Rather, we need to see how they differ and how they are used in conjunction with one another—because that's how they're typically cast in a design pattern.

The clearest way we've seen composition distinguished from inheritance is through describing the relationship between components in an application. If ClassB is subclassed from ClassA, ClassB is described as *being a* ClassA. However, if ClassB delegates to ClassA through composition, then ClassB can be said to *have a* ClassA.

You may have a class set up for loading SWF files in a desired configuration. You want the functionality of loading the SWF files in that configuration, but you also want to play audio using MP3 files. Using composition, you could simply create a class that delegates each function to the appropriate classes. Figure 1-7 shows this relationship:

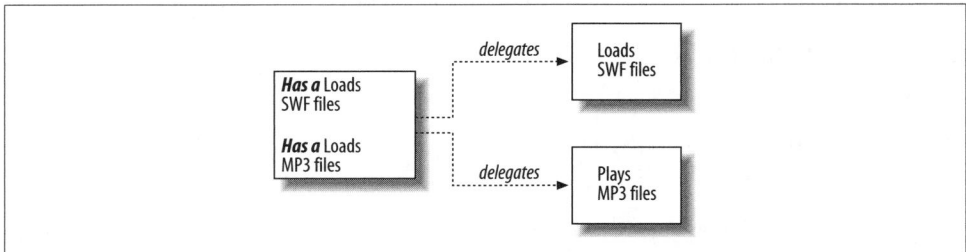

Figure 1-7. Delegating to different classes

In this situation, inheritance would not be too helpful. You could subclass one class but not both. Of course you could instantiate an instance of each class in the third class, or simply subclass one class and then create an instance of whichever class you didn't subclass. That would be a new class with an "is-a" and a "uses-a" different class for the other functionality. A class is considered a "uses-a" when it creates an instance of another class but does not hold a reference to it.

To understand and best use composition, you need to understand how delegation really works, and to explain, you need to see it in a slightly more realistic example of its use. The application will simulate a media application for playing and recording media files using Flash and Flash Media Server 2 (FMS2). You can play either FLV or MP3 files using FMS2. While you can record FLV files using FMS2, you can't publish MP3 files by themselves. This application is designed for adding future features and reducing dependencies at the same time.

If you are pretty sure that both the media server and your application will change, then you'll want to minimize dependencies by using composition and delegation. For example, suppose that a future version of FMS2 changes, and you can record MP3 files directly. You'd only have to change the RecordAudio class so that it would record audio. By making that change, nothing else in the application would be affected. Alternatively, suppose you have a holographic player that you want to add to the mix. You can easily add another class that will play and/or record holographic images without disturbing the rest of the application.

Examples 1-45 though 1-54 make up the application. Save all the .as files in the same folder. It represents a typical use of composition.

Example 1-45. Media.as

```
package
{
    //Abstract class
    class Media
    {
        //Composition: Reference to two interfaces
        var playMedia:PlayMedia;
        var recordMedia:RecordMedia;

        public function Media() {}

        public function doPlayMedia():void
        {
            //Delegates to PlayMedia
            playMedia.playNow();
        }
        public function doRecordMedia():void
        {
            //Delegates to RecordMedia
            recordMedia.recordNow();
        }
    }
}
```

Example 1-46. VideoFlash.as

```
package
{
    //Concrete Media subclass: Video
    class VideoFlash extends Media
    {
        public function VideoFlash()
        {
            //Inherits composition references from superclass
            playMedia = new PlayVideo();
            recordMedia = new RecordVideo();
        }
    }
}
```

Example 1-47. Mp3.as

```
package
{
    //Concrete Media subclass: Audio
    public class Mp3 extends Media
    {
```

Example 1-47. Mp3.as (continued)

```
    public function Mp3( )
    {
        //Inherits composition references from superclass
        playMedia = new PlayAudio( );
        recordMedia = new RecordAudio( );
    }
  }
}
```

Example 1-48. PlayMedia.as

```
package
{
    //Interface for playing media
    interface PlayMedia
    {
        function playNow( ):void;
    }
}
```

Example 1-49. PlayVideo.as

```
package
{
    //Concrete PlayMedia: Video
    class PlayVideo implements PlayMedia
    {
        public function playNow( ):void
        {
            trace("Playing my video. Look at that!");
        }
    }
}
```

Example 1-50. PlayAudio.as

```
package
{
    //Concrete PlayMedia: Audio
    class PlayAudio implements PlayMedia
    {
        public function playNow( ):void
        {
            trace("My MP3 is cranking out great music!");
        }
    }
}
```

Example 1-51. RecordMedia.as

```
package
{
    //Interface for recording media
    interface RecordMedia
    {
        function recordNow( ):void;
    }
}
```

Example 1-52. RecordVideo.as

```
package
{
    //Concrete RecordMedia: Video
    class RecordVideo implements RecordMedia
    {
        public function recordNow( ):void
        {
            trace("I'm recording this tornado live! Holy....crackle, crackle\n");
        }
    }
}
```

Example 1-53. RecordAudio.as

```
package
{
    //Concrete RecordMedia: Audio
    class RecordAudio implements RecordMedia
    {
        public function recordNow( ):void
        {
            trace("Rats! I can't record MP3 by itself.\n");
        }
    }
}
```

Example 1-54. TestMedia.as

```
package
{
    import flash.display.Sprite;

    public class TestMedia extends Sprite
    {
        public function TestMedia( )
        {
            var delVideo:Media=new VideoFlash( );
            delVideo.doPlayMedia( );
            delVideo.doRecordMedia( );
```

Example 1-54. TestMedia.as (continued)

```
        var delAudio:Media = new Mp3();
        delAudio.doPlayMedia();
        delAudio.doRecordMedia();
    }
  }
}
```

Create a Flash document, save it in the same folder with the class files, and, in the Document class window, type in **TestMedia**. When you test it, the Output window simulates the behaviors.

```
Playing my video. Look at that!
I'm recording this tornado live! Holy....crackle, crackle

My MP3 is cranking out great music!
Rats! I can't record MP3 by itself.
```

The algorithms you'd have in an actual application would be more complex than the simple trace statements. However, no matter how complex they got, the dependencies are set up so that a change in one would only affect those elements in the application that you want to change, and not those you don't want to change.

Making Composition, Inheritance, and Instantiation Work Together

We haven't compared the relative advantages and disadvantages between composition and inheritance because with composition, both composition and inheritance operate in the same environment. For that matter, so too does instantiation where one class simply instantiates an instance of another class. The idea that one would work with one and exclude the other was never the point made by GoF in their principle to *favor composition over inheritance*. Yes, stated that way, that's what the principle sounds like. However, in explaining the principle, the founders of design patterns not only explicitly point out that composition and inheritance work together, their design patterns show it.

The application in Example 1-45 through Example 1-54 was used to illustrate composition. It also shows inheritance and instantiation at work. To see this relationship better, consider Figure 1-8.

In Figure 1-8, you can see that the Media class *delegates* to the RecordMedia class. It does this by holding a reference to that class in its definition. (See Example 1-45.)

```
    var recordMedia:RecordMedia;
```

In the VideoFlash class, you can see that it *inherits* from the Media class. At the same time, though, VideoFlash *instantiates* RecordVideo.

```
    recordMedia = new RecordVideo();
```

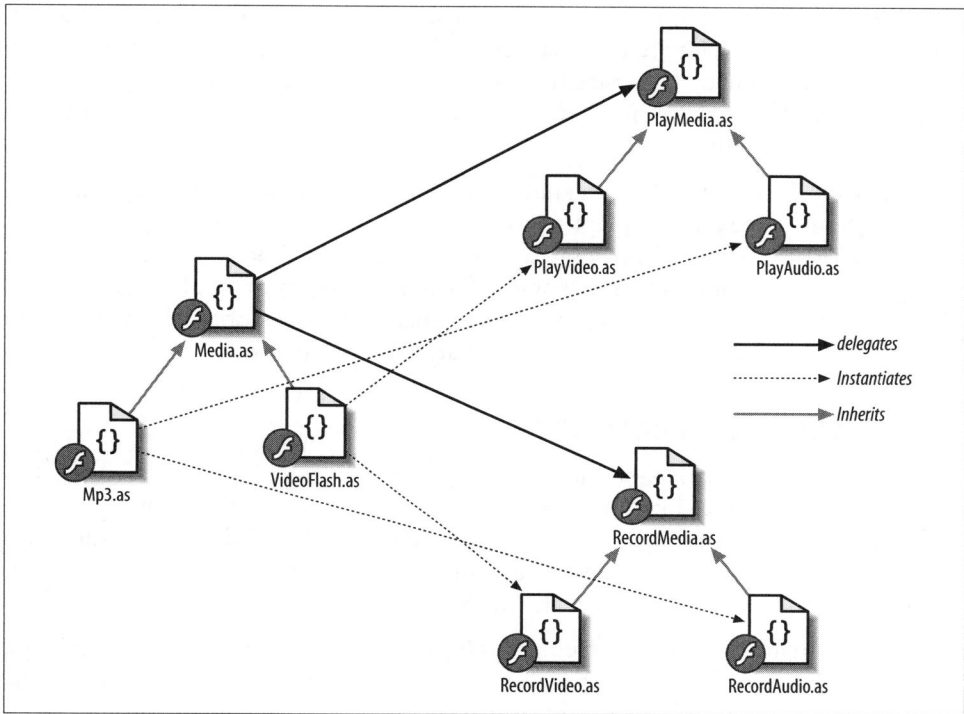

Figure 1-8. Relationships of composition, inheritance, and instantiation

In turn, `RecordVideo` *inherits* from `RecordMedia`. At this point, we're right back to the class to which the `Media` class first delegated, `RecordMedia`.

Using composition without inheritance is difficult to imagine in most practical applications. Thus, instead of focusing on the relative advantages of each, for now consider composition and inheritance a team. In Chapter 11, we again consider this issue of favoring composition over inheritance in the context of using composition with design patterns.

Maintenance and Extensibility Planning

A number of years ago, we built a web site designed for change. At the time, no thought was given to design patterns, but instead we knew that the site would change based on experience, and were acutely aware of making sure that the site was set up for accepting change without having to redo it.

This was a case where the plan worked too well. The site is easy to update and as a result, we really haven't bothered to take the time to rework the site to incorporate new concepts. It's starting to look a little old-fashioned, and we'd like to upgrade the version of Flash so that we can optimize video and all the new features in Flash CS3 and ActionScript 3.0. However, the plan illustrates a basic truth about software in general and web development in particular. You're going to spend more time on maintenance and changing a site than you are building it in the first place. As a result, you need to plan for maintenance and extensibility, and not just to get things working right in the first place.

Had the web site that had been planned for change been done with design patterns, not only would it be able to adapt to change, we wouldn't have to scrap the current design and start all over from scratch to extend the site. That is, only part of the planning process should address change of a static category. You also need to plan for extending the site to incorporate more than what you originally planned to change. That is, you may need to add new materials to change.

Planning Only for Maintenance

While the web site described as *built for change* has persisted, it has not evolved. The site has been easy to maintain because its main function loads an image, a text file, and menu items for a given product. By either changing the label on an existing button or adding a button, changing and adding products is pretty simple as well. So it has a little extensibility in the sense that its not fixed to a single product.

However, the site really isn't set up for robust extensibility. For instance, adding a blog to the site or changing the way that the menus work would take the same amount of re-structuring as it would to start from scratch. So, while changing products in the site is simple, changing the site is not. Structurally, the site looks something like Figure 1-9—The Big Function.

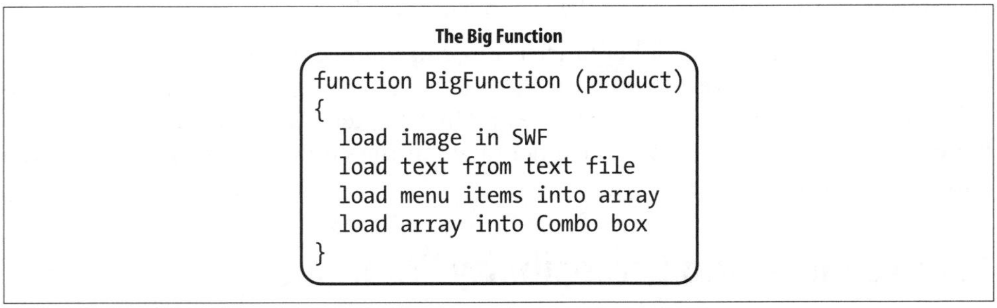

The Big Function

```
function BigFunction (product)
{
   load image in SWF
   load text from text file
   load menu items into array
   load array into Combo box
}
```

Figure 1-9. The Big Function

It doesn't matter whether the big function is directly instantiated, gained through inheritance, or a delegate of composition. It has no flexibility other than the parameter to tell it what to place on the stage. If its algorithm is changed, it could wreck havoc on its use. You can view it as tough and inflexible because it gets one job done in one way. Alternatively, the big function can be seen as dainty and fragile because of its dependency on a single routine, and because it is subject to freeze up when interacting with new elements in the application. In any case, it doesn't lend itself to a flexible site, and we should rethink it.

Adding Extensibility to a Plan with Granularity

The plan using The Big Function, even though it has limited flexibility, is bound to break down and fail in the long run. To avoid getting stuck with an inalterable application, you need to consider some granularity in your design. In this context *granularity* refers to the amount of functionality each of your classes has. The trade-off between full functionality and granularity is that the more functionality a class has, the more it will do all by itself. After all, most classes we create are developed to add the functionality of several built-in classes. However, sometimes less is better. The less functionality a class has, the more components in your application its functionality can employ. Figure 1-10 shows how this granularity might work.

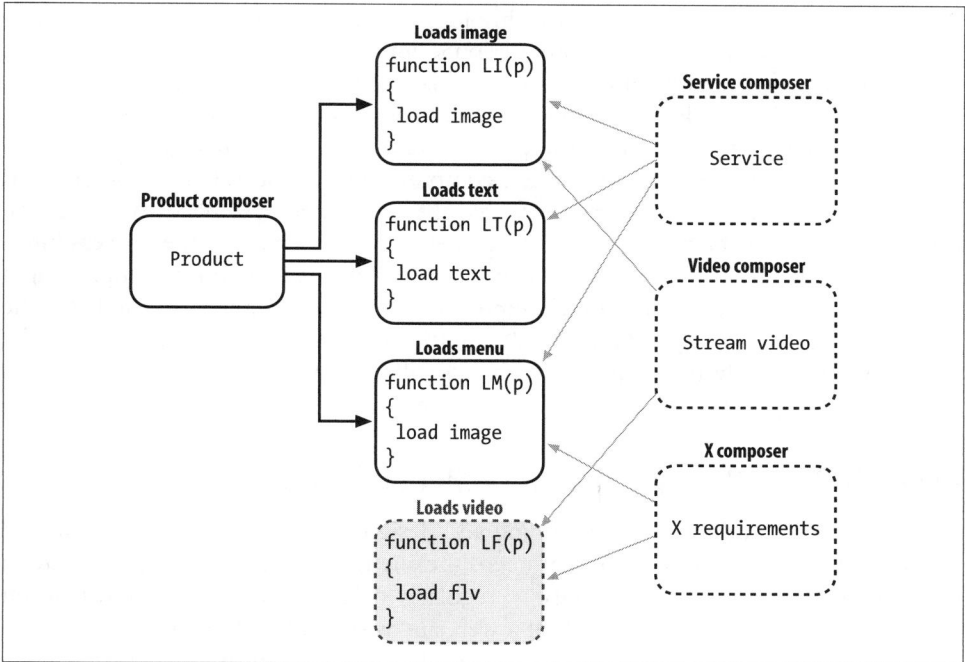

Figure 1-10. Granular functions

The Big Function from the last section has been broken down into three smaller (more granular) functions. Using composition, the functionality of the Big Function is duplicated. However, the granularity gives the developer far more options in the future. In the context of developing a real-world application, your design must *look over the horizon*. That is, you need to plan for both possible and unknown changes.

Figure 1-10 shows some possible future extensions to the application (those with dashed lines). The value of granularity is that the new classes can use some or all of the more granular functions. That would be impossible with the single Big Function from the previous section. Likewise, new functions can be added and used with the old ones.

Your Application Plan: It Ain't You Babe

Jennifer Tidwell, in talking about interface design, reminds the designer that whatever else is true, the designer/developer is *not* the audience (or the client for that manner). Before pulling out your program development tools, you really need to get together with the client and find out what the client wants. The image of the programmer as the guy in the basement with a ponytail (*whom we don't let talk to our clients*) simply isn't a workable model, especially when you're planning for the Web.

Because the Web and Web-related technology are always changing, as clearly evidenced by the changes in Flash and ActionScript over recent years, what can and cannot be accomplished by any software tool is always changing. Because the developer is responsible for knowing the limits and possibilities of software better than anyone, she needs to be part of the process. In larger firms, this role is part of a graphic design, interface design, human computer interaction (HCI) designers, and information design team. In smaller firms, the developer may have to fill several roles, but whatever the arrangement, developers need to be part of the process interacting with the client whose business or organization depends on accomplishing a goal. The better the developer understands what the client wants and the better he can communicate the opportunities and limitations of the software to accomplish the goals, the more likely the software produced will accomplish what the client needs for success.

Using OOP and Design Patterns to Meet Client Goals

The role of object-oriented programming and design patterns is to help the software developer plan for creating a site that keeps the client's site healthy. Keeping a site in good shape depends on the capacity to regularly update it, and to expand it when needed. Too often developers think of a web site as static, but sites are dynamic, living entities—or at least need to be conceived that way. Design patterns constitute a set of plans—architectural designs if you will—that provide the tools to keep web sites alive.

Flexibility is inherent in software reusability. Both OOP and design patterns were developed with the goal of both reusability and flexibility, and if an application is approached in the most practical manner imaginable, then design patterns make a great deal of sense. So rather than being a set of strict rules for creating great software, design patterns represent flexible tools for creating exactly the kind of site your client needs.

Choosing the Right Design Pattern

Choosing the best design pattern for a particular situation is as much an art as it is a formula. Throughout the book, you'll see that we've included a wide variety of examples, and you may even see a few similar examples with different design patterns. The reason is that most development challenges can be approached from more than a single angle. From one angle, a solution seems good and natural, but from a different angle, another solution seems better. For example, a major project employing a design pattern involved a video player that would be able to play, record, stop, and pause a video using Flash Media Server 2. The solution originally seemed to lie in state machine because of a related project. The "fit" between what needed to be done and the concepts in a state machine seemed to be perfect. From there it was a simple step to the State design pattern. It was tested as a solution, and it worked so well, and had the required flexibility, that it was adopted as the right solution.

As you go through the examples in the book, you'll see that the patterns have been organized into three parts: creational, structural, and behavioral. The parts in the book describe the general categories for the design patterns. The chapters within the parts explain how to create the designs in ActionScript 3.0, and give examples and explanations of their actual use.

In addition to organizing the design patterns into the purposes for which the patterns are designed, the Gang of Four also classified the patterns by *scope*. Scope refers to whether the pattern applies primarily to object or class. In selecting the design patterns for this book, we selected representative patterns from each of the matrices that these class and object classifications represent. Table 1-1 shows the design patterns chosen for this book organized by purpose and scope.

Table 1-1. Design pattern classifications

		Purpose		
		Creational	Structural	Behavioral
Scope	Class	Factory Method	Adapter (class)	Template Method
	Object	Singleton	Adapter (object)	Command
			Composite	Observer
			Decorator	State
				Strategy

Achieving Better OOP Through Design Patterns

While this chapter has provided an introduction to key OOP concepts for those who are relatively new to OOP, learning the design patterns should prove useful in learning OOP as well. We might even venture to add that if this is your initial introduction to OOP, you will find what some consider the *correct* way to understand OOP. (Others might even contend that it is the *only* way to understand OOP.) We spent time on OOP because a sizable portion of ActionScript programmers may not have gotten around to its use yet. After all, ActionScript itself is relatively new to OOP structures.

Alternatively, if you're an old trooper with OOP, either from ActionScript or another language such as Java or C++, we hope that our discussion of design patterns will help you better apply OOP concepts in a design pattern.

Whatever your background in OOP, the Gang of Four recommend the following design patterns for those of you who are relatively inexperienced in object-oriented programming:

- Adapter (Chapter 5)
- Composite (Chapter 6)
- Decorator (Chapter 4)
- Factory Method (Chapter 2)
- Observer (Chapter 8)
- Strategy (Chapter 11)
- Template Method (Chapter 9)

However, if these patterns seem in any way daunting, do not worry. We don't know of anyone who fully grasped design patterns on the first go-around, including the patterns suggested by GoF. We certainly didn't. However, by using, changing and experimenting with the examples we have provided, along with going over the explanation of OOP and design pattern concepts in the chapters, we believe that you'll come to see them in the same light as we do—the best friend a programmer could have.

PART II

Creational Patterns

*If the Lord Almighty had consulted me before
embarking on creation thus, I should have
recommended something simpler.*
—Attributed to Alfonso the Wise (13th century Castilian
king and wise guy)

*To exist is to change, to change is to mature, to
mature is to go on creating oneself endlessly.*
—Henri Bergson

There is nothing like a dream to create the future.
—Victor Hugo

This first section examines design patterns that abstract the instantiation process. The creator pattern separates the use of objects from their creation. The separation process is accomplished by encapsulation. The concrete class uses the encapsulated information, but has no direct knowledge of that information. At the same time, the concrete class masks how the instances themselves are created and constructed.

Figure Part II-1 shows a general figure of the two main features of creational patterns.

The two design patterns we examine as representatives of the creational patterns are very different. The Factory Method pattern solves the problem of the tight coupling between the Client and the Product by delegating the object creation to a separate method called a *factory*; hence the name Factory Method. The Singleton method is charged with making sure that a *single* instance and only a single instance of a class is created, and so derives its name from the single instance it instantiates. The Singleton design pattern is often used in conjunction with other design patterns as a gateway when the developer needs to make sure that only one instance of some aspect of the pattern is instantiated.

Chapter 2, *Factory Method Pattern*
Chapter 3, *Singleton Pattern*

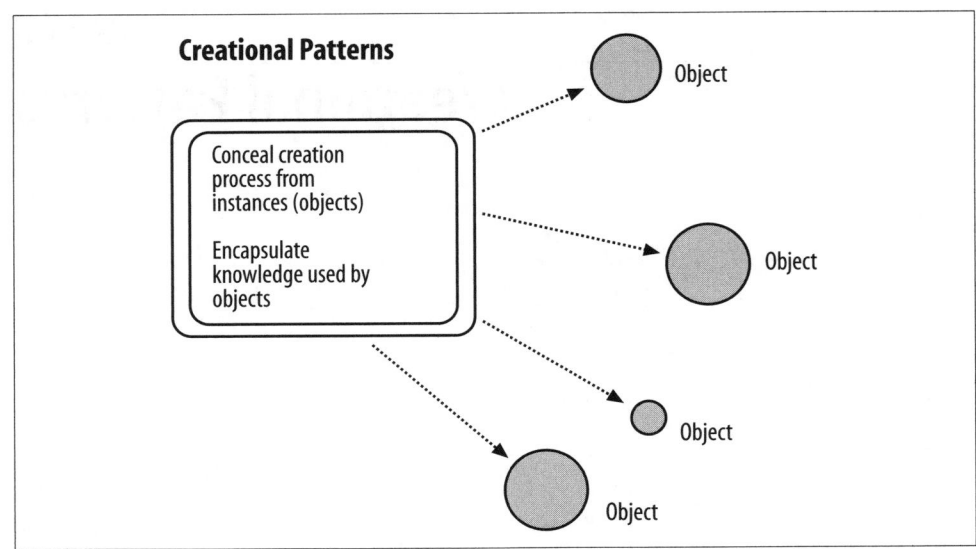

Figure Part II-1. Model of creational patterns

Factory Method Pattern

*As experimentation becomes more complex, the need
for the cooperation in it of technical elements from
outside becomes greater and the modern laboratory
tends increasingly to resemble the factory and to
employ in its service increasing numbers of purely
routine workers.*

—John Desmond Bernal

*The medieval university looked backwards; it
professed to be a storehouse of old knowledge. The
modern university looks forward, and is a factory of
new knowledge.*

—Thomas Huxley

*One cannot walk through an assembly factory and not
feel that one is in Hell.*

—W. H. Auden

What Is the Factory Method Pattern?

One of the most common statements in object-oriented programming (OOP) uses
the new keyword to instantiate objects from concrete classes. ActionScript applications that have multiple classes can have an abundance of code that looks like the
following:

```
public class Client
{
    public function doSomething()
    {
        var object:Object = new Product();
        object.manipulate();
    }
}
```

The Client class creates a new instance of the Product class and assigns it to the
variable object. There's nothing wrong with this code, but it does create a *coupling*

or *dependency* between the Client and Product classes. Simply put, the Client class depends on the Product class to function properly. Any changes to the Product class in terms of class name changes or change in the number of *parameters* passed to it will require changes in the Client class as well. This situation is exacerbated if multiple clients use the Product class, and requires changing code in multiple locations.

The solution to this common problem is to loosen the tight coupling between the client and the concrete classes it uses. This is where the factory method pattern offers a robust solution. It introduces an intermediary between the client and the concrete class. The intermediary is called a *creator* class. It allows the client to access objects without specifying the exact class of object that will be created. This is accomplished by delegating object creation to a separate method in the creator called a *factory*. The primary purpose of the factory method is to instantiate objects and return them.

Model of the Factory Method Pattern

Figure 2-1 shows the high-level model of the factory method pattern. Multiple *clients* can use the factory method in a *creator* to access and use multiple *products*. The intermediary nature of the creator is clear in this model, as it forces the creation of multiple types of objects (different products) through a common point.

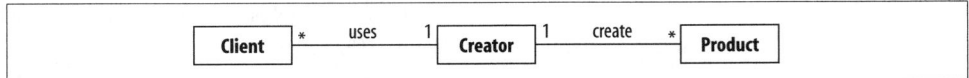

Figure 2-1. Logic model of factory method pattern

This high-level model doesn't show how clients can use a factory method to access objects without specifying their concrete classes. Let's write some code for the creator class to create and return product objects.

```
public class Creator
{
    public static function simpleFactory(product:String)
    {
        if (product == "p1")
        {
            return new product1();
        } else if (product == "p2") {
            return new product2();
        }
    }
}
```

The parameterized method called simpleFactory( ) instantiates product classes and returns them. The client would call this method and pass the product identifier, which in this case is the String value "p1" or "p2". This loosens the coupling between the client and the product classes. However, it's a very commonly used code segment, and doesn't offer the reusability and flexibility offered by the factory method pattern. This code segment is commonly known as a *simple factory*.

To add a new product, we'll have to modify the simpleFactory( ) method and add another IF clause. This goes against the open-closed principle in OOP where code such as classes and methods should be *open for extension,* but *closed for modification.* One of the primary advantages of the factory method pattern is indeed the extensibility it affords to accommodate change. Let's look at the class diagram of the classic factory method pattern.

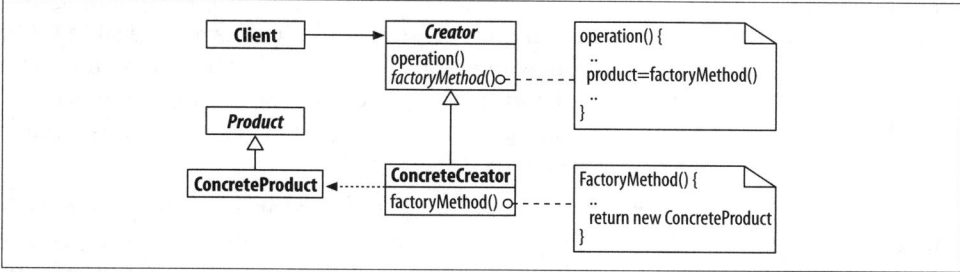

Figure 2-2. Class diagram of the factory method pattern

The creator and the product are both defined as *interfaces* and not concrete classes (interfaces are indicated by italicized class names in class diagrams). Interfaces define the type and method signatures for classes. Classes that implement an interface have to implement the methods declared in the interface. A pure interface does not provide any implementation for declared methods. However, there is a special kind of interface called an *abstract interface.* Abstract interfaces can provide default implementations for methods. They're also called *abstract classes,* and cannot be instantiated, but can be extended by other classes.

The Creator class in Figure 2-2 is an abstract class. It declares a *factory method* (called factoryMethod( ) in this case). This is where most of the action takes place. The factory method is defined as an *abstract method* without any implementation. This puts the onus on subclasses (classes that extend the abstract class such as ConcreteCreator) to provide the implementation details for the factory method. The Creator class also defines and implements a public method (called operation( ) in this case) that calls the factory method.

```
operation( )
{
    ..
    product = FactoryMethod( )
    ..
}
```

The operation( ) method calls FactoryMethod( ) to create product objects.

```
factoryMethod( ) {
    ..
    return new ConcreteProduct
}
```

The primary responsibility of the factory method is to instantiate and return product objects. The interesting issue is that even though *factoryMethod( )* is declared in the abstract class Creator, it's implemented in ConcreteCreator. Therefore, it is the ConcreteCreator class that knows about the product classes, essentially hiding the product classes from the client.

The reason for using interfaces and abstract classes will be clear when we look at a real application as it allows the addition of new products and corresponding creators by extending, as opposed to changing, existing code. This is a big deal in OOP because it allows a safe way to add new functionality without breaking anything. The ConcreteCreator class extends the Creator abstract class. The Product interface can be either a pure interface or abstract class depending on whether there is default functionality that needs to be implemented for all products.

Clients access the ConcreteProduct classes through the Creator interface. To force clients to access products through the factory methods, the product classes are generally hidden from outside access. We can see how this is implemented in ActionScript by developing a minimalist example.

Abstract Classes in ActionScript 3.0

Before developing an example factory method pattern, we need to tackle the issue of *abstract* classes, or more specifically, lack of support for them in ActionScript 3.0. The factory method pattern defines creators as abstract classes, and there's no way around this. In fact, much of the usefulness of the pattern can be attributed to this abstraction.

Abstract classes cannot be instantiated. They have to be extended by subclasses. They can contain abstract methods or unimplemented method declarations that subclasses need to implement. The methods implemented in an abstract class will in most cases be default behaviors, and much of the class will be unimplemented. Before a class derived from an abstract class can be instantiated, it must implement all unimplemented methods. The advantage of deriving from an abstract class is that the subclass does not have to implement a method if the default behavior implemented in the abstract class is what it needs.

Defining the creator class as abstract enables us to concentrate on a few concepts that change, but leave others at their default functionality. This reduces complexity—one of the key benefits of OOP. For example, from our model, we can use the default implementation for the operation( ) method, but override the *FactoryMethod( )*.

Unfortunately, ActionScript 3.0 does not support abstract classes. The alternative is to implement abstract classes as concrete classes in ActionScript without the instantiation and method implementation checks. These checks are conducted at compile time in languages that support abstract classes. We can add code to concrete classes in ActionScript 3.0 to do these checks at runtime and throw violation errors. In addition, commenting the classes and methods that should behave as abstract is also important. It must be emphasized that this puts the burden on the programmer as opposed to the compiler to check if all methods that should behave as abstract are implemented.

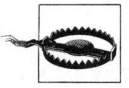 We will define *abstract* classes as *concrete* classes with the knowledge that they will not be instantiated, but will be extended by subclasses. *Abstract methods* will be defined simply as a function declaration that will throw an `IllegalOperationError` error if called. Both abstract classes and methods will be clearly identified using comments.

Minimalist Example

We will develop a minimalist example of a factory method pattern in ActionScript 3.0 using Flash CS3. The Project window shown in Figure 2-3 mirrors the file structure for the example.

Figure 2-3. Project window for the minimalist example

The *Factory Method Minimalist.fla* is a Flash document whose document class is defined as `Main`. The *document class* is a new feature in Flash CS3 that can be set from the Properties tab in the Properties panel of a Flash document (*.fla* file). This represents the class whose constructor will be automatically run by the Flash Player when the Flash movie (*.swf* file) is loaded. The `Main` class is defined in the Action-Script file called *Main.as*. The project also contains a *package* called `example`. Packages allow you to bundle classes together to facilitate code sharing. They also allow control over the visibility of classes and method names outside the package by using identifiers. This minimizes naming conflicts that can occur when developing applications. We will use packages to hide the product classes from direct access by clients in this example.

The example package contains the `Product1` and `Product2` classes that implement the `IProduct` interface. It also contains the *abstract* class `Creator` that is extended by two subclasses `CreatorA` and `CreatorB`. Each class is defined in its own file, as is the convention with ActionScript 3.0. First, let's take a look at the product classes.

Product Classes

Example 2-1 through Example 2-3 show the product interface and concrete product classes. All three classes belong to the `example` package as indicated by the *package* declaration. The `IProduct` interface declares a method called `manipulate( )` that is implemented by both product classes. True to a minimalist example, the product classes don't do much of anything. However, make note of the class attribute.

Example 2-1. IProduct.as

```
package example
{
    public interface IProduct
    {
        function manipulate( ):void;
    }
}
```

Example 2-2. Product1.as

```
package example
{
    internal class Product1 implements IProduct
    {
        public function manipulate( ):void
        {
            trace("Doing stuff with Product1");
        }
    }
}
```

Example 2-3. Product2.as

```
package example
{
    internal class Product2 implements IProduct
    {
        public function manipulate( ):void
        {
            trace("Doing stuff with Product2");
        }
    }
}
```

The product classes are defined as *internal* (the default class attribute in Action-Script 3.0). This means that they're not publicly visible. They can only be called from within the example package. Now, let's examine the creator classes.

Creator Classes

Example 2-4 through Example 2-6 show the creator classes. As with the product classes, all creators belong to the package example. The creator classes are defined as *public*, which indicates that they are publicly accessible from outside the package. The creator class, as indicated by the comments, should behave as an abstract class. It should be subclassed and not be instantiated. It also defines the factory method that should behave as an abstract method. Note that the two concrete creator classes CreatorA and CreatorB extend Creator. They also override and implement the factoryMethod( ) method, each returning a corresponding product object. In addition, the factoryMethod( ) declared in the Creator class has to return null to prevent a compile-time error. It will also throw an IllegalOperationError if called directly. This is a runtime check to make sure that this method is overridden.

Example 2-4. Creator.as

```
package example
{
    import flash.errors.IllegalOperationError;

    // ABSTRACT Class (should be subclassed and not instantiated)
    public class Creator
    {
        public function doStuff( ):void
        {
            var product:IProduct = this.factoryMethod( );
            product.manipulate( );
        }

        // ABSTRACT Method (must be overridden in a subclass)
        protected function factoryMethod( ):IProduct
        {
            throw new IllegalOperationError("Abstract method:
                                    must be overridden in a subclass");
            return null;
        }
    }
}
```

Example 2-5. CreatorA.as

```
package example
{
    public class CreatorA extends Creator
    {
        override protected function factoryMethod( ):IProduct
        {
```

Example 2-5. CreatorA.as (continued)

```
            trace("Creating product 1");
            return new Product1( ); // returns concrete product
        }
    }
}
```

Example 2-6. CreatorB.as

```
package example
{
    public class CreatorB extends Creator
    {
        override protected function factoryMethod( ):IProduct
        {
            trace("Creating product 2");
            return new Product2( ); // returns concrete product
        }
    }
}
```

Note that the doStuff( ) method in the Creator class is declared as *public* because we need to allow clients to get to it from outside the package. In contrast, the factoryMethod( ) is declared as *protected*. The *protected* attribute makes the method visible only within the same class or derived classes. Finally, we can take a look at the document class called Main, which is the client described in the class diagram shown in Figure 2-2 that uses the creator to access products.

Clients

The document class Main does not belong to a named package. Therefore, it must import the packages that contain the classes it uses. The example package needs to be imported, as it contains the creator classes. The document class Main is the client described in the high-level model of the factory method pattern shown in Figure 2-1. In Example 2-7, the document class calls a static method called run( ) in the static Test class to run some tests.

Example 2-7. Main.as

```
package
{
    import flash.display.Sprite;
    import example.*;

    /**
    *    Main Class
    *    @ purpose: Document class for movie
    */
    public class Main extends Sprite
    {
```

Example 2-7. Main.as (continued)

```
    public function Main( )
    {
        // instantiate concrete creators
        var cA:Creator = new CreatorA( );
        var cB:Creator = new CreatorB( );

        // creators operate on different products
        // even though they are doing the same operation
        cA.doStuff( );
        cB.doStuff( );
    }
  }
}
```

We get the following output after running the project.

```
Creating product 1
Doing stuff with Product1
Creating product 2
Doing stuff with Product2
```

Let's step through the code to see how we end up with the output. The client (document class Main) does not know anything about the product classes. It only knows about the creator classes and what they do. Therefore, the client instantiates CreatorA and CreatorB, and asks them both to doStuff( ). The Creator class behaving as an abstract class knows how to doStuff( ), but it has allowed subclasses to determine the product that it does stuff to. The doStuff( ) method calls factoryMethod( ) to return a product object. It then calls the manipulate( ) method in the product object.

The primary task of the subclasses CreatorA and CreatorB is to create and return product objects. They know about the product classes to operate on, and they override the factory method to instantiate the appropriate products and return them to the doStuff( ) method. Knowledge about object creation has been encapsulated within the concrete creator classes.

The factory method pattern has essentially created a firewall between clients and the concrete product classes they use. Is the firewall bulletproof? Have we fully accomplished what we set out to do? Are the product classes only accessible through the creators? We will have to check this.

Hiding the Product Classes

Let's check if the product classes are truly hidden and accessible only through the creator classes. We can try to instantiate a product by accessing its creator class and the factory method directly. Add the following statements to the Test class in the *Main.as* file (Example 2-7) to try and directly instantiate products:

```
// instantiate concrete products
var p1 = new Product1( );
var p2 = CreatorB.factoryMethod( );
```

The following compile-time errors shown in Figure 2-4 are produced when we run the project.

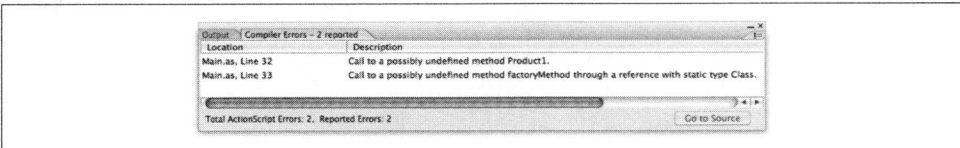

Figure 2-4. Compile-time errors when directly accessing product classes

The errors indicate that the product classes and the factory method aren't visible to the client. The product classes are encapsulated within the package, as they were defined with *attribute internal*. Internal classes can only be accessed from within the package. Similarly, the factoryMethod( ) is not accessible as it a *protected* class. Therefore, external access to the product classes is only possible through the doStuff( ) *public* method.

You may wonder why it's necessary to use this complex design just to prevent clients from directly instantiating concrete classes. The alternative would be much simpler. The client could have instantiated Product1 and Product2 and fed it to a doStuff( ) method. Let's address this issue after we develop a simple application using the factory method pattern. It will be easy to see the advantages when there is real context instead of generic products and creators.

Example: Print Shop

Let's develop an example application to dispatch print jobs at a hypothetical print shop (think copy center with printers). Think of the shop as a place where customers bring what they want to print on portable media. The clerk at the counter will initiate a print job on the computer for dispatch and billing, based on the type of print job. We will build the application in Flash and ActionScript 3.0 as a generic example to illustrate the utility of the factory method pattern.

Our print shop is a small time operation with only two printers. We have a workgroup printer and an inkjet that prints in black and white. In order to streamline operations, the manager has a bright idea to create separate print centers in the shop. One print center will handle high-volume jobs that will be sent to the workgroup printer. The other will handle low-volume jobs that will be dispatched to the inkjet. We design the print shop application using the factory method pattern, as we had heard somewhere that it allows for flexibility and expansion. We are hoping to make a profit and add more printers in the future. Figure 2-5 shows the class structure for the print shop example.

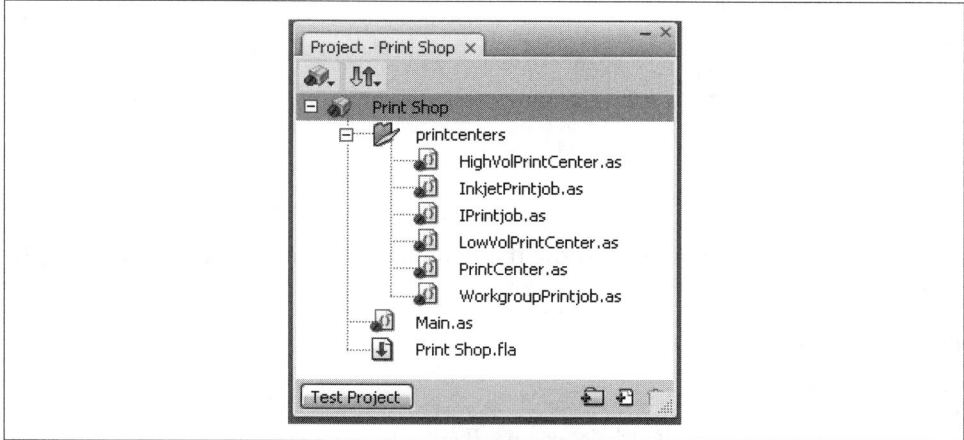

Figure 2-5. Project window for the print shop example

The class structure is very similar to the minimalist example shown in Figure 2-3. The products will be print jobs that will be created and the creators will be the print centers (see class diagram in Figure 2-6).

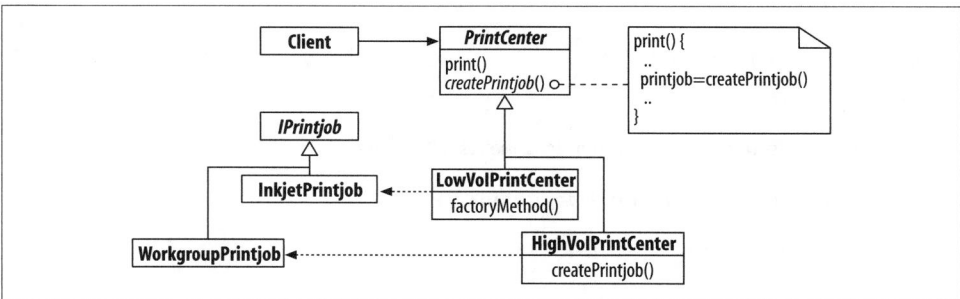

Figure 2-6. Class diagram for the print shop example

Product Classes: Print Jobs

The product classes don't do anything at this point, but in a real application they will initiate billing and dispatch print jobs to a print server. The print job classes belong to the printcenters package. Example 2-8 shows the IPrintjob interface that declares a parameterized method called start( ) that takes a file name of a document to print.

Example 2-8. IPrintjob.as

```
package printcenters
{
    public interface IPrintjob
    {
        function start(fn:String):void;
    }
}
```

Example 2-9 and Example 2-10 show the two concrete print job classes that implement the IPrintjob interface.

Example 2-9. InkjetPrintjob.as

```
package printcenters
{
    internal class InkjetPrintjob implements IPrintjob
    {
        public function start(fn:String):void
        {
            trace("Printing '" + fn + "' to inkjet printer");
        }
    }
}
```

Example 2-10. WorkgroupPrintjob.as

```
package printcenters
{
    internal class WorkgroupPrintjob implements IPrintjob
    {
        public function start(fn:String):void
        {
            trace("Printing '" + fn + "' to workgroup printer");
        }
    }
}
```

Creator Classes: Print Centers

Example 2-11 shows the class PrintCenter that should behave as an abstract class. The factory method is called createPrintjob( ), and client access to the printer centers is through the print( ) method.

Example 2-11. PrintCenter.as

```
package printcenters
{
    import flash.errors.IllegalOperationError;

    // ABSTRACT Class (should be subclassed and not instantiated)
    public class PrintCenter
```

Example 2-11. PrintCenter.as (continued)

```
    {
        public function print(fn:String):void
        {
            var printjob:IPrintjob = this.createPrintjob();
            printjob.start(fn);
        }

        // ABSTRACT Method (must be overridden in a subclass)
        protected function createPrintjob():IPrintjob
        {
            throw new IllegalOperationError("Abstract method:
                                    must be overridden in a subclass");
            return null;
        }
    }
}
```

Example 2-12 and Example 2-13 show the `LowVolPrintCenter` and `HighVolPrintCenter` classes that extend the `PrintCenter` class, and override and implement the createPrintjob() factory method.

Example 2-12. LowVolPrintCenter.as

```
package printcenters
{
    public class LowVolPrintCenter extends PrintCenter
    {
        override protected function createPrintjob():IPrintjob
        {
            trace("Creating new printjob for the inkjet printer");
            return new InkjetPrintjob();
        }
    }
}
```

Example 2-13. HighVolPrintCenter.as

```
package printcenters
{
    public class HighVolPrintCenter extends PrintCenter
    {
        override protected function createPrintjob():IPrintjob
        {
            trace("Creating new printjob for the workgropup printer");
            return new WorkgroupPrintjob();
        }
    }
}
```

Clients

Note that the client doesn't know what specific printers the copy shop has in use. The client only knows about the type of print job defined by the creator classes. Based on the volume of the print job brought in by the customer, the application would instantiate the corresponding concrete print center class (LowVolPrintCenter or HighVolPrintCenter) and call the print( ) method passing the filename of the document to be printed.

To test our design we run the following code from the client.

```
var pcHighVol:PrintCenter = new HighVolPrintCenter();
var pcLowhVol:PrintCenter = new LowVolPrintCenter();

pcHighVol.print("LongThesis.doc");
pcLowhVol.print("ShortVita.doc");
```

As in the minimalist example, we get the following output.

```
Creating new printjob for the workgropup printer
Printing 'LongThesis.doc' to workgroup printer
Creating new printjob for the inkjet printer
Printing 'ShortVita.doc' to inkjet printer
```

Looking at the output, it's clear that the print( ) method operates on different objects (WorkgroupPrintjob and InkjetPrintjob objects). This is an elegant solution, as the client simply chooses the proper print center and requests it to print. The print center classes take care of instantiating the correct print job. There is a clear separation between creating an object and using the created object. Object creation is handled by the factoryMethod( ), and the created object is used by the print( ) method. Object creation is completely hidden from the client.

Print Shop Extension

The real utility of the factory method pattern is evident when extending or adding more functionality to an application. Because the print shop is doing good business, the manager decides to add a fancy multi-function printer that has a sorting bin, a built-in stapler, and double-sided (duplex) printing features. How do we add this new printer to our existing application? We need a new print center in the print shop for anyone who needs additional features such as stapling or duplex printing. In terms of code, we need to create a new subclass of the PrintCenter class to handle the fancy print jobs. We will call this class FancyPrintCenter (Example 2-15). We also need to subclass Printjob and develop a new concrete class called MultifunctionPrintJob (Example 2-14) to dispatch jobs to the new printer. Let's look at the code changes needed to do this.

Example 2-14. MultifunctionPrintJob.as

```
package printcenters {

    internal class MultifunctionPrintJob implements IPrintjob {

        public function start(fn:String):void {
            trace("Printing '" + fn + "' to multifunction printer");
        }
    }
}
```

Example 2-15. FancyPrintCenter.as

```
package printcenters {

    import printcenters.*;

    // High Volume Print Center (subclass of PrintCenter)
    public class FancyPrintCenter extends PrintCenter {

        override protected function createPrintjob():IPrintjob {
            trace("Creating new printjob for the multifunction printer");
            return new MultifunctionPrintJob();
        }
    }
}
```

We added two new classes, but didn't have to modify existing code at all. We added a new product class by implementing the Printjob interface and a new creator class by extending the PrintCenter abstract class. This is the big advantage of the factory method pattern when compared to the simple factory discussed previously. By declaring both the product and creator classes as interfaces, we were able to extend the code to add new functionality without changing existing code. To access the new multifunction printer, clients need to instantiate a FancyPrintCenter class, and call its print() method.

Parameterized Factory Methods

The examples we've seen have used non-parameterized factory methods. *Non-parameterized* factory methods don't take any parameters in their function declarations. *Parameterized* factory methods take a parameter that specifies a kind of product that will be created. For example, in the print shop application, you can pass an extra *parameter* to the factory method to indicate a particular kind of print job (like multiple kinds of high volume print jobs). Parameterized factory methods allow further encapsulation and illustrate the ultimate utility of the factory method pattern. We will further extend the print shop example to incorporate a parameterized factory method.

Extended Example: Color Printing

The print shop has been going gangbusters! The manager decided to add the single most requested feature at the shop—color printing. We end up purchasing two new color printers: a color inkjet printer for low volume jobs, and a color laser printer for high volume printing. Unfortunately, we didn't think about color printing when first designing the application. How do we add this feature to our application? It's a good thing that we know about parameterized factory methods.

We still have the two print centers for high and low volume printing. However, we now have to specify a kind of print job. Customers can request a color or black and white print job that can be high or low volume. To indicate the kind of print job, we can pass a parameter to the print( ) method.

New Product Classes

We add two new product classes for the new printers, called `ColorInkjetPrintjob` (Example 2-16) and `ColorLaserPrintjob` (Example 2-17). Again, we're not changing existing code, but extending the application by implementing to the `IPrintjob` interface show in Example 2-8.

Example 2-16. ColorInkjetPrintjob.as

```
package printcenters
{
    internal class ColorInkjetPrintjob implements IPrintjob
    {
    public function start(fn:String):void
        {
            trace("Printing '" + fn + "' to color laser printer");
        }
    }
}
```

Example 2-17. ColorLaserPrintjob.as

```
package printcenters
{
    internal class ColorLaserPrintjob implements IPrintjob
    {
        public function start(fn:String):void
        {
            trace("Printing '" + fn + "' to color laser printer");
        }
    }
}
```

New Creator Classes: Integrating a Parameterized Factory Method

As with the product classes, we can add a parameterized factory method to our application without modifying existing code. We won't change the original PrintCenter abstract class and its derived classes, LowVolPrintCenter and HighVolPrintCenter. By letting these be, we don't break the functionality of the old interface, and clients using it will continue to function. We will define a new abstract interface called NewPrintCenter with a parameterized factory method (Example 2-18).

Example 2-18. NewPrintCenter.as

```
package printcenters
{
    import flash.errors.IllegalOperationError;

    // ABSTRACT Class (should be subclassed and not instantiated)
    public class NewPrintCenter
    {

        public function print(fn:String, cKind:uint):void
        {
            var  printjob:IPrintjob = this.createPrintjob(cKind);
            printjob.start(fn);
        }

        // ABSTRACT Method (must be overridden in a subclass)
        protected function createPrintjob(cKind:uint):IPrintjob
        {
            throw new IllegalOperationError("Abstract method:
                                   must be overridden in a subclass");

            return null;
        }
    }
}
```

The factory method createPrintjob( ) takes a parameter of type uint that represents a kind of print job (color or black and white). In addition, the print( ) method also takes this as an additional parameter.

We next create two concrete classes (Example 2-19 and Example 2-20) that extend the NewPrintCenter abstract class for low and high volume printing.

Example 2-19. NewLowVolPrintCenter.as

```
package printcenters
{
    public class NewLowVolPrintCenter extends NewPrintCenter
    {
        public static const BW       :uint =  0;
        public static const COLOR    :uint =  1;

        override protected function createPrintjob(cKind:uint):IPrintjob
```

Example 2-19. NewLowVolPrintCenter.as

```
        {
            if (cKind == BW)
            {
                trace("Creating new printjob for the b/w inkjet printer");
                return new InkjetPrintjob( );
            } else if (cKind == COLOR) {
                trace("Creating new printjob for the color inkjet printer");
                return new ColorInkjetPrintjob( );
            } else {
                throw new Error("Invalid low volume print job");
                return null;
            }
        }
    }
}
```

Example 2-20. NewHighVolPrintCenter.as

```
package printcenters
{
    public class NewHighVolPrintCenter extends NewPrintCenter
    {
        public static const BW        :uint = 0;
        public static const COLOR     :uint = 1;

        override protected function createPrintjob(cKind:uint):IPrintjob
        {
            if (cKind == BW)
            {
                trace("Creating new printjob for the b/w workgroup printer");
                return new WorkgroupPrintjob( );
            } else if (cKind == COLOR) {
                trace("Creating new printjob for the color laser printer");
                return new ColorLaserPrintjob( );
            } else {
                throw new Error("Invalid high volume print job");
                return null;
            }
        }
    }
}
```

We have created a new hierarchy of related classes for the new print centers, with parameterized factory methods. The abstract class is NewPrintCenter, and its derived subclasses are NewLowVolPrintCenter and NewHighVolPrintCenter. Note the public static constants to identify the different kinds of print jobs. These constants are publicly accessible and should be used as the parameters passed to the print( ) method.

Clients

Clients need to instantiate the new print center classes to access the color printers. The `print( )` method takes a parameter that specifies a color or black and white print job. They operate on different print job objects based on the passed parameters.

```
var pcNewHighVol:NewPrintCenter = new NewHighVolPrintCenter( );
var pcNewLowhVol:NewPrintCenter = new NewLowVolPrintCenter( );

pcNewHighVol.print("LongThesis.doc", NewHighVolPrintCenter.BW);
pcNewHighVol.print("SalesReport.pdf", NewHighVolPrintCenter.COLOR);
pcNewLowhVol.print("ShortVita.doc", NewLowVolPrintCenter.BW);
pcNewLowhVol.print("SalesChart.xlc", NewLowVolPrintCenter.COLOR);
```

The old print center classes, `LowVolPrintCenter` and `HighVolPrintCenter`, which implement a non-parameterized factory method, will continue to work. They'll continue to use the `WorkgroupPrintjob` and `InkjetPrintjob` print job classes without disruption. The power of the factory method design pattern to handle changing requirements is very evident in this example.

Parallel Class Hierarchies

Take a look at the class diagram for the extended print center application (Figure 2-7). You will see two distinct concrete product class hierarchies. The `WorkgroupPrintjob` and `ColorLaserPrintjob` classes represent the high volume print jobs. Likewise, the `InkjetPrintjob` and `ColorInkjetPrintjob` classes represent the low volume print jobs. In addition, knowledge about these class hierarchies is encapsulated within their corresponding creator classes. Note that the product classes cannot be accessed directly. They can only be accessed through the creator classes. The `NewLowVolPrintCenter` and `NewHighVolPrintCenter` know about their corresponding product class hierarchy. We can think of the factory method pattern as sets of *parallel class hierarchies*: the concrete creator classes and their corresponding products. This is a powerful way of encapsulating knowledge and managing dependencies within software applications.

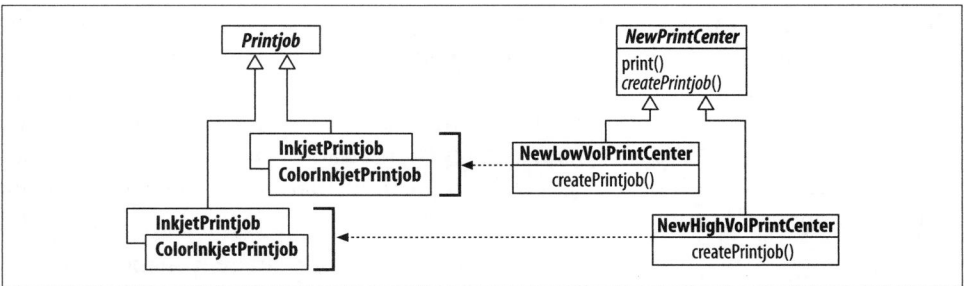

Figure 2-7. Class diagram for the extended print shop example

Key OOP Concepts Used in the Factory Method Pattern

Incorporating changes that were not anticipated in the original software design can sometimes require changes to existing code. Modifying existing code that works well should be avoided if at all possible as it can result in unintended consequences such as the introduction of new bugs. A slight change in a dependant module can result in breaking a program in several places if there's tight coupling between code segments.

Code that handles change well is possible using good OO design. The factory method pattern is an excellent solution to this recurring requirement. The factory method pattern is a solution to one of the most common reasons for tight coupling, which is caused by one class instantiating another class and using the resultant object. Of course, classes need to be instantiated—there's no way to write code that does not instantiate classes. So, what are we talking about?

We're not going to eliminate coupling caused by instantiating concrete classes. However, we can manage the dependency between classes by reducing the coupling. To do this, the factory method pattern lets you separate the *creation* of objects from their *use*.

Here lies the crucial concept. Clients can *use* objects created from another class, but the factory method handles the *creation* of objects by introducing an intermediary called a creator class between the client and the concrete class that is instantiated. The client does not have to specify the class name of the object that it wants to use because the creator class encapsulates that knowledge. This encapsulation allows managing change by extension, as the print shop example showed.

All in all, the factory method pattern allows the creation of loosely coupled designs that stand the test of changing requirements.

Example: Sprite Factory

ActionScript 3.0 introduced the Sprite class, which is a lightweight building block for interactive objects on stage. MovieClips are now derived from the new Sprite class. The factory method pattern can come in handy when developing applications that utilize sprites in Flash. Sprites are frequently added, and their behavior and appearance modified, during the course of Flash application development. Therefore, managing the dependencies between sprites and the rest of the application can be advantageous. We will create a simple example application called Shapes that manages sprite creation by introducing a factory method that enables clients to create sprites without explicitly specifying their class names.

The application shown in Figure 2-8 will simply draw four different shapes based on the Sprite class on the Flash stage. The first set of shapes will consist of an *unfilled* rectangle and circle. The second set will be a *filled* rectangle and circle. The example is not a productive application, but it will serve as a springboard to the *vertical shooter game* that we'll develop later in the chapter.

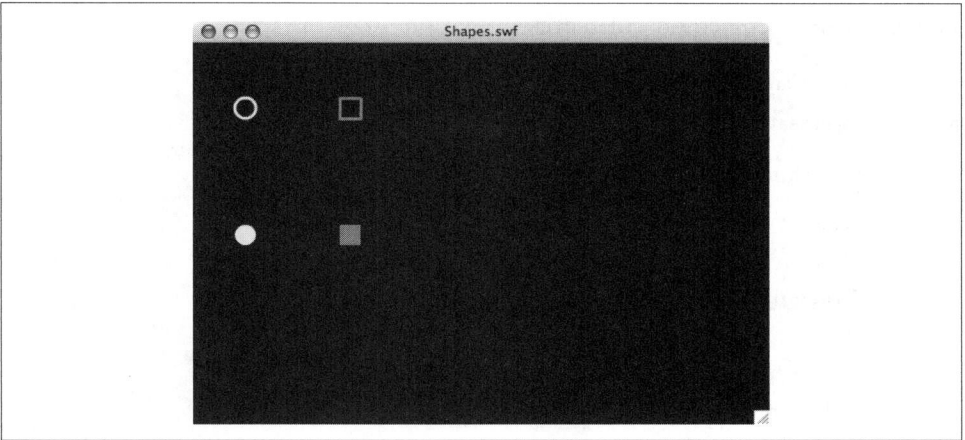

Figure 2-8. Screenshot of Shapes example stage

The Project window in Figure 2-9 shows the file structure of the Shapes example.

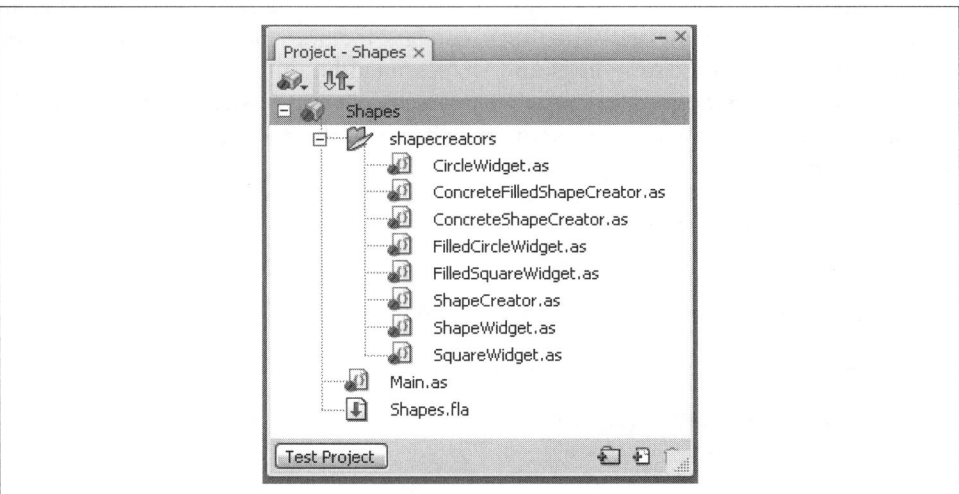

Figure 2-9. Shapes example Project window

Product Classes: Shape Widgets

The shapes on the stage (Figure 2-9) are the products in this example. These concrete shape widgets extend the ShapeWidget abstract class (Example 2-21). Unlike in previous examples, we define ShapeWidget as an abstract interface because we want to implement default behavior common to all shape widgets in the definition. In addition, ShapeWidget also subclasses Sprite. The default behavior is defined in a method called setLoc( ) to set the X and Y coordinates of the sprite. ShapeWidget also defines an abstract method called drawWidget( ) to draw the sprite.

Example 2-21. ShapeWidget.as

```
package shapecreators
{
    import flash.display.Sprite;

    // ABSTRACT Class (should be subclassed and not instantiated)
    internal class ShapeWidget extends Sprite
    {
        // ABSTRACT Method (should be implemented in subclass)
        internal function drawWidget( ):void {}

        internal function setLoc(xLoc:int, yLoc:int):void {
            this.x = xLoc;
            this.y = yLoc;
        }
    }
}
```

Each Shape, Sprite, and MovieClip object has a property called graphics that is an instance of the Graphics class. The Graphics class includes properties and methods for drawing and manipulating lines and shapes including fills, colors, and patterns. The concrete classes derived from the ShapeWidget class are listed in Examples 2-22 through 2-25. They draw the corresponding shapes in the *constructor* using methods accessed through the graphics property.

Example 2-22. SquareWidget.as

```
package shapecreators {

    internal class SquareWidget extends ShapeWidget {

        override internal function drawWidget( ):void
        {
            graphics.lineStyle(3, 0xFF00FF);
            graphics.drawRect(-10, -10, 20, 20);
        }
    }
}
```

Example 2-23. CircleWidget.as

```
package shapecreators {

    internal class CircleWidget extends ShapeWidget {

        override internal function drawWidget():void
        {
            graphics.lineStyle(3, 0xFFFF00);
            graphics.drawCircle(0, 0, 10);
        }
    }
}
```

Example 2-24. FilledSquareWidget.as

```
package shapecreators {

    internal class FilledSquareWidget extends ShapeWidget {

        override internal function drawWidget():void
        {
            graphics.beginFill(0xFF00FF);
            graphics.drawRect(-10, -10, 20, 20);
            graphics.endFill();
        }
    }
}
```

Example 2-25. FilledCircleWidget.as

```
package shapecreators {

    internal class FilledCircleWidget extends ShapeWidget {

        override internal function drawWidget():void
        {
            graphics.beginFill(0xFFFF00);
            graphics.drawCircle(0, 0, 10);
            graphics.endFill();
        }
    }
}
```

Creator Classes: Shape Creators

The ShapeCreator class shown in Example 2-26 defines the abstract interface for the creator classes. The publicly accessible draw( ) method is the real workhorse of this class. It calls the createShape( ) factory method, and operates on the returned ShapeWidget object. The parameterized factory method createShape( ) should behave as an abstract method, and must be overridden by the concrete creator classes.

Example 2-26. ShapeCreator.as

```
package shapecreators
{
    import flash.display.DisplayObjectContainer;
    import flash.errors.IllegalOperationError;

    // ABSTRACT Class (should be subclassed and not instantiated)
    public class ShapeCreator
    {
        public function draw(cType:uint, target:DisplayObjectContainer,
                             xLoc:int, yLoc:int):void {
            var  shape = this.createShape(cType);
            shape.drawWidget();
            shape.setLoc(xLoc, yLoc); // set the x and y location
            target.addChild(shape); // add the sprite to the display list
        }

        // ABSTRACT Method (must be overridden in a subclass)
        protected function createShape(cType:uint):ShapeWidget
        {
            throw new IllegalOperationError("Abstract method:
                                    must be overridden in a subclass");
            return null;
        }
    }
}
```

The draw( ) method takes four parameters: the kind of shape to be created, the stage object, and the shape's X and Y location. Even though the shape widget classes draw the shapes, they're not visible until added to the *display list* of the stage via the addChild( ) method. Clients will pass an instance of the *Stage* object as the display object container to draw shapes on the stage. The concrete creator classes UnfilledShapeCreator (Example 2-27) and FilledShapeCreator (Example 2-28) extend the ShapeCreator (Example 2-26) class and implement the createShape factory method.

Example 2-27. UnfilledShapeCreator.as

```
package shapecreators
{
    public class UnfilledShapeCreator extends ShapeCreator
    {
        public static const CIRCLE       :uint =  0;
        public static const SQUARE       :uint =  1;

        override protected function createShape(cType:uint):ShapeWidget
        {
            if (cType == CIRCLE)
            {
                trace("Creating new circle shape");
                return new CircleWidget();
            } else if (cType == SQUARE) {
```

Example 2-27. UnfilledShapeCreator.as

```
                trace("Creating new square shape");
                return new SquareWidget( );
            } else {
                throw new Error("Invalid kind of shape specified");
                return null;
            }
        }
    }
}
```

Example 2-28. FilledShapeCreator.as

```
package shapecreators
{
    public class FilledShapeCreator extends ShapeCreator
    {
        public static const CIRCLE        :uint =  0;
        public static const SQUARE        :uint =  1;

        override protected function createShape(cType:uint):ShapeWidget
        {
            if (cType == CIRCLE)
            {
                trace("Creating new filled circle shape");
                return new FilledCircleWidget( );
            } else if (cType == SQUARE) {
                trace("Creating new filled square shape");
                return new FilledSquareWidget( );
            } else {
                throw new Error("Invalid kind of shape specified");
                return null;
            }
        }
    }
}
```

Clients

Note that when a client calls the creator classes, it needs to pass an instance of the stage to the draw( ) method as a parameter. If your client is the document class for a Flash document, it should have access to the stage using the this.stage property. In ActionScript 3.0, the stage isn't globally accessible. It can only be accessed by objects that are already attached to the display list.

```
// instantiate concrete shape creators
var unfilledShapeCreator:ShapeCreator = new UnfilledShapeCreator( );
var filledShapeCreator:ShapeCreator = new FilledShapeCreator( );

// draw unfilled shapes
unfilledShapeCreator.draw(UnfilledShapeCreator.CIRCLE, this.stage, 50, 75);
unfilledShapeCreator.draw(UnfilledShapeCreator.SQUARE, this.stage, 150, 75);
```

```
// draw filled shapes
filledShapeCreator.draw(FilledShapeCreator.CIRCLE, this.stage, 50, 200);
filledShapeCreator.draw(FilledShapeCreator.SQUARE, this.stage, 150, 200);
```

As in previous examples, you can extend this application to draw different kinds of sprites with different behaviors without much effort. We will use the sprite factory in our final example, a vertical shooter game.

Example: Vertical Shooter Game

The next application will demonstrate the usefulness of the factory method pattern when designing fast-paced action games, as many sprites on the screen are created at runtime based on user input. When an application doesn't know which objects to create until runtime, the factory method design pattern light bulb should go off in your head. We will develop a portion of a vertical shooter game in the best traditions of the original Space Invaders. The game will be based on the sprite factory example, as all interactive objects that appear on the Flash Stage are derived form the Sprite class. This will not be a complete game, but the parts that show the utility of the factory method pattern, such as creating different space ships, including the different projectiles that the ships shoot at each other, will be fully developed.

The game will consist of one hero ship located at the bottom of the stage (see Figure 2-10) that can be moved horizontally using the mouse. Five alien ships are placed in a row at the top of the stage. The alien ships shoot alien cannon balls (unfilled circles) and alien mines (unfilled squares that rotate). Clicking the mouse will make the hero ship shoot hero cannon balls (filled circles). In this example, we will not implement collision detection (aka hit testing) to figure out if projectiles hit the ships.

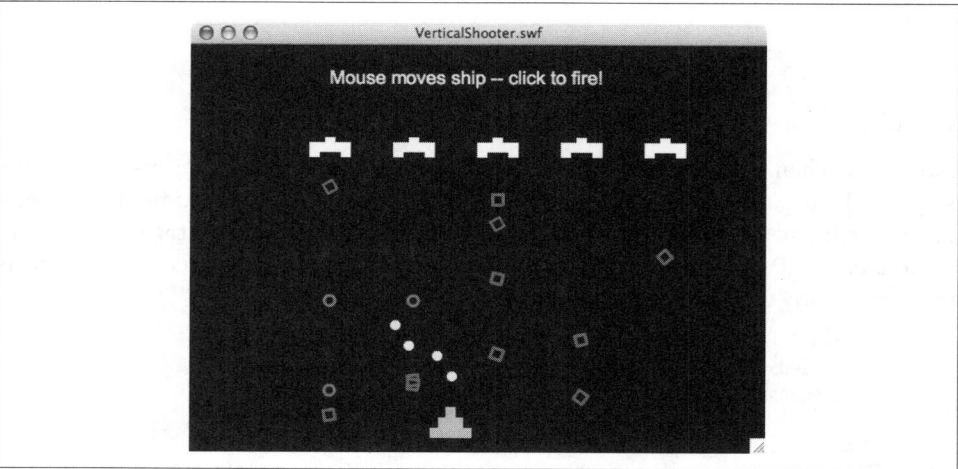

Figure 2-10. Screenshot of Vertical Shooter example showing space ships and projectiles

Figure 2-11 shows the Project window for the example. It consists of two packages that encapsulate space ships and projectiles. The weapons package makes use of the factory method pattern, and defines creator classes (weapons platforms) that produce different projectiles. The ships package uses a variation on the factory method pattern to create different spaceships.

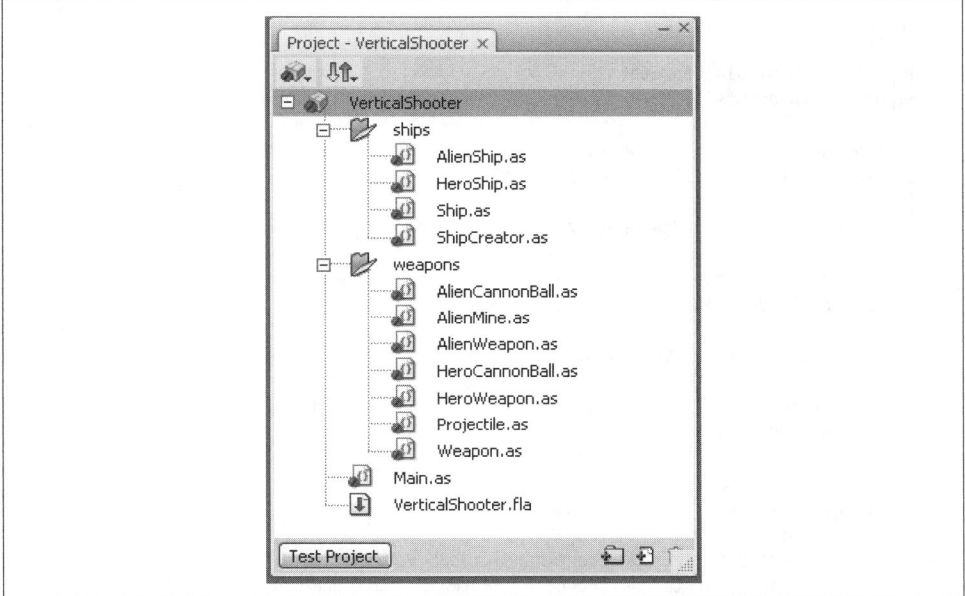

Figure 2-11. Vertical Shooter Project window

Product Classes

The example consists of two different products: projectiles and space ships. Each product is visible as a sprite on the Stage.

Projectiles

The Projectile class shown in Example 2-29 defines the abstract interface for the concrete projectile classes. It should behave as an abstract class and is declared as a subclass of Sprite. The class defines the nSpeed property to hold the speed of the projectile in pixels per second. The drawProjectile( ) method should behave as abstract and has to be implemented in a subclass. The class also defines several methods with default implementations. The setLoc( ) method sets the X and Y coordinates of the sprite. The arm( ) method specifies the default speed of the projectile and sets it to 5 pixels per frame. The release( ) method attaches an EnterFrame event handler called doMoveProjectile( ) to move the projectile vertically by nSpeed pixels on each EnterFrame event. The doMoveProjectile( ) also performs the important function of checking if the projectile has gone beyond the top or bottom boundaries of the stage. If so, it removes the sprite object as an event listener, and removes it from the display list of the stage. Because there are no references to the projectile object at this point, the Flash garbage collector will recover the memory it occupied.

Example 2-29. Projectile.as

```
package weapons
{
    import flash.display.Sprite;
    import flash.events.*;

    // ABSTRACT Class (should be subclassed and not instantiated)
    internal class Projectile extends Sprite
    {
        internal var nSpeed:Number // holds speed of projectile

        // ABSTRACT Method (must be overridden in a subclass)
        internal function drawProjectile( ):void {}

        internal function arm( ):void
        {
            // set the default speed for the projectile (5 pixels / fame)
            nSpeed = 5;
        }

        internal function release( ):void
        {
            // attach EnterFrame event handler doMoveProjectile( )
            this.addEventListener(Event.ENTER_FRAME, this.doMoveProjectile);
        }

        internal function setLoc(xLoc:int, yLoc:int):void
        {
            this.x = xLoc;
            this.y = yLoc;
        }

        // update the projectile sprite
        internal function doMoveProjectile(event:Event):void
        {
            this.y += nSpeed; // move the projectile
            // remove projectile if it extends off the top or bottom of the stage
            if ((this.y < 0) || (this.y > this.stage.stageHeight))
            {
                // remove the event listener
                this.removeEventListener(Event.ENTER_FRAME,
                                    this.doMoveProjectile);
                this.stage.removeChild(this); // remove sprite from stage
            }
        }
    }
}
```

The default behaviors defined in the Projectile class are suitable for most of the derived concrete projectile classes (Examples 2-30 through 2-32). So the derived projectile classes are much simpler. They simply draw the projectile by overriding and implementing the drawProjectile( ) method. The arm( ) method is overridden to set a different speed. The advantage of using abstract classes should be noted here, as the code required to add new projectiles is minimal because in most cases, the desired action will be to inherit default behavior.

Example 2-30. HeroCannonBall.as

```
package weapons {

    internal class HeroCannonBall extends Projectile {

        override internal function drawProjectile():void
        {
            graphics.beginFill(0xFFFF00);
            graphics.drawCircle(0, 0, 5);
            graphics.endFill();
        }

        override internal function arm():void {
            nSpeed = -10; // set the speed
        }
    }
}
```

Example 2-31. AlienCannonBall.as

```
package weapons {

    internal class AlienCannonBall extends Projectile {

        override internal function drawProjectile():void
        {
            graphics.lineStyle(3, 0xFF00FF);
            graphics.drawCircle(0, 0, 5);
        }

        override internal function arm():void {
            nSpeed = 8; // set the speed
        }
    }
}
```

Example 2-32. AlienMine.as

```
package weapons {

    import flash.events.*;


    internal class AlienMine extends Projectile {
```

Example 2-32. AlienMine.as (continued)

```
      override internal function drawProjectile( ):void
      {
          graphics.lineStyle(3, 0xFF0000);
          graphics.drawRect(-5, -5, 10, 10);
      }

      override internal function arm( ):void {
          nSpeed = 2; // set the speed
      }

      override internal function doMoveProjectile(event:Event):void {
          super.doMoveProjectile(event);
          this.rotation += 5; // rotate
      }
   }
 }
}
```

Projectiles are drawn using methods available in the Graphics class accessible via the graphics property. The projectile speed is set to a negative value for the HeroCannonBall class as it moves from the bottom to top of the stage (Example 2-30). In contrast, alien projectiles move from top to bottom (See Figure 2-10 to see the locations of the space ships). Also note the overridden doMoveProjectile( ) method in the AlienMine class. It calls the default behavior in the superclass using the *super* property, but adds a statement to make the sprite rotate. So, alien mines spin slowly as they move.

Space ships

The Ship class shown in Example 2-33 defines the abstract interface for the concrete space ship classes. The Ship class should behave as an abstract class and is declared as a subclass of Sprite. It defines a setLoc( ) method to set the X and Y coordinates of the sprite. It also defines two methods without implementations that should behave as *abstract* methods. The drawShip( ) method should be overridden and implemented to draw the ship. Similarly, the initShip( ) method should be overridden to initialize ship behavior such as attach event handlers.

Example 2-33. Ship.as

```
package ships
{
    import flash.display.Sprite;
    import flash.events.*;

    // ABSTRACT Class (should be subclassed and not instantiated)
    internal class Ship extends Sprite
    {
        internal function setLoc(xLoc:int, yLoc:int):void
        {
            this.x = xLoc;
```

Example 2-33. Ship.as (continued)

```
            this.y = yLoc;
        }

        // ABSTRACT Method (must be overridden in a subclass)
        internal function drawShip():void {}

        // ABSTRACT Method (must be overridden in a subclass)
        internal function initShip():void {}
    }
}
```

The AlienShip (Example 2-34) and HeroShip (Example 2-35) classes extend the Ship (Example 2-33) class.

Example 2-34. AlienShip.as

```
package ships
{
    import flash.display.*;
    import flash.events.*;
    import weapons.AlienWeapon;

    public class AlienShip extends Ship
    {
        private var weapon:AlienWeapon;
        // available projectiles
        private const aProjectiles:Array = [AlienWeapon.CANNON, AlienWeapon.MINE];

        override internal function drawShip():void
        {
            graphics.beginFill(0xFFFFFF); // white color
            graphics.drawRect(-5, -10, 10, 5);
            graphics.drawRect(-20, -5, 40, 10);
            graphics.drawRect(-20, 5, 10, 5);
            graphics.drawRect(10, 5, 10, 5);
            graphics.endFill();
        }

        override internal function initShip():void
        {
            // instantiate the alien projectile creator
            weapon = new AlienWeapon();
            // attach the doFire() method on this object
            // as an ENTER_FRAME handler of the stage
            this.stage.addEventListener(Event.ENTER_FRAME, this.doFire);
        }

        protected function doFire(event:Event):void
        {
            // fire randomly (4% chance of firing on each enterframe)
            if (Math.ceil(Math.random() * 25) == 1)
            {
                // select random projectile
```

Example 2-34. AlienShip.as

```
            var cProjectile:uint =
              aProjectiles[Math.floor(Math.random( ) * aProjectiles.length)];
            weapon.fire(cProjectile, this.stage, this.x, this.y + 15);
        }
    }
  }
}
```

Example 2-35. HeroShip.as

```
package ships
{
    import flash.display.*;
    import weapons.HeroWeapon;
    import flash.events.*;

    internal class HeroShip extends Ship
    {
        private var weapon:HeroWeapon;

        override internal function drawShip( ):void
        {
            graphics.beginFill(0x00FF00); // green color
            graphics.drawRect(-5, -15, 10, 10);
            graphics.drawRect(-12, -5, 24, 10);
            graphics.drawRect(-20, 5, 40, 10);
            graphics.endFill( );
        }

        override internal function initShip( ):void
        {
            // instantiate the hero projectile creator
            weapon = new HeroWeapon( );
            // attach the doMoveShip() and doFire() methods on this object
            // as MOUSE_MOVE and MOUSE_DOWN handlers of the stage
            this.stage.addEventListener(MouseEvent.MOUSE_MOVE, this.doMoveShip);
            this.stage.addEventListener(MouseEvent.MOUSE_DOWN, this.doFire);
        }

        protected function doMoveShip(event:MouseEvent):void
        {
            // set the x coordinate of the sprite to the
            // mouse relative to the stage
            this.x = event.stageX;
            event.updateAfterEvent( ); // process this event first
        }

        protected function doFire(event:MouseEvent):void
        {
            weapon.fire(HeroWeapon.CANNON, this.stage, this.x, this.y - 25);
            event.updateAfterEvent( ); // process this event first
        }
    }
}
```

Note the initShip( ) methods in both derived classes attach event handlers to intercept events. The event handlers on the HeroShip class respond to MOUSE_MOVE and MOUSE_DOWN events sent to the stage. Intercepting these stage events is necessary as the hero ship should respond to mouse events even when the mouse focus is not on the sprite. In addition, the initShip( ) method initializes the corresponding creator class for creating projectiles. The ENTER_FRAME event handler on the AlienShip class is the doFire( ) method. It fires a random projectile from the available projectile list using the projectile creator class.

Creator Classes

We end up with two sets of creator classes corresponding to the two product types. One creator class encapsulates the creation of projectiles and the other encapsulates space ship creation.

Weapon

The Weapon class (Example 2-36) is the abstract interface that encapsulates projectile creation. The weapon is better described as a weapons platform that can fire different kinds of projectiles. The publicly accessible fire( ) method calls the createProjectile( ) factory method.

Example 2-36. Weapon.as

```
package weapons
{
    import flash.display.Stage;
    import flash.errors.IllegalOperationError;

    // ABSTRACT Class (should be subclassed and not instantiated)
    public class Weapon
    {

        public function fire(cWeapon:uint, target:Stage, xLoc:int, yLoc:int):void
        {
            var  projectile:Projectile = this.createProjectile(cWeapon);
            trace("Firing " + projectile.toString( ));
            // draw projectile
            projectile.drawProjectile( );
            // set the starting x and y location
            projectile.setLoc(xLoc, yLoc);
            // arm the projectile (override the default speed)
            projectile.arm( );
            // add the projectile to the display list
            target.addChild(projectile);
            // make the projectile move by attaching enterframe event handler
            projectile.release( );
        }
```

Example 2-36. Weapon.as (continued)

```
        // ABSTRACT Method (must be overridden in a subclass)
        protected function createProjectile(cWeapon:uint):Projectile
        {
            throw new IllegalOperationError("Abstract method:
                                        must be overridden in a subclass");
            return null;
        }
    }
}
```

The AlienWeapon (Example 2-37) and HeroWeapon (Example 2-38) classes extend the Weapon class (Example 2-36) and implement the createProjectile( ) factory method.

Example 2-37. AlienWeapon.as

```
package weapons
{
    public class AlienWeapon extends Weapon
    {
        public static const CANNON    :uint =  0;
        public static const MINE      :uint =  1;

        override protected function createProjectile(cWeapon:uint):Projectile
        {
            if (cWeapon == CANNON)
            {
                trace("Creating new alien cannonball");
                return new AlienCannonBall( );
            } else if (cWeapon == MINE) {
                trace("Creating new alien mine");
                return new AlienMine( );
            } else {
                throw new Error("Invalid kind of projectile specified");
                return null;
            }
        }
    }
}
```

Example 2-38. HeroWeapon.as

```
package weapons
{
    public class HeroWeapon extends Weapon
    {
        public static const CANNON    :uint =  0;

        override protected function createProjectile(cWeapon:uint):Projectile
        {
            if (cWeapon == CANNON)
            {
                trace("Creating new Hero cannonball");
```

Example 2-38. HeroWeapon.as (continued)

```
                return new HeroCannonBall( );
            } else {
                throw new Error("Invalid kind of projectile specified");
                return null;
            }
        }
    }
}
```

ShipCreator

The concrete class ShipCreator (Example 2-39) encapsulates ship creation. We don't need to encapsulate knowledge about hero ships and alien ships at this point. After all, we have only one hero ship and one kind of alien ship.

Example 2-39. ShipCreator.as

```
package ships
{
    import flash.display.Stage;

    public class ShipCreator
    {
        public static const HERO        :uint =  0;
        public static const ALIEN    :uint =  1;

        public function addShip(cShipType:uint, target:Stage, xLoc:int, yLoc:int):void
        {
            var ship:Ship = this.createShip(cShipType);
            ship.drawShip( ); // draw ship
            ship.setLoc(xLoc, yLoc); // set the x and y location
            target.addChild(ship); // add the sprite to the stage
            ship.initShip( ); // initialize ship
        }

        private function createShip(cShipType:uint):Ship
        {
            if (cShipType == HERO)
            {
                trace("Creating new hero ship");
                return new HeroShip( );
            } else if (cShipType == ALIEN) {
                trace("Creating new alien ship");
                return new AlienShip( );
            } else {
                throw new Error("Invalid kind of ship specified");
                return null;
            }
        }
    }
}
```

Concrete Creator Classes

Until we encountered the ShipCreator class (Example 2-39), the examples defined creator classes as abstract. Concrete creator classes implement the factory method as opposed to leaving the implementation to subclasses. So, adding new products requires changing the factory method in a concrete class. Changing existing code is not as elegant a solution as extending an abstract class to accommodate changes. Concrete creator classes are useful when the design's only motivation is to decouple concrete classes from the clients that use them. When you add the possibility of changing requirements to this equation, in most cases the abstract creator classes are the more prudent choice.

Clients

We have multiple clients accessing the creator classes. Clients can use the ShipCreator class (Example 2-39) to place space ships on the stage.

```
// instantiate ship creator
var shipFactory:ShipCreator = new ShipCreator();

// place hero ship
shipFactory.addShip(ShipCreator.HERO, this.stage,
                this.stage.stageWidth / 2, this.stage.stageHeight - 20);
// place alien ships
for (var i:Number = 0; i < 5; i++)
{
    shipFactory.addShip(ShipCreator.ALIEN, this.stage,
        120 + 80 * i, 100);
}
```

In addition, the hero and alien spaceships access their corresponding weapons classes to create and fire projectiles. The spaceships are the clients for the projectile classes.

Summary

Change is inevitable in software design. Requirements change during the course of application development, and, in some cases, ugly hacks are used to effect changes that the original design didn't anticipate. The antidote to this common issue is robust design that stands up to changes and modifications. The best way to handle changing requirements is to manage the dependencies between code segments. Consider the example of a Client class creating a new instance of a Product class using the new keyword, and saving the resulting object in a variable. This is a very common practice that creates a strong dependency between the two classes. This is also known as strong or *tight coupling*. Changes to either class will most likely propagate to the other class as well. The factory method pattern is an excellent way to manage these types of dependencies, as it introduces a firewall between classes that depend on each other. The pattern does not prevent the classes from depending on each other, but it provides a framework by which this dependency can be managed.

CHAPTER 3

Singleton Pattern

*The aspects of things that are most important to us are
hidden because of their simplicity and familiarity.*
—Ludwig Wittgenstein
*Above all be of single aim; have a legitimate and
useful purpose, and devote yourself unreservedly to it.*
—James Allen

What Is the Singleton Pattern?

The Singleton pattern is used all the time, even if you don't realize you're using it.
For example, if you have some kind of class that keeps the total number of points in
a game, you want only a single instance of that total. It doesn't make any sense to
have two totals where the game records only a single total score, like you find in a
single-player pinball game. Likewise, if you create a music application, you want the
application to play only one tune at a time, and so you want only a single instance of
the class that actually plays the music. In fact, most applications have at least some
feature where you want to make sure that there's only a single instance, and that's
where you'll want to use the Singleton design pattern.

Key Features

In a nutshell, the Singleton has two key features:

1. One and only one instance of the class can be instantiated at any one time.
2. The class must have a single, global access point.

You may be thinking, "How hard can that be? As the developer, I can just instantiate a single instance and use a global variable. Bob's your uncle, and it's all done.
Next pattern."

First of all, as you saw in Chapter 1, OOP and design patterns were devised for teams
of developers, and not just one person working independently. So if you're involved

in teamwork, the Singleton can be used to make sure another developer on the team doesn't create an instance of the class when you've already done so. The Singleton design pattern tells other developers not to create more than a single instance of the base class associated with the pattern.

Second, using global variables in no way restricts their usage to a single instance. They can be instantiated anywhere from a top-level package to within a function inside a class. Global access must go hand-in-hand with single instantiation.

This is not to say creating a Singleton class is difficult. You can create the class using a single file, and there's not a lot of code in the basic class. You can add all the methods and properties you want, and so a Singleton isn't restrictive in that sense. The main issue to wrap your head around is that of making sure only a single instance is invoked at any one time.

The Singleton Model

Looking at the Singleton structure in the class diagram notation, we see no abstract classes or interfaces. A key point to note is the use of a static Instance( ) and the connection to the implementation pseudocode. As you will see, the pattern uses static class variables and methods for the global implementation and the uniqueness of the instantiation of the class. Figure 3-1 shows this simple but powerful structure.

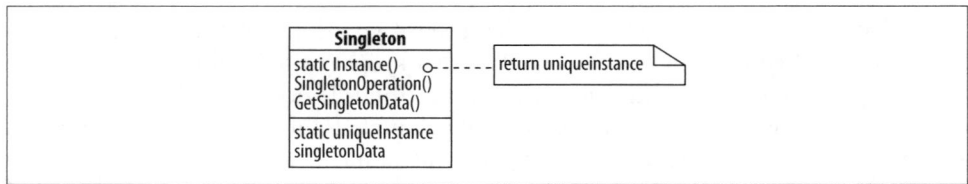

Figure 3-1. Singleton structure

To move from the diagram structure to a working model, we need to get a couple of OOP issues straightened out using ActionScript 3.0. Primarily, we need to work out how to get a self-instantiated class set up. With most of the other patterns, the different parts work together with one part implementing or extending the other. So we need to take a look at the basics.

Key OOP Concepts Used with the Singleton Pattern

One of the first issues we need to address is that of using private functions as constructors. In the Singleton pattern implemented in ActionScript 2.0 and Java, the "classic" Singleton is created using a private constructor so that, given the structure of the constructor, only a single instance can be created. Example 3-1 shows a typical implementation:

Example 3-1. Classic Singleton

```
class Singleton
{
    private static var instance:Singleton;
    private function Singleton()
    {
    }
    public static function getInstance():Singleton
    {
        if (instance == null) {
            Singleton.instance = new Singleton();
        }
        return Singleton.instance;
    }
}
```

That looks pretty simple. However, looking at it carefully, you'll find a lot going on. Let's go over the key points:

Private static instantiation of the instance variable typed as Singleton
> The private characteristic of the variable means you can't access it outside the class. Being static means you can access it by the method in the class set up to instantiate a Singleton object.

Private class constructor
> Example 3-1 is pretty straightforward in ActionScript 2.0. In ActionScript 3.0, we are faced with the dilemma that private functions cannot be used as constructors in packages. Classes to be instantiated need to be public and part of a package. This will be discussed further when creating the equivalent of a private class constructor.

Public static function for creating a class instance
> The getInstance() method is a wonderfully simple function. It checks to see if an instance has been created, and, if it hasn't, then it creates one. Otherwise it simply returns the existing Singleton instance.

The simplicity of the Singleton is clearer after seeing how it actually works in a concrete example. However, working with ActionScript 3.0, we're stuck because we can't create a private class constructor. This next section provides a workaround to this dilemma.

Creating and Using a Private Class Constructor

Rather than showing how your code will fail if you attempt to create a private constructor function inside a package, you're going to see how to effectively make your very own private class, and use it as a constructor. In fact, you will see how to implement it in a script.

To create a class, we need a public constructor function within a package. Because we cannot create a private class within a package, we'll have to create one outside a package, and then somehow get it to work inside a package. So, using a single *.as* file, the following script first creates a public class, closes the package, and then creates a private class outside the package. The private class is then called from within the public class. Example 3-2 shows how this is done.

Example 3-2. PublicClass.as

```
 1  package
 2  {
 3      import flash.display.Sprite;
 4      public class PublicClass extends Sprite
 5      {
 6          public function PublicClass()
 7          {
 8              PrivateClass.alert();
 9          }
10      }
11  }
12  //End of Package
13  //**************
14  //Private class
15  class PrivateClass
16  {
17      public function PrivateClass()
18      {
19
20       public static function alert():void
21       {
22          trace("This is from a private class");
23       }
24  }
```

Save the file as *PublicClass.as,* and, in an FLA file, type in **PublicClass** as the Document class, and save the FLA file as *TestPrivate.fla.* When you test the program, you will see:

```
    This is from a private class
```

in the Output panel. Notice in Line 8 that the class, PrivateClass, is employed simply by typing the class name and the method. No constructor statement is used at all.

Creating a Private Class Instance

Keeping in mind the implementation in Example 3-1, we have to work out a way for the class constructor to act like a private class. If the private class can be part of the instantiation method (getInstance()), then we'll be able to have the same effect as a private class constructor.

 Why aren't there any private classes in ActionScript 3.0? Private classes haven't yet been implemented in ECMAScript, and Action-Script 3.0 has been following the current ECMAScript standards. Because of a number of non-trivial issues, it turns out that both ECMAScript and ActionScript 3.0 will have to wait for private classes. The alternatives were to hold up releasing ActionScript 3.0 or engineer a hack to create a private class constructor.

Consider Example 3-3:

Example 3-3. Using a private class in a public class constructor

```
package
{
    public class PublicClass
    {
        private static var instance:PublicClass;
        public function PublicClass(pvt:PrivateClass) {
        }
        public static function getInstance():PublicClass
        {
            PublicClass.instance=new PublicClass (new PrivateClass());
        }
        return PublicClass.instance;
        }
    }
}
class PrivateClass
{
    public function PrivateClass() {
        trace("Private class is up");
    }
}
```

The real key is that the private class is assigned as a parameter in the constructor. Then, when a new instance is created with the getInstance() method, the instance includes the parameter made up of a new instance of the private class.

Minimalist Abstract Singleton

To illustrate the Singleton design pattern as simply as possible, Figure 3-4 uses the classic Singleton with very little change. The added else statement shows what happens when more than a single instance is instantiated at the same time. It will be removed in the remaining discussion of the Singleton. The other trace statements in the script shown in Example 3-4 help to demonstrate how the script runs through the code.

Example 3-4. Singleton.as

```
package
{
    public class Singleton
    {
        private static var _instance:Singleton;
        public function Singleton(pvt:PrivateClass) {
        }
        public static function getInstance():Singleton
        {
            if(Singleton._instance == null)
            {
                Singleton._instance=new Singleton(new PrivateClass());
                trace("Singleton instantiated");
            }
            else
            {
                trace("Sorry--already have a Singleton instantiated")
            }
            return Singleton._instance;
        }
    }
}
class PrivateClass
{
    public function PrivateClass() {
        trace("Private class is up");
    }
}
```

Save the files as Singleton.as. You now have a Singleton to work with. The next step is actually using it.

Instantiation with a Private Class Parameter

When the Singleton class is instantiated as an object in a program, you cannot successfully use the following format:

```
var mySingleton:Singleton = new Singleton();
```

This format runs into the ironic problem of needing an argument in the constructor. Right now, the declaration line has 0 arguments, and you need 1. The argument you need is a reference to a private class that can be accessed only through the public class you're trying to instantiate. (There's a paradox if there ever was one!) Look at Example 3-5 for a bad implementation of the Singleton class:

Example 3-5. BadImplementation.as

```
package
{
    import flash.display.Sprite
    public class BadImplementation extends Sprite
```

Example 3-5. BadImplementation.as (continued)

```
    {
        public function BadImplementation( )
        {
            var mySingleton=new Singleton( );
        }
    }
}
```

Save the file as *BadImplementation.as* in the same folder as the *Singleton.as*. In a Flash document, type in **BadImplementation** in the Document class window, and test the application. As predicted, you get a compiler error as shown in Figure 3-2.

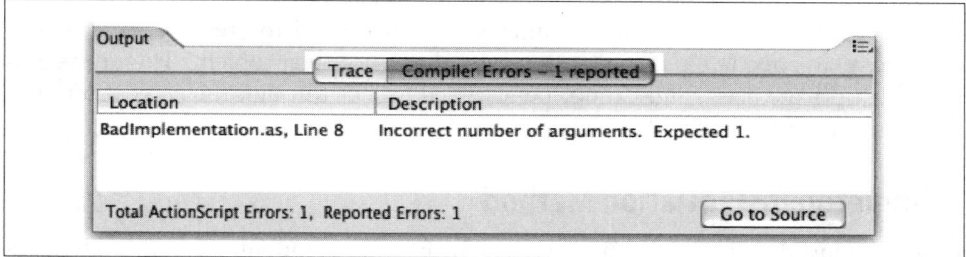

Figure 3-2. Compiler error expecting argument

Immediately you see that the Singleton constructor contains an argument, a PrivateClass, and so the natural response is to change the code to include a PrivateClass argument as shown in Example 3-6.

Example 3-6. Attempt to add private class parameter

```
package
{
    import flash.display.Sprite
    public class BadImplementation extends Sprite
    {
        public function BadImplementation( )
        {
            var mySingleton=new Singleton(new PrivateClass( ));
        }
    }
}
```

Re-save the *BadImplementation.as* file and test it again. This time, you get a different error as shown in Figure 3-3:

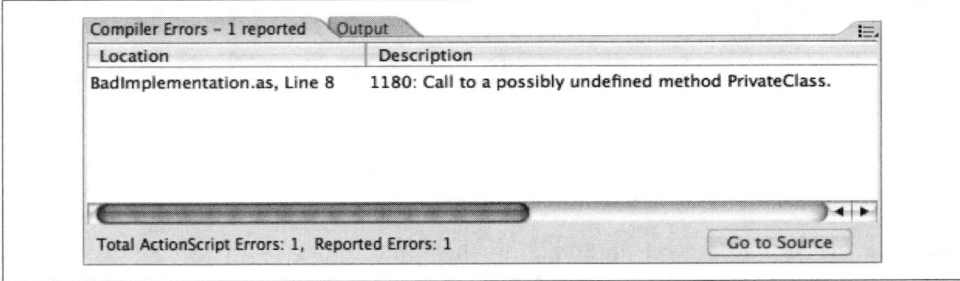

Figure 3-3. Compiler not finding class

So what does this mean? Essentially, the compiler does not recognize the class named PrivateClass, and doesn't think you remembered to create it, or that you don't have an adequate path to it. However, that's not the problem. The problem is that it's a private class, and cannot be accessed except through the class you're trying to instantiate—the Singleton class.

A Singleton Instantiation Method

In developing the Singleton class, we had to include a special method in the constructor to instantiate the class. As you've seen, the standard methods used to create a class instance just don't work. The getInstance( ) function solves the instantiation problem. The following code segment shows this essential part of the program, which allows access to the private class necessary for the instantiation of the class:

```
public static function getInstance( ):Singleton
{
    if(Singleton._instance == null)
    {
        Singleton._instance=new Singleton(new PrivateClass( ));
        trace("Singleton instantiated");
    }
    ............
    return Singleton._instance
}
```

The _instance variable is a private static one that will hold an instance of the Singleton class. Because we want only one instance, the code checks to see if there's an instance already. Any ActionScript 3.0 user-defined class data type that has not been assigned a value is null by default. So after making sure that Singleton._instance is null (no other instance exists), the script creates one. Here we see the instantiation line we tried outside of the class:

```
....new Singleton(new PrivateClass( ));
```

This is possible because the PrivateClass is referenced from within the Singleton class.

Now, we can write a class that instantiates the Singleton class. Open a new Action-Script file, and enter the code shown in Example 3-7. The script attempts to instantiate two instances of the Singleton class. If the class is set up correctly, it'll allow you only one instance.

Example 3-7. Instantiating Singleton class

```
package
{
    import flash.display.Sprite;
    public class SingletonTest extends Sprite {
        public function SingletonTest() {
            var firstSingleton:Singleton = Singleton.getInstance();
            var secondSingleton:Singleton=Singleton.getInstance();
        }
    }
}
```

Save the file as *SingletonTest.as*, open a new Flash document, and type **SingletonTest** in the Document class window. Both files should be saved in the same directory as the *Singleton.as* file. Now test the application in the Flash document. Figure 3-4 shows what you should see:

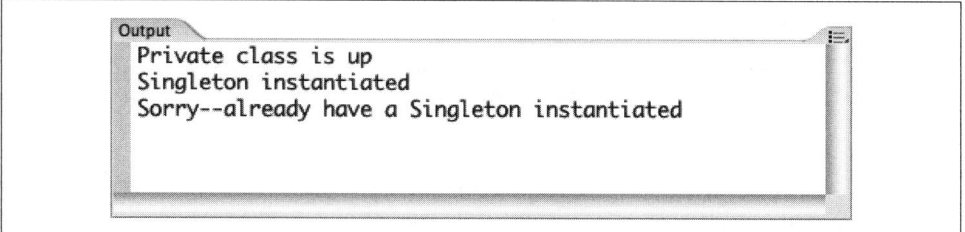

Figure 3-4. Single class instance created

The fact that you can see the message, "Sorry--already have a Singleton instantiated" means that only one of the two instances was successfully created. That's exactly what we were hoping for. Had both instances been created successfully, we'd have to go back to the drawing board. However, after the first one was created, as indicated by the messages, "Private class is up" and "Singleton instantiated," the second one was blocked.

One Instance and Different References

In reviewing the classic Singleton design pattern application, you may have noticed that no matter what happens during an attempted instantiation of the class, the program always passes through to a statement that returns a Singleton._instance. We know that if the conditional statement finds that a Singleton._instance exists, it doesn't create another one, but still returns whatever instance has been instantiated.

However, does that mean that only a single reference can be associated with the single instance? What happens, for example, if I first create one instance with one label, and then attempt to create another instance with a different label?

To see that a single instance can be associated with more than one reference (name or label), some changes have to be made to the primary Singleton class. Using a separate folder from the Singleton class, in Example 3-4 open a new ActionScript file and add the script in Example 3-8. Save it as *Singleton.as* in the newly created folder.

Example 3-8. Singleton.as

```
package
{

    public class Singleton
    {
        private var _msg:String;
        private static var _instance:Singleton;
        public function Singleton(pvt:PrivateClass)
        {
        }
        public static function getInstance():Singleton
        {

            if(Singleton._instance == null)
            {
                Singleton._instance=new Singleton(new PrivateClass());
                trace("Singleton instantiated");
            }
            return Singleton._instance;
        }

        //Get and set methods

        public function getMsg():String
        {
            return _msg;
        }
        public function setMsg(alert:String):void
        {
            _msg = alert;
        }
    }
}

class PrivateClass
{
    public function PrivateClass() {
    trace("PrivateClass called");
    }
}
```

This second Singleton has getter and setter methods. If we attempt to create two different instances using two different object names and set different string values to the _msg variable, we should see only one when we ask for the value, if both use the get method after the second one has set a different value than the first. That is, we can have as many names associated with one instance as we want, and they'll all function. However, they'll be referencing only one Singleton instance. The following pseudocode shows the logic:

- Label A instantiates a Singleton (succeeds).
- Label A uses the set method to add "Message A" (succeeds).
- Label B instantiates a Singleton (Returns the currently instantiated instance).
- Label B uses the set method to add "Message B" (succeeds).
- Label A uses the get method to display the most recently set image. (What will appear?)

To resolve this issue, open a new ActionScript file and add the code shown in Example 3-9.

Example 3-9. SingletonTest.as

```
package
{
    import flash.display.Sprite;
    public class SingletonTest extends Sprite {
        public function SingletonTest( ) {

            var firstSingleton:Singleton = Singleton.getInstance( );
            firstSingleton.setMsg("Singleton instance: firstSingleton");
            var secondSingleton:Singleton = Singleton.getInstance( );
            secondSingleton.setMsg("Singleton instance: secondSingleton");

            trace(firstSingleton.getMsg( ));
            trace(secondSingleton.getMsg( ));

        }
    }
}
```

Save the file as *SingletonTest.as* in the same folder as the new *Singleton.as* file. Open a new Flash document, type in **SingletonText** in the Class document window, and save the FLA file in the same folder as the two ActionScript (.as) files. When you test the movie, your output window shows that only a single instance exists as in Figure 3-5.

It's clear from the output that only a single instance was created, which must have been the first one because of the code structure. However, both the instance labels (firstSingleton and secondSingleton) typed as Singleton data are returning the value of the second instance. Both instance labels will always have the same value because they are merely references to the instance, and not actually instances themselves.

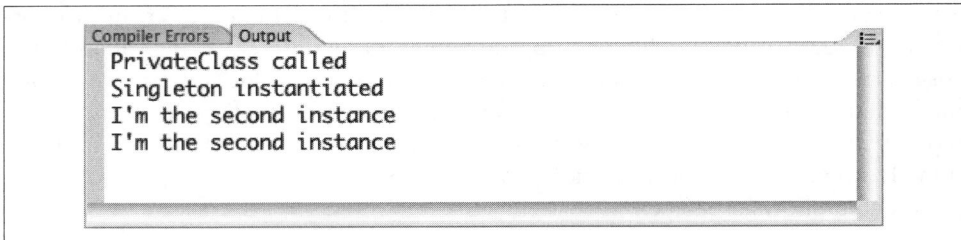

Figure 3-5. Two instance labels and one instance

You may be wondering how this was possible, because the second instance did not drop into the part of the constructor that actually created the Singleton instance:

```
Singleton._instance=new Singleton(new PrivateClass());
```

However, it did not have to because the line,

```
return Singleton._instance
```

contains the Singleton instance that had already been created, and simply returned that instance to the reference name.

While you can guarantee that only one instance of the Singleton class will exist at any one time, more than a single reference to that instance can exist at the same time as well. For a shared property used with either increments or decrements, this can be a very handy way of making sure that only a single source is used by all of the references. If, for instance, you're making a game to save miners trapped in a mineshaft, you need to keep track of the amount of oxygen available for the miners. So if you create an Oxygen class as a Singleton, all of the miner characters can create a reference to it, and each one can access a method in the single instance that decrements the amount of air. Because the amount of air has to be the same for all, the Singleton becomes a handy tool for keeping track of the many references to the single instance of the class.

When to Use the Singleton Pattern

As noted at the beginning of this chapter, the Singleton design pattern is best employed when you need one and only one instance of a class in an application. A couple of examples were discussed, but the use of the Singleton is so ubiquitous in object-oriented programming that it's sort of like asking when to use a variable.

Moreover, developers often combine the Singleton design pattern with other patterns. Where the developer needs a single, global entry point and a single instance, you'll often find a Singleton class. Likewise, multiple Singleton classes can be used in conjunction when you have several different objects where only a single instance of each object should be instantiated at any one time.

In order to provide a broad but by no means exhaustive view of how the Singleton can be employed, we will step through three examples. First, the Alert example is a simple one that shows how a single message can be placed on the stage. It is meant to represent those kinds of interfaces where the user gets a message, such as in a dialog box or similar feedback mechanism. Only a single instance of the feedback should be instantiated, to avoid contradictory messages. However, the example also shows how to connect the class to display objects on the stage. As such, it is instructive for working with display programming in ActionScript 3.0.

The second example is used for playing an MP3 file. In most situations where you play media, whether it's a MP3 file or a video, you want to hear or see only one media element at a time. Playing Bach and a song by Gnarls Barkley simultaneously may create a racket that neither Johann Sebastian nor Gnarls would want to hear. A Singleton class helps to keep the play sequential, with no more than one playing at the same time.

The third example uses a simple shopping cart to illustrate how a single instance can be used to keep track of a running total. In situations where your application needs an absolutely no-questions-about-it single instance for keeping track of financial accumulations, a Singleton can be crucial. The example also shows how to link a class to a stage-created movie clip and embedded text field.

A Single Alert Message

Because clear communication is the crux of good site design, mixed messages need to be kept out of all web applications. By using a Singleton pattern, you can help assure that you have a single source for messages to the user. This way, you're less likely to send two contradictory messages. The following application uses a Singleton for that purpose. It's designed so that no matter where a message originates, it has only this one instance to deliver it.

To get started, open a new ActionScript file, and type in the script shown in Example 3-10.

Example 3-10. Alert.as

```
package
{
    public class Alert
    {
        private var _msg:String;
        private static var _instance:Alert;
        public function Alert(pvt:PrivateClass) {

        }
        public static function getInstance():Alert
        {
            if(Alert._instance == null)
```

Example 3-10. Alert.as

```
            {
                Alert._instance=new Alert(new PrivateClass());
                trace("Alert instantiated");
            }
            return Alert._instance;
        }
        //Alert Property
         public var colorFont:uint;
        //Alert Methods
        public function getMsg():String
        {
            return _msg;
        }
        public function setMsg(alert:String):void
        {
            _msg = alert;
        }
    }
}

class PrivateClass
{
    public function PrivateClass() {
    trace("PrivateClass called");
    }
}
```

Save the file as *Alert.as*. As you can see, this Singleton design pattern doesn't have to be saved as "Singleton," and the only reason that name was used in the previous examples was to help you better see its structure, and where it belonged in the application. In fact, it's almost identical to the other *Singleton.as* files used as examples in this chapter, and even has the same methods as in Example 3-8. However, this example includes a property used as a variable in the font color of the text field used here. Conceivably, your application may need different colored messages to differentiate categories of advisements your application might employ.

In ActionScript 3.0, you can create a TextField instance in one of two ways. First, you can create it dynamically in the script, as we will do in this example. Alternatively, you can create a MovieClip object on the stage, embed a TextField in the movie clip, and then reference the embedded TextField. Unless you have a good reason for doing so, it's more practical and uses less memory to just write the script for the TextField. (Further on in this chapter, a movie clip in the shape of a shopping cart with an embedded text field shows how to create and dynamically use a TextField object on the stage.)

Open a new ActionScript file and after entering the code in Example 3-11, name the file *AlertText.as* and save it in the same folder as *Alert.as*.

Example 3-11. AlertText.as

```
package
{
    import flash.text.TextField;
    import flash.text.TextFormat;
    import flash.text.TextFieldAutoSize;
    import flash.display.Sprite;
    public class AlertTest extends Sprite
    {
        public function AlertTest( )
        {
            var reminder:Alert = Alert.getInstance( );
            reminder.setMsg("Remember to use addChild( )");
            var announce:TextField=new TextField( );
            announce.text=reminder.getMsg( );
            announce.autoSize=TextFieldAutoSize.LEFT;
            var format:TextFormat=new TextFormat( );
            reminder.colorFont=0x990099;
            format.color=reminder.colorFont;
            format.font="Arial Black";
            announce.setTextFormat(format);
            announce.x=200;
            announce.y=150;
            this.addChild(announce);
        }
    }
}
```

When using something other than trace( ) statements in your applications, you need to import the necessary packages and classes for your application. Also, anything that you plan to place on the stage needs to be at least a Sprite or MovieClip. Because our application has no Timeline, we can use a Sprite. Thus, the AlertTest extends the Sprite class.

We need to mention a couple of concepts here for OOP beginners and those new to ActionScript 3.0. They include *package parsimony* and *abstraction*. As noted in Chapter 1, abstraction is a pillar of OOP, and you can see it in the Alert class where parameters and return values are abstract variables. The concept *package parsimony* reminds us that when importing packages from the core set, you should import only what you need, and not the whole package. As you can see in the AlertTest class, only the necessary classes were imported. While it can be tempting to use the wild-card asterisk (*) to bring in the whole package and save some typing time, this carries with it a lot of baggage. For example, instead of typing in the three lines,

```
import flash.text.TextField;
import flash.text.TextFormat;
import flash.text.TextFieldAutoSize;
```

we could have just typed in,

```
import flash.text.*;
```

However, had we done that, we would have added 15 classes of excess baggage. So while we would have saved a few strokes typing, we would have burdened the application with those unused classes.

You can see a somewhat odd example of abstraction at work in the single property colorFont included in the Alert Singleton class. The colorFont property is an abstraction of any unsigned integer (uint). First, the colorFont property is assigned a literal value, and second, that instance property is assigned to the format.color property. Obviously, we could have assigned the color value directly to the format.color property as a literal, but the purpose of putting the colorFont property in the Singleton is to insure that only a single instance will be available for coloring the fonts. Thus, the abstraction of an unsigned integer in the Alert Singleton class insured that no color mix-up occurs.

To finish up, open a new Flash document, and type **AlertTest** as the Document class name. Save the FLA file in the same folder as the *Alert* and *AlertTest* files. Figure 3-6 shows what you will see on both the stage and Output window.

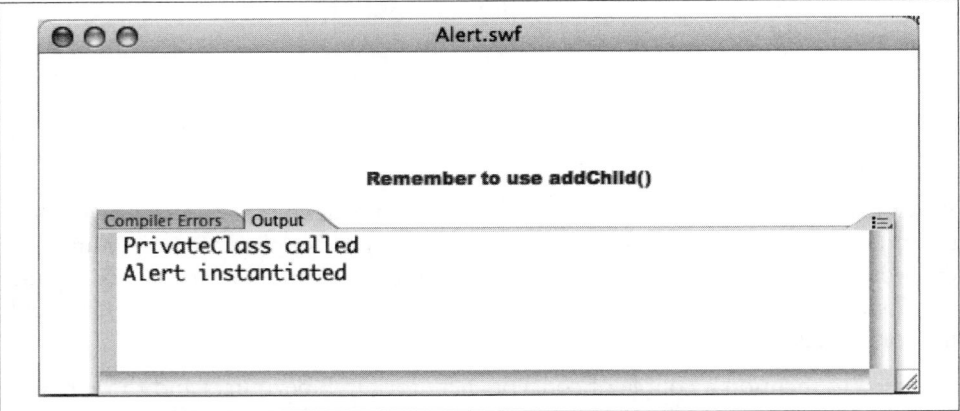

Figure 3-6. Alert message on the stage

In a typical application, you would use dynamic input for the message and color. For example, you might set up a user feedback system using different error or information messages, depending on what action the user takes. However, in the example you can see the fundamentals of setting up such a system using a Singleton and text field.

Just One Tune at a Time

Since the advent of MP3 and MP3 players, music has migrated from the CD to MP3 players and devices like Apple's iPod. Imagine cranking up your iPod to listen to your favorite tunes, and instead of one at a time, they all start playing simultaneously. The software that runs your iPod won't let that happen, and you shouldn't let it happen to your applications either. Here's another situation where a Singleton can come in handy.

To get started, we need to take a look at how we can play an MP3 file in Flash CS3. We won't even consider the idea of importing an MP3 file into the main Timeline and bloating our SWF file. Rather, we need to take a quick look at how ActionScript 3.0 deals with sound and externally accessed MP3 files.

The classes relating to sound can be found in the flash.media package. Of the five sound-related classes, we'll need only the Sound and SoundChannel classes. We're going to access an external file (the MP3 file), so we'll need the flash.net.URLRequest class as well. The necessary minimum sequence can be seen in the following pseudocode:

```
var mySound:Sound = new Sound( );
var myChannel:SoundChannel = new SoundChannel;
var myTune:URLRequest= new URLRequest(string);
mySound.load(myTune);
myChannel=mySound.play( );
```

Using the following script, we can create the actual method:

```
public function playMe(song:String):void
{
    _tuneUp=new Sound( );
    _tuneIn=new URLRequest(song);
    _tuneUp.load(_tuneIn);
    _goChannel=_tuneUp.play( );
}
```

The function has a single parameter, which is a string variable that will be the name of the song (MP3 file). You might want to think of the song parameter as a URL, because that's actually what it is. However, it makes perfect sense to reference it as a song because the individual MP3 files are individual tunes. Given the way the function's designed, there's a place for only a single sound. Because the method resides in a Singleton class, there's also going to be only a single instance, guaranteeing that only one tune at a time will be played.

However, before we go further, we need to consider how the SoundChannel class works. As soon as the Sound.play( ) method is assigned to the SoundChannel instance, the song starts playing. If, using the same instance of the Sound and SoundChannel classes, you load and play another MP3 file, it's going to start playing as well. As far as the instances are concerned, there's no contraction because they've done their job and set the first MP3 file merrily on its way. So they're finished. Using exactly the same instance, they're willing to do it again with another MP3 file even if the first one's still playing. The two will overlap, and because that's one of the things we want to prevent, the code will have to find whether there's a SoundChannel instance with an assigned value around. This is done by testing the SoundChannel instance for a null value. If a null value is found, the script just goes ahead and activates the code for playing the selected tune. If it finds a non-null value, it means it better stop any current sounds associated with the SoundChannel instance before loading up and playing a new MP3 file. In that way, you ensure that you won't have multiple tunes playing simultaneously. The moral to this particular application is this:

> Just because you use a Singleton design pattern does not mean that your application will work with the single outcome you want. You must design your Singleton to ensure that the single outcome you want takes place in the way you want.

With the moral in mind, you can now create your Singleton for making sure that only one MP3 file is allowed to play at once. Enter the script shown in Example 3-12 in an ActionScript file, and save it as *Tuner.as*.

Example 3-12. Tuner.as

```
package
{
    import flash.net.URLRequest;
    import flash.media.Sound;
    import flash.media.SoundChannel;
    public class Tuner
    {
        private var _goChannel:SoundChannel;
        private var _tuneUp:Sound;
        private var _tuneIn:URLRequest;
        //Singleton instance
        private static  var _instance:Tuner;

        //Singleton constructor
        public function Tuner (pvt:PrivateClass)
        {
        }
        //Singleton constructor method
        public static  function getInstance ():Tuner
        {
            if (Tuner._instance == null)
            {
                Tuner._instance=new Tuner(new PrivateClass );
                trace ("Tuner instantiated");
            }
            return Tuner._instance;
        }
        //Start Play
        public function playMe (song:String):void
        {
            if (_goChannel != null)
            {
                _goChannel.stop ();
            }
            _tuneUp=new Sound  ;
            _tuneIn=new URLRequest(song);
            _tuneUp.load (_tuneIn);
            _goChannel=_tuneUp.play();
```

Example 3-12. Tuner.as

```
        }
        //Stop Play
        public function stopMe ():void
        {
            if (_goChannel != null)
            {
                _goChannel.stop ();
            }
        }
    }
}

class PrivateClass
{
    public function PrivateClass ()
    {
        trace ("PrivateClass called");
    }
}
```

The first thing to note about this Singleton script is that it imports packages and classes. Up to this point, all of the imports were done in the scripts that called the Singleton class. However, whenever a method or property has a reference, including abstract ones, to a class in a package, it needs to import that class. Likewise, you'll see that the class (DoMusic) that implements the Singleton class (Tuner) requires no further import of the objects associated with the packages and classes already imported in the Singleton class.

Because this application simply makes sure that only one MP3 file is played at any time, the Singleton implementation is very simple. Example 3-13 shows the code for this class:

Example 3-13. DoMusic.as

```
package
{
    import flash.display.Sprite;
    public class DoMusic extends Sprite {
        public function DoMusic() {
            var playOne:Tuner = Tuner.getInstance();
            //Use any MP3 file you have available
            playOne.playMe("blues.mp3");
        }
    }
}
```

Save Example 3-13 as *DoMusic.as* in the same folder as *Tuner.as*. Open a Flash document file, type **DoMusic** in the Class document window in the Properties panel, and save it as *Music.fla* in the folder with the two ActionScript files. Finally, place any

MP3 file in the same folder, and rename it *blues.mp3*. (You may keep the MP3 file's original name and change the reference name in the script from *blues.mp3* to the name of your MP3 file—just make sure that the reference name and the filename are the same.) When you test your movie, you should hear your MP3 file play.

In a more realistic example, the application is likely to have several sound selections from which to choose, and the Singleton ensures that only one plays at one time. Because the method for playing an MP3 file is abstracted in the Singleton class, if another tune is called through the Singleton, it employs the single instance of the class to start the new tune. This particular Singleton takes care of the sound "house-keeping" by making sure that any currently playing SoundChannel instances are stopped, and so it does more than just ensure that only a single instance of the class is instantiated. Example 3-14 provides the necessary code. Save the file as *DoMusicBtn.as* in the same folder as the *Tuner.as* file.

Example 3-14. DoMusicBtn.as

```
package
{
    import flash.events.MouseEvent;
    import flash.display.Sprite;

    public class DoMusicBtn extends Sprite
    {
        private var _playOne:SongPlay=new SongPlay();
        private var _playTwo:SongPlay=new SongPlay();
        private var _stopSong:SongPlay=new SongPlay();
        private var playTune:Tuner;

        public function DoMusicBtn ()
        {
            playTune = Tuner.getInstance();
            //Set up buttons
            addChild (_playOne);
            _playOne.x=30;
            _playOne.y=50;
            addChild (_playTwo);
            _playTwo.x=30;
            _playTwo.y=150;
            addChild (_stopSong);
            _stopSong.x=130;
            _stopSong.y=100;

            //Set up event listeners
            _playOne.addEventListener (MouseEvent.CLICK,doOne);
            _playTwo.addEventListener (MouseEvent.CLICK,doTwo);
            _stopSong.addEventListener (MouseEvent.CLICK,doStop);
        }
        //Methods
        function doOne (e:MouseEvent):void
        {
```

Example 3-14. DoMusicBtn.as

```
        playTune.playMe ("blues.mp3");
    }
    function doTwo (e:MouseEvent):void
    {
        playTune.playMe ("class1.mp3");
    }
    function doStop (e:MouseEvent):void
    {
        playTune.stopMe ();
    }
  }
}
```

To test this particular implementation, you will need a slightly more elaborate Flash document file. The following steps show what you need to do.

1. Open a new Flash document and save it in the same folder as your *Tuner.as* file.

2. Using the Oval tool, draw an oval with a radius of 15 on the stage. Select the oval, and then press the F8 button to open the Convert to Symbol dialog box. Type in **SongPlay** in the Name window, and select Button for the Type. Click the Export for ActionScript checkbox in the Linkage group. The class name should show SongPlay and the base class will show flash.display.SimpleButton. Click OK. Delete the button from the stage. (It still remains in the Library.)

3. Open the Properties panel, and, in the Document class window, type in **DoMusicBtn**. Save the file once more.

4. In the folder where you've saved the ActionScript (*.as*) and Flash document files (*.fla*), add two MP3 files using the file names shown in Example 3-14. (You can change the names in your MP3 files or the names in Example 3-14.)

5. Test the application by pressing Ctrl + Enter (Command + Return on the Mac).

You should see three buttons appear. The two buttons on the left let you select one of the two MP3 files, and the one on the right will stop whatever is currently playing. If you click either of the buttons on the left while a tune is still playing, it'll stop the tune and start play from the beginning of the selected tune.

Using Multiple References in a Shopping Cart

This final example of a Singleton design pattern shows how a Singleton instance can have multiple references and still maintain accuracy. Like the previous examples, this one's also simple, with the focus on both the role of the Singleton design and some insights into the Singleton structure

The online Shopping Cart is really nothing more than a conceptual image of a digital accumulator. As each new item is added to the cart, the most current entry is accumulated, and at the time of checkout, this total is computed with applicable tax and shipping costs. It constitutes a good example of how a Singleton should be used, because you want to be sure there's only one shopping cart, and no matter where you add an entry, or take something out, it needs to be from the same instance.

To get started, Example 3-15 shows a Singleton design with a single method for adding to a running total. Open a new folder, copy the code from Example 3-15, and save the file as *ShopCart.as*.

Example 3-15. ShopCart.as

```
package
{
    public class ShopCart
    {
        private static var _cartTotal:Number=0;
          private static var _instance:ShopCart;
        public function ShopCart(secure:PrivateClass) {
            trace("ShopCart instantiated");
        }
        public static function getInstance( ):ShopCart
        {
            if(ShopCart._instance == null)
            {
                var security:PrivateClass=new PrivateClass( );
                ShopCart._instance=new ShopCart(security);
            }
            return ShopCart._instance;
        }
        //Method
        public function kaChing(cart:Number):Number
        {
            _cartTotal+=cart;
            return _cartTotal;
        }
    }
}

class PrivateClass
{
    public function PrivateClass( ) {
        trace("private class installed");
    }

}
```

Like the previous examples, this one uses a private static variable in a method. The variable, _crtTotal, is incremented using a compound operator, and then returns the current amount when the kaChing( ) method is called.

To see the value of a Singleton structure in this application, the script in Example 3-16 generates an instance with two reference names. The first reference name is myCart. Three values are then placed in the "cart" using the kaChing( )

method, and the output is placed into a movie clip's text field. Then, a second cart, named ghostCart, uses the Output window to add to the sum already placed in the movie clip shopping cart. As you will see, the second name reference is using the same instance because all that happens is that the ghostCart instance's value is added to the value in the graphic shopping cart, and displayed in the Output window. This clearly demonstrates the unity of the single instance, and ensures that even with a second cart reference name, the total will be correct. Enter the script in Example 3-16, and save it as *TestCart.as* in the same folder as the *ShopCart.as* file.

Example 3-16. TestCart.as

```
package
{
    import flash.display.Sprite;
    public class TestCart extends Sprite
    {
        private var cartNow:Cart=new Cart();
        public function TestCart ()
        {
            var myCart:ShopCart = ShopCart.getInstance();
            var apples:Number=2.45;
            var oranges:Number=3.50;
            var blackberries:Number=4.11;
            myCart.kaChing (apples);
            myCart.kaChing (oranges);
            myCart.kaChing (blackberries);
            var total:String=String(myCart.kaChing(0));
            cartNow.total_txt.text="$"+total;
            this.addChild (cartNow);
            cartNow.x=(550/2)-(321.6/2);
            cartNow.y=(400/2)-(316.6/2);
            //Attempt to create new instance and introduce new amount
            var ghostCart:ShopCart = ShopCart.getInstance();
            trace ("Ghost cart adds 25.33 for a total of $"+ghostCart.kaChing(25.33));
        }
    }
}
```

The final task is to create a movie clip and text field on the stage to represent our shopping cart. While it's fairly easy to code a text field and place it on the stage, it's a little more difficult to draw a shopping cart using code exclusively. Of course, that's one of the nice features in Flash. You can create images, and control those images with code. Because this step involves a little more than just entering a Document class name, use the following steps to create the shopping cart module:

1. Open a new Flash document, and save it as *TestCart.fla* in the same folder as your *ShopCart.as* file.
2. With the drawing tools, draw a shopping cart. Using static text, label the middle of the cart, "Total." Select the completed shopping cart, and press the F8 key to

open the Convert to Symbol dialog box. Type **Cart** as the Name, and select Movie clip as the Type. Click the Export for ActionScript checkbox, and click OK. (See Figure 3-7 for a visual idea of the cart.)

3. Double-click the Shopping Cart movie clip on the stage to open it for editing. Use the Text tool to add a Dynamic text field. Give it the instance name total_txt in the Properties panel.

4. Exit the Symbol Editing Mode by clicking on the Scene 1 icon. Delete the movie clip from the stage. (Don't worry; it'll still be in the Library panel.)

5. Test the application by pressing Ctrl + Enter (Command + Return on the Mac.)

When the application runs, it creates a single ShopCart class instance, and, using the kaChing( ) method, it adds a total of $10.06 to the text field in the shopping cart movie clip as shown in Figure 3-7.

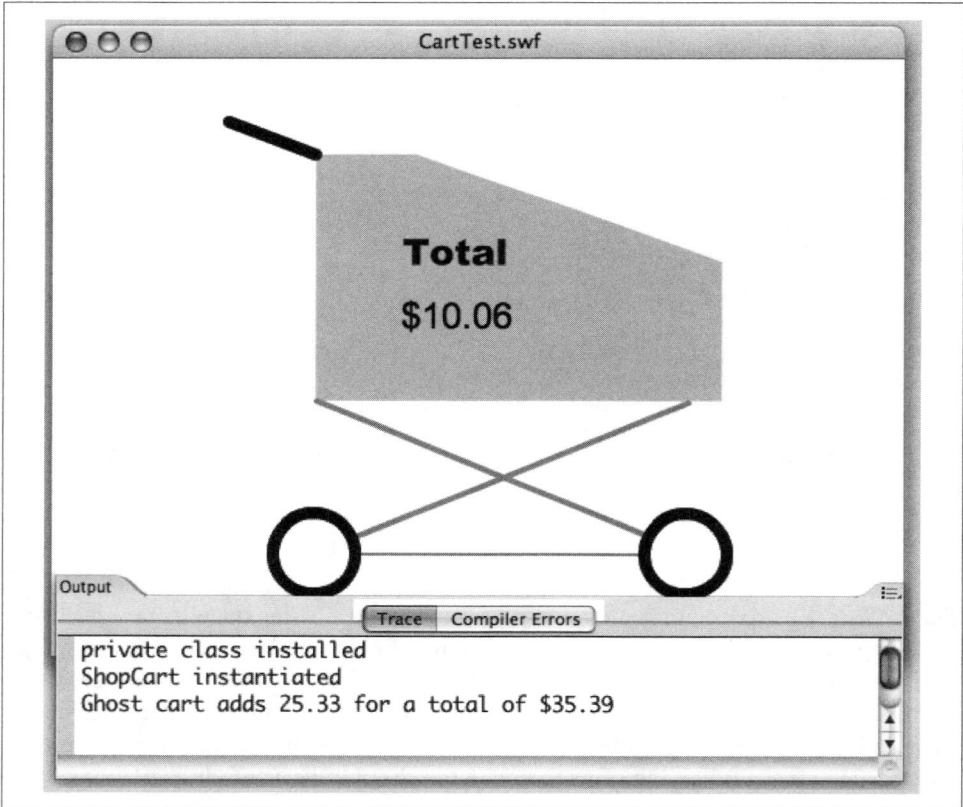

Figure 3-7. Correct results with two references to a single instance

Figure 3-7 also shows the Output window with the ghostCart instance adding another $25.33 for a total of $35.39. The final total is simply the sum of 25.33 and 10.06. The $10.06 value is the amount in the myCart reference, and, added to the amount in the ghostCart reference, we arrive at 35.39, just as predicted.

Summary

The Singleton focuses on ensuring that only a single instance of a class is instantiated and having global access to the class of the Singleton's origin. While certain aspects of the Singleton appear simple, other features show it to be a subtle and complex design pattern. To be sure, one can find more than one way to design a Singleton, and the ones developed for this chapter certainly have no claim to originality. However, they do represent a very standard implementation of the Singleton, and one that resolves some of the unique elements of ActionScript 3.0 specifically, and ECMAScript more generally.

The Singleton, especially the "classic" model on which we based the ones used in this chapter, has well-reasoned detractors. A short search of design pattern books and articles, including many excellent ones available online, finds many different ideas of how to best design a Singleton class or wholly replace it with a different conceptual structure. The fact that the Singleton provokes such thought has merit in its own right, and we certainly have wrestled with certain limitations ourselves. So if you've got a better Singleton design or better alternative, by all means pursue it.

The most common complaint about the Singleton is its incorrect use, or use in a context where it gets in the way of flexibility and reusability. Another complaint is that the pattern's overused. Some of the overuse can be attributed to its simplicity, but overuse also happens when people don't fully understand the pattern. One reason we provided so many different examples of the Singleton is to show that it does have clear uses. As a rule of thumb—do not use the Singleton where a good deal of change and reusability are likely. A Singleton's purpose is clear—limiting one and only one instantiation, and providing a global entry point. Beyond that, they have limited utility, and while popular as part of more robust design patterns, you must be careful not to let them get in the way of another pattern's utility.

However, as we have demonstrated in this chapter, the Singleton has some very practical uses, and you should never lose sight of that. Like all design patterns, the Singleton's only redeeming purpose is to accomplish certain recurring programming tasks. The fact that you can't use it every time these tasks appear to be necessary does not mean it's been rendered obsolete. Rather, it means simply that the Singleton isn't the best way to do it. These tasks, especially common ones, should either serve to prompt adaptation of the Singleton, use another design pattern, or develop and adjust certain aspects of the classical Singleton design.

PART III

Structural Patterns

*True ornament is not a matter of prettifying externals.
It is organic with the structure it adorns, whether a
person, a building, or a park.*
—Frank Lloyd Wright

*The importance of certain problems concerning the
facts will be inherent in the structure of the system.*
—Talcott Parsons (20th Century Sociologist)

*If the structure and the program components were
well chosen, then often many of the constituent
instructions can be adopted unchanged.*
—Niklaus Wirth

Structural patterns are strategies that use classes and objects to build larger structures. In part, the process entails using abstract classes as interfaces, with derivative classes making up the larger structures. Using both inheritance and composition, the Structural patterns provide rich flexibility for designing applications. The class patterns tend toward using inheritance in generating larger structures, and object structures tend to be built using composition. However, both kinds of approaches have the same general approach. Figure Part III-1 illustrates the overall Structural pattern.

As a mental image, you can think of constructing applications with Structural patterns as pulling parts out of different bins. The bins represent different class extensions and object compositions. The structure itself is built from the parts gathered from the bins, but it becomes a new phenomenon distinct from the parts used to build it.

This section examines three different Structural patterns. First, the Decorator pattern adds responsibilities to an object. A single component is *wrapped* with new functionalities and properties while remaining fundamentally unchanged as far as its internal structure is concerned. The Adapter pattern provides a way for two unrelated interfaces to work together. When adding a new object to an otherwise incompatible structure, the Adapter is an alternative to rebuilding an application from scratch to accept a new feature. You will find out how to create Adapter applications

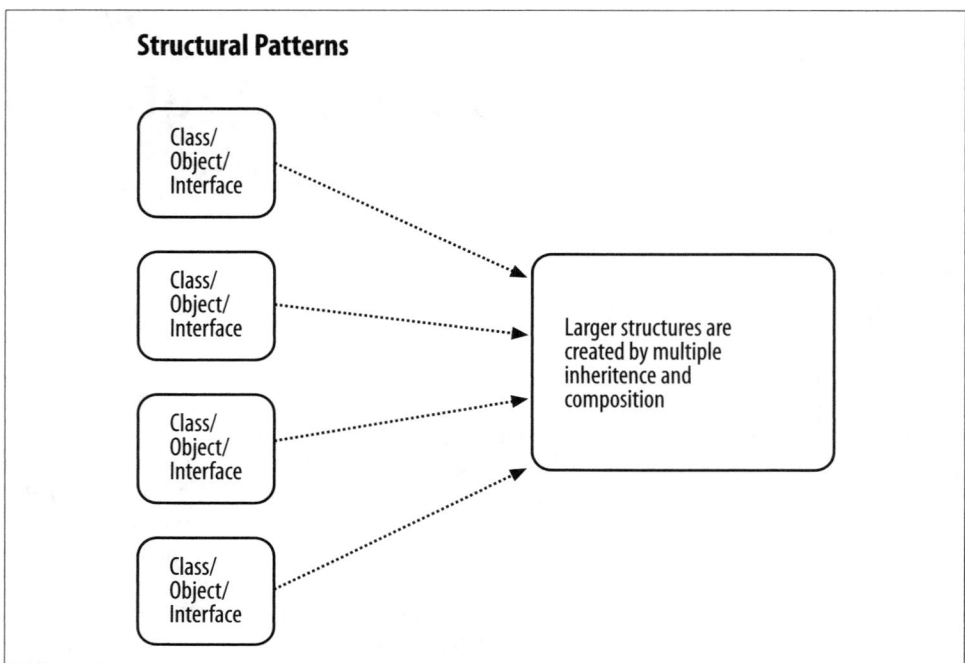

Structural Patterns

Class/Object/Interface

Class/Object/Interface

Class/Object/Interface

Class/Object/Interface

Larger structures are created by multiple inheritence and composition

Figure Part III-1. Structural design pattern

using both *inheritance* and *composition*. Finally, the Composite pattern composes objects in a tree-structure. In this way, clients can treat objects and composition (of objects) in the same way. By structuring objects in this way, the Composite pattern greatly simplifies creating complex structures.

CHAPTER 4

Decorator Pattern

I try to decorate my imagination as much as I can.
—Franz Schubert
Pictures deface walls more often than they decorate them.
—William Wordsworth (Poet and a guy who really understood bandwidth)

What Is the Decorator Pattern?

The Decorator pattern wasn't developed with a web designer or developer in mind, but it could well have been. A few years back, we developed a web site and were cognizant that periodically we'd have to update it. The design was set up so that substitution of one element for an updated one was fairly simple, and it required no major change in the code or structure. Because we didn't have to update it too often, this wasn't much of a problem. However, had we needed to update elements or features on a fairly regular basis, our design would have left a good deal to be desired.

Imagining situations where you need to update or change certain parts of a web site on a regular basis isn't difficult. If your client is a retailer with regular advertising such as weekly specials and new products introduced periodically, you want to have flexibility in your web design and structure. You may want to use features of your basic structure that assure change is easily accommodated, but you don't have to alter the basic structure itself in any way.

The Decorator pattern addresses the issue of maintaining the structure while having the ability to make changes by decorating the different components that make up the application. The decorations are composed of descriptions and/or methods used to wrap different objects in the application. As you will see, this design pattern allows you to mix and match all the different components and decorations to optimize flexibility and expandability, while core structure classes remain unaltered.

Key Features

We can understand the Decorator pattern in terms of two key features. Often, developers want to add unique responsibilities for an object without adding those same responsibilities to the whole class. Among other design patterns, the Decorator pattern's characterized by adding unique responsibilities. The identifying characteristic of the Decorator pattern is to add responsibilities in a uniquely Decorator fashion. Wrapping a component in an object that adds a responsibility follows a couple of guidelines:

- Decorators can appear wherever a component object can.
- At runtime, you can mix and match combinations of decorators as needed.

To understand the Decorator design pattern's key features, you need to consider some alternatives to implementing the work the pattern does. Essentially, your project requires that you add new features and responsibilities to individual *objects* rather than the entire *class*. To do so using inheritance would bloat the class and change the structure with each new feature. Every single object would inherit all the features and functionality of every other object, and that's not what you want.

 In this chapter, you will see the term "component" a good deal. The reference to component here is wholly unrelated to the components in Flash, used for UIs, Media, Data and other purposes. In the context of this chapter, a component refers to a concrete instance that is decorated with another concrete instance called a *decorator*. So, for the time being, don't think of components as anything other than something that gets decorated. (In the last application example of a Decorator design pattern in this chapter, you'll be using Flash UI components, but by then you'll be able to distinguish the different kind of components.)

Imagine you're setting up an automobile dealership site. You can choose between different models of autos and add different features—options. You can set up options such as an MP3 player, Global Positioning System (GPS), cloth, vinyl or leather seat covers, and different kinds of alarm systems. If you use inheritance, every one of those options would have to be in every object. What's more, you'd need to have all the models in your main class as well. That's absurd! Why would anyone need both cloth and vinyl seats or be both a Ford Escape and a Chevrolet Malibu? Then, if a new option were introduced, you'd have to bloat the class with yet another option for every single object. However, if you can just wrap a single responsibility around a component when and if you need it, you can keep your program slim, trim and ready to adapt.

The key to understanding the Decorator design pattern is to understand that it uses inheritance and employs *abstract classes*; however, as you know from Chapter 2, ActionScript 3.0 doesn't support abstract classes. You *can* create classes that work *like* abstract classes, simply by not instantiating them directly. In fact, that's what an abstract class is to some extent—a class that you do not instantiate but can extend. They work something like an interface, but while you can implement an interface and its abstract methods, you cannot extend it. (You were introduced to using interfaces in Chapter 1, and in Chapter 5, you will be using a design pattern that employs interfaces.)

Lack of support of abstract classes is a sore point with some Flash and Flex developers. Before firing off an impassioned email to Adobe, though, first take a look at the ECMAScript Rev 4 specs. These specifications don't exactly support abstract classes either, at this point in time.

Why are abstract classes important for the Decorator pattern? Like interfaces, you can create abstract methods that can be implemented in different ways. At the same time, you can use them to create subclasses so that core properties can be inherited in ways not possible with interfaces alone.

The Decorator Model

The Decorator outlined in the class diagram notation shows two key elements: component and decorator. The component represents what's to be decorated, and the decorator is the abstract class for the concrete decorations. The concrete component is what's actually decorated, and the concrete decorations are the actual decorations. All the concrete decorations and the concrete component are subclassed from the same source. Keeping that in mind, take a look at the class diagram in Figure 4-1.

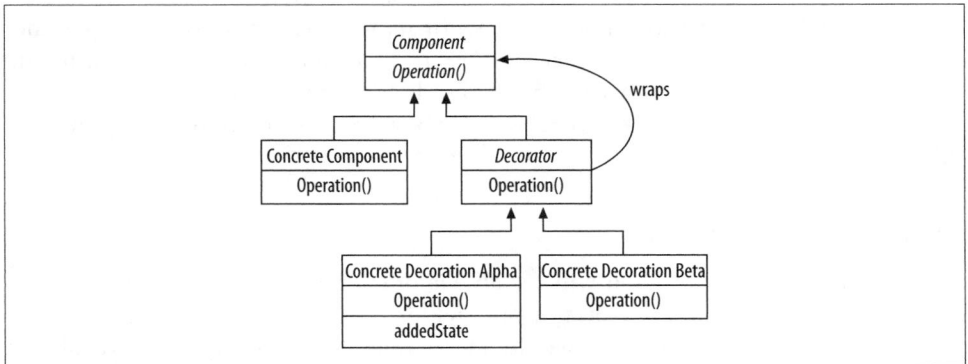

Figure 4-1. Decorator design pattern

In the most basic sense, the component is the Christmas tree, and the decorations are the ornaments. Each concrete decorator wraps the tree and is subclassed from the same source as the tree. A better way to think about components and decorators is more like the nesting dolls from Japan and Russia. The innermost doll is the component, and it's placed into a decorator. Then the component and decorator are placed into another decorator, and then into the next decorator. Figure 4-2 shows this model.

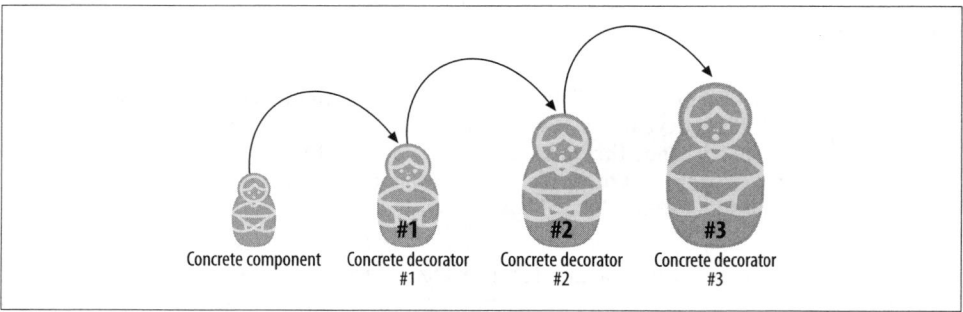

Figure 4-2. Component wrapped in series of decorators

Probably the most important thing to remember about the Decorator pattern is that its purpose is to allow additional elements to be added to a class without altering the base class. So instead of making changes by changing the class, the class is decorated with subclasses that don't interfere with the class from which the decorators were derived.

Key OOP Concepts Used with the Decorator Pattern

Sometimes when you think about key OOP concepts such as *inheritance*, you have to consider its larger consequences. The upside of inheritance is that once a superclass has been established, all the subclasses inherit its features. However, you may not want or need all the "stuff" for every subclass from a superclass. If you want to add functionality to an object, subclassing may not be the way to go, because everything else subclassed from the same superclass may be unnecessarily burdened by unused functionality.

Unwanted Inheritance

At the end of this chapter, you will see an example of a car dealership where users select models of cars with a choice of options for those cars. If all the options were derived from a superclass, that would mean that every car would have all the options, whether or not you wanted them. One option in the example is a rear view camera used with minivans and large SUVs with limited rear vision. Such an option would be superfluous on a sports car such as a Chevrolet Corvette, Morgan, or Ferrari. However, with subclassing, that's exactly what would happen. Every subclass gets everything from the superclass. So here's a case where we'd have to look beyond simple inheritance. Depending on how the application's written, even the components would all have the same features. A pickup truck would be subclassed from the same component as a luxury car—both inheriting features they don't want and wouldn't use.

Wrapping Responsibilities

The Decorator design pattern is also known as the Wrapper pattern. The concept of "wrapping" is at the heart of the Decorator design pattern. So what does it mean to "wrap" one object in another? One way to think about wrapping is to imagine wrapping a gift. The wrapper transforms the gift, but the gift does not inherit the characteristics of the wrapper—it only uses the wrapping. Unlike subclassing, which extends one class into another, wrapping allows one object to use another's characteristics without extending either the wrapped object or the object doing the wrapping.

The wrapping with which most ActionScript programmers are familiar is that used for transforming data types from one type to another. For example, the Number class can wrap a string variable, and then that variable has the characteristics of the Number class. Figure 4-3 illustrates a common wrapper function:

```
1  var k:uint=5;
2  var s:String="7";
3  var l:uint;
4  l=Number(s);
5  trace(k+l);
```

Output
12
Now variable **s** has Number characteristics. It acts like a number.

Number class wraps string variable.

Figure 4-3. Number class wrapping String class

 When we look at wrapping one object with another object, we can think of it as a class intercepting API calls intended for a specific instance of another class. The example in Figure 4-3 shows that the Number class is intercepting a call to an instance of the String class. The result is that the l variable, an unsigned integer, is able to accept the assignment of the s variable as a number. That's because the s variable is wrapped in a Number class and treated as a number.

Using the Decorator class, components are wrapped in decorators. The wrapping class is a concrete instance of a decorator, and the wrapped class is an instance of the concrete component class. Thus, the concrete component now "contains" the characteristics of the wrapper, but the characteristics are not inherited. Figure 4-4 shows an example.

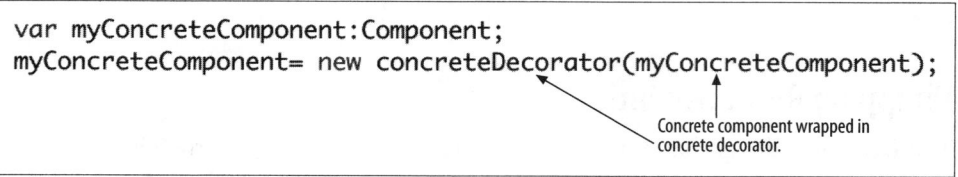

```
var myConcreteComponent:Component;
myConcreteComponent= new concreteDecorator(myConcreteComponent);
```

Concrete component wrapped in concrete decorator.

Figure 4-4. Concrete decorator wrapping concrete component

The concrete component that's wrapped by another class borrows characteristics of the wrapping class. When those characteristics are not needed, the instance of the concrete class is simply instantiated without being wrapped.

Flexibility and Adaptability

One good OOP practice is to create your classes so that they can be extended but not changed. If a class is changed, especially one with subclasses, you can quickly destroy an application. So the trick is to set up your classes so that it's easy to extend them, yet keep them safe from alteration.

The Decorator design pattern allows you to do this. The model is grounded in a single class that is the superclass to all others. This core class is an abstract component class. An abstract decorator class is subclassed from this class, re-implementing the core methods. (In the context of ActionScript 3.0, the *abstract* nature of the class is simulated by using the override statement when re-implementing methods in subclasses.) All the other concrete component and decorator classes have the same root superclass, even though the decorator classes are subclassed from the abstract decorator class, and the component classes are directly from the abstract component class. So, when the concrete component objects are wrapped in concrete decorator objects, both objects share the same root superclass. Thus, the decorated objects can keep the core object unmodified while changing its responsibilities.

In a larger OOP framework, the Decorator pattern can add and subtract functionality from an object by wrapping selected components with selected decorators. Second, it can add more than a single functionality to an object by wrapping one wrapper inside another wrapper. As a result, the design pattern can change functionality without changing structure.

Minimalist Abstract Decorator

To get started with the Decorator design pattern, a minimum implementation needs the following:

- An abstract component
- An abstract decorator
- A concrete component
- Concrete decorators

For the sake of clarity, two decorators will be devised so that you can better see how the structure works (and it's closer to the model shown in Figure 4-1.) Of all the classes devised in this pattern, by far the most important is the initial abstract class modeling the component. Every other class is subclassed from this initial class.

Abstract Component Class

To begin the process of creating a Decorator design pattern, create a component. You might think of a component as an undecorated Christmas tree, or even a person deciding what to wear. It's simple because all the added features are handled by decorators. Example 4-1 has only a single string variable that will be used to describe the component. Save the script as `Component.as`.

Example 4-1. Component.as

```
package
{
    //Abstract Component in Decorator Design Pattern
    //**************
    //Abstract class
    public class Component
    {
        internal var information:String;

        public function getInformation():String
        {
            return information;
        }
    }
}
```

From this point on, all the classes will extend the Component class. Keeping in mind that the class is an abstract one—or at least is treated as one—its primary function is to establish a basic structure for the rest of the application. It contains a single variable, `information`, and a single getter function, `getInformation()`. These elements set up both the concrete components and decorations. Both components and decorations need to display information about their characteristics. A concrete Christmas tree displays information that lets you know that it's a Christmas tree instead of another kind of object that can be decorated, such as a front yard to be decorated with gnomes and pink plastic flamingoes. Additionally, you want to be able to retrieve information, and so it has a getter function.

Abstract Decorator Class

Next, the abstract decorator is a subclass class of the Component class that inherits the information variable, so nothing is needed as far as the information variable is concerned. In fact, nothing's required for this simple example other than defining the class as an extension of the Component class. However, the getInformation() method is re-implemented independently of the Component class, using the override statement—which does what it says on the tin; it overrides parent class methods. This is done to distinguish the same method being used for the Decorator class from the method being used for the Component class. All the concrete decorations are subclassed from the Decorator class, and all concrete components are subclassed directly from the Component class. Further on, the concrete components will be wrapped in concrete decorators, and such distinctions become important in more complex implementations of the Decorator design pattern. The trace( ) statement is used to show you where in the process the abstract Decorator class appears. Save Example 4-2 as Decorator.as.

Example 4-2. Decorator.as

```
package
{
    //Abstract Decorator in Decorator Design Pattern
    //*************
    //Abstract class
    public class Decorator extends Component
    {
        trace("|*|Decorator|*|");
        override public function getInformation( ):String
        {
            return information;
        }
    }
}
```

Once the two abstract classes, Component and Decorator, have been established, it's time to work with the concrete classes. For this example, only a single concrete component is created. Cleverly named ConcreteComponent, this class represents whatever will be decorated in a Decorator design pattern. You can have multiple concrete components that all use the same set of decorations, or only a single one. Later in this chapter, you will see an application where multiple concrete classes are decorated by a single set of decorators. The nice thing about the Decorator is that you can add as many concrete components as you want. Imagine a business web site where the concrete component represents an e-business site that you've worked on for several months. Using a Decorator design pattern, you've developed several useful and tested elements that are applied using decorators. Shortly after the project is complete, you get a request to develop another site with a different main product and an overlapping set of elements. Rather than starting from scratch, all you have to do is to add a different concrete component class and some new decorators that aren't available in the original set.

Example 4-3 shows that the concrete component does little more than extend the Component class and add a constructor. It inherits all of the features of the Component class, and uses the `information` variable to place a message in the Output window to point to the decorators. Save the code in Example 4-3 as `ConcreteComponent.as`.

Example 4-3. ConcreteComponent.as

```
package
{
    //Concrete Component
    public class ConcreteComponent extends Component
    {
        public function ConcreteComponent( )
        {
            //\u2794 is Unicode for a right-pointing arrow
            information = "Concrete Component is decorated with \u2794";
        }
    }
}
```

In Example 4-3, you see that Unicode is inserted using the format \u + character code value. In the example, an arrow character is formed using Unicode 2794. To search for a character you may want to use, see *http://www.fileformat.info/info/unicode/char/search.htm*. You'll find several different arrow characters you can use, including \u0363, \u2192, \u21aa, and \u21d2.

The next step is to build concrete decorator classes. In this abstract example, two concrete decorators will wrap themselves around the concrete component. So, to get started, we'll need a Component instance variable to hold the component we're wrapping.

```
var components:Component;
```

The variable is named `components`, with an "s," because `component` is a built-in word in ActionScript 3.0. This variable is referenced in the decorator's methods. Next, we need a way to affix the `components` variable to the object being wrapped. The following code shows how the component being wrapped is passed to the decorator's constructor.

```
public function DecConA(components:Component)
{
    this.components=components;
}
```

Finally, you need a getter function to get the *unique* information from the concrete decorator. The public method inherited from the `Decorator` class must be set up using the override statement. Here, the method gets both the concrete component's information [`components.getInformation( )`], and adds on that of the concrete decoration [`+ " Decoration Alpha:"`]:

```
override public function getInformation( ):String
{
    return components.getInformation( ) + " Decoration Alpha:";
}
```

Concrete Decorations

Now, we're all set to write the concrete decorator classes. Save Examples 4-4 and 4-5 as `DecConA.as` and `DecConB.as`, respectively.

 In several of the decorator classes, you'll see:

```
    this.components = components;
```

Such code is a non-standard use of the `this` identifier, but it makes sense in this context because it differentiates the variable and parameter. Normally, you wouldn't use the `this` identifier in this manner. The variable and parameter names are identical to emphasize the use of the abstract class in both cases, with one passing the value to the other.

Example 4-4. DecConA.as

```
package
{
    //Concrete Decorator "Alpha"
    public class DecConA extends Decorator
    {
        private var components:Component;
        public function DecConA(components:Component)
        {
            this.components=components;
        }
        override public function getInformation( ):String
        {
            return components.getInformation( ) + " Decoration Alpha:";
        }
    }
}
```

Example 4-5. DecConB.as

```
package
{
    //Concrete Decorator "Beta"
    public class DecConB extends Decorator
    {
        var components:Component;
        public function DecConB(components:Component) {
            this.components=components;
        }
        override public function getInformation():String
        {
            return components.getInformation() + " Decoration Beta:";
        }
    }
}
```

Wrapping Up

To execute the Decorator design pattern, the whole key lies in knowing how to wrap a component in a concrete decorator. First, you need to instantiate a concrete component.

```
var testComponent:Component = new ConcreteComponent();
```

Then, you wrap the component in one or more decorations using the following format:

```
componentInstance=new ConcreteDecorator(testComponent);
```

So, in our example, with two concrete decorations, we'd write:

```
testComponent=new DecConA(testComponent);
testComponent=new DecConB(testComponent);
```

At this point, `testComponent` is decorated with two decorations. We could duplicate the above lines adding the same two decorations as often as we wanted. Think of the decorations as red and green Christmas tree ornaments. The tree could be covered with nothing but red and green ornaments, rather than just one of each. The Decorator design pattern is employed cumulatively. That is, as you add each decoration, it's added to those already wrapping the concrete component.

Finally, to see what havoc we've wrought, we use the getter method—`getInformation()`:

```
trace(testComponent.getInformation());
```

To see how all of this works, save Example 4-6 as `DecTest.as` in an ActionScript file. Then open a new Flash document file, and type **DecTest** in the Document class window in the Properties panel.

Example 4-6. DecTest.as

```
package
{
    import flash.display.Sprite;
    public class DecTest extends Sprite
    {
        public function DecTest()
        {
            //Instantiate Concrete Component
            var testComponent:Component = new ConcreteComponent();
            //Wrap first decorator around component
            testComponent=new DecConA(testComponent);
            //Wrap second decorator around component
            testComponent=new DecConB(testComponent);
            //Output results
            trace(testComponent.getInformation());
        }
    }
}
```

Figure 4-5 shows what you should see in your Output window when you test the movie.

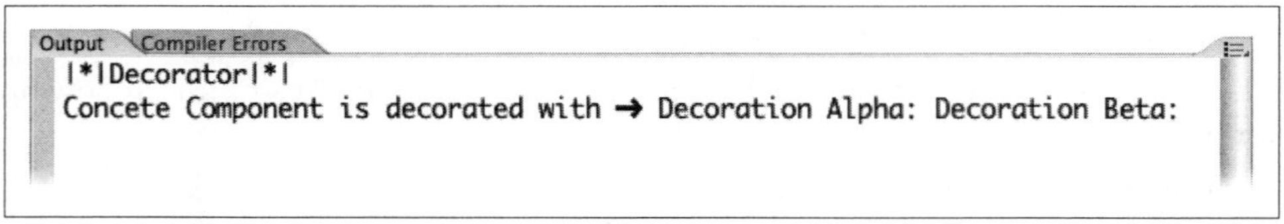

Figure 4-5. Decorations on component

To understand what's going on in the Decorator pattern, go back and look at Figure 4-2. The example application first instantiated a ConcreteComponent() object. That object displays a message pointing to its decorations. Imagine that object (testComponent) as the smallest can to the far left in Figure 4-2. That can is then placed into decorator Can #1. At this point, the concrete component object (testComponent) is decorated with Can #1, but retains its original properties –much in the same way that a lawn decorated with a family of gnomes still retains its property of green grass. Next, Can #1, which now contains the concrete component, is dropped into Can #2. Now Can #2 has both Can #1 and the Concrete component Can. Thus, Can #2 has all of the properties of itself plus those of the cans inside.

In a sense, the whole process works like the compound operator, plus-equal (+=). Each decorator attaches itself to the existing component and its decorator. As each decorator is added, all the previous ones are retained but not duplicated, unless you add the same decorator more than once. So, as the output shows, you can add as many decorations as you want simply by wrapping them in the existing object in one of the decorators.

Applying a Simple Decorator Pattern in Flash: Paper Doll

You can move from a conceptual example to a concrete one with a computerized paper doll game. The paper doll component is the doll being dressed, and the decorations are clothing items selected for the doll. Using ActionScript's new Loader class, different GIF files are used to decorate a base GIF image of a Victorian paper doll. As in the previous abstract example, this example uses a single concrete component and several decorations.

This concrete example does not have an interface—keeping the focus on the application's use of a Decorator pattern. However, it does have a graphic output so you can see the pattern's ultimate output. (Later in this chapter, there's an example with a full interface.)

Setting Up the Component Class

The first class is the component class, Model. From this, all other classes are subclasses. It's very simple but key to the success of the application. As you can see, it's very close to the previous abstract Decorator. It consists of a method, getDressed( ), and a string variable, whatToWear, as shown in Example 4-7. Save the file as Model.as.

Example 4-7. Model.as

```
package
{
    //Abstract class
    public class Model
    {
        protected var whatToWear:String;
         public function getDressed( ):String
        {
            return whatToWear;
        }
    }
}
```

Keep in mind that Example 4-7 should be treated as an abstract class. So the method getDressed( ) needs to be created as an override public function for it to work the way we want. However, the property whatToWear doesn't need to be changed from its inherited characteristics.

Decorator Class: Dressing the Dolls

Example 4-8 is the abstract Decorator class, Dresser, which extends the component class, Model. The major contribution here is simply re-implementing the getDressed( ) method with a reference to the inherited whatToWear property.

Example 4-8. Dresser.as

```
package
{
    //Abstract class
    public class Dresser extends Model
    {
        override public function getDressed():String
        {
            return whatToWear;
        }
    }
}
```

All of the concrete decorators will be subclassed for this class.

The Concrete Classes

Once the two main abstract classes in the Decorator pattern have been established, you're all set to create the concrete ones. In the previous minimalist Decorator example, you saw the output using the trace( ) statement. Instead of trace( ) statements, both the concrete component and decorators need to be formatted for later parsing, so a tilde character (~) has been added as a demarcation point. Because all the strings from both the concrete component and decorators are grouped together into a single large string, the tilde serves as cutting point.

Concrete component class

The concrete component class is the only concrete class that extends directly from the abstract concrete class. All the other classes in this application extend from the abstract decorator class. Using a simple constructor function, Sue( ), the class assigns a value to the whatToWear variable. This is enough to identify the class as an instance of the main abstract component class, Model, and to establish a unique name. All decorations use the concrete component as the target for the decorations. Save Example 4-9 as Sue.as.

Example 4-9. Sue.as

```
package
{
    public class Sue extends Model
    {
        public function Sue()
        {
            whatToWear="~sue";
        }
    }
}
```

If you want to create more concrete component classes, all you need to do is create a similar class with a different name and value for the whatToWear variable. With this structure, you have no limit to the number of new concrete components you can add.

Concrete decorator classes

Moving from the minimalist example previously shown in this chapter, it's a little easier to see how the Decorator pattern works by actually seeing something happening in a graphic display. When the initial instance of the concrete component is created, all references in the concrete decorator class are to that instance. (See example 4-16, where the concrete component is wrapped in the decorators.) In all the concrete decorator classes, the reference to the model variable is a reference to the concrete component object. In this case, that's the instance of the Sue( ) class, but it can be any instance of any concrete component. That's why, if you wish to expand the application to include more concrete components (paper dolls to dress), you don't have to make any fundamental changes. Just add another concrete component class. In Examples 4-10 to 4-15, the captions are the filenames.

Example 4-10. OrangeDress.as

```
package
{
    public class OrangeDress extends Dresser
    {
        private var model:Model;
        public function OrangeDress(model:Model)
        {
            this.model=model;
        }
        override public function getDressed( ):String
        {
            return model.getDressed( ) + "~orangedress";
        }
    }
}
```

Example 4-11. BlueDress.as

```
package
{
    public class BlueDress extends Dresser
    {
        private var model:Model;
        public function BlueDress(model:Model)
        {
            this.model=model;
        }
        override public function getDressed( ):String
        {
            return model.getDressed( ) + "~bluedress";
        }
    }
}
```

Example 4-12. Bow.as

```
package
{
    public class Bow extends Dresser
    {
        private var model:Model;
        public function Bow(model:Model)
        {
            this.model=model;
        }
        override public function getDressed():String
        {
            return model.getDressed() + "~bow";
        }
    }
}
```

Example 4-13. Umbrella.as

```
package
{
    public class Umbrella extends Dresser
    {
        private var model:Model;
        public function Umbrella (model:Model)
        {
            this.model=model;
        }
        override public function getDressed():String
        {
            return model.getDressed() + "~ umbrella ";
        }
    }
}
```

Example 4-14. Hat.as

```
package
{
    public class Hat extends Dresser
    {
        private var model:Model;
        public function Hat(model:Model)
        {
            this.model=model;
        }
        override public function getDressed():String
        {
            return model.getDressed() + "~hat";
        }
    }
}
```

Example 4-15. Muff.as

```
package
{
    public class Muff extends Dresser
    {
        private var model:Model;
        public function Muff(model:Model)
        {
            this.model=model;
        }
        override public function getDressed( ):String
        {
            return model.getDressed( ) + "~muff";
        }
    }
}
```

All six decorations can be used in any combination you want with the instance of the Model class. This next section shows how to implement the Decorator pattern using the different decorators.

Implementing the Paper Doll Decorator

As noted, no interface was created for implementing this application, and so you can see clearly how the concrete component is wrapped by the decorators. Then, on the stage, you can see the effects of the different combinations.

The sequence is:

1. Instantiate a concrete component.
2. Wrap the concrete component in the desired decorator instance using the format:

   ```
   componentInstance = new DecoratorInstance(componentInstance)
   ```

3. Apply the getter method (getDressed( )) to the concrete component instance initiated to get the fully wrapped values. The values will include those of the concrete component instance and the applied decorations.

Example 4-16 illustrates how to implement the paper doll decorator.

Example 4-16. FashionShow.as

```
package
{
    import flash.display.Loader;
    import flash.net.URLRequest;
    import flash.display.Sprite;
    public class FashionShow extends Sprite
    {
        var ensemble:Array=new Array( );
        public function FashionShow( )
        {
```

Example 4-16. FashionShow.as (continued)

```
                trace("||--Working--||");
                var doll:Model = new Sue( );
                doll=new Hat(doll);
                doll=new OrangeDress(doll);
                //doll=new BlueDress(doll);
                //doll=new Umbrella(doll);
                doll=new Bow(doll);
                doll=new Muff(doll);
                var ready2wear:String=doll.getDressed( );
                sewingMachine(ready2wear);
                for (x=0; x < ensemble.length; x++)
                {
                    clothesOn(ensemble[x]);
                }
        }
        private function sewingMachine(wardrobe:String):Array
        {
            ensemble=wardrobe.split("~");
            ensemble.shift( );
            return ensemble;
        }
        private function clothesOn(outfit:String)
        {
            var clothier:Loader=new Loader( );
            var item:String="clothes/" + outfit + ".gif";
            var getItem:URLRequest=new URLRequest(item);
            clothier.load(getItem);
            this.addChild(clothier);
        }
    }
}
```

Once you've got everything ready to go, you'll need some GIF files. The model (concrete component) should be an image of a doll that you will clothe with the Decorator pattern. Each filename needs to be the name of the value assigned to the whatToWear variable in the concrete component or decorator listing, minus the tilde (~) character. For example, the concrete component, Sue, whatToWear variable is assigned the string value "~sue" and so the GIF filename for that component would be sue.gif. The decorator BlueDress has a whatToWear value of "~bluedress," and so the image with the blue dress would be named bluedress.gif. Place all the GIF files, including the file representing the doll model, in a folder named clothes.

Finally, open up a new Flash document and set the stage dimensions to 300 × 650. In the Properties panel's Document class window, type in **FashionShow**. The size and shape of your stage will depend on the size of the paper dolls you use.

Figure 4-6 shows two different combinations of decorations on the paper doll. The image on the left decorates with the hat, bow, orange dress, and muff, while the second is the blue dress, the bow and an umbrella. Each appears very different just by changing the combination of decorations.

Figure 4-6. Paper doll with two different decoration sets

Instead of paper dolls, any component could be decorated with any characteristics. Also, you can include more than a single property or method in a decoration. In the next section, we'll take a look at adding additional properties with the Decorator design pattern.

Decorating with Deadly Sins and Heavenly Virtues

Action gaming pits different kinds of heroes and villains against one another, and the combatants have different weapons and shields. That is, they're *decorated* with different characteristics and abilities. In order to see how to add some more functions to a Decorator pattern, what could be more appropriate than pitting good against evil?

Table 4-1 shows a list of deadly sins and heavenly virtues. (The list is considerably updated from Dante's *Inferno* and Prudentius' epic poem, *Psychomachia*, both of whom I understand were using Commodore-64's to make their lists.)

Table 4-1. Decorations of good and evil

Deadly Sin	Description	Virtue	Description
Rage	Uncontrolled anger—striking out at syntax errors	Compassion	Caring about others—Helping procedural programmers transition to OOP
Malice	Meanness, malevolence, ill will, cruelty, and hatred toward others—unkind remarks about Linux.	Courage	Doing the right thing regardless of the danger—taking on object-oriented programming
Obfuscation	Hiding the truth— redefining an act, knowledge by adding confusion—coding without comments	Hope	Belief in eventual success of good over evil—you really can complete the project on time
Arrogance	Excessive pride, not considering others' beliefs, feelings, or knowledge—belief that Microsoft Windows is the only real OS	Justice	A fair balance and even chance—using Windows, Mac OS, and Linux
Prejudice	Judging others on the basis of stereotypes and not their actions—teasing Mac users	Openness	Capacity to consider new knowledge, ideas, and contrary ideas—writing a program on a Mac
Dogmatisms	Narrow, inflexible belief even in light of evidence to the contrary—continue to use procedural programming methods	Integrity	Maintaining values even when tempted to abandon them for short term gains—foregoing hacks even though they'd get the job done and the client would never know
Indifference	Seeing suffering and doing nothing or not even caring to help—unwilling to offer help in learning OOP	Diligence	Willingness to stick with an especially difficult task to complete it—learning design patterns

Thinking about what has been presented so far in this chapter, the first thing that comes to mind is a property that describes each of the deadly sins and heavenly virtues. That's easy enough, because just like the paper doll example, all we have to do is to assign a property value to each decorator. However, we can do more with the Decorator design pattern, as you'll see in the next two sections.

Adding Properties and Methods

Up to now, we've used a single string variable with a single getter method for the basic abstract component class. However, like any other class, this basic structure can accommodate more than a single variable or function. Example 4-17 shows three variables and getter functions. Save the script as Component.as.

Example 4-17. Component.as

```
package
{
    //Abstract class
    public class Component
    {
        protected var soul:String="All that is inside a spirit";
        protected var goodness:Number;
        protected var vice:Number;

        public function getSoul():String
        {
            return soul;
        }
        public function good():Number
        {
            return goodness;
        }
        public function evil():Number
        {
            return vice;
        }
    }
}
```

Like the previous examples, we begin with a string property, soul. (It's assigned a string literal, but that's really not necessary because it's an abstract class and will never be seen or used—just a clarification.) Next, two numeric properties are defined, goodness and vice. These two properties will collect all the accumulated good and evil in a soul.

Next, three getter functions are supplied to get the values of the string and two numeric variables. Now the abstract component class is all set to go.

Multiple Concrete Components

We could look at one soul at a time, but what fun is that? More important, in a lot of applications, having a single component to decorate isn't too useful either. So instead of having a single soul to decorate, we'll add two. For the time being, we'll forego any debates about original sin and start our souls with a clean slate. Both goodness and vice will be set to zero. Just give them different soul values so they can be differentiated.

Examples 4-18 and 4-19 provide the concrete components for Dick and Jane classes. Each class just needs a string value for soul and numeric values for goodness and vice—all inherited properties from the Component class. Save Example 4-18 as Dick.as, and Example 4-19 as Jane.as.

Example 4-18. Dick.as

```
package
{
    public class Dick extends Component
    {
        public function Dick( )
        {
            soul = "Dick's soul\n";
            goodness=0;
            vice=0;
        }
    }
}
```

Example 4-19. Jane.as

```
package
{
    public class Jane extends Component
    {
        public function Jane( )
        {
            soul = "Jane's soul\n";
            goodness=0;
            vice=0;
        }
    }
}
```

These concrete component classes are exactly like the previous examples we've examined, except we have two instead of one. Furthermore, instead of using a single string variable, two additional numeric variables are added, along with their assigned values. Otherwise, they're just the same.

In these two concrete classes, the properties are inherited directly from the abstract Component class. No overrides or other special adjustments are needed. This is because the Dick and Jane classes are components, both to be decorated by the decorator classes. The overrides that generate unique methods and characteristics for the concrete decorators are accomplished *by the decorator classes*. Therefore, overrides by the concrete component classes are unnecessary.

Decorating with Multiple Properties

Multiple properties and methods are not difficult to add to components, and the same is true for decorator classes. Instead of a single property and method, you do essentially the same thing using multiple methods and classes. Example 4-20 shows the abstract `Decorator` class, subclassed from the `Component` class. Save the script as `Decorator.as`.

Example 4-20. Decorator.as

```
package
{
    //Abstract class
    public class Decorator extends Component
    {
        override public function getSoul():String
        {
            return soul;
        }
        override public function good():Number
        {
            return goodness;
        }
        override public function evil():Number
        {
            return vice;
        }
    }
}
```

As a subclass of the `Component` class, this `Decorator` abstract class does nothing more than re-implement the getter functions—one returning a string, and the other two returning a number. The properties that are to be returned were originally defined as properties in the `Component` class, and as a subclass of `Component`, the `Decorator` class doesn't have to re-implement them. However, as you've seen in previous examples, the getter functions are re-implemented. The only difference is that there are more of them. However, the process and logic are the same.

Multiple Method Concrete Decorations

When it comes to the concrete decorations in this example application, we're going to see something slightly new. First, take a look at example 4-21. It's a generic example and should *not* be placed in as actual code. Just look at it. Several actual concrete elements with working code will replace generic values.

Example 4-21. Generic concrete decoration

```
package
{
    //Generic-NOT implemented
    public class GoodEvil extends Decorator
    {
        private var components:Component;
        public function GoodEvil(components:Component)
        {
            this.components=components;
        }
        override public function getSoul():String
        {
            return components.getSoul() + "|GoodEvil";
        }
        override public function good():Number
        {
            return +/-00 + components.good();
        }
        override public function evil():Number
        {
            return +/-00 + components.evil();
        }
    }
}
```

If you break down Example 4-21, the first part looks exactly like the previous examples. A Component instance, components, is instantiated, and the constructor function wraps the components object in itself:

```
var components:Component;
public function GoodEvil(components:Component)
{
    this.components=components;
}
```

Next, the script re-implements the getter function, getSoul( ), to return both the current value of the concrete component's decorations plus its own decoration value. Again, this is what previous examples have done.

```
override public function getSoul():String
{
    return components.getSoul() + "|GoodEvil";
}
```

The next two functions add or subtract numeric values using the good( ) and evil( ) methods. Each good adds to a good and subtracts from an evil, and *vice versa* for a vice—adds to evil and subtracts from good. So depending on the concrete decorator, you add or subtract from each of the two return values, and add that to the current value of the concrete component.

```
override public function good():Number
{
    return +/-00 + components.good();
```

```
    }
    override public function evil():Number
    {
        return +/-OO + components.evil();
    }
```

Examples 4-22 through 4-35 make up the seven deadly (revised) sins and seven heavenly (revised) virtues. However, what they really represent is the flexibility of the Decorator design pattern. (Also, they illustrate the complex issue of saving souls.)

The Good and Evil Concrete Decorators

Following are 14 concrete decorator classes. They're all the same except for the names and values assigned to the numeric properties. It's a lot easier just to do one, and then paste it into a new ActionScript file and edit in changes rather than doing them all from scratch. Once you've completed all 14, go ahead and add two more—good and evil concrete decorators of your own making. In Examples 4-22 through 4-35, the filename is in the caption.

Heavenly virtues

Example 4-22. Integrity.as

```
package
{
    public class Integrity extends Decorator
    {
        private var components:Component;
        public function Integrity(components:Component) {
            this.components=components;
        }
        override public function getSoul():String
        {
            return components.getSoul() + "|Integrity";
        }
        override public function good():Number
        {
            return 14 + components.good();
        }
        override public function evil():Number
        {
            return -6 + components.evil();
        }
    }
}
```

Example 4-23. Hope.as

```
package
{
    public class Hope extends Decorator
    {
        private var components:Component;
        public function Hope(components:Component)
        {
            this.components=components;
        }
        override public function getSoul():String
        {
            return components.getSoul() + "|Hope";
        }
        override public function good():Number
        {
            return 5 + components.good();
        }
        override public function evil():Number
        {
            return -10 + components.evil();
        }
    }
}
```

Example 4-24. Courage.as

```
package
{
    public class Courage extends Decorator
    {
        private var components:Component;
        public function Courage(components:Component)
        {
            this.components=components;
        }
        override public function getSoul():String
        {
            return components.getSoul() + "|Courage";
        }
        override public function good():Number
        {
            return 10 + components.good();
        }
        override public function evil():Number
        {
            return -8 + components.evil();
        }
    }
}
```

Example 4-25. Compassion.as

```
package
{
    public class Compassion extends Decorator
    {
        private var components:Component;
        public function Compassion(components:Component)
        {
            this.components=components;
        }
        override public function getSoul():String
        {
            return components.getSoul() + "|Compassion";
        }
        override public function good():Number
        {
            return 7 + components.good();
        }
        override public function evil():Number
        {
            return -15 + components.evil();
        }
    }
}
```

Example 4-26. Openness.as

```
package
{
    public class Openness extends Decorator
    {
        private var components:Component;
        public function Openness(components:Component)
        {
            this.components=components;
        }
        override public function getSoul():String
        {
            return components.getSoul() + "|Openness";
        }
        override public function good():Number
        {
            return 12 + components.good();
        }
        override public function evil():Number
        {
            return -15 + components.evil();
        }
    }
}
```

Example 4-27. Diligence.as

```
package
{
    public class Diligence extends Decorator
    {
        private var components:Component;
        public function Diligence(components:Component)
        {
            this.components=components;
        }
        override public function getSoul():String
        {
            return components.getSoul() + "|Diligence";
        }
        override public function good():Number
        {
            return 10 + components.good();
        }
        override public function evil():Number
        {
            return -5 + components.evil();
        }
    }
}
```

Example 4-28. Justice.as

```
package
{
    public class Justice extends Decorator
    {
        private var components:Component;
        public function Justice(components:Component)
        {
            this.components=components;
        }
        override public function getSoul():String
        {
            return components.getSoul() + "|Justice";
        }
        override public function good():Number
        {
            return 9 + components.good();
        }
        override public function evil():Number
        {
            return -9 + components.evil();
        }
    }
}
```

Deadly sins

Example 4-29. Rage.as

```
package
{
    public class Rage extends Decorator
    {
        private var components:Component;
        public function Rage(components:Component)
        {
            this.components=components;
        }
        override public function getSoul():String
        {
            return components.getSoul() + "|Rage";
        }
        override public function good():Number
        {
            return -9 + components.good();
        }
        override public function evil():Number
        {
            return 8 + components.evil();
        }
    }
}
```

Example 4-30. Malice.as

```
package
{
    public class Malice extends Decorator
    {
        private var components:Component;
        public function Malice(components:Component)
        {
            this.components=components;
        }
        override public function getSoul():String
        {
            return components.getSoul() + "|Malice";
        }
        override public function good():Number
        {
            return -14 + components.good();
        }
        override public function evil():Number
        {
            return 12 + components.evil();
        }
    }
}
```

Example 4-31. Prejudice.as

```
package
{
    public class Prejudice extends Decorator
    {
        private var components:Component;
        public function Prejudice(components:Component)
        {
            this.components=components;
        }
        override public function getSoul():String
        {
            return components.getSoul() + "|Prejudice";
        }
        override public function good():Number
        {
            return -10 + components.good();
        }
        override public function evil():Number
        {
            return 15 + components.evil();
        }
    }
}
```

Example 4-32. Obfuscation.as

```
package
{
    public class Obsfuscation extends Decorator
    {
        private var components:Component;
        public function Obsfuscation(components:Component)
        {
            this.components=components;
        }
        override public function getSoul():String
        {
            return components.getSoul() + "|Obsfuscation";
        }
        override public function good():Number
        {
            return -12 + components.good();
        }
        override public function evil():Number
        {
            return 7 + components.evil();
        }
    }
}
```

Example 4-33. Dogmatisms.as

```
package
{
    public class Dogmatisms extends Decorator
    {
        private var components:Component;
        public function Dogmatisms(components:Component)
        {
            this.components=components;
        }
        override public function getSoul():String
        {
            return components.getSoul() + "|Dogmatisms";
        }
        override public function good():Number
        {
            return -12 + components.good();
        }
        override public function evil():Number
        {
            return 15 + components.evil();
        }
    }
}
```

Example 4-34. Arrogance.as

```
package
{
    public class Arrogance extends Decorator
    {
        private var components:Component;
        public function Arrogance(components:Component)
        {
            this.components=components;
        }
        override public function getSoul():String
        {
            return components.getSoul() + "|Arrogance";
        }
        override public function good():Number
        {
            return -5 + components.good();
        }
        override public function evil():Number
        {
            return 5 + components.evil();
        }
    }
}
```

Example 4-35. Indifference.as

```
package
{
    public class Indifference extends Decorator
    {
        private var components:Component;
        public function Indifference(components:Component)
        {
            this.components=components;
        }
        override public function getSoul():String
        {
            return components.getSoul() + "|Indifference";
        }
        override public function good():Number
        {
            return -9 + components.good();
        }
        override public function evil():Number
        {
            return 10 + components.evil();
        }
    }
}
```

At this point you can add your own concrete decorators. Use the same format as the others. You can also add additional concrete components. So instead of just Dick and Jane, you can add others you'd like to decorate with good and evil.

Implementing the Good and Evil Decorator

Instead of a single implementation, you can try out two different implementations. The first one dresses up the two different concrete components, and sends the results to the output window. The second takes the results, uses them to place movie clips on a "soul graph," and adds a label to an angel or devil movie clip—depending on whether good or evil is predominant.

Dual implementation

The first implementation decorates both the Dick and Jane concrete components. This one is set up to use all 14 deadly sins and heavenly virtues, but you can use any combination you want. As each concrete component (life and light) is wrapped, the good and evil properties are incremented or decremented, depending on which decorator wraps the concrete component. The reference to the components object in each of the decorators is a reference to the concrete component being wrapped. With each new decorator, then, the value goes up and down depending on the wrapping decorator. Save Example 4-36 as MainDual.as in an ActionScript file. Open a new Flash document file, and save it as a Dual.fla. Type in **MainDual** in the Document class window in the Dual.fla Properties panel, and resave it as *MainDual.as*. Now test the movie.

Example 4-36. MainDual.as

```
package
{
    import flash.display.Sprite;
    public class MainDual extends Sprite
    {
        public function MainDual()
        {
            trace("||--Judging--||");
            var life:Component=new Dick();
            var light:Component=new Jane();
            //***Add Good
            life=new Courage(life);
            light=new Hope(light);
            light=new Compassion(light);
            life=new Openness(life);
            life=new Diligence(life);
            light=new Justice(light);
            //***Add Evil
            light=new Malice(light);
            life=new Prejudice(life);
            life=new Dogmatisms(life);
            life=new Arrogance(life);
            life=new Indifference(life);
            life=new Rage(life);
            light=new Obsfuscation(light);
            trace(life.getSoul()+"\nTotal Virture: "+
                (life.good()-life.evil()));
            trace(light.getSoul()+"\nTotal Virture: "+
                (light.good()-light.evil()));
        }
    }
}
```

The output for all of the good and evil together is:

```
||--Judging--||
Dick's soul
|Courage|Openness|Diligence|Prejudice|Dogmatisms|Arrogance
    |Indifference|Rage
Total Virture: -38
Jane's soul
|Hope|Compassion|Justice|Malice|Obsfuscation
Total Virture: 10
```

Because the trace() statement subtracts the evil() method from the good() method total value, any positive results indicate an abundance of good characteristics, and a negative result shows a plethora of negative traits.

You can "multi-wrap" using the same decorator more than once on the same concrete component. (Someone who thinks he can get the month-behind project done on time by not sleeping for a week is doubly hopeful, has a triple dose of diligence, and perhaps a double dose of arrogance.)

Charting souls

Like any of the other design patterns, what you do with the output is up to you. However, because ActionScript 3.0 is part of Flash, this next implementation shows how to place the output into different formats with graphic elements. The getSoul( ) generates a string, and the good( ) and evil( ) methods generate numbers. The string will be placed in a text field embedded in a movie clip, and the vertical position of the movie clip will be determined by the values generated by the good( ) and evil( ) methods. To get started, save the script in Example 4-37 in an ActionScript file named Soul.as.

Example 4-37. Soul.as

```
package
{
    import flash.display.Sprite;
    import flash.display.MovieClip;
    public class Soul extends Sprite
    {
        //Instantiate the two MovieClip objects in
        //the Library
        var devil:Devil=new Devil( );
        var angel:Angel=new Angel( );
        public function Soul( )
        {
            var life:Component=new Jane( );
            //***Add Good***
            life=new Courage(life);
            life=new Compassion(life);
            life=new Hope(life);
            //life=new Integrity(life);
            life=new Openness(life);
            life=new Diligence(life);
            life=new Justice(life);
            //***Add Evil***
            life=new Malice(life);
            life=new Prejudice(life);
            //life=new Dogmatisms(life);
            life=new Arrogance(life);
            //life=new Indifference(life);
            //life=new Rage(life);
            //life=new Obsfuscation(life);
            setAngelDevil(life.good(),life.evil(),life.getSoul( ));
        }
        private function setAngelDevil(right:Number,wrong:Number,
            eternalsoul:String)
        {
            this.addChild(devil);
            this.addChild(angel);
            var booWrong:Number=Number(wrong>0);
```

Example 4-37. Soul.as (continued)

```
        var booRight:Number=Number(right>0);
        devil.x=330;
        devil.y=270-((wrong*booWrong)*(270/72));
        angel.x=96;
        angel.y=270-((right*booRight)*(270/60));
        if (booWrong)
        {
            devil.soul_txt.text=eternalsoul;
        } else
        {
            angel.soul_txt.text=eternalsoul;
        }
    }
  }
}
```

In looking at the script, all it does is pass the three different values generated by the getter methods, good( ), evil( ) and getSoul( ), to the setAngelDevil( ) function. The setAngelDevil( ) function uses two movie clips from the library and positions them on the stage. Depending on the outcome, the concrete component's name appears in the angel or devil icon. Figure 4-7 shows what the output will look like. Use it as a guide for setting up your stage.

Figure 4-7. Decorator generated values used for placement and labels

The following steps guide you through the process of preparing the two MovieClip classes in the Flash IDE and setting the stage as a "soul chart."

1. Open a new Flash document file, type in **Soul** in the Document class window, and save the file as SoulChart.fla.

2. Add a layer to the existing layer, and name the top layer, **Labels** and the bottom layer "Lines." (Say that last sentence fast three times!)

3. Select Insert → New Symbol from the menu bar. Type **Angel** in the Name window, and click the Export for ActionScript checkbox. Click OK. You are now in the Symbol Edit Mode. (Be sure to capitalize the "A" in "Angel" because this is a class name.)

4. In the Symbol Edit window, draw or import an image of an angel.

5. Click the Text icon in the Tools panel, and select Dynamic Text for the type of text. In the Properties panel, provide the instance name soul_txt for the dynamic text object.

6. Exit the Symbol Edit Mode by clicking the Scene 1 icon. You should now see a movie clip icon in the Library named "Angel."

7. Repeat steps 3 to 6, substituting "Devil" for "Angel." Once you're finished, you should see both Devil and Angel movie clip icons in the Library panel.

8. Click the Lines layer and add 11 horizontal lines and one vertical line as shown in Figure 4-7. Lock the layer.

9. Click the Labels layer, number the lines from 0 to 100, and place a "Good" and "Evil" label at the top of the stage as shown in Figure 4-7. Lock the layer and save the file once again.

By adding and removing the comment lines in the Soul.as file, you can change the vertical positions of the angel and devil images. You may have to make some adjustments depending on the size of your angel and devil movie clips and/or if you change the default size of the stage from 550 by 400.

Dynamic Selection of Concrete Components and Decorations: A Hybrid Car Dealership

Up to this point, the examples have focused on different dimensions of the Decorator design pattern, with the emphasis on how the different elements in the Decorator design pattern can be used with different components and decorations. Both concrete and abstract output has shown different ways to display information, but no example has illustrated how to input data dynamically. This Decorator example uses the case of selecting automobiles and their options to illustrate how to dynamically input data for both decorators and concrete components.

Imagine that you are responsible for creating and maintaining a web site for a car dealership. With each year, new models appear, and different options are made available. You never know what options are going to be added or dropped, or even if the same car models will be around from one year to the next. You've decided to use the Decorator pattern because you can easily add or drop both concrete components and concrete decorators. The concrete components will be the different models, and the options are the different decorations for any model selected. So whenever a new model appears, you simply update the concrete component to reflect those changes. Likewise with the options available for any of the models, all you need to change are the concrete decorations. You can easily add or change decorations without altering the program's basic structure.

Setting Up the Hybrid Car Components

This particular dealership has decided to specialize in four hybrid model cars. This example uses four such cars, the Prius, Mercury Mariner, Ford Escape and Honda Accord hybrids. So in addition to an abstract Component class, this example requires four concrete components.

Auto abstract component

To get started, the abstract component is cast as a class named Auto. It needs only a string for the name of the car and a numeric variable for the car's price. Two getter functions for auto type and price make up the rest of the abstract component. Example 4-38 shows the code saved as Auto.as.

Example 4-38. Auto.as

```
package
{
    //Abstract class
    public class Auto
    {
        protected var information:String;
        protected var bucks:Number;

        public function getInformation():String
        {
            return information;
        }
        public function price():Number
        {
            return bucks;
        }
    }
}
```

As with all Decorator design patterns, all other classes are derived from this abstract component class. In the next section, you'll see that all of the concrete component classes are subclasses of the Auto class.

Hybrid car classes concrete component

The four hybrid autos are placed into separate concrete component classes that are all subclassed from the Auto class. The constructor function assigns a value to the information property, and the price( ) function returns a value representing the car's price. In Examples 4-39 to 4-42, the captions are the filenames to use for saving each class.

Example 4-39. Prius.as

```
package
{
    public class Prius extends Auto
    {
        public function Prius()
        {
            information = "Toyota Prius Hybrid~\n";
        }
        override public function price():Number
        {
            return 21725.00;
        }
    }
}
```

Example 4-40. Mariner.as

```
package
{
    public class Mariner extends Auto
    {
        public function Mariner()
        {
            information = "Mercury Mariner Hybrid~\n";
        }
        override public function price():Number
        {
            return 29225.00;
        }
    }
}
```

Example 4-41. Accord.as

```
package
{
    public class Accord extends Auto
    {
```

Example 4-41. Accord.as (continued)

```
        public function Accord( )
        {
            information = "Accord Hybrid~\n";
        }
        override public function price( ):Number
        {
            return 30990.00;
        }
    }
}
```

Example 4-42. Escape.as

```
package
{
    public class Escape extends Auto
    {
        public function Escape( )
        {
            information = "Ford Escape Hybrid\n~";
        }
        override public function price( ):Number
        {
            return 26240.00;
        }
    }
}
```

The prices here are based on prices found on the Internet, but they may or may not reflect prices at a later date. If you want to update prices or even use different autos, feel free to do so.

The \n escape character and the tilde (~) characters are used for formatting purposes. The \n is a line break, and the tilde (~) helps in separating out all the different models that become a big string as the decorator merges them altogether. Without these, the output would be a mess.

Using Auto Options as Decorators

With all the concrete components in place, the next step will be to construct the decorator class and the concrete decorators. Like the components they decorate, they too will need an identification and price property as well as methods to return them. The abstract decorator will set that up so that the derived classes have the necessary properties and methods.

The options abstract decorator

As you have seen with other abstract decorator classes in this chapter, it's one of the simplest classes. Because it extends the abstract concrete component class, it inherits all the class' properties. However, we need to re-implement the getter function so that we can further reimplement it for the delegations the different concrete decorators use. Example 4-43 shows the abstract decorator class to be saved as `Decorator.as`.

Example 4-43. Decorator.as

```
package
{
    //Abstract class
    public class Decorator extends Auto
    {
        override public function getInformation( ):String
        {
            return information;
        }
    }
}
```

Because the `information` variable is inherited from the Auto class, we need not redefine it here. It represents an abstract string.

The options concrete decorators

The concrete decorators generate the information that adds the `information` property and price value to each option. As a concrete component is wrapped in each, the string data are added to any other strings that wrap the component. So, when the `getInformation( )` method launches, it first gets the delegated information from all other options and the concrete component it wraps. In order not to get a huge string that we cannot unravel, a tilde (~) on the end of the added string will help separate all the different decorations. Examples 4-44 through 4-47 are labeled with the filenames used to save the class.

Example 4-44. HeatedSeat.as

```
package
{
    public class HeatedSeats extends Decorator
    {
        private var auto:Auto;
        public function HeatedSeats(auto:Auto)
        {
            this.auto=auto;
        }
        override public function getInformation( ):String
        {
            return auto.getInformation( ) + " Heated Seats~";
        }
        override public function price( ):Number
        {
            return 350.78 + auto.price( );
        }
    }
}
```

Example 4-45. GPS.as

```
package
{
    public class GPS extends Decorator
    {
        private var auto:Auto;
        public function GPS(auto:Auto)
        {
            this.auto=auto;
        }
        override public function getInformation( ):String
        {
            return auto.getInformation( ) +
                " Global Positioning System~";
        }
        override public function price( ):Number
        {
            return 345.88 + auto.price( );
        }
    }
}
```

Example 4-46. RearViewVideo.as

```
package
{
    public class RearViewVideo extends Decorator
    {
        private var auto:Auto;
        public function RearViewVideo(auto:Auto)
        {
            this.auto=auto;
        }
        override public function getInformation( ):String
        {
            return auto.getInformation( ) + " Rear View Video~";
        }
        override public function price( ):Number
        {
            return 560.75 + auto.price( );
        }
    }
}
```

Example 4-47. MP3.as

```
package
{
    public class MP3 extends Decorator
    {
        private var auto:Auto;
        public function MP3(auto:Auto)
        {
            this.auto=auto;
```

Example 4-47. MP3.as (continued)

```
        }
        override public function getInformation( ):String
        {
            return auto.getInformation( ) + " MP3 Player~";
        }
        override public function price( ):Number
        {
            return 267.55 + auto.price( );
        }
    }
}
```

For this particular application, we're not concerned with separating the individual costs. In fact, we want each cost to be accumulated with the others, including the cost of the concrete component we're decorating. So while the string value needs the tilde (~) for demarcation purposes, we don't need it for the numeric value.

Setting Up the User Interface

The largest single class we're going to use is the one to create the user interface. The line numbers appear in the Example 4-48 for the purpose of referencing lines in the code. A lot of the work done by this class, named Deal, is to set up the interface objects. These include the radio button, checkbox, and button components. Additionally, a good hunk of code is required for the text field output window and formatting for the output. So while the interface to the decorator pattern may look unwieldy, it's not decorator pattern's fault. In fact, only the getCar( ) (beginning on line 115) and getOptions( ) (beginning on line146) private functions are employed to pull out the information generated by the Decorator pattern.

To get a handle on what the class does, enter the code from Example 4-48 and save it as Deal.as.

Example 4-48. Deal.as

```
 1  package
 2  {
 3      import fl.controls.CheckBox;
 4      import fl.controls.RadioButton;
 5      import fl.controls.Button;
 6      import flash.display.Sprite;
 7      import flash.display.MovieClip;
 8      import flash.events.MouseEvent;
 9      import flash.text.TextField;
10      import flash.text.TextFormat;
11
12      public class Deal extends Sprite
13      {
14          internal var checks:Array=[];
15          internal var cars:Array=[];
```

Example 4-48. Deal.as

```
16          internal var carDeal:Auto;
17          public var dealText:TextField=new TextField( );
18
19          //Constructor Function
20          public function Deal ( ):void
21          {
22              getRadios ( );
23              getChecks ( );
24              doDealButton ( );
25              showDeal ( );
26          }
27          //Add button from Library
28          private function doDealButton ( ):void
29          {
30              var doDeal:Button=new Button( );
31              this.addChild (doDeal);
32              doDeal.x=215;
33              doDeal.y=195;
34              doDeal.label="Make Deal";
35              doDeal.addEventListener (MouseEvent.CLICK,getPackage);
36          }
37          //**
38          //Get information from Decorator and display it
39          //**
40          private function getPackage (e:MouseEvent):void
41          {
42              getCar ( );
43              getOptions ( );
44              if (carDeal == null)
45              {
46                  return;
47              }
48              else
49              {
50                  var nowDrive:String=carDeal.getInformation( )+"\nTotal=$"+carDeal.price( );
51              }
52              dealText.text=formatMachine(nowDrive);
53          }
54          //Format Output
55          private function formatMachine (format:String):String
56          {
57              if (format.indexOf("~") != -1)
58              {
59                  format=format.split("~").join("\n");
60              }
61              return format;
62          }
63          //Text Field & Format
64          private function showDeal ( ):void
65          {
66              dealText.width=150;
67              dealText.height=100;
```

Example 4-48. Deal.as

```
68              dealText.wordWrap=true;
69              dealText.multiline=true;
70              dealText.x=165;
71              dealText.y=230;
72              dealText.border=true;
73              dealText.borderColor=0xcc0000;
74              var dealerFormat:TextFormat=new TextFormat();
75              dealerFormat.leftMargin=4;
76              dealerFormat.rightMargin=4;
77              dealText.defaultTextFormat=dealerFormat;
78              this.addChild (dealText);
79          }
80          //Add Check boxes for Options (Concrete Decorators)
81          private function getChecks ():void
82          {
83              var gizmos:Array=new Array("MP3","Heated Seats","GPS",  "Rear View Video");
84              var saloon:uint=gizmos.length;
85              var giz:uint;
86              for (giz=0; giz<saloon; giz++)
87              {
88                  checks[giz]=new CheckBox();
89                  this.addChild (checks[giz]);
90                  checks[giz].width=150;
91                  checks[giz].x=250;
92                  checks[giz].y=80+(giz*30);
93                  checks[giz].label=gizmos[giz];
94              }
95          }
96          //Add Radio buttons Auto (Concrete Components)
97          private function getRadios ():void
98          {
99              var car:Array=new Array("Escape","Mariner","Prius","Accord");
100             var saloon:uint=car.length;
101             var ride:uint;
102             for (ride=0; ride<saloon; ride++)
103             {
104                 cars[ride]=new RadioButton();
105                 cars[ride].groupName="deals";
106                 this.addChild (cars[ride]);
107                 cars[ride].x=150;
108                 cars[ride].y=80+(ride*30);
109                 cars[ride].label=car[ride];
110             }
111         }
112         //Select Auto and create Concrete Component
113         private function getCar ():void
114         {
115             var tracker:String;
116             var hybrid:uint;
117             for (hybrid=0; hybrid<cars.length; hybrid++)
118             {
119                 if (cars[hybrid].selected)
```

Example 4-48. Deal.as

```
120                 {
121                     tracker=cars[hybrid].label;
122                     switch (tracker)
123                     {
124                         case "Escape" :
125                             carDeal = new Escape( );
126                             break;
127
128                         case "Mariner" :
129                             carDeal = new Mariner( );
130                             break;
131
132                         case "Prius" :
133                             carDeal = new Prius( );
134                             break;
135
136                         case "Accord" :
137                             carDeal = new Accord( );
138                             break;
139                     }
140                 }
141             }
142         }
143         //Select options -- wrap Concrete Component in Decorator
144         private function getOptions ( ):void
145         {
146             var tracker:String;
147             var toy:uint;
148             for (toy=0; toy<checks.length; toy++)
149             {
150                 if (checks[toy].selected)
151                 {
152                     tracker=checks[toy].label;
153                     switch (tracker)
154                     {
155                         case "MP3" :
156                             carDeal = new MP3(carDeal);
157                             break;
158
159                         case "Heated Seats" :
160                             carDeal = new HeatedSeats(carDeal);
161                             break;
162
163                         case "GPS" :
164                             carDeal = new GPS(carDeal);
165                             break;
166
167                         case "Rear View Video" :
168                             carDeal = new RearViewVideo(carDeal);
169                     }
170                 }
171             }
```

Example 4-48. Deal.as

```
172        }
173     }
174 }
175
```

Creating the document and setting the stage

Once you've saved the Deal.as file, you'll need to do a little work on a Flash document file. The following steps will guide you.

1. Open a new Flash document and save it as *AutoDealer.fla* in the same folder as the *.as* files.

2. In the Document class window, type in **Deal,** and resave the file.

3. Using Figure 4-8 as a guide, use Static text to add the header "2 Guys From Connecticut Hybrid Cars." Beneath the header, at horizontal position 150, type in **Select Car**, and on the same line at horizontal position 250, type in **Select Options**.

4. Open the Components and Library panels and drag a copy of the radio button and the checkbox to the Library.

5. Select Insert → Symbol in the menu bar, and select Button as Type. In the Name window, type in **Button** (which is the default name), and click the Import for ActionScript checkbox. Click OK to enter the Button Symbol editor indicated by the special four-frame Timeline.

6. In the Button Symbol editor, add a layer, and, selecting the top layer, use the Rectangle Tool to draw a rectangle with colors to suit your tastes with 8-point rounded corners located at x=0, y=0. Size it to W=43, H=13. Add keyframes to all the frames in the top layer. Select the object in the Over frame and swap (reverse) the stroke and fill colors.

7. Add keyframes to the first three frames in the lower layer. In the Up frame, using a Static text and narrow sans serif 10-point font type, type "Calculate" centered below the button. In the Over frame, do the same thing, but type in **Total Cost**. Leave the Down frame empty.

8. Check to make sure your Library shows the following: CheckBox, CheckBoxSkins, Component Assets, Button, RadioButton, RadioButtonSkins. If it does, you should be all set.

The next step is to test the application. All the buttons and the text field are automatically placed on the stage. Figure 4-8 shows what you can expect to see if everything is working as expected.

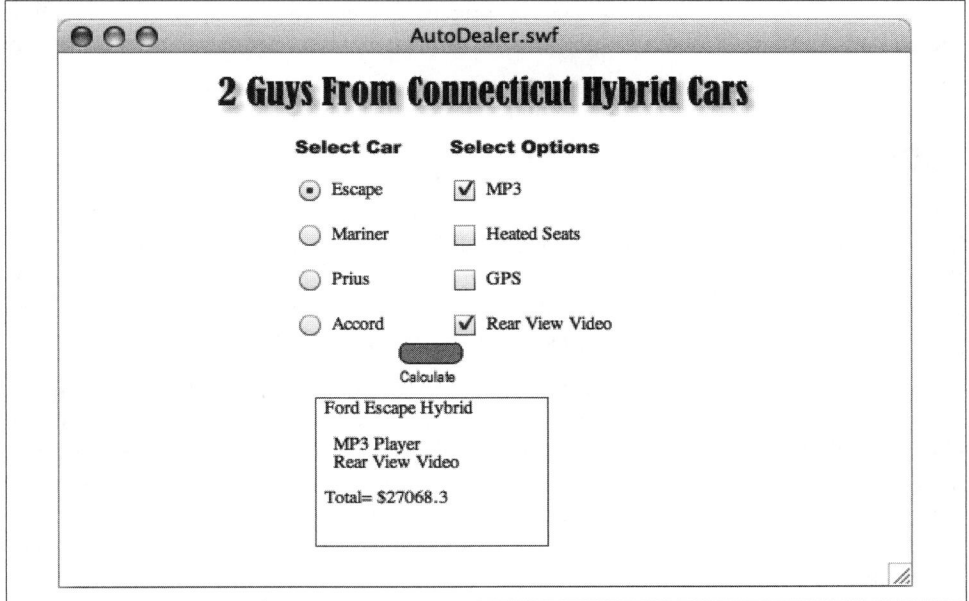

Figure 4-8. Decorator user interface and output

Implementing the concrete components and their decorators

The pattern implementation process requires that certain things are in place so that the user can choose what she wants as far as both concrete components (car model) and concrete decorators are concerned. Initially, the script must first find which car has been selected. So the function getCar( ) loops through the radio buttons until it finds which one is selected. When it locates it, it simply assigns an instance of carDeal with one of the concrete components such as:

```
carDeal = new Mariner();
```

The carDeal object has to be instantiated outside a function so that it can be used by more than a single private function. On line 16 of Example 4-48, the carDeal object is instantiated as an Auto data type. (The internal statement is added to draw attention to the fact that the variable is available to any caller in the same package—even though it is the default state when instantiating variables.)

Once the carDeal object has been created, the script looks at the options selected. Using the getOptions( ) function, each of the checkboxes is compared to its selection state. When a selected option is found, the option, a concrete decorator, wraps the concrete object carDeal. For example, if one of the selections is heated seats, the code section in the switch statement looks like the following:

```
case "Heated Seats":
carDeal = new HeatedSeats(carDeal);
break;
```

Because more than one decorator can be selected, as each selected option is located, the concrete object can be wrapped more than once. Thus, any or all of the options can be added to the selected auto.

Summary

The Decorator design pattern excels in adding features to core objects without having to fundamentally change those objects. Like the ornaments on a Christmas tree, the ornaments change the appearance of the tree, but the tree itself is not changed at all. Anything from the appearance of a web site to the contents of an online shopping cart can be structured using a Decorator pattern.

The Decorator should be considered a core design pattern when your project has to be updated with the addition of new objects and new features for those objects. We like to think of the Decorator as a "100-year" pattern. Imagining concrete components as types of people and decorations as the clothes they wear, it's not too difficult to envision a web site being updated with different kinds of people spanning a century—from a blacksmith at the beginning of the 20th century to a nanotechnologist at the beginning of the 21st century. Likewise, all kinds of people can be styled with a range of clothing over the same time span, from a blacksmith's leather apron in 1900 to an astronaut's spacesuit in 2000. However, the programmer who is thinking ahead from one century to the next is able to use a Decorator pattern, and doesn't have to change the core component at all. He just adds more concrete components and decorators as needed.

At the same time that the Decorator pattern is open to adding new features without changing the structure of the program, both components and decorators can be deleted when they're no longer needed. Further, changes to existing components and decorators are easy to make without altering anything other than their specifics, such as a string's label or a number's value.

The Decorator pattern, though, has certain drawbacks. For example, in this chapter, some readers may have been thinking that they could have programmed the same exact functionality for some of the sample applications using a fraction of the code and far fewer classes. That's definitely true, and for specific applications, the Decorator design pattern may be like swatting a fly with an elephant gun. However, like all design patterns, the developer has to be judicious in selecting which, if any pattern, he wants to employ. That decision needs to be made not just on the current size of the application, though. When starting any project where the Decorator pattern is considered, you have to ask yourself: are the concrete components and decorators going to grow and change or are they going to be fairly static? So, even though your application may begin as an acorn, you have to envision the oak tree as a possibility and plan accordingly.

CHAPTER 5

Adapter Pattern

*Adapt or perish, now as ever, is nature's inexorable
imperative.*
—H. G. Wells

*The presentations and conceptions of the average man
of the world are formed and dominated, not by the full
and pure desire for knowledge as an end in itself, but
by the struggle to adapt himself favorably to the
conditions of life.*
—Ernst Mach

What Is the Adapter Pattern?

The basic motivation for the adapter pattern is to enable wider use of existing
classes. For example, let's assume that there's a class that does a particular job, and
does it well. We want to use this class in an application, but it just doesn't fit all the
current requirements. We may want to expand its features, or combine it with some
other classes to provide additional functionality. The bottom line is that we must
adapt this existing class to fit new requirements. This is what the adapter pattern
does; it allows a client to use an existing class by converting its *interface* into one that
fits a new context. The key point to remember is that the existing class isn't modified, but an *adapter class* that has the right interface uses it or extends it to provide
the necessary functionality.

A Design Pattern for Potty Training

A good example of an adapter is the *toilet seat adapter* used by toddlers that fits on
top of a traditional toilet seat. Let's take a look at the context. We have a *legacy
object* that is the toilet seat, whose basic design hasn't changed in years. It functions
well for its original adult users (probably why the design hasn't changed). Let's look
at the new context in Figure 5-1. We now need to adapt it for use by a toddler. The
problem is obvious—*incompatible interfaces*! The legacy toilet seat was designed to

fit an adult's bottom, and we now need to convert that interface to fit a toddler's smaller bottom. We need an adapter that presents the correct interface to fit the current context. The toilet seat adapter was built to do precisely that. We get to use an existing object whose interface has been converted to one that the client expects.

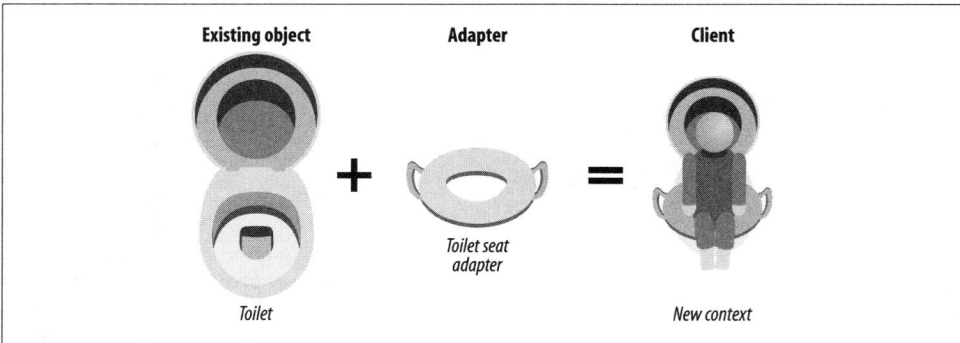

Figure 5-1. Toilet seat adapter

How is this analogous to an adapter pattern? We have an existing object (toilet seat); a new interface it needs to conform to (a toddler's bottom); an adapter that converts the interface (toilet seat adapter); and a new client (toddler).

Let's extend this analogy to computer code. The existing object would be analogous to an existing class that creates objects. The new interface would represent new requirements for this class. The adapter would be another class that implements the new interface by using the existing class.

What would be the alternative to using an adapter in this case? We could rewrite or modify the code in the existing class to fit the new interface. This is analogous to buying one of those small potties built for toddlers (with no plumbing). I think most people would rather not have to deal with the additional cost and the disposal issue. This can be as painful as changing existing code that already works, introducing bugs, and breaking dependencies. An adapter would be a better option in both cases.

Key Features of the Adapter Pattern

Before considering an adapter pattern for a project, a couple conditions should exist:

- An existing class that meets some of the implementation requirements, but whose interface is incompatible in the new context of use
- A target interface for the new context

If these conditions exist, then we can develop an adapter class that uses the existing class to implement the target *interface*. The new context should be thoroughly analyzed, and the new requirements defined, before thinking about implementation. In other words, we should know the desired interface before we look at existing classes and their functionality to figure out if they'll fit the bill. We can then develop an adapter class that implements the target interface. There's no point to adapting an existing class if it doesn't provide some benefit, such as savings in development time compared to developing a whole new class.

Object and Class Adapters

An adapter can exploit an existing class to implement functionality in two ways. The adapter can use either *composition* or *inheritance* to access an existing class. If the adapter subclasses the existing class, it will inherit the methods and properties. If the adapter uses composition to access the existing class, the adapter class will hold a reference to an instance of the existing class, and use its methods and properties for implementation. In OOP, composition is generally preferred over inheritance. However, as we will see in subsequent examples, there are good arguments for both approaches depending on the context. Either way, the idea is to use the properties and methods of the existing class to provide most or some of the functionality required.

Object Adapters

When the adapter uses *composition* to access the existing class, it's known as an *object adapter*. Object adapters store a reference to an instance of the existing class. Therefore, an object adapter *uses* an existing class.

All adapter classes implement an *interface*. In the class diagram shown in Figure 5-2, the interface called ITarget declares a single method called request( ). The class diagram shows that a reference to an instance of the Adaptee class is stored in the variable adaptee. When implementing the request( ) method, the adapter references this instance.

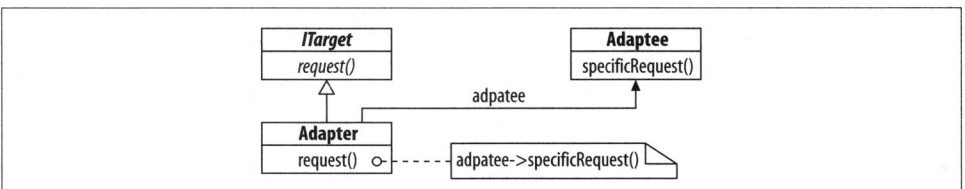

Figure 5-2. Class diagram of an object adapter

Minimalist example of an object adapter

Example 5-1 through Example 5-4 show the implementation of an object adapter in ActionScript 3.0. The different files are called: *Adaptee.as* (existing class), *ITarget.as* (required interface), *Adapter.as* (adapter), and *Main.as* (client; also the *document class* for the Flash document).

Example 5-1. Adaptee.as

```
package
{
    public class Adaptee
    {
        public function specificRequest():void
        {
            trace("Called Adaptee:specificRequest()");
        }
    }
}
```

Example 5-2. ITarget.as

```
package
{
public interface ITarget
    {
        function request():void
    }
}
```

Example 5-3. Adapter.as

```
Package
{
    public class Adapter implements ITarget
    {
        private var adaptee:Adaptee;

        public function Adapter()
        {
            this.adaptee = new Adaptee();
        }

        public function request():void
        {
            adaptee.specificRequest();
        }
    }
}
```

Example 5-4. Main.as

```
package
{
    import flash.display.MovieClip;

    /**
    *    Main Class
    *    @ purpose:        Document class for movie
    */
    public class Main extends MovieClip
    {
```

Example 5-4. Main.as (continued)

```
    public function Main( )
    {
        var target:ITarget = new Adapter( );
        target.request( );
    }
  }
}
```

The client class `Main` creates an instance of the adapter class and calls the method `request( )` defined in the `ITarget` interface. The client sees only the interface that's implemented by the adapter. Object adapters are like traffic cops, as they intercept method calls and decide what to do with them. Some of the method calls are directed to the appropriate methods in the `Adaptee` class. The `Adaptor` class keeps tight control of access to the existing class by implementing only the `ITarget` interface. The client doesn't even know that the adapter's using an existing class. The `Adaptee` class could have many public methods and properties that aren't accessible through the adapter.

Because the `Adaptor` class creates an instance of the `Adaptee` class, there's *tight coupling* between them. This doesn't allow the adapter to use a subclass of `Adaptee` or use a totally different existing class without modifying existing `Adapter` code.

Using a parameterized adapter class

A variation on the previous example of the adapter is to require the client to pass an instance of the existing class when creating an adapter. You can do this by using a parameterized constructor in the adapter class. The following changes are needed in the `Adapter` class constructor.

```
    public function Adapter(a:Adaptee)
    {
        this.adaptee = a;
    }
```

This is desirable in many cases, as it reduces the coupling between the `Adapter` and `Adaptee` classes, providing more flexibility. However, this puts the burden on the client to create an instance of `Adaptee` class and pass it to the adapter.

```
    var adaptee:Adaptee = new Adaptee( );
    var target:ITarget = new Adapter(adaptee);
```

The disadvantage of doing it this way is that the existing class is no longer hidden from the client. The client creates the instance of `Adaptee` that is passed to the `Adaptor`. This could potentially cause disruption if the client inadvertently manipulates the `Adaptee` instance.

Class Adapters

When the adapter uses *inheritance* to access an existing class, it's known as a *class adapter*. The adapter class extends the existing class and has an *is-a* relationship with it. Extending the existing class allows the adapter to inherit its properties and methods.

As is evident from the class diagram, implementing a class adapter requires *multiple inheritance*. Multiple inheritance is an OOP feature that enables a class to inherit from more than one superclass. In Figure 5-3, the Adapter class inherits from both the Target and the Adaptee classes.

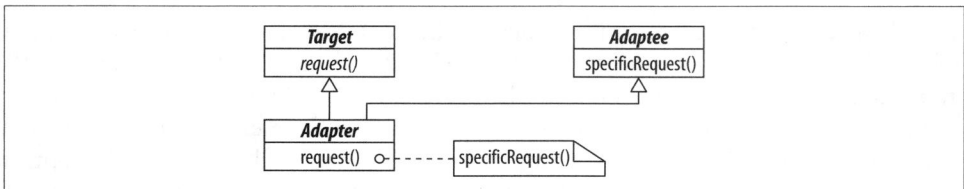

Figure 5-3. Class diagram of class adapter

According to the classic treatise on design patterns written by the group affectionately known as the Gang of Four (GoF), one inheritance branch of a class adapter is used to inherit the *interface,* and the other to inherit *implementation.* They also point out that in most cases, the class adapter inherits the interface *publicly* while the implementation branch is inherited *privately.* This hides the implementation branch of the inheritance from public view, resulting in the desirable situation where only the public interface is left visible to clients. In Figure 5-3, the Adapter class would inherit publicly from the Target class and privately from the Adaptee class. This implies that the Adapter would be a subclass of Target, and it would make use of Adaptee methods and properties to implement required operations.

Implementing *multiple inheritance* in a programming language is not an easy task, and ActionScript 3.0 doesn't support it. Therefore, implementing a classic class adapter is not possible using ActionScript 3.0. However, an ActionScript 3.0 class can subclass and implement an interface at the same time. If the required interface is defined at ITarget, then the class declaration will be:

```
public class Adapter extends Adaptee implements ITarget
```

The Adapter class will implement the ITarget interface and inherit from the Adaptee class at the same time. The big difference is that inheritance of Adaptee will be public, exposing its functionality. Although not a pure class adapter, this implementation does have its uses and can be desirable in certain contexts.

Minimalist example of a class adapter

5-5 through Example 5-8 show the implementation of a class adapter in ActionScript 3.0. The different files are called: *Adaptee.as* (existing class), *ITarget.as* (required interface), *Adapter.as* (adapter), and *Main.as* (client).

Example 5-5. Adaptee.as

```
package
{
    public class Adaptee
    {
        public function requestA( ):void
        {
            trace("Called Adaptee:requestA( )");
        }

        public function requestB( ):void
        {
            trace("Called Adaptee:requestB( )");
        }

        public function requestC( ):void
        {
            trace("Called Adaptee:requestC( )");
        }
    }
}
```

Example 5-6. ITarget.as

```
package
{
    public interface ITarget
    {
        function renamedRequestA( ):void
        function requestB( ):void
        function requestC( ):void
        function requestD( ):void
    }
}
```

Example 5-7. Adapter.as

```
package
{
    public class Adapter extends Adaptee implements ITarget
    {
        public function renamedRequestA( ):void
        {
            this.requestA( );
        }

        override public function requestB( ):void
        {
            trace("Called Adapter:requestB( )");
        }

        public function requestD( ):void
```

Example 5-7. Adapter.as (continued)

```
        {
            trace("Called Adapter:requestD( )");
        }
    }
}
```

Example 5-8. Main.as

```
package
{
    import flash.display.MovieClip;

    /**
    *    Main Class
    *    @ purpose:        Document class for movie
    */
    public class Main extends MovieClip
    {
        public function Main( )
        {
            var target:ITarget = new Adapter( );

            target.renamedRequestA( );
            target.requestB( );
            target.requestC( );
            target.requestD( );
        }
    }
}
```

The client would generate the following output. These are trace statements that indicate which class and method produced the output.

```
Called Adaptee:requestA( )
Called Adapter:requestB( )
Called Adaptee:requestC( )
Called Adapter:requestD( )
```

The method declaration renamedRequestA( ) is simply a name change to a method whose implementation is already available in the Adaptee. This conversion is implemented by directing the request to requestA( ) in the Adaptee.

Method requestB( ) is available in Adaptee, but the Adapter has overridden and re-implemented it because the existing functionality wasn't what was needed.

Method requestC( ) is available in Adaptee and the method call passes directly to it. This is the primary advantage of using inheritance: you don't have to implement a method if you need the functionality and *method signature* implemented in the Adaptee.

Method requestD( ) is implemented in the Adapter. The Adaptor class isn't required to use the Adaptee class to implement everything. The adapter can have custom methods and properties to accomplish what it needs to do. The `ITarget` interface could declare methods that are needed in the new context, but have no relation to the existing class.

Key OOP Concepts in the Adapter Pattern

Comparing the advantages and disadvantages of object and class adapters enables us to clearly understand the merits of *composition* versus *inheritance* in OO (object-oriented) design.

Object and Class Adapters Compared

Choosing between object and class adapters depends on the context in which they are used. Object adapters that use parameterized constructors are flexible because the `Adaptee` object is passed to them. This decouples the `Adaptor` and `Adaptee` classes, allowing instances of subclasses of `Adaptee` class to be passed to the adapter.

For their part, class adapters generally have less code, resulting in quicker implementation. Because they subclass the `Adaptee`, they have an *is-a* relationship with the `Adaptee` class. The `Adapter` class is therefore the same *Type* as the `Adaptee`, and easier to deal with from a client standpoint. Clients need to create only one instance of the `Adapter` class (as opposed to both an `Adaptee` and `Adapter` instance, in the case of parameterized object adapters). Class adapters can also be less time-consuming to implement if the target interface is large, because most methods will be inherited.

The decision to choose either an object or adapter class to implement an adapter depends on many factors: flexibility required, the size of the interface, ease of implementation, and match between the required interface and the `Adaptee`.

As a general rule, *composition* is better than *inheritance* because of its flexibility and loose coupling. However, the adapter pattern shows that there can be instances where you can save time and gain coding efficiency by using *inheritance*.

Example: Car Steering Adapter

Adapter patterns are commonly used when there is an existing legacy class that provides the functionality you require, but whose interface doesn't conform to what you need. Let's assume that we have a legacy class called `LegacyCar`, which is a car sprite from an old game. The `LegacyCar` class was initially developed for use with a steering wheel input device to provide an authentic driving experience. We will change the interface to the `LegacyCar` class so that we can steer the car using different input devices such as a keyboard and mouse.

The Existing Class

The LegacyCar class shown in Example 5-9 is a subclass of the Sprite class, and is saved as *LegacyCar.as*.

Example 5-9. LegacyCar.as

```
 1  package {
 2
 3      import flash.display.*;
 4      import flash.events.*;
 5      import flash.geom.*;
 6
 7      public class LegacyCar extends Sprite
 8      {
 9
10          internal var nSpeed:Number; // holds speed of car in pixels/frame
11          internal var nSteeringWheelAngle:Number; // steering rotation in Degrees
12
13          public function LegacyCar(xLoc:int, yLoc:int)
14          {
15              nSpeed = 5;
16              nSteeringWheelAngle = 0;
17              this.drawCar();
18              this.setLoc(xLoc, yLoc);
19          }
20
21          private function drawCar():void
22          {
23              // draw car body
24              graphics.beginFill(0x00FF00); // green color
25              graphics.drawRect(-20, -10, 40, 20);
26              graphics.endFill();
27              // draw tires
28              drawTire(-12, -15);
29              drawTire(12, -15);
30              drawTire(-12, 15);
31              drawTire(12, 15);
32          }
33
34          private function drawTire(xLoc:int, yLoc:int)
35          {
36              graphics.beginFill(0x000000); // black color
37              graphics.drawRect(xLoc - 4, yLoc - 2, 8, 4);
38              graphics.endFill();
39          }
40
41
42          // method to set the x and y location of the sprite
43          private function setLoc(xLoc:int, yLoc:int):void
44          {
45              this.x = xLoc;
46              this.y = yLoc;
```

Example 5-9. LegacyCar.as

```
47        }
48
49        // method to attach event handlers and get the car moving
50        public function start():void
51        {
52            if (this.stage)
53            {
54                // attach EnterFrame event handler doMoveCar()
55                this.addEventListener(Event.ENTER_FRAME, this.doMoveCar);
56            } else {
57                throw new Error("Add car to display list first");
58            }
59        }
60
61        // method to set the steering wheel angle (in Degrees)
62        public function setSteeringWheelAngle(nAngle:int):void
63        {
64            nSteeringWheelAngle = nAngle;
65        }
66
67        // move the car
68        private function doMoveCar(event:Event):void
69        {
70            this.rotation += nSteeringWheelAngle * 0.01; // rotate sprite
71            trace(nSteeringWheelAngle);
72            var newLocOffset:Point = Point.polar(nSpeed,
73                                    this.rotation * Math.PI / 180);
74            this.x += newLocOffset.x; // move by the x offset
75            this.y += newLocOffset.y; // move by the y offset
76            // place Sprite in center of stage if it goes off screen
77            if ((this.y < 0) || (this.y > this.stage.stageHeight) ||
78                ((this.x < 0)) || (this.x > this.stage.stageWidth))
79            {
80                this.setLoc(this.stage.stageWidth * 0.5,
81                            this.stage.stageHeight * 0.5);
82            }
83        }
84    }
85 }
```

The parameterized *constructor* (lines 13-19) gets the initial location of the car through xLoc and yLoc parameters. The constructor sets the property nSpeed to its default value of 5, and sets nSteeringWheelAngle to zero indicating that the steering wheel is held straight. It then calls the drawCar() method to draw the car, and the setLoc() method with the passed x and y coordinates to place the Sprite.

The drawCar() method (lines 21-32) uses the graphics property of the Sprite class to draw the car from the perspective of looking down on it from above (map view). The car is a green rectangle with four black wheels (also rectangles) drawn using the drawTire( ) method (lines 34-39). The car is drawn so that its *registration point* is in the center of the sprite.

The LegacyCar class has two public methods. The start( ) method (lines 50-59) checks whether the sprite has been added to the *display list* by checking the existence of the stage object (a sprite can be added to the display list using the addChild( ) method). If the stage object exists, it registers the doMoveCar( ) listener method to respond to *enter frame* events (line 55). The doMoveCar( ) method essentially gets the car moving forward by nSpeed pixels per frame. The LegacyCar class was not designed to control the speed of the car or stop it from moving.

The other public method (lines 62-65) is setSteeringWheelAngle( ), which takes the angle of the steering wheel in degrees as a parameter, and sets the nSteeringWheelAngle property to it. The nSteeringWheelAngle property represents the rotation angle of the steering wheel in degrees.

The doMoveCar( ) method (lines 68-83) is the *enter frame* event handler (it was registered as the enter fame handler in line 55). An enter fame event is generated each time the playhead in Flash enters a new frame. The frame rate can be set within the Flash document. The doMoveCar( ) method is executed on each enter frame event. It rotates the car sprite by 1 percent of the rotation angle of the steering wheel (stored in nSteeringWheelAngle). For example, if the rotation angle of the steering wheel is negative 200 degrees, the car sprite will rotate 2 degrees anticlockwise each time an *enter frame* event is received. It then uses the polar( ) method in the Point class to figure out the next location of the car sprite, based on its speed (nSpeed) and current direction (rotation property of the Sprite class). It then moves the sprite to its new location. The final task of the doMoveCar( ) function is to check whether the car sprite has moved offscreen. If so, it simply moves it back to the center of the stage.

The LegacyCar class is not the most functional car we've come across, but it provides a solid implementation for steering a car using a steering wheel input device. We hope to make use of this in our new context that requires us to steer the car using different input devices.

Interface Conversion

The primary function of an adapter pattern is to convert the interface of an existing class to fit into a new context. First, we need to figure out the original interface, and then determine the requirements of the new context. After this, we can determine if converting the interface of the existing class using an adapter is a viable option.

The original interface

The LegacyCar class has two public methods that represent its interface. Public methods are the primary way by which a client can access and manipulate an object. The public start( ) method simply gets the car moving. Therefore, it functions like the ignition key of the car (assume that the car is in gear all the time). The `setSteeringWheelAngle( )` public method takes in the angle of the steering wheel and rotates the car accordingly. The interface is illustrated in Figure 5-4.

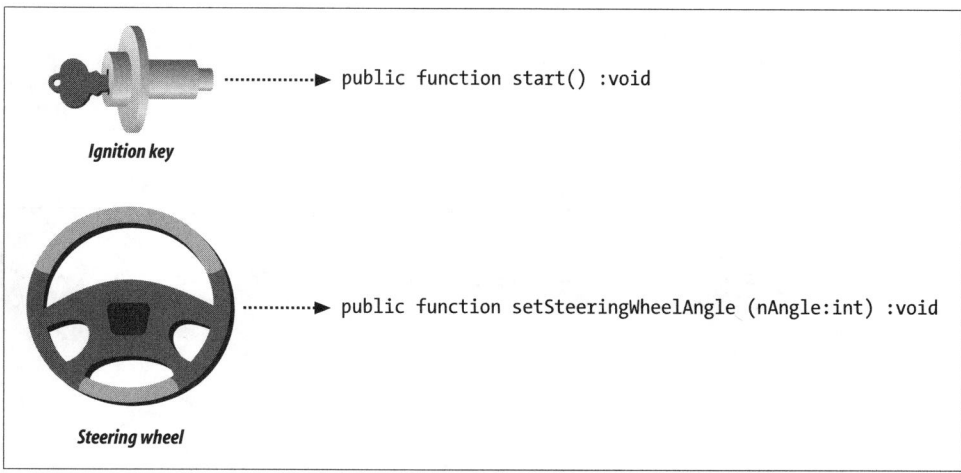

Figure 5-4. The original interface of the LegacyCar class

The new context

Let's assume that the new context requires the car to be driven, not only by a steering wheel, but by alternative input devices as well. For example, we need to drive the car using the keyboard or the mouse. Think of the new context as an effort to modify the car to be driven by someone disabled who can't use a steering wheel. The original interface allowed the car to be steered with very fine-grained movements using the `setSteeringWheelAngle( )` method. You could make the steering wheel turn half a degree or 900 degrees (2.5 complete rotations of the steering wheel). However, generating such a wide range of values is not possible with key presses. A key press essentially has two values, key down and key up. It is evident that we'll have to turn the steering wheel in discrete steps. For example, we can assume that every press of the left-arrow key represents turning the steering wheel by 50 degrees counterclockwise. The right-arrow key will, in turn, represent turning the steering wheel in the clockwise direction. It will also be helpful to have a way to get the steering wheel back to its original position. The up arrow key can be used to set the steering wheel angle to zero. We need to convert the interface to fit this new context.

The new interface

Based on the previous analysis, the new interface needs several methods to meet the requirements of the new context. The `ICar` target interface, shown in Example 5-10 and depicted in Figure 5-5, is designed for the new context.

Example 5-10. ICar.as

```
package
{
    public interface ICar
    {
        function start( ):void
        function turnMoreToTheLeft( ):void
        function turnMoreToTheRight( ):void
        function goStraight( ):void
    }
}
```

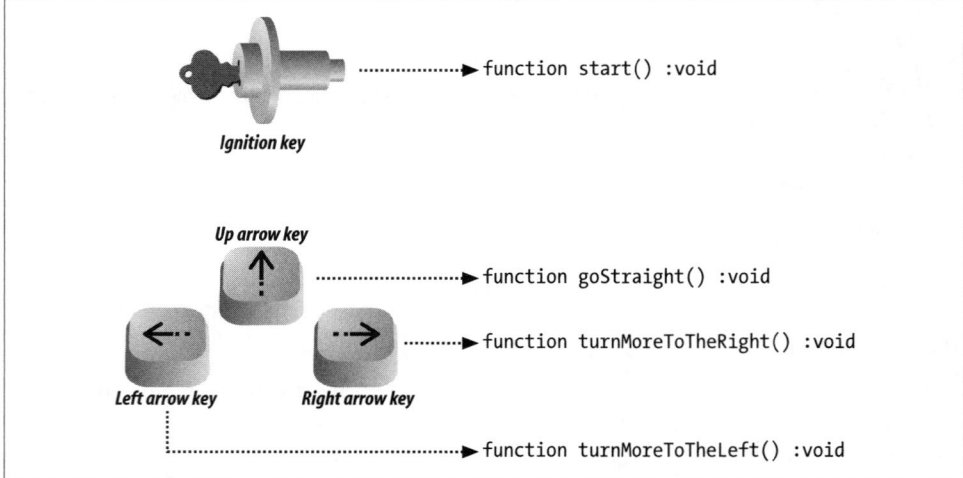

Figure 5-5. The interface showing keyboard input

The Adapter Class

We now have a target interface. The next step is to figure out if an object or class adapter is the most suitable option. Because the existing class is small with only two public methods, we won't get any benefits from using a class adapter. If there were methods in the existing class that could be directly used by the client in the new context, a class adapter would make sense. Therefore, the CarAdapter shown in Example 5-11 will be implemented as an object adapter.

Example 5-11. CarAdapter.as

```
package
{
    public class CarAdapter implements ICar
    {

        private var legacyCar:LegacyCar;
        private var nSteeringAngle:Number;
```

Example 5-11. CarAdapter.as (continued)

```
        public function CarAdapter(car:LegacyCar)
        {
            this.legacyCar = car;
            this.nSteeringAngle = 0;
            this.goStraight();
        }

        public function start():void
        {
            legacyCar.start();
        }

        public function turnMoreToTheLeft():void
        {
            legacyCar.setSteeringWheelAngle(nSteeringAngle -= 50);
        }

        public function turnMoreToTheRight():void
        {
            legacyCar.setSteeringWheelAngle(nSteeringAngle += 50);
        }

        public function goStraight():void
        {
            legacyCar.setSteeringWheelAngle(nSteeringAngle = 0);
        }

    }
}
```

The CarAdapter class implements the ICar interface and has a parameterized constructor that receives a LegacyCar instance. It contains four public methods as specified in the interface. All four methods use one of the public methods in the LegacyCar
class for implementation. The steering angle is set in discrete steps of 50 degrees, as
discussed previously. Note the nSteeringAngle property that keeps track of the current steering angle of the car. Adapter classes can have their own properties and
methods to support implementation.

The Client

All that's left to accomplish is to develop a client to test the adapter. The client
(*Main.as* shown in Example 5-12) creates a new instance of LegacyCar and passes
two parameters to the constructor that places it on the center of the stage. Next, it
creates an instance of CarAdapter and passes the previously created LegacyCar
instance to it. The client also has to receive input from the keyboard to steer the car.
To do this, the client attaches the onKeyPress() listener function to respond to *key
down* events. This listener function calls appropriate methods on the adapter class
based on keyboard input. The onKeyPress() listener function responds to the left,

right, and up arrow *key down* events, and calls turnMoreToTheLeft( ),
turnMoreToTheRight( ), and goStraight( ) methods implemented in the adapter.

Example 5-12. Main.as (document class)

```
package
{
    import flash.display.MovieClip;
    import flash.text.*;
    import flash.events.*;
    import flash.ui.*;

    public class Main extends MovieClip
    {
        private var carAdapter:ICar; // declare adapter

        public function Main( )
        {
            // Create a legacy car instance
            var legacyCar:LegacyCar =
                new LegacyCar(this.stage.stageWidth * 0.5,
                                this.stage.stageHeight * 0.75);
            addChild(legacyCar); // add legacy car to stage display list

            // Wrap legacy car with the CarAdapter
            this.carAdapter = new CarAdapter(legacyCar);

            // attach KEY_DOWN event listener onKeyPress( ) to the stage
            this.stage.addEventListener(KeyboardEvent.KEY_DOWN,
                this.onKeyPress);

            carAdapter.start( );
        }

        private function onKeyPress(event:KeyboardEvent):void
        {
            switch (event.keyCode)
            {
                case Keyboard.LEFT :
                    this.carAdapter.turnMoreToTheLeft( );
                    break;
                case Keyboard.RIGHT :
                    this.carAdapter.turnMoreToTheRight( );
                    break;
                case Keyboard.UP :
                    this.carAdapter.goStraight( );
                    break;
            }
        }
    }
}
```

Note that the new interface turns the car in discrete steps (50 degrees on each key press). Therefore, to make a hard turn right, the right arrow key should be pressed and held down (to generate multiple key down events). A quick press and release of the appropriate keys results in small turns.

Extended Example: Steering the Car Using a Mouse

If the target interface is designed with flexibility and future use in mind, the adapter can be used in multiple contexts. Because steering is accomplished in discrete steps using the turnMoreToTheLeft( ), turnMoreToTheRight( ), and goStraight( ) methods implemented in the adapter, it can be used with different input devices such as a joystick or mouse. Let's look at how a client can use mouse input to steer the car. For example, we can use a mouse click to straighten the steering and make the car go straight. How can a left and right turn be accomplished using the mouse? One way is by keeping track of the horizontal movement of the mouse as shown in Figure 5-6. If the mouse moves to the left, we can call turnMoreToTheLeft( ). If the mouse moves to the right, we can call turnMoreToTheRight( ).

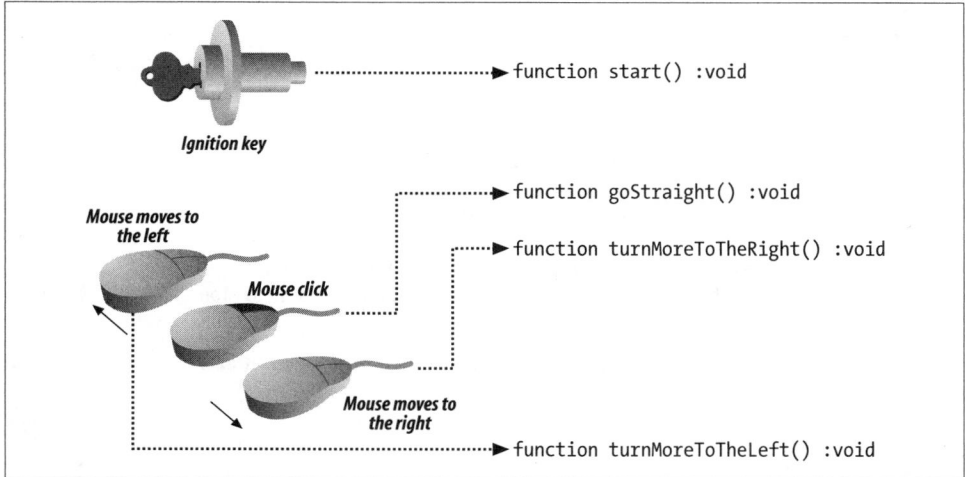

Figure 5-6. The interface showing mouse input

The basic client is similar to the Main class (Example 5-12) that used keyboard input to steer the car. The following changes need to be made to the Main class in order to steer the car using the mouse. We need to add a new property to keep track of the previous horizontal location of the mouse on the stage, to figure out if the mouse moved to the left or right. The initial horizontal location will be zero.

```
private var oldMouseStageX:Number = 0;
```

An additional change is to attach different listener functions that respond to mouse events rather than keyboard events. Instead of attaching a listener function to intercept *key down* events, we need to attach listeners to intercept *mouse down* and *mouse move* events. Note that the listeners should be attached to the stage rather than the LegacyCar object. This enables the listener functions to receive mouse clicks over the broad area of the stage, as opposed to directly over the car object.

```
this.stage.addEventListener(MouseEvent.MOUSE_MOVE, this.doMouseMove);
this.stage.addEventListener(MouseEvent.MOUSE_DOWN, this.doMouseDown);
```

All that's required now is to implement the listener functions that call the appropriate methods in the adapter. The doMouseDown( ) function listens to *mouse down* events and calls the goStraight( ) method in the adapter.

```
private function doMouseDown(event:MouseEvent):void
{
    this.carAdapter.goStraight( );
}
```

The doMouseMove( ) function listens to *mouse move* events. It checks whether the mouse has moved to the left or right from its last position. The last mouse position is saved in the oldMouseStageX property. Based on whether the mouse moved to the left or right, the adapter methods turnMoreToTheLeft( ) and turnMoreToTheRight( ) are called.

```
private function doMouseMove(event:MouseEvent):void
{
    // change in horizontal mouse position
    var xDiff = event.stageX - this.oldMouseStageX;
    if (xDiff > 0) {
        this.carAdapter.turnMoreToTheRight( );
    } else {
        this.carAdapter.turnMoreToTheLeft( );
    }
    event.updateAfterEvent( ); // process this event first
    this.oldMouseStageX = event.stageX // save old mouse x position
}
```

As is evident from this example, that well-thought-out design of adapters can be used in multiple contexts.

Example: List Display Adapter

Adapter patterns also come in handy to create reusable classes that use existing classes to implement some of the required functionality. For example, think about when you would want to display a list of values on the *Stage*. There may be many instances when you want to do this: lists of names, lists of high scores in a game, lists of products in a shopping cart, etc. In Flash you can use a TextField to display a list, putting each item on a separate line. However, this requires that the display text be preformatted with a carriage return character ('\r', ASCII 13) separating each list item before sending it out to the TextField object for display. The following code snippet will display a list using a TextField object.

```
var listField = new TextField( );
listField.x = 20;
listField.y = 20;

var sList:String = "Bread";
sList += "\r" + "Butter";
sList += "\r" + "Cheese";

listField.text = sList;

addChild(listField);
```

This works, but what if you want to delete an item from the list? You essentially have to recreate the list again. Thinking more about this, it becomes apparent that holding the list items in an array and splitting the array to create a string separated by return characters would be a better option. This would require more code, and our little code block ceases to become a "snippet" and screams out for a generic solution.

Wouldn't it be nice to have a reusable ListDisplayField where you can add one list item at a time? It would function very much like a TextField with built-in list item functionality. This is a good context in which to develop an adapter because we'll be using an existing class and converting its interface to fit a new context.

The Existing Class

The TextField class is used for text display and input in ActionScript 3.0. We will use it as the existing class. It has a detailed interface with many properties and methods that allow low-level manipulation of rendered text. The ActionScript 3.0 documentation (accessible online) describes this class at length.

Interface Conversion

We need to convert the TextField class interface to enable adding and deleting list items as required in the new context. The deleteItemAt(n:uint) method defines a return type signifying the success or failure of the operation. The interface also defines a method to clear the field. The IListDisplay interface in Example 5-13 defines the new target interface.

Example 5-13. IListDisplay.as

```
package
{
    public interface IListDisplay
    {
        function addItem(s:String):void;
        function deleteItemAt(n:uint):Boolean;
        function clear( ):void;
    }
}
```

The Adapter Class

Before we implement the IListDisplay interface, a decision regarding which type of adapter, class or object, needs to be made. The existing interface of the TextField class is quite extensive and contains several methods that would be directly useful in the new context. For example, the TextField interface defines many properties such as backgroundColor and border that enable formatting the text field display object. In addition, it also defines methods such as setTextFormat( ) that allows formatting the text in the field using a TextFormat object. If the ListDisplayField adapter is implemented as a class adapter, we can benefit from less code and implementation efficiency. However, if we implement ListDisplayField as a class adapter in ActionScript 3.0 using inheritance, all the public methods and properties in TextField will be exposed. We will need to carefully override some of the methods and properties in the TextField class that allow direct manipulation of text in the field. The adapter implementation is shown in Example 5-14.

Example 5-14. ListDisplayField.as

```
 1  package
 2  {
 3      import flash.text.*;
 4
 5      // Adapter
 6      public class ListDisplayField extends TextField implements IListDisplay
 7      {
 8
 9          private var aList:Array;
10
11          public function ListDisplayField( )
12          {
13              super( ); // Call the TextField constructor
14              this.clear( );
15          }
16
17          public function addItem(s:String):void
18          {
19              this.aList.push(s);
20              this.update( );
21          }
22
23          public function deleteItemAt(i:uint):Boolean
24          {
25              if ((i > 0) && (i <= aList.length)) {
26                  aList.splice(i-1, 1);
27                  this.update( );
28                  return true;
29              } else {
30                  return false;
31              }
32          }
33
```

Example 5-14. ListDisplayField.as

```
34          public function clear( ):void
35          {
36              aList = [];
37              this.update( );
38          }
39
40          internal function update( )
41          {
42              var listText:String = "";
43              // split the array to create a string separated by returns
44              for (var i:Number = 0; i < aList.length; i++) {
45                  listText += aList[i] + "\r";
46              }
47              super.text = listText;
48          }
49
50          override public function set text(s:String):void
51          {
52              throw new Error("Cannot directly set text property - use
                            addItem( ) method");
53          }
54
55          override public function set htmlText(s:String):void
56          {
57              throw new Error("Cannot directly set htmlText property");
58          }
59
60          override public function appendText(s:String):void
61          {
62              throw new Error("Cannot append text - use addItem( ) method");
63          }
64
65          override public function replaceSelectedText(s:String):void
66          {
67              throw new Error("Cannot replace selected text");
68          }
69
70          override public function replaceText(beginIndex:int, endIndex:int,
                            newText:String):void
71          {
72              throw new Error("Cannot replace text");
73          }
74      }
75  }
```

The ListDisplayField adapter extends the TextField class, and implements the
IListDisplay interface. The constructor calls the super( ) method to invoke the constructor in the superclass TextField (line 13). The implementation is straightforward
in that the list of items to display is stored in an array called aList that is a property
of the class. The addItem(s:String) method appends the passed string value to the
end of the aList array. The deleteItemAt(i:uint) method deletes the item at the

requested location in aList (list index starts at 1). This method checks to see if the delete location is within array bounds, and returns a Boolean value accordingly. Note the use of the qualifier super to set the text in the update( ) method (line 47). This allows the method to access the superclass property, listText, directly. This is necessary as the setter method for the text property is overridden (lines 50–53). In fact, several public methods in the TextField class that allow direct setting of field contents are overridden to prevent clients from breaking IListDisplay functionality. The overridden methods are: setter methods to the text and htmlText properties including appendText( ), replaceSelectedText( ), and replaceText( ).

The Client

Clients would use the ListDisplayField adapter class just as they would a TextField class. This is the big advantage to implementing class adapters in ActionScript 3.0, as the public methods and properties of the existing class behave as expected (unless overridden). The following client, *Main.as* shown in Example 5-15, uses a TextFormat object to set the font and font size of the display object. In addition, the border property of the text field is set to show the field boundary.

Example 5-15. Main.as (document class)

```
package
{
    import flash.display.MovieClip;
    import flash.text.*;

    public class Main extends MovieClip
    {
        public function Main( )
        {
            // create ListDisplayField
            var shoppingListField:ListDisplayField = new ListDisplayField( );

            // develop field formatting
            var format:TextFormat = new TextFormat( );
            format.size = 18;
            format.font = "Arial";

            // set field location and format
            shoppingListField.x = 20;
            shoppingListField.y = 20;
            shoppingListField.border = true;
            shoppingListField.defaultTextFormat = format;

            // create list
            shoppingListField.addItem("Bread");
            shoppingListField.addItem("Butter");
            shoppingListField.addItem("Broccoli");
            shoppingListField.addItem("Cheese");
            // changed mind about Broccoli
```

Example 5-15. Main.as (document class) (continued)

```
        shoppingListField.deleteItemAt(3);

        addChild(shoppingListField);
    }
  }
}
```

This client code will display a text field located at point (20,20) on the stage, showing Bread, Butter, and Cheese in three separate lines in Arial font size 18. Displaying lists and deleting list items by location is now especially easy for clients. There is no need to keep items in a list or traverse this list to delete items. All this is implemented by the adapter and encapsulated. Note that additional methods to manipulate the list can be easily added to the adapter class. For example, a method to delete items by content rather than location, or a method to replace or insert a list item can be implemented by extending the adapter. We have therefore created a generic class that is reusable in multiple contexts by converting the interface of an existing class.

Extended Example: Displaying the O'Reilly New Books List

To further illustrate the utility of the ListDisplayField adapter, we'll use it to display the list of new books published by O'Reilly Media, Inc. Because this list changes often, it makes sense to access the list dynamically using network methods, and display the book titles using the ListDisplayField adapter.

The new books list is published from the O'Reilly web site as a *web feed*. A web feed is a data format used to publish content that changes frequently. The content publisher *syndicates* a web feed, allowing users to *subscribe* to it.

The O'Reilly new books *web feed,* shown in Example 5-16, is published using the *Atom Syndication Format*, commonly known as *Atom*. Another common web feed format is RSS (the RSS 2.0 acronym stands for Really Simple Syndication). Syndication formats are specified using XML (Extensible Markup Language), which is a way to create special-purpose markup languages to describe data.

Example 5-16. Condensed version of new books web feed from O'Reilly showing two book entries

```
<?xml version='1.0' encoding='utf-8'?>

<feed xmlns='http://www.w3.org/2005/Atom'
xmlns:itunes='http://www.itunes.com/dtds/podcast-1.0.dtd'
xml:lang='en-US'>

<title>O'Reilly Media, Inc. New Books</title>
<link rel="alternate" type="text/html" href=http://www.oreilly.com/
    hreflang="en" title="O'Reilly Media, Inc. New Books" />
```

Example 5-16. Condensed version of new books web feed from O'Reilly showing two book entries

```
<rights>Copyright O'Reilly Media, Inc.</rights>
<updated>2006-09-28T22:45:16-08:00</updated>
<link rel="self" type="application/atom+xml" href=
    "http://www.oreillynet.com/pub/feed/29"/>

<entry>
    <title>Designing and Building Enterprise DMZs</title>
    <id>http://www.oreilly.com/catalog/1597491004</id>
    <link rel='alternate' href='http://www.oreilly.com/
        catalog/1597491004'/>
    <summary type='html'>
    &lt;i>Building DMZs for Enterprise Networks&lt;/i> covers a
        sorely needed area in critical business infrastructure:
        the Demilitarized Zone. DMZs play a crucial role in any
        network consisting of a Hosted Internet Web Server, internal
        servers which need to be segregated, External to Internal DNS
        Server, and an E-mail SMTP Relay Agent. This book covers what
        an administrator needs to plan out and integrate a DMZ into a
        network for small, medium, and Enterprise networks.
    </summary>
    <author><name>Hal Flynn</name></author>
    <updated>2006-09-28T22:45:16-08:00</updated>
</entry>

<entry>
    <title>Windows PowerShell Quick Reference</title>
    <id>http://www.oreilly.com/catalog/windowspowershell</id>
    <link rel='alternate' href='http://www.oreilly.com/catalog/
        windowspowershell'/>
    <summary type='html'>
    For years, support for scripting and command-line administration
        on the Windows platform has paled in comparison to the
        support offered by the Unix platform. Unix administrators
        enjoyed the immense power and productivity of their command
        shells, while Windows administrators watched in envy.
        Windows PowerShell, Microsoft's next-generation command shell
        and scripting language, changes this landscape completely.
        This Short Cut contains the essential reference material to
        help you get your work done-including the scripting language
        syntax, a regular-expression reference, useful .NET classes,
        and much more.
    </summary>
    <author><name>Lee Holmes</name></author>
    <updated>2006-09-27T22:46:17-08:00</updated>
</entry>
</feed>
```

We will subscribe to the web feed, extract the book titles using ECMAScript for XML (E4X), and display them using the ListDisplayField adapter. ActionScript 3.0 fully supports E4X, making it possible to access and manipulate XML documents in a form that mimics XML syntax. Example 5-17 shows the implementation.

Example 5-17. Main.as (document class)

```
1  package
2  {
3      import flash.display.MovieClip;
4      import flash.text.*;
5      import flash.events.*;
6      import flash.net.*;
7
8      /**
9       *     Main Class
10      *     @ purpose:          Document class for movie
11      */
12     public class Main extends MovieClip
13     {
14         var xml:XML;
15         var xmlLoader:URLLoader;
16         var newBookListField:ListDisplayField;
17
18         public function Main()
19         {
20             // create ListDisplayField (Adapter)
21             newBookListField = new ListDisplayField();
22
23             // develop field formatting
24             var format:TextFormat = new TextFormat();
25             format.size = 14;
26             format.font = "Arial";
27
28             // set field location and format
29             newBookListField.x = 20;
30             newBookListField.y = 20;
31             newBookListField.width = 500;
32             newBookListField.height = 300;
33             newBookListField.border = true;
34             newBookListField.defaultTextFormat = format;
35
36             // create list from O'Reilly New Books Feed (Atom)
37             var newBooksURL = "http://www.oreillynet.com/pub/feed/29";
38             xml = new XML();
39             var xmlURL:URLRequest = new URLRequest(newBooksURL);
40             xmlLoader = new URLLoader(xmlURL);
41             xmlLoader.addEventListener(Event.COMPLETE, xmlLoaded);
42
43             addChild(newBookListField); // add field to display list
44         }
45
46         function xmlLoaded(evtObj:Event)
47         {
48             xml = XML(xmlLoader.data);
49             // set the default XML namespace
50             if (xml.namespace("") != undefined)
51             {
52                 default xml namespace = xml.namespace("");
```

Example 5-17. Main.as (document class)

```
53              }
54              // populate the ListDisplayField with new book titles
55              for each (var bookTitle:XML in xml..entry.title)
56              {
57                  newBookListField.addItem(bookTitle.toString());
58              }
59          }
60      }
61  }
```

The feed URL (*http://www.oreillynet.com/pub/feed/29*) is specified in line 37. The URLLoader( ) method (line 40) loads this document over the Internet, and calls the xmlLoaded( ) function when loading is complete. The xmlLoaded( ) method is registered as a listener function (line 41) because loading data is an asynchronous operation requiring notification when the process is completed. It is important that the default namespace be set if a namespace is specified in the XML document (lines 50-53). This enables E4X to do proper validation while parsing the XML document. The for each statement accesses each book title (lines 55-58) and adds it to the ListDisplayField adapter. Figure 5-7 shows the output from the example.

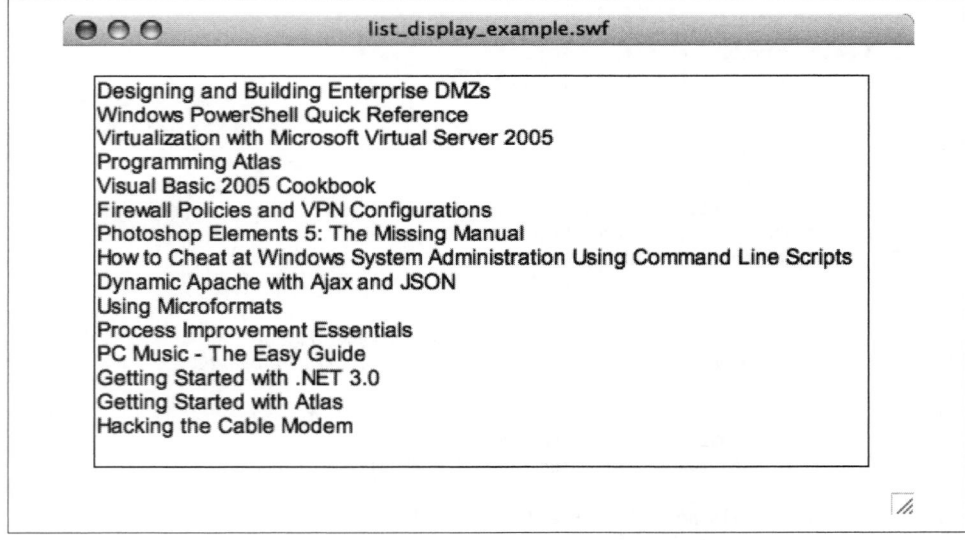

Figure 5-7. The O'Reilly new books list displayed using the ListDisplayField adapter

Summary

The adapter pattern allows existing classes to be used in situations that didn't exist or weren't anticipated when they were developed. For example, an application can have a lot of legacy code, code that is no longer supported or maintained, but needs to be used for various reasons. Adaptor classes use or extend existing code to fit new requirements. The main focus of the adapter pattern is to convert the interface of the existing class to one that fits a new context.

Adapter patterns are very close in intent and in function to several other patterns such as the façade, decorator (see Chapter 4), and bridge. The primary distinctions are that the adapter requires a target interface to which the adapter provides the implementation, there has to be an existing class that the adapter uses or extends to provide the implementation, and there is no requirement to simplify the interface.

There are two types of adapters, and choosing between object and class adapters highlights the advantages and disadvantages of composition versus inheritance in implementation. They also illustrate the importance of interfaces, and how they allow the designer to encapsulate implementation details.

CHAPTER 6

Composite Pattern

What we need to do is learn to work in the system, by which I mean that everybody, every team, every platform, every division, every component is there not for individual competitive profit or recognition, but for contribution to the system as a whole on a win-win basis.

—W. Edwards Deming

In a logically perfect language, there will be one word and no more for every simple object, and everything that is not simple will be expressed by a combination of words, by a combination derived, of course, from the words for the simple things that enter in, one word for each simple component.

—Bertrand Russell

A complex system that works is invariably found to have evolved from a simple system that works.

—John Gaule

What Is the Composite Pattern?

The composite pattern provides a robust solution to building complex systems that are made up of several smaller components. The components that make up the system may be individual objects or containers that represent collections of objects. Think of a car as a complex system that is made up of several smaller components. The car contains an engine, body, chassis, seats, tires, etc. For the sake of simplicity, let's consider a tire as an indivisible or primitive object. A car would be composed of four tires (in reality a tire contains several smaller components such as hubcap, rim, tube, etc.). Similarly, a car contains one steering wheel. However, the engine contains several smaller components such as cylinders, compressor, radiator, etc. The engine is a component of the car, but the engine itself is a collection of components. We refer to a component that is a collection of other components as a composite object. The beauty of the composite pattern is that it allows clients to treat primitive objects and composite objects the same way. For example, when adding, or removing a component, the client doesn't have to bother with figuring out if the object is a primitive or composite object. The client can just as easily remove the engine or a tire through a common interface.

A useful way to understand the composite pattern is to think of complex composite objects as hierarchical trees. We're talking about upside-down trees as in Figure 6-1, where the system begins with a root node and cascades down, subdividing into several branches.

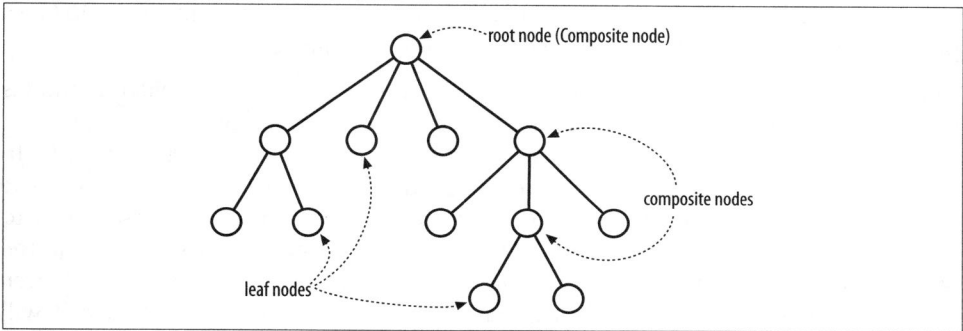

Figure 6-1. A hierarchical tree structure showing nodes and leaves

In Figure 6-1, the nodes that contain other components are composite objects. The leaf nodes are indivisible or primitive components that cannot have any children. Each leaf node is a *child* of a composite node and each composite node can have multiple children, including other composite nodes. Likewise, the composite node that's immediately up the hierarchy from a leaf is called its *parent*. As shown in the class diagram in Figure 6-2, the composite pattern provides a common interface to deal with both composite and leaf nodes.

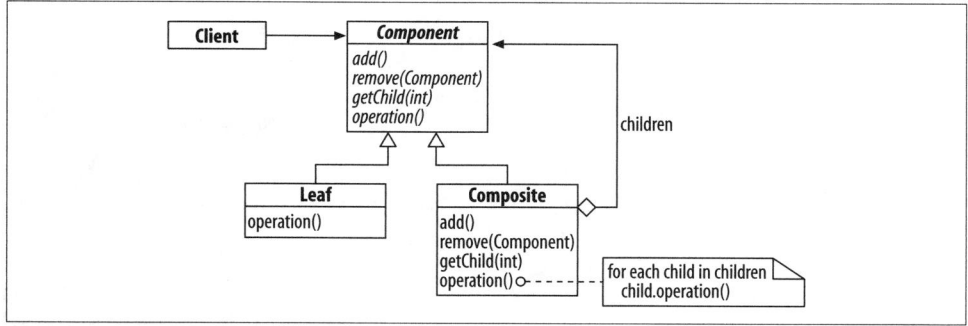

Figure 6-2. Class diagram of a composite pattern

The common interface for both composite and leaf nodes is the Component class. The component class is usually defined as an abstract class. Therefore, the Component class can define default implementations for both composite and leaf nodes. At a minimum, the Component class declares: add( ), remove(child:Component), and getChild(n:int) methods. These methods allow clients to build the composite system. The Leaf and Composite classes extend the Component class and override necessary methods. The default implementation defined in the component usually applies to the concrete Leaf classes. Because adding, removing, and getting child nodes aren't relevant to leaf nodes, the default implementation for these methods in the Component class is to raise an exception (throw an error). However, these methods should be overridden and implemented in the Composite class. Note how a composite object can be composed of several children of type component. The children property in the Composite class aggregates child components.

The real power of the composite pattern is evident in how the operation( ) method is implemented both in the Leaf and Composite classes in the diagram in Figure 6-2. Operations that apply to both leaves and nodes are defined in the Component class. In most cases, these operations are defined as abstract methods, forcing both the Leaf and Composite classes to provide implementations. The composite classes need to provide a recursive implementation for the operation( ) method. It needs to call the operation( ) method in each of its child components referenced by the children property. When we think of hierarchical trees, the operation( ) method call will traverse the tree calling the operation( ) method in all child components.

To understand how common operations apply to all children recursively, look at the similarities between the composite pattern and a mobile (Figure 6-3).

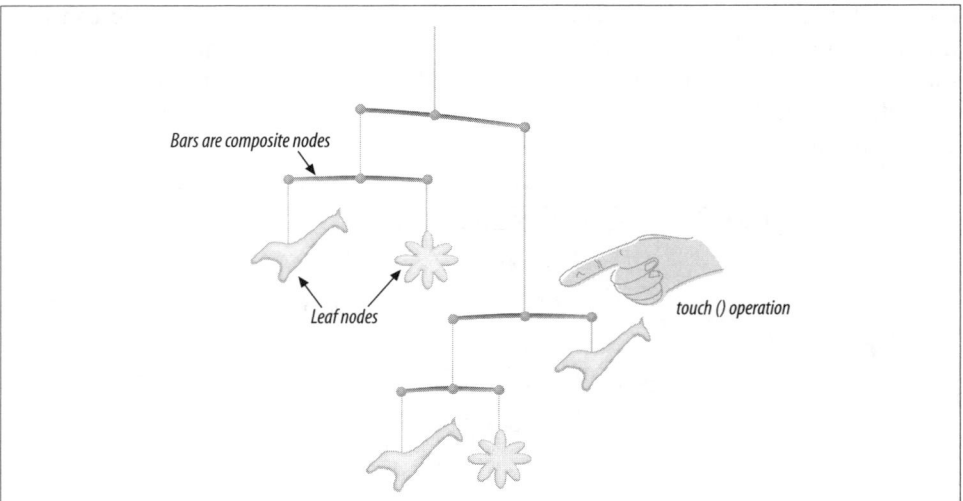

Figure 6-3. A mobile implements a composite pattern

The bars represent composite nodes, and the fish and starfish are leaf nodes. The interesting aspect of the mobile is to visualize what happens when you touch one of the components. We can think of touch( ) as a common operation that applies to all components in the mobile. Generally, the touch operation makes the mobile component rotate. If you touch a composite node, it will rotate not only itself, but all its children as well. Touching a leaf node such as a fish will rotate only that component, as leaf nodes have no children. The fact that the client manipulating the composite structure does not have to worry about whether the operation's being carried out on a leaf or a composite node is one of the key features of the composite pattern.

Key Features of the Composite Pattern

The composite pattern streamlines the building and manipulation of complex structures that are composed of several related pieces.

- Complex structures are built as hierarchical trees.
- The components of the structure can be individual components (primitives or indivisible objects) or composite components that hold a collection of other components.
- They allow clients to treat both individual components (leaf nodes) and composite components (composite nodes) the same way, simplifying the interface.

Minimalist Example of a Composite Pattern

This example implements the composite shown in the class diagram in Figure 6-2. The *Component.as* file (Example 6-1) contains the Component abstract class that defines the interface for both leaf and composite nodes. The *Leaf.as* file (Example 6-2) contains the Leaf class, and the *Composite.as* file (Example 6-3) contains the Composite class. Both Leaf and Composite classes extend the Component class and provide necessary implementations. The *Main.as* file (Example 6-4) contains the client class Main (also known as the *document class* for the Flash document).

Example 6-1. Component.as

```
package
{
    import flash.errors.IllegalOperationError;

    // ABSTRACT Class (should be subclassed and not instantiated)
    public class Component
    {
        public function add(c:Component):void
        {
            throw new IllegalOperationError
                ("add operation not supported");
        }

        public function remove(c:Component):void
        {
```

Example 6-1. Component.as (continued)

```
        throw new IllegalOperationError
            ("remove operation not supported");
    }

    public function getChild(n:int):Component
    {
        throw new IllegalOperationError
            ("getChild operation not supported");
        return null;
    }

    // ABSTRACT Method (must be overridden in a subclass)
    public function operation( ):void {}

    }
}
```

The Component class should behave as an abstract class and should not be instantiated. It also defines the abstract interface for managing child components, and provides default implementations for the add(c:Component), remove(c:Component) and getChild(n:int) methods. The default implementations for these methods are designed for leaf nodes and will raise an exception by throwing an IllegalOperationError. This should be the case as leaf nodes cannot have children and should not implement operations that deal with child nodes. In addition, the operation( ) method is defined as an abstract method without implementation. It is left up to the classes that subclass Component to provide an implementation for it.

Example 6-2. Leaf.as

```
package
{
    public class Leaf extends Component
    {
        private var sName:String;

        public function Leaf(sNodeName:String)
        {
            this.sName = sNodeName;
        }

        override public function operation( ):void
        {
            trace(this.sName);
        }
    }
}
```

The Leaf class extends the Component class. It declares a property called sName that holds the name of the leaf. It also implements a parameterized constructor that takes a string value that's then set to the sName property. It implements the operation( )

method by tracing sName. When operation( ) is called in a leaf node, it will output its name in the output panel.

Example 6-3. Composite.as

```
package
{
    public class Composite extends Component
    {
        private var sName:String;
        private var aChildren:Array;

        public function Composite(sNodeName:String)
        {
            this.sName = sNodeName;
            this.aChildren = new Array( );
        }

        override public function add(c:Component):void
        {
            aChildren.push(c);
        }

        override public function operation( ):void
        {
            trace(this.sName);
            for each (var c:Component in aChildren)
            {
                c.operation( );
            }
        }
    }
}
```

The Composite class extends the Component class. It also declares a property called sName that holds the name of the composite node and sets it to the value passed to it in the parameterized constructor. A unique feature of the Composite class is that it needs to define a structure to hold references to child components and implement the methods that operate on child nodes. The simplest structure to hold references to child nodes is an array. The array called aChildren is initialized in the constructor. Whenever a component is added to a composite node via the add(c:Component) method, it's added to the aChildren array using the push( ) method. The operation( ) method is also unique in the sense that, it not only implements it by tracing sName, but calls operation( ) in all of its children. This ensures that the operation( ) method call recursively traverses all child nodes in the tree structure.

Example 6-4. Main.as

```
package
{
    import flash.display.MovieClip;

    public class Main extends MovieClip
    {
        public function Main()
        {
            var root:Composite = new Composite("root");

            // create a node
            var n1:Composite = new Composite("composite 1");
            n1.add(new Leaf("leaf 1")); // add a child leaf
            n1.add(new Leaf("leaf 2")); // add a child leaf
            root.add(n1); // add node to root as child

            // create another node
            var n2:Composite = new Composite("composite 2");
            n2.add(new Leaf("leaf 3")); // add a child leaf
            n2.add(new Leaf("leaf 4")); // add a child leaf
            n2.add(new Leaf("leaf 5")); // add a child leaf
            root.add(n2); // add node to root as child

            // add a child leaf to the root node
            root.add(new Leaf("leaf 6"));

            root.operation(); // call operation on root node
        }
    }
}
```

The Main class shown in Example 6-4 represents the *client*. It creates a composite *root* node and adds several composite and leaf nodes to it. The resulting composite structure is shown graphically in Figure 6-4.

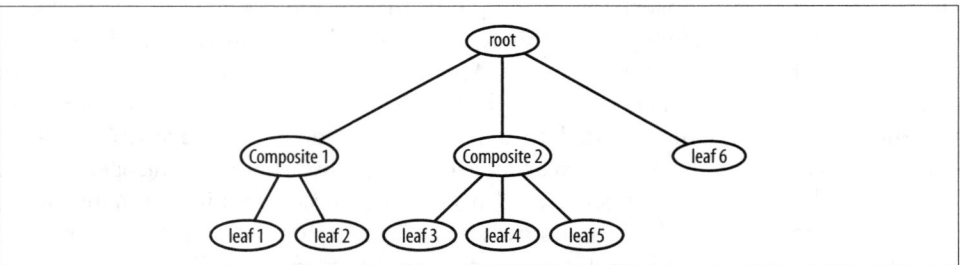

Figure 6-4. Composite tree structure built by the client

The Main class constructor ends with a call to the operation( ) method on the root node. This method recursively traces the names of all subsequent components in the structure. The following is the output from this operation.

```
root
composite 1
leaf 1
leaf 2
composite 2
leaf 3
leaf 4
leaf 5
leaf 6
```

It is important to note that the *client* sees only the interface defined by the Component class. The client doesn't need to differentiate between composite and leaf nodes, and isn't tied to how the operation( ) method is implemented. It can simply call operation( ) on any leaf or composite node and get consistent results.

Accessing Child Nodes

You may have noticed that we didn't override and implement the getChild(n:int) method in the Composite class. However, this method's very important to the composite pattern, as it allows the client to develop a composite structure by not declaring variables, as in the previous example. This ensures proper garbage collection when removing nodes. Garbage collection allows the application to recover memory and resources allocated to deleted nodes, and will be discussed in more detail later in the chapter. The getChild( ) method allows the client to access the children of any composite node. The following getChild( ) method is implemented in the Composite class.

```
override public function getChild(n:int):Component
{
    if ((n > 0) && (n <= aChildren.length))
    {
        return aChildren[n-1];
    } else {
        return null;
    }
}
```

The parameterized getChild( ) method returns the child object by the position indicated by the parameter n (index starts from 1). After doing a range check, the method returns the child node or null if no children exist. The client can now leverage the getChild( ) method and build the same composite structure more efficiently.

```
// create root node
var root:Composite = new Composite("root");

// add a node to root
root.add(new Composite("node 1"));
root.getChild(1).add(new Leaf("leaf 1"));
root.getChild(1).add(new Leaf("leaf 2"));

// add another node
root.add(new Composite("node 2"));
```

```
root.getChild(2).add(new Leaf("leaf 3"));
root.getChild(2).add(new Leaf("leaf 4"));
root.getChild(2).add(new Leaf("leaf 5"));

// add a child leaf to the root node
root.add(new Leaf("leaf 6"));

root.operation( ); // call operation on root node
```

Removing Nodes

Implementing the remove( ) method in the Composite class can be a little tricky. The safe way to remove nodes is to do it from the parent. In order to implement node removal, we need to create a reference to its parent from each node.

Creating a parent reference

Because all nodes, excluding the root node, will have parent references, it makes sense to declare the parent reference, and the methods that access it, in the Component class. The parentNode property can be declared as follows.

```
protected var parentNode:Composite = null;
```

Note that the parentNode property is declared as type Composite, and defaults to null. This does introduce a dependency between the Component and Composite classes. However, the tradeoff is type safety over class dependency. The parent reference is also declared as *protected* to make it accessible only to the current class and its subclasses. Two methods to set and get the parent reference should also be implemented in the Component class.

```
internal function setParent(compositeNode:Composite):void
{
    this.parentNode = compositeNode;
}

public function getParent( ):Composite
{
    return this.parentNode;
}
```

Note that the getParent( ) method is declared as *public* to make it accessible to clients. However, the setParent( ) method is declared as *internal* to prohibit setting the parent from outside the *package*. This is important as the parent link should only be set in the add( ) method implementation in the Composite class. The add( ) method should be modified as follows to set the parent reference of the child node to the current composite node.

```
override public function add(c:Component):void
{
    aChildren.push(c);
    c.setParent(this);
}
```

Executing the following statements accesses the *third child of the second child of the root node*; which is *leaf 5*. The parent of *leaf 5* is the second child of the root node (see Figure 6-4).

```
var leaf5:Component = root.getChild(2).getChild(3);
var leaf5Parent:Composite = l5.getParent();
```

Calling the operation( ) on the parent of *leaf 5* should give the following output.

```
composite 2
leaf 3
leaf 4
leaf 5
```

Implementing the remove method

The primary concern with removing nodes has to do with removing all references to deleted objects so that the garbage collector can recover the memory they used. For example, before removing a composite node, all its child nodes need to be deleted. If one of the child nodes is itself a composite, then the remove method should recursively delete its children as well. Therefore, the remove method will work similar to the operation( ) method.

From the previous scenario, it is evident that we need to treat leaf nodes and composite nodes differently when deleting them. Therefore, it's useful to declare a getComposite( ) method in the Component class to return the composite object if it is indeed a composite, and null if not. The default behavior would be to return null. The following method would be defined with its default implementation in the Component class.

```
internal function getComposite():Composite
{
    return null;
}
```

The Composite class would override this method and return the actual composite object.

```
override internal function getComposite():Composite
{
    return this;
}
```

In addition, the parent references of components should be removed before components can be removed. The following method to remove the parent reference should be defined and implemented in the Component class.

```
internal function removeParentRef():void
{
    this.parentNode = null;
}
```

The default remove(c:Component) method declared with its default implementation in the Component class is overridden and implemented in the Composite class (Example 6-5).

Example 6-5. The remove() method

```
 1  override public function remove(c:Component):void
 2  {
 3      if (c === this)
 4      {
 5          // remove all my children
 6          for (var i:int = 0; i < aChildren.length; i++)
 7          {
 8              safeRemove(aChildren[i]); // remove children
 9          }
10          this.aChildren = []; // remove references to children
11          this.removeParentRef(); // remove my parent reference
12      } else {
13          for (var j:int = 0; j < aChildren.length; j++)
14          {
15              if (aChildren[j] == c)
16              {
17                  safeRemove(aChildren[j]); // remove child
18                  aChildren.splice(j, 1); // remove reference
19              }
20          }
21      }
22  }
```

The remove( ) method takes one parameter that is an instance of the Component class. Based on the passed component instance, the remove( ) method has to deal with two situations: (a) what to do when the component to delete is the current object, and (b) what to do if it isn't. If the passed component is the current object, then the current object has to recursively remove all child components (lines 6–9), and then remove references to its parent (line 11) and children (line 10). In the second scenario, if the passed component is not the current object, it's assumed to be one of its children. In this case, the program loops though all its child nodes (lines 13–20) and checks if one of its children needs to be removed. If so, it removes the child component (line 17), and deletes the reference to the removed child from the aChildren array (line 18).

The remove( ) method uses safeRemove( ), shown in Example 6-6, to safely remove child components. The safeRemove( ) method first checks if the passed component is a composite, and if so, calls its remove method. If the passed component is not a composite (it's a leaf node), it removes its parent reference.

Example 6-6. The safeRemove() method

```
private function safeRemove(c:Component)
{
    if (c.getComposite())
    {
        c.remove(c); // composite
    } else {
        c.removeParentRef();
    }
}
```

Following the proper sequence when removing parent and child references is essential, so that deleted objects are left isolated without incoming or outgoing references. This is a necessary condition for the garbage collector to dispose of the object and recycle the memory used by it.

Building and Manipulating a Composite Structure

Let's test how the remove() method works by building the composite structure shown in the first column of Figure 6-4 and removing selected leaves and composite nodes. From the *client*, execute the statements in Example 6-7.

Example 6-7. Main.as (client code to remove nodes)

```
package
{
    import flash.display.MovieClip;

    public class Main extends MovieClip
    {
        public function Main()
        {
            var root:Composite = new Composite("root");

            // create a node
            var n1:Composite = new Composite("composite 1");
            n1.add(new Leaf("leaf 1")); // add a child leaf
            n1.add(new Leaf("leaf 2")); // add a child leaf
            root.add(n1); // add node to root as child

            // create another node
            var n2:Composite = new Composite("composite 2");
            n2.add(new Leaf("leaf 3")); // add a child leaf
            n2.add(new Leaf("leaf 4")); // add a child leaf
            n2.add(new Leaf("leaf 5")); // add a child leaf
            root.add(n2); // add node to root as child

            // add a child leaf to the root node
            root.add(new Leaf("leaf 6"));

            root.operation(); // call operation on root node
```

Example 6-7. Main.as (client code to remove nodes) (continued)

```
            trace("display tree");
            trace("============");
            root.operation();

            trace("remove first child of the second child of root");
            trace("=================================================");
            root.getChild(2).remove(root.getChild(2).getChild(1));
            root.operation();

            trace("remove the second child of root");
            trace("===============================");
            root.remove(root.getChild(2));
            root.operation();          }
    }
}
```

Executing the statements in Example 6-7 will generate the following output. The operation( ) method traverses the tree structure recursively using a depth-first approach, and prints the component names accordingly.

```
display tree
============
root
composite 1
leaf 1
leaf 2
composite 2
leaf 3
leaf 4
leaf 5
leaf 6
remove first child of the second child of root
=================================================
root
composite 1
leaf 1
leaf 2
composite 2
leaf 4
leaf 5
leaf 6
remove the second child of root
===============================
root
composite 1
leaf 1
leaf 2
leaf 6
```

You can easily visualize what happens to the component tree by looking at what happens graphically in Figure 6-5.

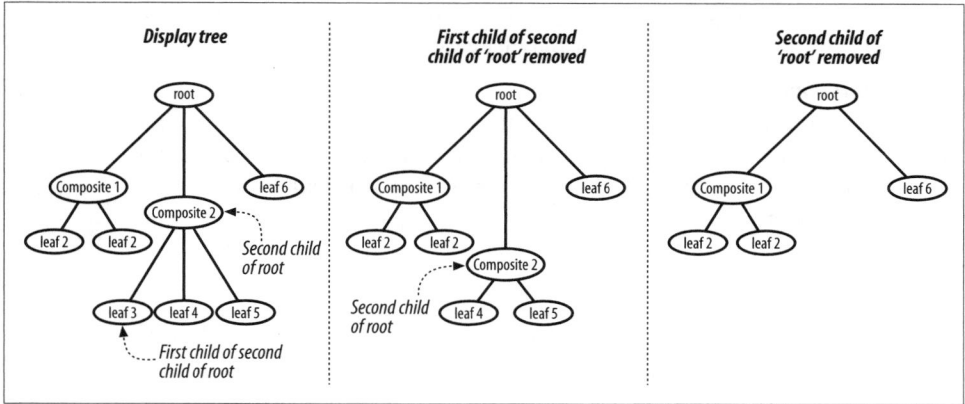

Figure 6-5. Deleting components from the tree structure

Key OOP Concepts in the Composite Pattern

The key OOP concept embedded in the composite pattern is *polymorphism*. Polymorphism can be broadly defined as the ability of objects instantiated from different classes to respond to the same method calls in specific ways. This is possible because the method signature's the same, even though the objects are instantiated from different classes. In short, the methods in the different classes show a common interface to clients.

Since the composite pattern allows clients to treat both leaf and composite nodes the same way through a common interface, it's a good example of polymorphism. This is due to both leaf and composite classes implementing the same component interface by subclassing the abstract component class.

Implementations of operations truly exemplify polymorphism. In the minimalist examples, the operation( ) method was implemented one way in the leaf nodes and another way in the composite nodes. The composite nodes have to forward the operation( ) call to all its child nodes. The operation( ) responds differently in both leaf and composite nodes, but the client doesn't need to know or care about these differences. The client doesn't see the different implementations; it sees only the interface.

Example: Music Playlists

Have you created music playlists in your favorite digital music jukebox? If so, have you taken the next step and embedded playlists inside other playlists to create ever larger playlists? This is a perfect application to implement a composite pattern. A library of digital music contains songs and playlists. A song is a primitive object, while a playlist is a composite object that contains a collection of songs. Let's first create the component class for our playlist example application.

The *Component.as* file (Example 6-8) contains the Component abstract class that defines the interface for both songs and playlists. The *Song.as* file (Example 6-10) contains the Song class, and the *Playlist.as* file (Example 6-9) contains the Playlist class. Both Song and Playlist classes extend the Component class and provide necessary implementations.

Example 6-8. Component.as

```
package
{
    import flash.errors.IllegalOperationError;

    // ABSTRACT Class (should be subclassed and not instantiated)
    public class Component
    {
        public function add(c:Component):void
        {
            throw new IllegalOperationError
                ("add operation not supported");
        }

        public function remove(c:Component):void
        {
            throw new IllegalOperationError
                ("remove operation not supported");
        }

        public function getChild(n:int):Component
        {
            throw new IllegalOperationError
                ("getChild operation not supported");
            return null;
        }

        // ABSTRACT Method (must be overridden in a subclass)
        public function play():void {}
    }
}
```

The Component class defines the abstract interface for both the Song and Playlist classes. It also defines the abstract method play( ).

Example 6-9. Playlist.as

```
package
{
    public class Playlist extends Component
    {

        private var sName:String;
```

Example 6-9. Playlist.as (continued)

```
    private var aChildren:Array;

    public function Playlist(sName:String)
    {
        this.sName = sName;
        this.aChildren = new Array( );
    }

    override public function add(c:Component):void
    {
        aChildren.push(c);
    }

    override public function play( ):void
    {
        trace("Queuing playlist: " + this.sName);
        for each (var c:Component in aChildren)
        {
            c.play( );
        }
    }
    }
}
```

The Playlist class extends the Component class and is almost identical to the composite class in the minimalist example.

Queuing Songs to Play in Sequence

Much of the Song class shown in Example 6-10 deals with queuing songs and handling events. Because songs need to be played in sequence and not simultaneously, several static properties are declared in the class. The soundChannel property is declared as *static* to ensure that only one sound channel is used to play music by all instances of the Song class. This ensures that different song objects don't open multiple sound channels simultaneously to play music. The Song class also declares a static property called aSongQueue, which is an array that holds the list of songs queued to play. Finally, a static property called songPlayingFlag holds a Boolean value that indicates whether a song's currently playing.

Example 6-10. Song.as

```
1  package
2  {
3      import flash.events.*;
4      import flash.media.Sound;
5      import flash.media.SoundChannel;
6      import flash.net.URLRequest;
7
8      public class Song extends Component
9      {
```

Example 6-10. Song.as

```
10          private var sName:String;
11          private var song:Sound;
12          private static var soundChannel:SoundChannel =  new SoundChannel();
13          private static var aSongQueue:Array = [];
14          private static var songPlayingFlag:Boolean = false;
15
16          public function Song(sName:String)
17          {
18              this.sName = sName;
19          }
20
21          override public function play():void
22          {
23              var request:URLRequest = new URLRequest
                    ("music/" + sName);
24              song = new Sound();
25              song.addEventListener(Event.COMPLETE, songLoaded);
26              song.addEventListener(IOErrorEvent.IO_ERROR, loadError);
27              song.load(request);
28          }
29
30          private function songLoaded(event:Event):void
31          {
32              aSongQueue.push(song);
33              playIfIdle();
34          }
35
36          private function loadError(event:Event):void
37          {
38              trace("Error loading song " + this.sName);
39          }
40
41          private function playDone(event:Event):void
42          {
43              songPlayingFlag = false;
44              playIfIdle();
45          }
46
47          private function playIfIdle():void
48          {
49              if (!songPlayingFlag)
50              {
51                  var s:Sound = aSongQueue.shift();
52                  if (s)
53                  {
54                      songPlayingFlag = true;
55                      trace("playing " + s.id3.songName);
56                          // from ID3 tag
57                      soundChannel = s.play();
```

Example 6-10. Song.as

```
58                       soundChannel.addEventListener
                             (Event.SOUND_COMPLETE, this.playDone);
59               }
60            }
61         }
62      }
63  }
```

The filename of the song clip is passed to the parameterized constructor and set to the sName property. The play( ) method loads the songs from a subfolder called *media*. The event handler called songLoaded is registered to listen to the Event.COMPLETE event (line 25). When the song is loaded, the songLoaded( ) method pushes the song into the aSongQueue play queue (line 32). It then calls the playIfIdle( ) method that determines if a song is playing and if not, gets the song from aSongQueue using the Shift function (line 51), starts to play the song, and assigns it to the soundChannel sound channel (line 56). The aSongQueue array functions as a song queue (first-in first-out). The event handler called playDone is registered to listen to the Event.SOUND_COMPLETE event (line 57).

When the sound stops playing, the Event.SOUND_COMPLETE event will trigger the playDone( ) method that calls the playIfIdle( ) method again.

We can now create some playlists and listen to some music.

Building Composite Playlists

Let's develop two playlists and embed them into a larger playlist. The following code should be executed from the document class of a Flash document.

```
// create playlist
var drumlicks:Playlist = new Playlist("drum licks");
drumlicks.add(new Song("bongo.mp3"));
drumlicks.add(new Song("tabla.mp3"));
drumlicks.add(new Song("djembe.mp3"));

// create another playlist
var guitariffs:Playlist = new Playlist("guitar riffs");
guitariffs.add(new Song("acousticguitar.mp3"));
guitariffs.add(new Song("electricguitar.mp3"));

// create composite playlist
var eclectic:Playlist = new Playlist("eclectic");
eclectic.add(drumlicks);
eclectic.add(new Song("balladpiano.mp3"));
eclectic.add(guitariffs);
eclectic.play();
```

The example application will first build the playlist named "drum licks." It will then build another playlist called "guitar riffs." Finally, it will build and play a new playlist called "eclectic" that includes both previous playlists and an additional song. The following text output shows the song play sequence.

```
Queuing playlist: eclectic
Queuing playlist: drum licks
Queuing playlist: guitar riffs
playing bongo
playing tabla
playing djembe
playing ballad piano
playing acoustic guitar
playing electric guitar
```

When the "eclectic" playlist is queued for play, it queues and plays the embedded "drum licks" and "guitar riffs" playlists as well. This is exactly the behavior we expect from our composite playlist structure. You can easily remove songs and playlists by implementing the remove( ) method as shown in the minimalist example.

Example: Animating Composite Objects Using Inverse Kinematics

There are many examples of excellent Flash games that use ActionScript to animate characters on stage. Even a simple animated figure can have independently functioning body parts such as arms and legs that can be animated to jump, run, and kick. Can we develop complex animated figures by treating body parts as composite and component objects? Do we gain an advantage by being able to treat component and composite parts of an animated figure in the same way? Indeed, the composite pattern brings several advantages to animation, as will be evident by the animated snake that will be developed in this example. Figure 6-6 shows a screenshot of the snake that moves by means of inverse kinematics.

Figure 6-6. Snake constructed using a composite pattern

Using Inverse Kinematics

Inverse kinematics is a method by which rigid objects interconnected by joints can move to form different poses. A good example of this type of object is a marionette: a puppet controlled by a puppeteer using strings. The hands and legs of the puppet consist of several parts connected by joints. For example, the upper arm would be connected to the torso at the shoulder. The upper arm would in turn be connected to the forearm through the elbow joint. The hand would be connected to the forearm at the wrist. These interconnected objects form a kinematic chain. Inverse kinematics allows kinematic chains to move, constrained by the range of motion allowed by the joints. The simplest form of a kinematic chain has a free end that's controlled externally. For example, the hand of a marionette would be a free end since it's attached to a puppeteer's string. Because joints connect them, the hand, forearm, and upper arm move when the puppeteer pulls this string. Try this yourself: let your left arm go limp, and pull it up by the hand using your right arm. Notice how the external force is pulling your left hand, which translates the pulling motion to the forearm, which in turn pulls the upper arm. The notion of interconnected objects pulling each other is the primary concept in inverse kinematics. This type of motion is very similar to the motion of the snake application we will develop.

In the example application, users will control the head of the snake using the keyboard. When the head moves, interconnected body segments will move based on inverse kinematic principles. The whole snake will be a kinematic chain.

Kinematic chains consist of one or more kinematic pairs. For example, the upper arm and forearm form a kinematic pair. Adjoining body segments in our snake will also form kinematic pairs. We will develop the snake as a composite object. The head of the snake will be the root node, and body segments will be connected to each other. Each node will be a composite object as they have child objects connected to them. The last segment of the snake, which is the tail (or the rattle for a rattlesnake), will be a component object.

Creating Component and Composite Nodes for the Snake

All our components will be *display objects* on the stage. Therefore we can develop the component class by extending the Sprite class. This allows us to inherit the properties and methods to manipulate components on the stage to make them move and respond to events. Example 6-11 shows the Component class that'll be used to create animated figures. The only difference in this class when compared to previous component classes is that it extends the Sprite class and declares a method called update( ).

Example 6-11. Component.as

```
package
{

    import flash.errors.IllegalOperationError;
    import flash.display.Sprite;

    // ABSTRACT Class (should be subclassed and not instantiated)
    public class Component extends Sprite
    {

        protected var parentNode:Composite = null;

        public function add(c:Component):void
        {
            throw new IllegalOperationError(
                "add operation not supported");
        }

        public function remove(c:Component):void
        {
            throw new IllegalOperationError(
                "remove operation not supported");
        }

        public function getChild(n:int):Component
        {
            throw new IllegalOperationError(
                "getChild operation not supported");
            return null;
        }

        // ABSTRACT Method (must be overridden in a subclass)
        public function update():void {}

        internal function setParent(aParent:Composite):void
        {
            parentNode = aParent;
        }

        public function getParent():Composite
        {
            return parentNode;
        }
    }
}
```

The Composite class shown in Example 6-12 extends the Component class and overrides the update( ) method.

Example 6-12. Composite.as

```
package
{
    public class Composite extends Component
    {
        protected var aChildren:Array;

        public function Composite()
        {
            this.aChildren = new Array();
        }

        override public function add(c:Component):void
        {
            aChildren.push(c);
            c.setParent(this);
        }

        override public function getChild(n:int):Component
        {
            if ((n > 0) && (n <= aChildren.length))
            {
                return aChildren[n-1];
            } else {
                return null;
            }
        }

        override public function update():void
        {
            for each (var c:Component in aChildren)
            {
                c.update();
            }
        }
    }
}
```

Both the Component and Composite classes should behave as abstract classes; they need to be subclassed. We will develop the Head and BodySegment classes that subclass Composite, and the Tail class that subclasses Component to build the snake.

Building the Snake Head

The head of the snake will be the root node of the snake's composite structure. Each component of the snake will consist of a line 20 pixels in length. Example 6-13 shows the Head class, which draws the head of the snake. The constructor receives a color parameter that represents the color of the snake's head.

Example 6-13. Head.as

```
package
{
    public class Head extends Composite
    {
        public function Head(color:uint = 0xC0C0C0)
        {
            graphics.lineStyle(20, color);
            graphics.moveTo(0, 0);
            graphics.lineTo(20, 0);
        }
    }
}
```

The snake's head will be controlled by keyboard events. The next step is to develop the document class that will build the snake, and register keyboard events to control the snake.

Controlling the Snake

Example 6-14 shows the `Main` class that builds the composite snake structure and registers event handler methods to control the snake. As a first step, only the snake's head will be created (lines 18-23). The arrow keys will make the snake head move forward, backward, rotate left, and right. The snake's head will be the free end of the kinematic chain that represents the snake. Just like the puppeteer's string pulling on the marionette's hand, key presses will pull on the snake's head and rotate it.

Example 6-14. Main.as

```
 1  package
 2  {
 3      import flash.display.Sprite;
 4      import flash.events.*;
 5      import flash.geom.*;
 6      import flash.ui.Keyboard;
 7
 8      /**
 9       *    Main Class
10       *    @ purpose:        Document class for movie
11       */
12      public class Main extends Sprite
13      {
14          private var snake:Composite;
15
16          public function Main()
17          {
18              // create snake
19              snake = new Head();
20              snake.x = snake.y = 200;
21
22              // add snake to stage
```

Example 6-14. Main.as

```
23            addChild(snake);
24
25            // register with the stage to receive key press events
26            stage.addEventListener(KeyboardEvent.KEY_DOWN, onKeyPress);
27        }
28
29        private function onKeyPress(event:KeyboardEvent):void
30        {
31            switch (event.keyCode)
32            {
33                case Keyboard.LEFT :
34                    snake.rotation -= 10;
35                    break;
36                case Keyboard.RIGHT :
37                    snake.rotation += 10;
38                    break;
39                case Keyboard.UP :
40                var newFWLocOffset:Point = Point.polar(5, snake.rotation * Math.PI / 180);
41                    snake.x += newFWLocOffset.x;
42                        // move forward by the x offset
43                    snake.y += newFWLocOffset.y;
44                        // move forward by the y offset
45                    break;
46                case Keyboard.DOWN :
47                  var newBKLocOffset:Point = Point.polar(5, snake.rotation * Math.PI / 180);
48                    snake.x -= newBKLocOffset.x;
49                        // move back by the x offset
50                    snake.y -= newBKLocOffset.y;
51                        // move back by the y offset
52                    break;
53            }
54        }
55    }
56 }
```

Line 26 in the Main class (Example 6-14) registers the onKeyPress handler method to respond to Key_DOWN events. The left and right arrow keys make the snake head rotate counter-clockwise and clockwise by 10 degrees. The up and down arrow keys make the snake head move forward or back by 5 pixels. The Point.polar method comes in handy here, as the snake needs to move in the direction that it's facing (rotation angle). The Point.polar() method returns a point that is the distance and angle from the origin (0, 0). Adding the coordinates of this point (x and y properties of the Point class) to the current location gives us the new location.

Before developing the body segments of the snake, we need to explore how a kinematic chain works.

Moving a Kinematic Pair

As discussed before, our snake will be a composite object consisting of several connected components that represent a kinematic chain. Kinematic chains are composed of kinematic pairs: two rigid segments connected by a joint. How do kinematic pairs move and orient themselves? The basic idea is that the parent segment pulls the child segment. In a simple kinematic pair, the only restriction on movement is the joint. Because it's the free end, the parent segment will move and rotate independent of the child. The child will strive to rotate and orient itself to face the joint, and move to keep up with its parent.

Figure 6-7 shows a four-step sequence by which a parent segment will pull a child in a kinematic pair. Even though the parent pulls, the child segment does all the work.

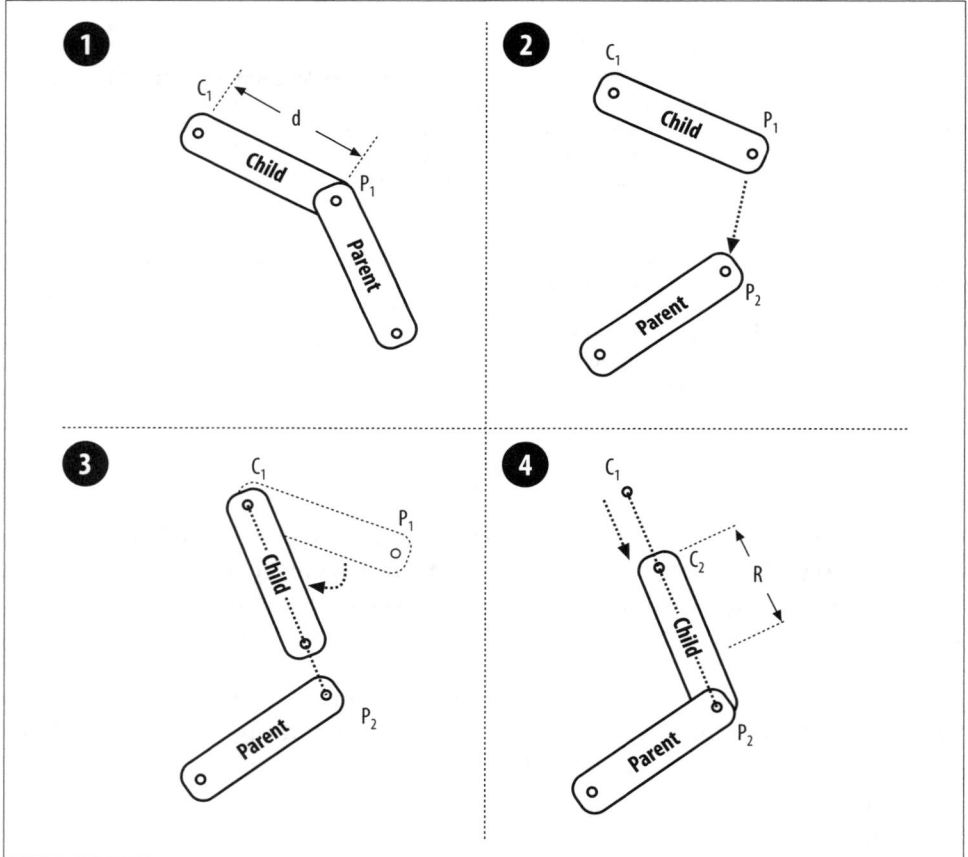

Figure 6-7. Child segment keeping up with parent in a kinematic pair

The following steps relate to Figure 6-7.

1. Initial condition where the kinematic pair consists of two line segments. The registration point of the segments is at the beginning of the lines (C1 for the child and P1 for the parent). The distance between the registration point of the child C1 and the joint is *d*.

2. Parent segment moves to position P2 and rotates (independent of the child segment).

3. Child segment rotates to orient itself to point to the joint.

4. Child segment moves towards point P2 to maintain distance *d*.

There is some trigonometry involved in this whole process. However, we will use the built-in Point class methods to accomplish much of the rotation and motion. We can now build the body segments for the snake.

Building the Body and Tail Segments

We didn't have to worry about inverse kinematic motion for the snake head as it was the root node of the composite structure. Head motion was controlled by the keyboard. However, the body segments that'll be attached to the head have to move as kinematic pairs. Example 6-15 shows the BodySegment class. It's a composite object and extends the Composite class shown in Example 6-12. The constructor draws the body segment, and the update( ) method is overridden to implemented inverse kinematic motion.

Example 6-15. BodySegment.as

```
 1  package
 2  {
 3      import flash.geom.Point;
 4
 5      public class BodySegment extends Composite
 6      {
 7          private var segLen:Number = 20;
 8
 9          public function BodySegment(color:uint = 0xC0C0C0)
10          {
11              graphics.lineStyle(10, color); // grey color
12              graphics.moveTo(0, 0);
13              graphics.lineTo(segLen, 0);
14          }
15
16          override public function update( ):void
17          {
18              var myParent:Composite = this.getParent( );
19              var parentLoc:Point = new Point(myParent.x, myParent.y);
20              var myLoc:Point = new Point(this.x, this.y);
21
22              // rotate to orient to parents new location
```

Example 6-15. BodySegment.as

```
23            var tempPoint:Point = parentLoc.subtract(myLoc);
24            var angle:Number = Math.atan2(tempPoint.y, tempPoint.x);
25            this.rotation = angle * 180 / Math.PI;
26
27            // move to maintain distance
28            var currentDistance:Number = Point.distance(
29                parentLoc, myLoc);
30            var myNewLoc:Point = Point.interpolate(myLoc, parentLoc,
                                        segLen / currentDistance);
31            this.x = myNewLoc.x;
32            this.y = myNewLoc.y;
33
34            super.update();
35        }
36    }
37 }
```

The update( ) method implements steps three and four described in Figure 6-7. Lines 18-20 access the current component's parent and create two points that represent C1 and P2 in step 3 of Figure 6-7.

Lines 22-25 calculate the new angle for the child component, so that it can orient to the new location of the joint. Subtracting point C1 from P2 in step 3 of Figure 6-7 provides a point whose x and y properties represent the horizontal and vertical distance between the two points. Thus the new angle of rotation for the child can be easily calculated by feeding these values to the arctangent function. Note that the Math.atan2 function returns the angle in *radians*. This has to be converted to *degrees* before assigning to the rotation property.

Lines 27-31 move the now correctly oriented child segment to maintain the joint and registration point distance (shown as *d* in step 3 of Figure 6-7). The current distance between points C1 and P2 is calculated first (line 28). Next, the Point.interpolate function is used to determine the intermediate point C2 that would maintain the correct segment length *d*. The third parameter in the Point.interpolate function is a ratio value (between 0 and 1) that represents a point between two points.

Finally, the update( ) method calls itself in the superclass (line 33) to update its child components.

The tail component, the last segment of the snake, is shown in Example 6-16. The Tail class subclasses Component (Example 6-11), draws the tail in its constructor, and implements the update( ) method. The tail is drawn as a rattle, transforming our generic snake into a rattlesnake. Unlike the BodySegment class, the update( ) method does not call itself in the superclass, as the tail is a component that can't have any children.

Example 6-16. Tail.as

```
package
{
    import flash.geom.Point;

    public class Tail extends Component
    {

        private var segLen:Number = 20;

        public function Tail(color:uint = 0xC0C0C0)
        {
            graphics.lineStyle(10, color);
            graphics.moveTo(0, 0);
            graphics.lineTo(segLen, 0);
            graphics.lineStyle(3, 0x000000);
            for (var i:uint = 1; i < 4; i++)
            {
                graphics.moveTo(i * 5, -5);
                graphics.lineTo(i * 5, 5);
            }
        }

        override public function update( ):void
        {
            var myParent:Composite = this.getParent( );
            var parentLoc:Point = new Point(myParent.x, myParent.y);
            var myLoc:Point = new Point(this.x, this.y);

            // rotate to orient to parents new location
            var tempPoint:Point = parentLoc.subtract(myLoc);
            var angle:Number = Math.atan2(tempPoint.y, tempPoint.x);
            this.rotation = angle * 180 / Math.PI;

            // move to maintain distance
            var currentDistance:Number = Point.distance(
                parentLoc, myLoc);
            var myNewLoc:Point = Point.interpolate(myLoc, parentLoc,
                segLen / currentDistance);
            this.x = myNewLoc.x;
            this.y = myNewLoc.y;
        }
    }
}
```

You may be wondering why the update( ) method was not implemented in the Component class. We implemented the most basic form of inverse kinematics in this case. Our snake is a real contortionist and is able to freely rotate around its joints. The real power of inverse kinematics is realized when limiting angles are introduced. Limiting angles bring constraints to joint rotation, just like the elbow joint restricts the angle of motion of the forearm. Introducing different limiting angles will make the update( ) method implementations unique for different segments. Therefore, declaring it as *abstract* in the Component class makes sense. We can now draw the whole snake.

Building the Composite Snake

Example 6-17 shows the updated constructor of the Main class from Example 6-14 that constructs the whole snake. Lines 10- 25 add the body segments to the snake in black and gray alternating colors. Finally, the tail component is added in lines 26 through 28. The update( ) method is called once (line 30) to fit and display all components on the stage as they're initially placed offscreen (line 22). The completed snake should look like Figure 6-6.

Example 6-17. Updated constructor in Main.as

```
 1 public function Main( )
 2 {
 3     // create snake
 4     snake = new Head( );
 5     snake.x = snake.y = 200;
 6
 7     // add snake to stage
 8     addChild(snake);
 9
10     // add multiple body segments
11     var parentNode:Composite = snake;
12     var color:uint;
13     for (var i:uint = 0; i < 10; i++)
14     {
15         if (i % 2) {
16             color = 0x000000; // black
17         } else {
18             color = 0xC0C0C0; // grey
19         }
20         var segment:Composite = new BodySegment(color);
21         parentNode.add(segment);
22         segment.x = segment.y = -50; // place it off screen
23         addChild(segment);
24         parentNode = segment;
25     }
26     var tail:Component = new Tail( );
27     addChild(tail);
28     parentNode.add(tail); // add rattle
29
30     snake.update( ); // to fit the segments together
31
32     // register with the stage to receive key press events
33     stage.addEventListener(KeyboardEvent.KEY_DOWN, onKeyPress);
34 }
```

Note how the snake is constructed using the composite pattern, by adding children to parent nodes. Construction is very straightforward as component and composite nodes are added the same way. The tail is added by calling the same add( ) method as you would a composite body segment. In addition, the update( ) method cascades down seamlessly through the structure to animate the snake. Here again, we don't need to call separate update methods or differentiate between component and composite objects. Even though our simple snake had only a single kinematic chain, this application can be extended to incorporate multiple kinematic chains and multiple children attached to the same parent. The construction of the structure and the update( ) call would not get any more complicated than this.

Using Flash's Built-in Composite Structure: the Display List

In the previous example, we extended the Sprite class to develop composite structures that display on stage. We first add the object to the composite structure, and subsequently add it to the *display list* using the addChild( ) method. What's the display list in ActionScript 3.0 applications? The display list is a tree structure with the *stage* as its root node. It consists of all the visible elements that'll be displayed on the stage. The display list consists of two types of objects: (1) display objects and (2) display object containers. Every element that appears on the stage is a type of *display object*. In contrast, *display object containers* not only have a visual representation on the stage, they can also have other display objects, and display object containers as children.

Close examination of the inheritance structure of the Sprite class will show two classes called DisplayObject and DisplayObjectContainer in its inheritance hierarchy.

The DisplayObject class consists of methods and properties that deal mainly with the visual presentation of an object such as the x and y properties that represent its position. The DisplayObjectContainer class inherits from DisplayObject, defines necessary properties, and implements methods to handle child objects (see the ActionScript 3.0 documentation for more detail). Some of the child handling methods implemented by the DisplayObjectContainer class are listed below.

```
addChild(child:DisplayObject):DisplayObject;
getChildAt(index:int):DisplayObject;
removeChild(child:DisplayObject):DisplayObject;
```

The display list is indeed a composite structure with the DisplayObject and DisplayObjectContainer representing the component and composite classes.

Both DisplayObject and DisplayObjectContainer are abstract classes and cannot be instantiated directly. We have to either extend these classes to define unique components or use the classes that inherit from them. The Shape and Bitmap classes extend the `DisplayObject` class. The more commonly used `Sprite` class extends `DisplayObjectContainer`, and is the preferred base class for composite objects.

The obvious question then is whether we can leverage the child handling methods in the `DisplayObjectContainer` class without having to re-implement them. We can indeed, and will develop a composite airplane to show how in some cases, it's better to use the built-in child-handling methods.

Creating a Composite Airplane

Figure 6-8 shows the composite airplane that will be developed in this example. We will leverage the *display list* to build the visual components. The utility of the composite pattern will be demonstrated by automatically calculating the weight of the total aircraft, by adding up component weights. In addition, the composite pattern implementation will help keep track of damage to each component, and figure out the overall damage to the aircraft. You will also see how particular components can be removed from the structure when damage exceeds a certain amount using the built-in methods of the `DisplayObjectContainer` class.

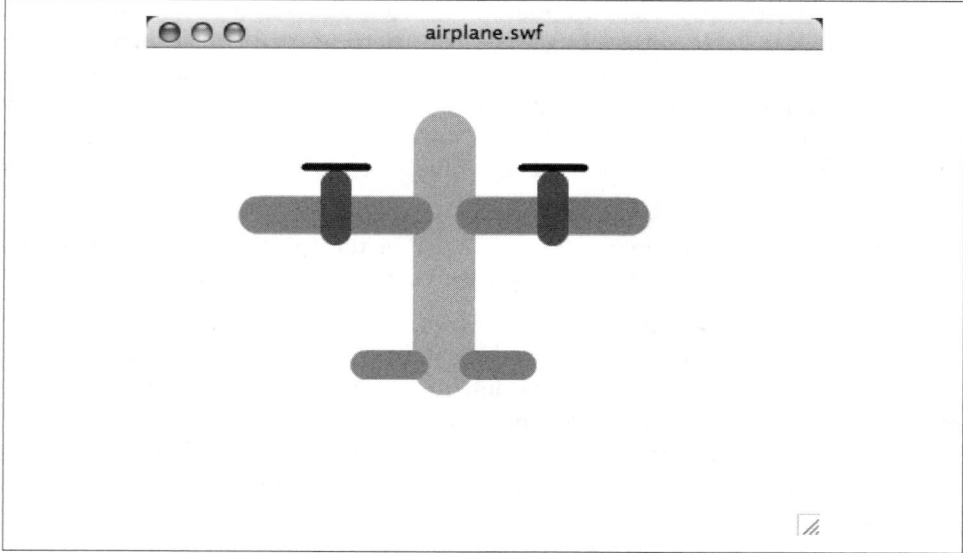

Figure 6-8. Twin-engine composite airplane (top-down view)

Developing the Component and Composite Classes for the Airplane

Because we will use the built-in methods of the `DisplayObjectContainer` class to manipulate child objects, the component and composite classes are simple to implement. We need only to define the *operations* for the composite structure. The first step is to define an interface for the operations supported by the airplane.

Example 6-18 shows the IPlane interface. It defines two operations, getDamage( )and getWeight( ), that return the weight and damage.

Example 6-18. IPlane.as

```
package
{
    public interface IPlane
    {
        function getDamage():Number;
        function getWeight():Number;
    }
}
```

Example 6-19 shows the component class for the airplane. It extends the Shape class and implements the IPlane interface. As explained previously, Shape subclasses the DisplayObject class. The constructor takes the weight and initial damage parameters, and assigns them to the nWeight and nDamage properties. The implementation for getWeight( ) and getDamage( ) is to simply return the requested property, as components do not have children.

Example 6-19. Component.as

```
package
{
    import flash.display.Shape;

    public class Component extends Shape implements IPlane
    {
        protected var nDamage:Number;
        protected var nWeight:Number;

        public function Component(weight:Number, damage:Number = 0)
        {
            this.nDamage = damage;
            this.nWeight = weight;
        }

        public function getDamage():Number
        {
            return nDamage;
        }

        public function getWeight():Number
        {
            return nWeight;
        }
    }
}
```

It is important to note that the Shape class doesn't inherit from the InteractiveObject class. Therefore, airplane component class cannot respond to user input such as mouse clicks and key presses.

Example 6-20 shows the composite class for the airplane. It extends the `Sprite` class and implements the `IPlane` interface. The `Sprite` class extends the `DisplayObjectContainer` class that inherits from `DisplayObject`. Therefore, our implementation follows the composite pattern framework. The significant difference between the composite and component classes is the implementation of operations. In the `Composite` class, both the `getWeight()` and `getDamage()` methods iterate across all their children, and return the aggregate weight and damage for the composite branch of the hierarchical tree. We do not have to implement any of the child handling methods, as they are inherited from the `DisplayObjectContainer` class.

Example 6-20. Composite.as

```
package
{
    import flash.display.*;

    public class Composite extends Sprite implements IPlane
    {
        protected var nDamage:Number;
        protected var nWeight:Number;

        public function Composite(weight:Number, damage:Number = 0)
        {
            this.nDamage = damage;
            this.nWeight = weight;
        }

        public function getDamage():Number
        {
            var localDamage:Number = nDamage;
            for (var i:uint = 0; i < this.numChildren; i++)
            {
                var child:DisplayObject = this.getChildAt(i);
                localDamage += IPlane(child).getDamage();
            }
            return localDamage;
        }

        public function getWeight():Number
        {
            var localWeight:Number = nWeight;
            for (var i:uint = 0; i < this.numChildren; i++)
            {
                var child:DisplayObject = this.getChildAt(i);
                localWeight += IPlane(child).getWeight();
            }
            return localWeight;
        }
    }
}
```

Unlike the Shape class, Sprite does inherit from InteractiveObject. Therefore, composite components in the airplane can respond to user interface events. We can now develop the component and composite classes that make up the airplane.

Creating the Fuselage, Wings, and Engines

Now that the Component and Composite classes have been developed, we can create the nodes that make up the airplane. Example 6-21 through Example 6-24 show the Fuselage, MainWing, TailWing, and Engine classes. The Fuselage and MainWing classes represent composite nodes that hold other components and extend the Composite class (see Example 6-20). The TailWing and Engine classes are leaf nodes and extend the Component class (see Example 6-19). The implementation of all these subclasses is very similar to each other. The component is drawn with simple lines, using the graphics property of the DisplayObject class. The first parameter of the constructor method is the weight, and the second is the initial damage (defaults to zero). Note the call to the superclass constructor using the super keyword in the last line of the constructor. This ensures proper initialization of properties defined in the superclass.

Example 6-21. Fuselage.as

```
package
{
    import flash.events.*;

    public class Fuselage extends Composite
    {
        public function Fuselage(weight:Number, damage:Number = 0)
        {
            graphics.lineStyle(40, 0xC0C0C0);
            graphics.moveTo(0, 0);
            graphics.lineTo(0, 150);
            super(weight, damage);
        }
    }
}
```

Example 6-22. MainWing.as

```
package
{
    public class MainWing extends Composite
    {
        public function MainWing(weight:Number, damage:Number = 0)
        {
            graphics.lineStyle(25, 0x999999);
            graphics.moveTo(0, 0);
            graphics.lineTo(100, 0);
            super(weight, damage);
        }
    }
}
```

Example 6-23. TailWing.as

```
package
{
    public class TailWing extends Component
    {
        public function TailWing(weight:Number, damage:Number = 0)
        {
            graphics.lineStyle(20, 0x999999);
            graphics.moveTo(0, 0);
            graphics.lineTo(30, 0);
            super(weight, damage);
        }
    }
}
```

Example 6-24. Engine.as

```
package
{
    public class Engine extends Component
    {
        public function Engine(weight:Number, damage:Number = 0)
        {
            graphics.lineStyle(20, 0x666666);
            graphics.moveTo(0, 0);
            graphics.lineTo(0, 30);
            graphics.lineStyle(5, 0x000000);
            graphics.moveTo(-20, -12);
            graphics.lineTo(20, -12);
            super(weight, damage);
        }
    }
}
```

Even though our airplane is a simple line drawing (to reduce complexity), it's possible to create the airplane components using high fidelity graphic images loaded from external files.

Building the Composite Structure

Figure 6-9 shows the hierarchical composite structure of the airplane. The fuselage and main wings are composite nodes. The fuselage contains two main wings and two tail wings. Each main wing contains an engine.

Example 6-25 shows the Main class that builds the composite airplane structure. This should be specified as the *document class* of the Flash document. The plane is displayed in top-down view, as shown in Figure 6-8. The build procedure is very straightforward. Each component is instantiated and positioned relative to its parent by assigning values to its x and y parameters. The component is then added to its parent composite node using the addChild( ) method. The airPlane variable refer-

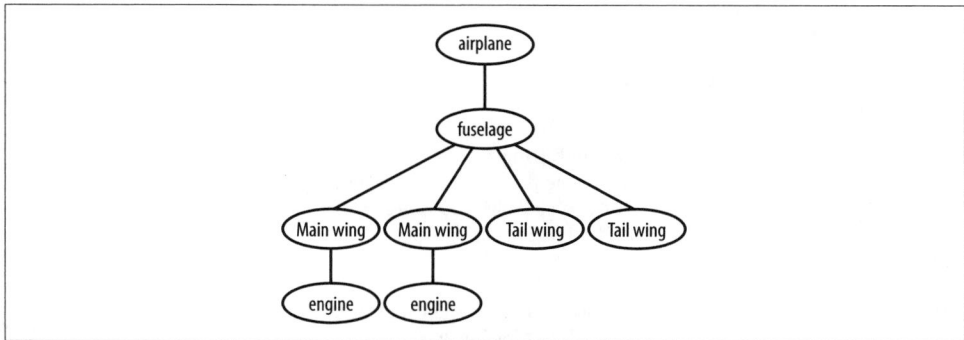

Figure 6-9. Hierarchical tree structure of the airplane

ences the root node of the airplane. The whole composite plane structure plane is then added to the display object container linked to the Main class (line 18). Because the Main class is the *document class* of the Flash document, the airplane is added to the *stage*, which is the root node of the display list.

Example 6-25. Main.as

```
 1 package
 2 {
 3     import flash.display.Sprite;
 4
 5     /**
 6      *    Main Class
 7      *    @ purpose:        Document class for movie
 8      */
 9     public class Main extends Sprite
10     {
11         private var airPlane:Composite;
12
13         public function Main( )
14         {
15             // create airplane
16             airPlane = new Composite(0.0);
17             airPlane.x = 250; airPlane.y = 100;
18             addChild(airPlane);
19
20             // add fuselage
21             var fuselage:Composite = new Fuselage(1000, 0)
22             airPlane.addChild(fuselage);
23
24             // add main wing on the left (port side)
25             var rightWing:Composite = new MainWing(200, 0);
26             rightWing.x = 20; rightWing.y = 50;
27             fuselage.addChild(rightWing);
28
29             // add main wing on the right (starbord side)
30             var leftWing:Composite = new MainWing(200, 0);
```

Example 6-25. Main.as (continued)

```
31            leftWing.scaleX = -1; // flip on vertical axis
32            leftWing.x = -20; leftWing.y = 50;
33            fuselage.addChild(leftWing);
34
35            // add engine to right wing
36            var rightEngine:Component = new Engine(300, 0);
37            rightEngine.x = 50; rightEngine.y = -20;
38            rightWing.addChild(rightEngine);
39
40            // add engine to left wing
41            var lefttEngine:Component = new Engine(300, 0);
42            lefttEngine.x = 50; lefttEngine.y = -20;
43            leftWing.addChild(lefttEngine);
44
45            // add tail wing on the right
46            var leftTailWing:Component = new TailWing(50, 0);
47            leftTailWing.scaleX = -1; // flip on vertical axis
48            leftTailWing.x = -20; leftTailWing.y = 150;
49            fuselage.addChild(leftTailWing);
50
51            // add tail wing on the left
52            var rightTailWing:Component = new TailWing(50, 0);
53            rightTailWing.x = 20; rightTailWing.y = 150;
54            fuselage.addChild(rightTailWing);
55
56            trace('Weight of airplane: ' + airPlane.getWeight());
57                //total weight
58        }
59     }
60 }
```

Calculating the Total Weight of the Airplane

Line 56 of the Main class shown in Example 6-25 calls the getWeight() method on the root node of the airplane. The following output is the result of this statement.

```
Weight of airplane: 2100
```

The getWeight() method calculates the weight iteratively by adding the weights of all components in the airplane structure. This is a very powerful way of keeping track of an overall parameter in a complex composite structure. If this airplane were used in a game, the weight is essential to craft realistic movement dynamics using motion physics. The weight of the plane can change dynamically. For example, the plane could be carrying passengers, bombs, and a fuel tank. Adding passengers will increase weight; dropping bombs will reduce weight, and flight will progressively reduce weight by using up fuel. The getWeight() method will work exactly the same way if we extend the airplane to add and remove other components such as passengers, fuel, etc.

Modifying Components to Reflect Damage

We will modify the composite components of the airplane to increase their damage property when clicked by the mouse. In a realistic game scenario, the source of damage will be bullets, missiles and random malfunctions in components. However, in the interest of keeping things simple, we'll imagine that a mouse click is a bullet hit. In Example 6-26 we will modify the Fuselage (Example 6-21) and MainWing (Example 6-22) classes to respond to mouse clicks.

Example 6-26. Fuselage.as with modifiedFuselage class

```
1  package
2  {
3      import flash.events.*;
4
5      public class Fuselage extends Composite
6      {
7          public function Fuselage(weight:Number, damage:Number = 0)
8          {
9              graphics.lineStyle(40, 0xC0C0C0);
10             graphics.moveTo(0, 0);
11             graphics.lineTo(0, 150);
12
13             addEventListener(MouseEvent.CLICK, doDamage);
14
15             super(weight, damage);
16         }
17
18         private function doDamage(evt:Event)
19         {
20             this.nDamage += 10;
21             trace('Damage to the fuselage is now ' + this.nDamage);
22             evt.stopPropagation(); // stop event propegation
23                 // to subsequent nodes
24         }
25     }
26 }
```

Line 13, in the modified Fuselage class constructor (Example 6-26), registers the doDamage( ) method to receive mouse click events. The doDamage( ) method simply increments the nDamage property defined in the superclass by 10. The stopPropagation( ) event call in line 22 is important to isolate event responses to embedded display objects such as this. If not, the event would propagate up the display list running other registered click event handlers in parent nodes. This statement ensures that the lowermost registered node in the clicked branch of the display list hierarchy handles the event. The ActionScript 3.0 documentation has more details on event propagation. In Example 6-27, we will now modify the MainWing class to exhibit similar behavior.

Example 6-27. MainWing.as with modifiedMainWing class

```
 1  package
 2  {
 3      import flash.events.*;
 4
 5      public class MainWing extends Composite
 6      {
 7          public function MainWing(weight:Number, damage:Number = 0)
 8          {
 9              graphics.lineStyle(25, 0x999999);
10              graphics.moveTo(0, 0);
11              graphics.lineTo(100, 0);
12
13              addEventListener(MouseEvent.CLICK, doDamage);
14
15              super(weight, damage);
16          }
17
18          private function doDamage(evt:Event)
19          {
20              this.nDamage += 20;
21              trace('Damage to this wing is now ' + this.nDamage);
22              if (this.nDamage > 50)
23              {
24                  trace('Wing detached from fuselage - fatal crash!');
25                  parent.removeChild(this);
26              }
27              evt.stopPropagation();
28                  // stop event propegation to subsequent nodes
29          }
30      }
31  }
```

Example 6-27 shows the modified MainWing class. Note the conditional statement in lines 22- 26. If the damage exceeds 50, this node removes itself from the display list (and the airplane composite structure) by calling removeChild in its parent. Before we can test our modified components, a few changes to the Main class are necessary to display total damage.

Calculating Total Damage to the Airplane

In the interests of keeping the example simple, we will register a mouse click handler called showDamage to the *stage* to display the total damage to the airplane. The following statement needs to be added at the end of the constructor in the Main class shown in Example 6-25.

```
stage.addEventListener(MouseEvent.CLICK, showDamage);
```

In addition, the following showDamage event handler method should be added to the Main class as well.

```
private function showDamage(evt:Event)
{
    trace('Total damage: ' + airPlane.getDamage());
}
```

Clicking on the stage will display the total damage to the airplane in the output panel. Likewise, clicking on either the fuselage or main wings will display the current damage to each of those components. The following output is a result of several clicks.

```
Damage to this wing is now 20          // clicked on right wing
Damage to this wing is now 40          // clicked on right wing
Damage to the fuselage is now 10       // clicked on fuselage
Damage to the fuselage is now 20       // clicked on fuselage
Damage to this wing is now 20          // clicked on left wing
Total damage: 80                       // clicked on stage
Damage to this wing is now 60          // clicked on right wing
Wing detached from fuselage - fatal crash!
```

The right wing was removed from the display list as its damage was more than 50. Ideally, the wing should not disappear, but drop off. If each component had additional routines for autonomous motion, then the wing component could have been removed from the fuselage and then added to the stage as a child, where it would fall off due to gravity and other simulated physical effects.

Leveraging the display list in ActionScript 3.0 to develop composite structures has many advantages because of its seamless integration with the Flash document object model. This method is preferable only when the composite object is rigid—when all component parts move with the larger whole. The airplane is a rigid body, even though it consists of several components. Assigning values to the x and y parameters of the root node will move the whole airplane. However, this method is not suitable when components move independent of each other as they did with the snake application. In the snake, the location of component nodes was not dependent on the location of the root node, but on their immediate parent. Additional geometric transformation would be required if its composite structure was implemented using the display list.

Summary

The composite pattern allows you to build complex systems that are made up of several smaller components. The components that make up the system may be individual components or containers that represent collections of components. The primary advantage of the composite pattern is that it allows clients to treat both individual components (leaf nodes) and composite components (composite nodes) the same way through a common interface. This pattern has particular utility in ActionScript, as the display list already implements the composite pattern, allowing developers to easily build and manipulate complex display objects.

PART IV

Behavioral Patterns

People's behavior makes sense if you think about it in terms of their goals, needs, and motives.

—Thomas Mann

Behavior which appears superficially correct but is intrinsically corrupt always irritates those who see below the surface.

—James Bryant Conant (An observation prompted by forgetting to implement one of an interface's methods.)

Insofar as international law is observed, it provides us with stability and order and with a means of predicting the behavior of those with whom we have reciprocal legal obligations.

—J. William Fulbright (Explanation of why you probably should avoid global variables when developing design patterns.)

There was no difference between the behavior of a god and the operations of pure chance.

—Thomas Pynchon (Description of an attempt to debug a program.)

Behavioral patterns focus on the interaction between classes and objects, and the distribution of responsibility. These patterns describe both the patterns of classes and objects and the communication between them. More than some of the other patterns, you will find a division of labor for the Behavioral design patterns. Rather than having a class doing all the work, tasks are more likely to be encapsulated and then used by the class or between classes. As a result, you'll find that these patterns tend to consider algorithms and the assignment of responsibilities between objects. Figure Part IV-1 illustrates this general idea.

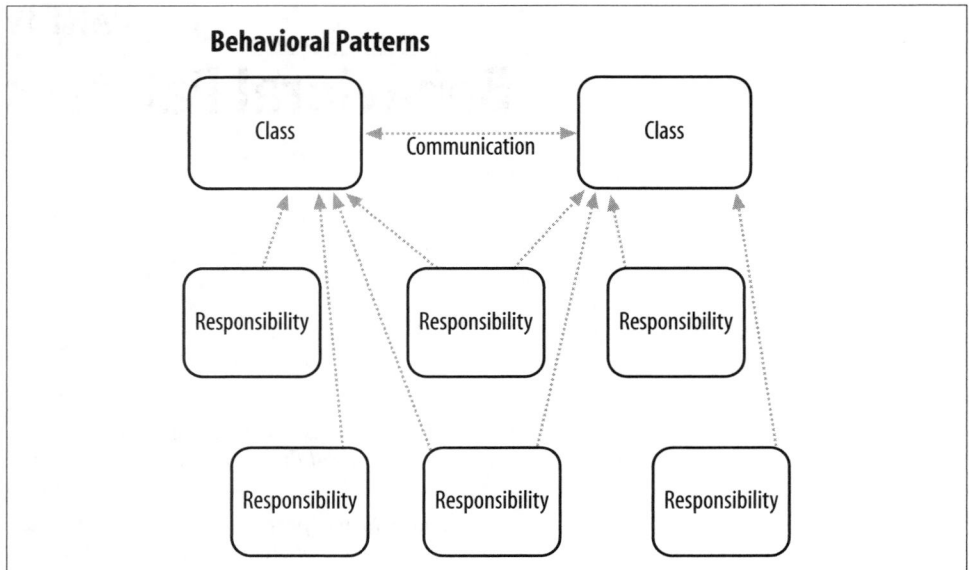

Figure Part IV-1. Behavioral patterns allocate responsibilities

The key to the Behavioral patterns is the allocation of responsibilities through either inheritance or object composition. First, only the *Template* design pattern in this section actually distributes responsibilities through inheritance. It's a simple pattern using an abstract class for the general outline of an algorithm, with the subclasses taking up the more detailed aspects. Second, and far more common among Behavioral patterns, is the use of object composition to allocate and distribute responsibilities. The *Command, Observer, State* and *Strategy* patterns all employ the object composition for distribution of tasks among the patterns classes and objects.

CHAPTER 7

Command Pattern

To command is to serve, nothing more and nothing less.
—Andre Malraux

When you do the common things in life in an uncommon way, you will command the attention of the world.
—George Washington Carver

Create like a god, command like a king, work like a slave.
—Constantin Brancusi

What Is the Command Pattern?

The command pattern allows a client to issue requests to an object without making any assumptions about the request, or the receiving object. Think of the request as a command sent to an object to engage in a known behavior. The straightforward way to do this would be to create an instance of the object, and call the method that implements the required command (or behavior). For example, let's assume that we're building a house that allows computer control of many of its components such as lights, doors, heating, etc. Let's look at the code that would turn on a light bulb. The Light class implements a method called on( ) that turns on a light. A client would execute the following code to turn the light on.

```
var light = new Light( );
light.on( );
```

Let's look at another command to open a door. In this case, the *receiver* of the command is an instance of the Door class, which implements a method called open( ) that opens the front door.

```
var frontdoor = new Door( );
frontdoor.open( );
```

Notice the tight coupling between the client and the receivers. By coupling, we mean the degree to which one section of code relies on another section. The client is tightly bound not only to the receiver classes (Light and Door), but to particular methods (on( ) and open( )) in those classes as well. This is not a good situation if we want to have a flexible system that allows future expansion.

What would happen if we replace our ordinary front door with a new sliding door? What if the new class that controls the door is called SlidingDoor, and the method in the class that opens the door is called slideOpen( )? We have to modify the code in the client to refer to the new receiver class. Avoid getting into situations that require modifying existing code. In addition, this new situation can require modifications in multiple places. For example, if the front door was controlled from two locations, a wall mounted control panel with buttons assigned to each controlled device and a handheld remote control (like a TV remote), changing the receiver class for the front door would require code changes in both control devices. Also, you couldn't reassign the buttons on the control to a different layout, as the control code is hard-coded to each button.

To have a flexible and extensible system, commands need to be assigned to buttons on the controls without explicitly specifying the receiver or the specific method in the receiver. This would decouple the client from the receiver, but how can we do this? It seems counterintuitive at first, but we need to encapsulate both the receiver and the receiving method in a command object. By encapsulation, we mean hiding the receiver and its method from where they're called. Let's look at a non-technical example to figure out what a command object looks like.

Mom Needs to Issue Some Commands

Parents assign household chores for children to keep them occupied in their younger years. Getting children to do their fair share of household work is a good thing anyway. Asking the children to do something is easy to do – just ask them. However, whether they do the assigned task is a different matter altogether. In our example, we're dealing with a model bunch of kids who are really conscientious and do their assigned tasks without raising a fuss. Let's assume that mom assigns the tasks for each person in the household. However, mom has to leave for a day on a business trip, and won't be around to assign tasks verbally. Mom needs to formalize a procedure to assign daily tasks for this and future instances when she will be away. This is a good opportunity to implement a command pattern structure.

Mom has several household chores in mind. She decides to write short notes for each task and assign them to a child. Dad will be the person who looks at each note and conveys what needs to be done to each child. Because Dad is notorious for losing reminders and notes, Mom makes the task notes more official and portable by putting each note into an envelope. This is analogous to a *command interface*, which is simply an interface that declares a method (generally called execute) that does some task. Figure 7-1 shows the household equivalent of a command interface. Mom's command interface is a note with the operative word "do," which will eventually describe what chore needs to be done, and who will do it.

Figure 7-1. Mom's command interface

Mom creates several *concrete commands* that conform to the *command interface* for the household tasks that need to be done while she is away. She puts notes, assigning each task to a different person, inside four envelopes. When the envelopes are sealed, it's not possible to tell which kid's responsibility it is to do the tasks, or even what tasks are enclosed in the envelopes. All we know is that the envelope contains a task. Therefore, the receiver and the task are hidden or *encapsulated* within the envelope.

Figure 7-2 shows Mom's concrete commands that implement her command interface declared in Figure 7-1. The four concrete commands: John will *load the dishwasher*, Jane will *walk the dog*, Jack will *do the laundry*, and Dad will *clean the garage* (Dad won't know what hit him). Mom has assigned each task to the person most appropriate to carry it out. She knows that Jane is the best person to walk the dog, as Brutus is on his best behavior when Jane is around. Dad is the best person to clean the garage, as it is his mess in the first place, and so on and so forth.

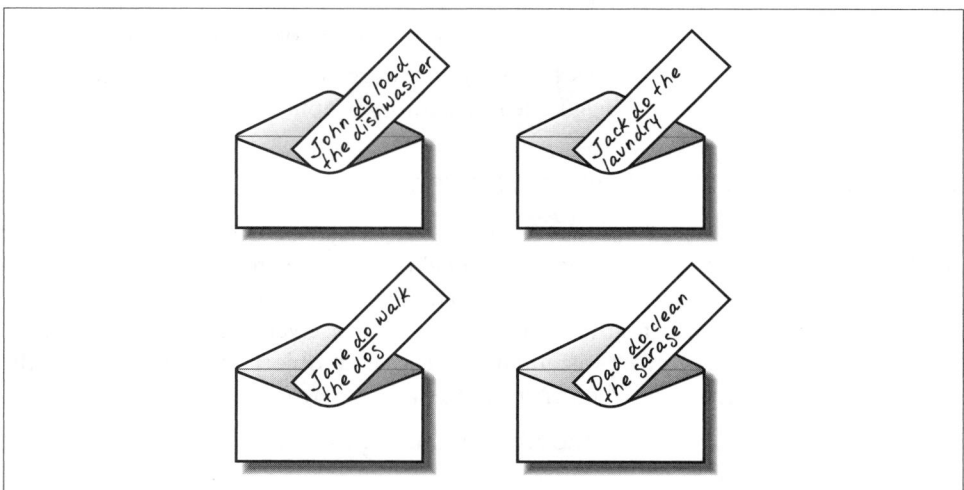

Figure 7-2. Household equivalent of concrete commands

Each envelope encapsulates a particular behavior that's assigned to a particular receiver. The envelopes, being very portable objects, can be simply given to someone (Dad) who will ask the assigned person to execute the indicated task. Mom hands the sealed envelopes to Dad, who will perform the task of *invoker*. He will hang on to each envelope until it's time to execute the tasks. Dad doesn't know what tasks the envelopes contain or who will execute the tasks or how they will do it. All he knows to do is open the sealed envelop and read the *do* instructions -"John *do* load the dishwasher" and "Jack *do* the laundry," etc. We have now decoupled the *receiver* and the *methods* that execute the task in the receiver by encapsulating both within a *command object* that is a sealed envelope. The *command object* is the envelope that hides both the receiver and the task.

It's time to do the assigned tasks when Dad brings the kids home from school. He opens each envelope, calls out the assigned tasks to each child, and then goes on to do his assigned task (mumbling to himself). Dad has no idea how the kids are doing their assigned tasks. Jane rides her bike while walking the dog. John asks his friend Mike to help him load the dishwasher. How each *receiver* executes its job is not the concern of the *invoker*.

Key Features of the Command Pattern

The primary usefulness of the command pattern is the flexibility and extensibility it affords when defining behavior in applications.

- The command pattern encapsulates behavior in a portable command object.
- The command pattern decouples the classes and which methods in those classes execute required behavior from the location where the behavior is called.
- The command pattern allows a client to dynamically create new behavior by creating new command objects and assigning them to invokers at runtime.
- The command pattern allows for straightforward implementation of command chaining, undo, redo and logging features into an application.

Class Diagram of the Command Pattern

The Command class (Figure 7-3) is an interface that declares, at a minimum, a single method called execute( ). The ConcreteCommand classes implement the Command interface. There can be multiple concrete commands. Concrete commands usually have *parameterized constructors* that take an instance of a receiver class to implement the required behavior. The client instantiates a Receiver object and passes it to the ConcreteCommand constructor when creating a new concrete command.

The ConcreteCommand references the receiver and delegates to it when implementing the execute( ) method.

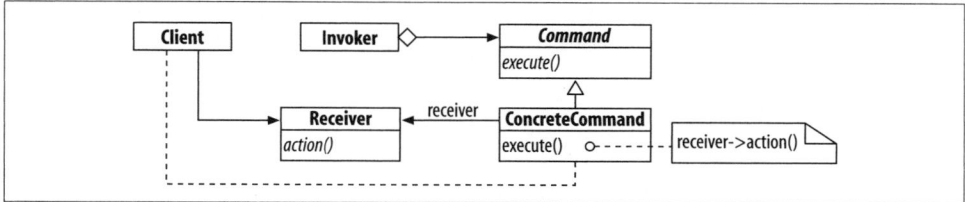

Figure 7-3. Command pattern class diagram

The client assigns each ConcreteCommand instance to specific triggers in *invokers*. Invokers are where the commands are called from. They hold on to the ConcreteCommand objects and call their execute( ) methods when it's time to execute the command. You'll clearly see how this is implemented in ActionScript 3.0 in the minimalist application.

Minimalist Example of a Command Pattern

This example implements the command pattern class diagram in Figure 7-3. The command pattern consists of the *command interface*, *concrete commands* that implement the command interface, *invokers* that call the execute( ) method in concrete commands, *receivers* that implement the behavior required of commands, and *clients* that create concrete commands and pass them on to invokers.

Code examples Examples 7-1 through 7-5 show the minimalist implementation of the command pattern.

The Command Interface

Example 7-1 shows the ICommand class that defines the interface for commands. It defines a single method called execute( ).

Example 7-1. ICommand.as

```
package
{
    public interface ICommand {
        function execute( ):void;
    }
}
```

The Concrete Command

Example 7-2 shows the ConcreteCommand class that implements the ICommand interface. The parameterized constructor takes a Receiver class instance and assigns it to the receiver property. The execute( ) command is implemented by delegating to the *receiver* instance by calling its action( ) method. Note that, because the receiver instance is passed to the constructor, the ConcreteCommand class and Receiver class are loosely coupled, allowing a subclass of Receiver to be passed if needed.

Example 7-2. ConcreteCommand.as

```
package
{
    class ConcreteCommand implements ICommand
    {
        var receiver:Receiver;

        public function ConcreteCommand(rec:Receiver):void
        {
            this.receiver = rec;
        }

        public function execute():void
        {
            receiver.action();
        }
    }
}
```

The Receiver

Example 7-3 shows the Receiver class. It implements a method called action(). Receiver classes implement required command behavior in the command pattern. The only elements that know about the receivers in the command pattern are the concrete commands and the client. Receivers are hidden from invokers.

Example 7-3. Receiver.as

```
package
{
    class Receiver
    {
        public function action()
        {
            trace("Receiver: doing action");
        }
    }
}
```

The Invoker

Example 7-4 shows the Invoker class. It has a method called setCommand() that takes a concrete command instance, which is saved in the currentCommand property. The executeCommand() method calls the execute() method in the concrete command instance. Note that the invoker does not refer to the receiver, and has no idea about its type.

Example 7-4. Invoker.as

```
package
{
    class Invoker
    {
        var currentCommand:ICommand;

        public function setCommand(c:ICommand):void
        {
            this.currentCommand = c;
        }

        public function executeCommand()
        {
            currentCommand.execute();
        }
    }
}
```

The Client

Example 7-5 shows the Main class (also the *document class* for the Flash document) that represents the *client*. The client does several tasks. It first creates an instance of the *receiver* (line 9) and passes it as a parameter when creating a ConcreteCommand instance (line 10). The instance of ConcreteCommand is called a *command object*. The client then creates an instance of the Invoker class (line 12) and passes the command object to it (line 13). Finally, the client executes the command by calling the execute( ) method on the command object.

Example 7-5. Main.as

```
 1 package
 2 {
 3     import flash.display.MovieClip;
 4
 5     public class Main extends MovieClip
 6     {
 7         public function Main()
 8         {
 9             var rec:Receiver = new Receiver();
10             var concCommand:ICommand = new ConcreteCommand(rec);
11
12             var invoker:Invoker = new Invoker();
13             invoker.setCommand(concCommand);
14             concCommand.execute(); // execute command
15         }
16     }
17 }
```

The output from the minimalist application will be the following trace from the receiver object indicating that its action( ) method has been called:

```
Receiver: doing action
```

Setting a Trigger to Invoke the Command

In most situations, the client does not call the execute( ) method in the command object. You wouldn't need to have an invoker if this were the case. Invokers hang on to command objects until it's time to execute them. There can be many triggers such as user events, and timers that would do this.

To make our minimalist example reflect the true nature of the invoker, we can implement a timer event that invokes the command. Example 7-6 shows the TimedInvoker class that extends the Invoker class (see Example 7-4). It implements the setTimer( ) method, which creates a timer that dispatches a timer event every second (1000 ticks equal 1 second) 5 times (line 10). It then registers the onTimerEvent( ) listener method to intercept timer events (line 11) and starts the timer. The onTimerEvent( ) method calls the executeCommand( ) method in the superclass.

Example 7-6. TimedInvoker.as

```
 1  package {
 2
 3      import flash.events.Event;
 4      import flash.events.TimerEvent;
 5      import flash.utils.Timer;
 6
 7      class TimedInvoker extends Invoker {
 8
 9          public function setTimer() {
10              var timer:Timer = new Timer(1000, 5);
11              timer.addEventListener(TimerEvent.TIMER, this.onTimerEvent);
12              timer.start();
13          }
14
15          public function onTimerEvent(evt:TimerEvent):void {
16              this.executeCommand();
17          }
18      }
19  }
```

Replace lines 12 through 14 in the Main class (see Example 7-5) with the following statements to use the new timed invoker.

```
var invoker:TimedInvoker = new TimedInvoker();
invoker.setCommand(concCommand);
invoker.setTimer();
```

This will cause the command to be executed every second for 5 seconds based on timer events. This is a more accurate representation of the command pattern where the invoker executes commands based on different triggers, independent of the client.

Key OOP Concepts in the Command Pattern

The key concept in the command pattern is encapsulation. Encapsulation is basically information hiding. You want to hide implementation details of parts of a program that are most likely to change from other parts.

Command objects, which are instances of concrete commands, embed behavior. However, which classes execute that behavior and which methods in those classes implement that behavior are hidden from where the behavior is called. This information is encapsulated within the command object.

We saw in the minimalist example that nowhere in the invoker (Example 7-4) is the type of the receiver mentioned. The invoker only knows what's implemented in the command interface (Example 7-1). It only knows that the command object has a method called execute( ). All the invoker knows is to call that method in the command object when it's time to do it.

This decouples the invoker from the receiver. If it becomes necessary to use a different receiver to implement a required behavior, we can modify the concrete command to delegate to a different receiver. The invoker won't know that anything has changed; it'll keep calling the execute( ) command in the same command object, oblivious to the fact that its behavior is now implemented using a different receiver.

Minimalist Example: Macro Commands

Macro commands are useful extensions of concrete commands. They allow the creation of composite commands that run several sub-commands in sequence. Consider what happens when you quit or exit an application. If there are open unsaved documents the application will ask if you want to save changes. The quit command is then a macro command that does several housekeeping tasks before quitting. These tasks are themselves commands, but are referred to as subcommands when invoked by a macro command.

Macro commands need to implement more functionality than a simple command does because they need to define interfaces to add and remove subcommands. We will extend the original command interface to fit the new requirements.

The Macro Command Interface

Example 7-7 shows the IMacroCommand interface. It extends the ICommand interface (Example 7-1) and declares the add( ) and remove( ) methods.

Example 7-7. IMacroCommand.as

```
package
{
    public interface IMacroCommand extends ICommand {
        function add(c:ICommand):void;
        function remove(c:ICommand):void;
    }
}
```

Two Concrete Subcommands

To demonstrate a macro command, we will implement two concrete command classes (ConcreteCommand1 and ConcreteCommand2) that use two receiver classes (Receiver1 and Receiver2). These are shown in Example 7-8 through Example 7-11.

Example 7-8. ConcreteCommand1.as

```
package {
    class ConcreteCommand1 implements ICommand
    {
        var receiver:Receiver1;

        public function ConcreteCommand1(rec:Receiver1):void
        {
            this.receiver = rec;
        }

        public function execute():void
        {
            receiver.action1();
        }
    }
}
```

Example 7-9. ConcreteCommand2.as

```
package {
    class ConcreteCommand2 implements ICommand
    {
        var receiver:Receiver2;

        public function ConcreteCommand2(rec:Receiver2):void
        {
            this.receiver = rec;
        }

        public function execute():void
        {
            receiver.action2();
        }
    }
}
```

Example 7-10. Receiver1.as

```
package {

    class Receiver1 {

        public function action1( ) {
            trace("Receiver 1: doing action 1");
        }
    }
}
```

Example 7-11. Receiver2.as

```
package {

    class Receiver2 {

        public function action2( ) {
            trace("Receiver 2: doing action 2");
        }
    }
}
```

The Concrete Macro Command

We will now develop a macro command that implements the IMacroCommand interface. The implementation is straightforward as Example 7-12 shows; it pushes commands into the commandObjectList array in the add( ) method, and executes them in sequence in the execute( ) method.

Example 7-12. ConcreteMacroCommand.as

```
package
{
    class ConcreteMacroCommand implements IMacroCommand
    {
        var commandObjectList:Array;

        public function ConcreteMacroCommand( )
        {
            this.commandObjectList = new Array( );
        }

        public function add(c:ICommand):void
        {
            commandObjectList.push(c);
        }

        public function remove(c:ICommand):void
        {
            for (var i:int = 0; i < commandObjectList.length; i++)
            {
```

Example 7-12. ConcreteMacroCommand.as (continued)

```
            if (commandObjectList[i] === c)
            {
                commandObjectList.splice(i, 1);
                break;
            }
        }
    }

    public function execute( ):void
    {
        for (var i:int = 0; i < commandObjectList.length; i++)
        {
            commandObjectList[i].execute( );
        }
    }
  }
}
```

A Macro Command Object Created from the Client

The client first creates the two subcommands. It then creates a new macro command and adds the two subcommands to it. Finally, it creates an invoker and sets it to execute the macro command. Example 7-13 shows how to create the macro command.

Example 7-13. Client code to create a macro command

```
var command1:ICommand = new ConcreteCommand1(new Receiver1( ));
var command2:ICommand = new ConcreteCommand2(new Receiver2( ));

// create a macro command and add commands
var macroCommand:IMacroCommand = new ConcreteMacroCommand( );
macroCommand.add(command1);
macroCommand.add(command2);

var invoker:TimedInvoker = new TimedInvoker( );
// assign macro command to the invoker
invoker.setCommand(macroCommand);
// invoke commands on timer events
invoker.setTimer( );
```

Note that macro commands do not delegate to receivers to implement required behavior. The primary purpose is to execute sub-commands. Since they implement the ICommand interface, invokers are indistinguishable from other command objects.

Example: Number Manipulator

The invoker in the previous examples can hold only one command object. However, in real applications, invokers need to hold multiple commands. For example, take the File menu of any application. It is a good example of an invoker. The File menu has Open, Save, and Save As menu items. Each of these menu items can be a command container that calls the execute( ) method of the embedded command object when triggered by the user. Toolbars in applications are also invokers. They generally consist of button icons that execute particular commands to manipulate elements in an application or document.

In the Number Manipulator application (Figure 7-4), we will create an invoker that contains buttons onto which command objects can be attached. When the button's clicked, the attached command will be executed. The example application will consist of two buttons and a text field. The two buttons will have embedded command objects that will increment and decrement the numerical value in the text field.

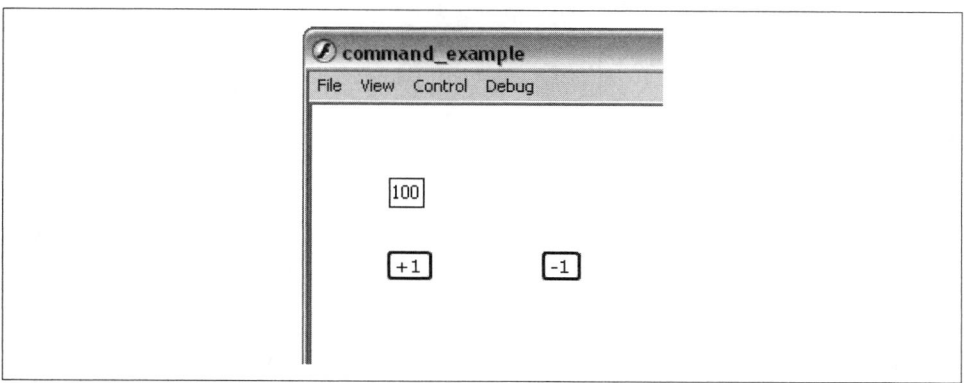

Figure 7-4. Number manipulator example

 We could have used the built-in Button component in Flash CS3 for the buttons in our application. However, we will implement our own button class to illustrate how easily you can create custom buttons with ActionScript 3.0. Use of components is demonstrated in Chapter 12, where we build an application that has several user interface elements to illustrate the Model-View-Controller pattern.

A Utility Button Class

First we need to create a button class that can be reused in subsequent examples. Example 7-14 shows the TextButton class that subclasses the built-in SimpleButton class in ActionScript 3.0. The TextButton constructor takes one parameter that defines the text on the button. The *TextButton.as* file contains an embedded class called TextButtonState that subclasses Sprite to draw required button states. The TextButtonState constructor takes two parameters: button state color, and button text. It creates a new text field with the passed text and draws a filled rounded rectangle around it, using the passed color. A new sprite is created and assigned to the up, down, and over states of TextButton.

Example 7-14. TextButton.as

```
package
{
    import flash.display.*;
    import flash.events.*;

    public class TextButton extends SimpleButton
    {
        public var selected:Boolean = false;

        public function TextButton(txt:String)
        {
            upState = new TextButtonState(0xFFFFFF, txt);
            downState = new TextButtonState(0x999999, txt);
            overState = new TextButtonState(0xCCCCCC, txt);
            hitTestState = upState;
        }
    }
}

import flash.display.*;
import flash.text.TextFormat;
import flash.text.TextField;
import flash.text.TextFieldAutoSize;

class TextButtonState extends Sprite
{
    public function TextButtonState(color:uint, labelText:String)
    {
        var label = new TextField();
        label.autoSize = TextFieldAutoSize.LEFT;
        label.text = labelText;
        label.x = 2;
        var format:TextFormat = new TextFormat("Verdana");
        label.setTextFormat(format);
        var buttonWidth:Number = label.textWidth + 10;
        var background:Shape = new Shape();
        background.graphics.beginFill(color);
        background.graphics.lineStyle(2, 0x000000);
        background.graphics.drawRoundRect(0, 0, buttonWidth, 18, 4);
        addChild(background);
        addChild(label);
    }
}
```

Triggering an Invoker by Button Clicks

Now that we have a button, let's use it to create a multibutton invoker. Example 7-15 shows the InvokerPanel class that contains buttons with commands assigned to them. Two arrays, commandList and buttonList, are declared to hold the button instances and corresponding command objects. The public setCommand( ) method takes two parameters, a slot position and command object (line 17), and assigns the command to the requested slot position in the commandList array. The setButton( ) method takes two parameters, a slot position as before, and button text (line 22). The setButton( ) method creates a new TextButton instance, and assigns it to the requested location on the buttonList array. It then draws the button, assigns an event handler to intercept mouse clicks, and adds it to the display list. The mouse click is the trigger for the button and its assigned command object. When there's a click on the button, the event is intercepted by the buttonClicked( ) method, which traverses the buttonList array to find the button clicked. And when the originating button is found, it executes the corresponding command object from the commandList array.

Example 7-15. InvokerPanel.as

```
1  package
2  {
3      import flash.display.*;
4      import flash.events.*;
5
6      class InvokerPanel extends Sprite
7      {
8          var commandList:Array;
9          var buttonList:Array;
10
11         public function InvokerPanel( )
12         {
13             this.commandList = new Array(5);
14             this.buttonList = new Array(5);
15         }
16
17         public function setCommand(nSlot:int, c:ICommand):void
18         {
19             this.commandList[nSlot] = c;
20         }
21
22         public function setButton(nSlot:int, sName:String):void
23         {
24             var btn:TextButton = new TextButton(sName);
25             this.buttonList[nSlot] = btn;
26             btn.x = nSlot * 100;
27             btn.addEventListener(MouseEvent.CLICK, this.buttonClicked);
28             this.addChild(btn);
29         }
30
31         private function buttonClicked(e:Event)
32         {
33             for (var i:int = 0; i < buttonList.length; i++)
34             {
35                 if (buttonList[i] === e.target)
36                 {
37                     this.commandList[i].execute( );
38                     break;
39                 }
40             }
41         }
```

Example 7-15. InvokerPanel.as (continued)

```
42      }
43  }
```

The Increment and Decrement Commands

Now that our InvokerPanel is complete, we can develop the command classes to increment and decrement a value in a text field. Examples 7-16 and 7-17 show the IncrementCommand and DecrementCommand classes, both of which implement the ICommand interface (Example 7-1). Note that the receiver is the built-in TextField class and the text in the field is assigned using its text property. The execute( ) method gets the text value from the receiver, casts it to a Number, and assigns the manipulated value back to the receiver.

Example 7-16. IncrementCommand.as

```
package {

    import flash.text.TextField;

    class IncrementCommand implements ICommand {

        var receiver:TextField;

        public function IncrementCommand(rec:TextField):void {
            this.receiver = rec;
        }

        public function execute( ):void {
            receiver.text = String(Number(receiver.text) + 1);
        }
    }
}
```

Example 7-17. DecrementCommand.as

```
package {

    import flash.text.TextField;

    class DecrementCommand implements ICommand {

        var receiver:TextField;

        public function DecrementCommand(rec:TextField):void {
            this.receiver = rec;
        }

        public function execute( ):void {
            receiver.text = String(Number(receiver.text) - 1);
        }
    }
}
```

The Client

The only remaining task is to develop the client code to create the command objects and assign them to the buttons on the invoker. Example 7-18 shows how the client first creates the receiver, which is a built-in text field (line 2), and assigns the number 100 to it. The receiver is then positioned and added to the display list (line 8). The client then creates two concrete commands to increment and decrement the receiver (lines 11-12). Next, the client creates the invoker button panel, and two buttons. Finally, the command objects are assigned to the proper button slots (lines 23-24). Note that the button slots are numbered from 0 through 4.

Example 7-18. Client code for number manipulator

```
 1  // create new receiver
 2  var numDisplayField:TextField = new TextField( );
 3  numDisplayField.autoSize = TextFieldAutoSize.LEFT;
 4  numDisplayField.text = '100'; // default value
 5  numDisplayField.border = true;
 6  numDisplayField.x = 50;
 7  numDisplayField.y = 50;
 8  this.addChild(numDisplayField);
 9
10  // concrete command objects
11  var incCommand:ICommand = new IncrementCommand(numDisplayField);
12  var decCommand:ICommand = new DecrementCommand(numDisplayField);
13
14  // create invoker button panel
15  var panel:InvokerPanel = new InvokerPanel( );
16  panel.setButton(0,"+1");
17  panel.setButton(1,"-1");
18  panel.x = 50;v
19  panel.y = 100;
20  this.addChild(panel);
21
22  // add commands to invoker buttons
23  panel.setCommand(0, incCommand);
24  panel.setCommand(1, decCommand);
```

Running the number manipulator example will produce a text field with the number 100 and two buttons labeled "+1" and "−1" (see Figure 7-4).

Extended Example: Sharing Command Objects

Portability is a significant advantage of command objects. They're portable because they encapsulate everything that's needed to execute a particular command. They're not tightly coupled to either the receiver or the invoker, and conform to a stable interface. Any code segment can execute a command by just calling the execute( ) method on a command object. Why is portability such a good thing?

Let's go back to our File menu example. We know that a File menu can be an invoker where the menu items are attached to command objects that can be executed. How about keyboard shortcuts for the File menu? The keyboard shortcut Ctrl-O on the PC and Command-O on a Mac will perform the same behavior as selecting the Open menu item. Ctrl-S on the PC and Command-S on a Mac will save a file exactly the same way as choosing the Save menu item. So, the keyboard shortcuts are invokers too, but do we need to create a whole new set of command objects for it? Not at all, we can create a single command object and share it with multiple invokers.

Triggering an Invoker by Key Presses

Let's extend our number manipulator example and add keyboard shortcuts to increment and decrement the number in the text field. The first step is to develop a new invoker to handle keyboard input. Example 7-19 shows the InvokerKeyboard class. Structurally, it's similar to previous multibutton invokers. However, unlike the InvokerPanel class, InvokerKeyboard does not have to subclass Sprite because it's not going to be added to the display list. The Stage instance is passed to InvokerKeyboard as the onKeyPress listener has to be registered with the stage. This is essential to intercept all key down events.

Two arrays, keyList and commandList, hold the shortcut key code and corresponding command objects. The public setCommand() method takes two parameters, a key code value and command object, and pushes them in tandem to the keyList and commandList arrays. If there is a key press and the keyList array contains the keycode for the key pressed, the corresponding command from the commandList array will be executed.

Example 7-19. InvokerKeyboard.as

```
package
{
    import flash.events.*;
    import flash.display.Stage;

    class InvokerKeyboard
    {
        var commandList:Array;
        var keyList:Array;

        public function InvokerKeyboard(stageTarget:Stage)
        {
            this.commandList = new Array();
            this.keyList = new Array();
            stageTarget.addEventListener(KeyboardEvent.KEY_DOWN,
                                this.onKeyPress);
        }

        public function setCommand(keycode:int, c:ICommand):void
```

Example 7-19. InvokerKeyboard.as (continued)

```
    {
        this.keyList.push(keycode);
        this.commandList.push(c);
    }

    private function onKeyPress(event:KeyboardEvent)
    {
        for (var i:int = 0; i < keyList.length; i++)
        {
            if (keyList[i] === event.keyCode)
            {
                this.commandList[i].execute();
                break;
            }
        }
    }
}
}
```

Sharing Command Objects from the Client

Now that the keyboard invoker has been implemented, we can add the following at the end of the client code shown in Example 7-18. This creates a new InvokerKeyboard instance, and assigns the same command objects to it that were used for the InvokerPanel.

```
var kb:InvokerKeyboard = new InvokerKeyboard(this.stage);
// add commands to keyboard shortcut invoker
kb.setCommand(Keyboard.RIGHT, incCommand);
kb.setCommand(Keyboard.LEFT, decCommand);
kb.setCommand(Keyboard.NUMPAD_ADD, incCommand);
kb.setCommand(Keyboard.NUMPAD_SUBTRACT, decCommand);
```

The keyboard right arrow key and the plus key on the numeric keypad should perform the increment command. Conversely, the left arrow key and negative key on the numeric keypad should perform the decrement command.

Command sharing is a powerful feature of the command pattern and makes extending applications much easier to manage. For example, if we decide to use a different receiver, we just need to pass an instance of the new receiver when creating the command object. Because the same command object is used in multiple invokers, the changes are seamlessly spread through the application. If command objects were not used and receivers were called directly from multiple invokers, code changes in multiple locations would be necessary.

Extended Example: Implementing Undo

Another powerful feature of the command pattern is the clear-cut means it provides for implementing undo, redo, queuing, and logging features. We all know how valuable the undo feature is in any productivity application, including games. Because the command object encapsulates execution of commands, it can just as easily encapsulate an undo( ) command to reverse itself and go back to its previous state.

We need to expand the command interface to declare an undo( ) command. However, before we proceed, let's stop and think about how to implement this feature. To implement undo, we need to keep track of executed commands using a command stack. A stack is a data structure that's based on the last-in-first-out (LIFO) principle. Stacks implement push( ) and pop( ) operations that store and retrieve items from it. The pop operation always retrieves the last item pushed. This is exactly what we need to implement undo, as it simply reverses the last command. Whenever a command is executed, its command object should be pushed into a stack. Ideally there should be only one command stack per application. When the user wants to undo the last command, the stack should be popped, and the undo( ) command of the popped command object should be executed.

An Abstract Interface for Commands

Instead of declaring a pure interface, we will declare an abstract interface for commands that support undo. We'll do this to implement the command stack feature within the command class. Example 7-20 shows the abstract interface for the CommandWithUndo class that implements this. Arrays in ActionScript support the push and pop operations. The command stack is a static array called aCommandHistory that'll hold the command objects that have already been executed. The default implementation for the execute( ) method is to push the current command object into the command stack. The undo( ) method has been declared as an abstract method requiring implementation by subclasses.

Note that ActionScript 3.0 language does not support abstract classes. It is up to the programmer to make sure that classes that need to behave as abstract are subclassed, and abstract methods implemented.

Example 7-20. CommandWithUndo.as

```
package
{
    // ABSTRACT Class (should be subclassed and not instantiated)
    public class CommandWithUndo implements ICommand
    {
        internal static var aCommandHistory:Array = new Array();

        public function execute():void
        {
```

Example 7-20. CommandWithUndo.as (continued)

```
            aCommandHistory.push(this);
        }

        // ABSTRACT Method (must be overridden in a subclass)
        public function undo( ):void {}
    }
}
```

Concrete Commands that Implement Undo

Now we will re-implement the increment and decrement concrete commands to the abstract interface declared by CommandWithUndo. The two new concrete command classes are IncrementCommandWithUndo (Example 7-21) and DecrementCommandWithUndo (Example 7-22). To implement the undo feature, we primarily need to push all executed command objects into the command stack. The execute( ) method does this by calling the execute( ) method in the superclass in the last statement (line 17), and implementing the undo( ) method. The undo( ) method simply reverses the effects of the execute( ) method (line 20).

Example 7-21. IncrementCommandWithUndo.as

```
 1  package
 2  {
 3      import flash.text.TextField;
 4
 5      class IncrementCommandWithUndo extends CommandWithUndo
 6      {
 7          var receiver:TextField;
 8
 9          public function IncrementCommandWithUndo(rec:TextField):void
10          {
11              this.receiver = rec;
12          }
13
14          override public function execute( ):void
15          {
16              receiver.text = String(Number(receiver.text) + 1);
17              super.execute( );
18          }
19
20          override public function undo( ):void
21          {
22              receiver.text = String(Number(receiver.text) - 1);
23          }
24      }
25  }
```

The DecrementCommandWithUndo class is similar, and shown in Example 7-22.

Example 7-22. DecrementCommandWithUndo.as

```
package
{
    import flash.text.TextField;

    class DecrementCommandWithUndo extends CommandWithUndo
    {

        var receiver:TextField;

        public function DecrementCommandWithUndo(rec:TextField):void
        {
            this.receiver = rec;
        }

        override public function execute():void
        {
            receiver.text = String(Number(receiver.text) - 1);
            super.execute();
        }

        override public function undo():void
        {
            receiver.text = String(Number(receiver.text) + 1);
        }
    }
}
```

We also need a new command object that'll be attached to an undo button on the invoker. Example 7-23 shows the UndoLastCommand class that will undo the last operation. The execute() method first checks if the aCommandHistory array contains any command objects, and pops the array to get the most recently executed command. It then proceeds to call the undo() method on the popped command object. Note that the undo command does not push itself into the command stack. It also throws an IllegalOperationError exception if its undo() method is called.

Example 7-23. UndoLastCommand.as

```
package
{
    import flash.errors.IllegalOperationError;

    class UndoLastCommand extends CommandWithUndo
    {
        override public function execute():void
        {
            if (aCommandHistory.length)
            {
                var lastCommand:CommandWithUndo = aCommandHistory.pop();
```

Example 7-23. UndoLastCommand.as (continued)

```
            lastCommand.undo( );
        }
    }

    override public function undo( ):void
    {
        throw new IllegalOperationError("undo operation not supported
            on this command");
    }
  }
}
```

Undoable Commands Assigned from the Client

In Example 7-24, the client can be modified to create command objects using the concrete commands that support undo (lines 11–13). A new "Undo" button is added (line 19), and the corresponding command object is attached to it (line 27).

Example 7-24. Client code for undoable number manipulator

```
1  // create new receiver
2  var numDisplayField:TextField = new TextField( );
3  numDisplayField.autoSize = TextFieldAutoSize.LEFT;
4  numDisplayField.text = '100'; // default value
5  numDisplayField.border = true;
6  numDisplayField.x = 50;
7  numDisplayField.y = 50;
8  this.addChild(numDisplayField);
9
10 // create concrete commands
11 var incCommand:CommandWithUndo = new IncrementCommandWithUndo(numDisplayField);
12 var decCommand:CommandWithUndo = new DecrementCommandWithUndo(numDisplayField);
13 var undo:CommandWithUndo = new UndoLastCommand( );
14
15 // create invoker button panel
16 var panel:InvokerPanel = new InvokerPanel( );
17 panel.setButton(0,"+1");
18 panel.setButton(1,"-1");
19 panel.setButton(2,"Undo");
20 panel.x = 50;
21 panel.y = 100;
22 this.addChild(panel);
23
24 // add commands to invoker
25 panel.setCommand(0, incCommand);
26 panel.setCommand(1, decCommand);
27 panel.setCommand(2, undo);
```

The example application will look like Figure 7-4 with an additional "Undo" button. Command "redo" functionality including logging features can be implemented in similar ways. Logging features are useful when the commands executed need to be saved on disk. For example, saving the installation command objects on disk when a new application is installed will facilitate an uninstall by loading the logged commands and undoing them in reverse order.

Example: Podcast Radio

This example implements a classic car radio with a twist. Instead of programming the push buttons to tune to a radio station, they will be attached to command objects that will download and play the latest episode from a podcast. Think of this as a futuristic car radio when long-range Wi-Fi becomes a reality. You can listen to the NPR hourly news summary on demand without waiting for the top of the hour. Figure 7-5 shows the screen layout of the application. It consists of labeled buttons that indicate the genre of the podcast assigned to each button, and a text field that displays the title of the podcast item that is currently playing.

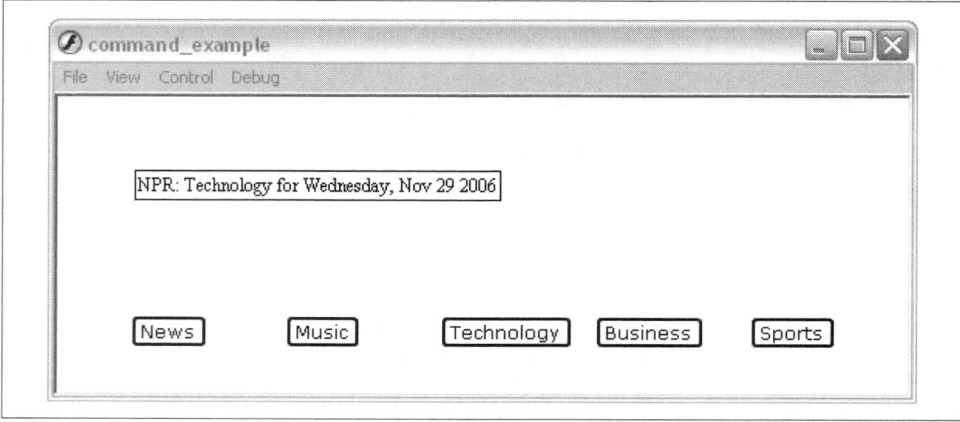

Figure 7-5. Screenshot of podcast radio

What Is a Podcast?

A podcast is a media file that is distributed over the Internet. Podcasts are distributed using a syndication feed, which is a standard way of distributing content that is regularly updated. The feed is an XML file just like a syndicated news feed that lists news stories with the most recent one first. The difference between news feeds and podcasts is that in podcasts, the story is not text but a URL to a media file. In an audio podcast, the linked media file is usually in MP3 format. Example 7-25 shows a fictitious podcast XML feed in RSS syndication format (with many elements deleted for clarity).

Example 7-25. Podcast XML feed

```
<?xml version="1.0" encoding="utf-8"?>
<rss version="2.0">
 <channel>
  <title>10AM ET News Summary</title>
  <item>
   <title>News Summary for Saturday, Nov 18 2006 at 10:00 AM EST</title>
   <pubDate>Sat, 18 Nov 2006 10:16:06 EST</pubDate>
   <enclosure url="http://news.podcasts.org/6507084.mp3">
  </item>
 </channel>
</rss>
```

To play an audio podcast, the podcast XML file has to be loaded and parsed to access the url attribute of the *enclosure* element that holds the URL to the audio file. Thereafter, the audio file has to be loaded from the Web and played.

Creating a Package with Utility Classes

First, we need to create two utility classes to create the button and text fields on the stage. The first is the same TextButton class shown in Example 7-14 that creates buttons on the stage. We also develop a class called TextDisplayField that subclasses TextField to format and display the title of the currently playing podcast item. We will add both classes into a package called utils.

The TextDisplayField class is shown in Example 7-26. The class is straightforward, and its main purpose is to set the initial text in the field, set the font size, and show the text field border.

Example 7-26. TextDisplayField.as

```
package utils {

    import flash.text.TextFormat;
    import flash.text.TextField;
    import flash.text.TextFieldAutoSize;

    public class TextDisplayField extends TextField {

        public function TextDisplayField(labelText:String = "",
                                         fontSize:int = 14,
                                         showborder:Boolean = true) {
            autoSize = TextFieldAutoSize.LEFT;
            text = labelText;
            border = showborder;
            var format:TextFormat = new TextFormat("Verdana");
            format.size = fontSize;
            setTextFormat(format);
        }
    }
}
```

Now that the utility classes have been created, we can develop the command pattern elements for the application.

Creating a Command to Play a Podcast

The command interface will be the same ICommand class defined in Example 7-1. The *concrete command* will be the PlayPodcastCommand class shown in Example 7-27. The constructor takes two parameters, the receiver of type Radio, and the URL of the podcast as type String.

Example 7-27. PlayPodcastCommand.as

```
package
{
    class PlayPodcastCommand implements ICommand
    {
        var receiver:Radio;
        var podCastURL:String;

        public function PlayPodcastCommand(rec:Radio, url:String):void
        {
            this.receiver = rec;
            this.podCastURL = url;
        }

        public function execute():void
        {
            this.receiver.playPodcast(this.podCastURL);
        }
    }
}
```

Developing the Radio Receiver

The *receiver* class shown in Example 7-28 is called Radio and subclasses Sprite. It uses the TextDisplayField class (see Example 7-26) from the previously developed utils package to display a text field to show the currently playing podcast item (lines 20-21). The audioDisplay property references the text field. In addition, it declares a static property called audioChannel of type SoundChannel (line 15). The reason the sound channel is declared as *static* is to make sure that only one podcast plays at a given moment, even if there are multiple instances of the Radio class in the application. The playPodcast() method loads the XML file for the podcast and registers the xmlLoaded listener method (line 28) to intercept the Event.COMPLETE event. After the XML file is loaded, it is parsed using the new E4X features in ActionScript 3.0 (ECMAScript for XML) to get the title element (line 42) and the enclosure attribute (line 44) of the first item element. The audio file is then loaded and played through the audioChannel sound channel (lines 46-51).

Example 7-28. Radio.as

```
1  package
2  {
3
4      import flash.display.*;
5      import flash.events.*;
6      import flash.media.Sound;
7      import flash.media.SoundChannel;
8      import flash.net.*;
9      import utils.*;
10
11     class Radio extends Sprite
12     {
13
14         private var audioDisplay:TextDisplayField;
15         private static var audioChannel:SoundChannel =  new SoundChannel( );
16         var xmlLoader:URLLoader;
17
18         public function Radio( )
19         {
20             audioDisplay = new TextDisplayField("click button to play", 14);
21             this.addChild(audioDisplay);
22         }
23
24         public function playPodcast(url:String)
25         {
26             var xmlURL:URLRequest = new URLRequest(url);
27             this.xmlLoader = new URLLoader(xmlURL);
28             xmlLoader.addEventListener(Event.COMPLETE, xmlLoaded);
29             xmlLoader.addEventListener(IOErrorEvent.IO_ERROR, loadError);
30         }
31
32         private function xmlLoaded(evtObj:Event)
33         {
34             var xml:XML = new XML( );
35             xml = XML(xmlLoader.data);
36             // set the default XML namespace to the source
37             if (xml.namespace("") != undefined)
38             {
39                 default xml namespace = xml.namespace("");
40             }
41             // set the display field to audio stream name
42             this.audioDisplay.text = xml..item[0].title;
43             // get audio url
44             var url = xml..item[0].enclosure.attribute("url");
45             // load audio and play
46             var request:URLRequest = new URLRequest(url);
47             var audio:Sound = new Sound( );
48             audio.addEventListener(IOErrorEvent.IO_ERROR, loadError);
49             audio.load(request);
50             audioChannel.stop( ); // stop previous audio
51             audioChannel = audio.play( );
52         }
53
```

Example 7-28. Radio.as

```
54          private function loadError(event:Event):void
55          {
56              trace("Load error " + event);
57          }
58      }
59  }
```

Push Button Invokers for the Radio

The ControlButtons class shown in Example 7-29 is identical to the InvokerPanel class (Example 7-15) discussed previously. The only difference is that now the TextButton class has to be imported from the *utils* package. Its main function is to hold push button instances and command objects associated with them, and execute the corresponding command when a button's clicked.

Example 7-29. ControlButtons.as

```
package
{
    import flash.display.*;
    import flash.events.*;
    import utils.*;

    class ControlButtons extends Sprite
    {
        var commandList:Array;
        var buttonList:Array;

        public function ControlButtons()
        {
            this.commandList = new Array(5);
            this.buttonList = new Array(5);
        }

        public function setCommand(nSlot:int, c:ICommand):void
        {
            this.commandList[nSlot] = c;
        }

        public function setButton(nSlot:int, sName:String):void
        {
            var btn:TextButton = new TextButton(sName);
            this.buttonList[nSlot] = btn;
            btn.x = nSlot * 100;
            btn.addEventListener(MouseEvent.CLICK,
                this.buttonClicked);
            this.addChild(btn);
        }

        private function buttonClicked(e:Event)
        {
```

Example 7-29. ControlButtons.as (continued)

```
            for (var i:int = 0; i < buttonList.length; i++)
            {
                if (buttonList[i] === e.target)
                {
                    this.commandList[i].execute( );
                    break;
                }
            }
        }
    }
}
```

The Client Assigns Podcasts to Push Buttons

In Example 7-30, the client first creates the receiver and adds it to the display list (lines 1-5). It then creates the push buttons that represent the invoker. The buttons' labels correspond to the podcast's genre. Finally, the concrete command objects are created, and assigned to the corresponding buttons in the invoker (lines 25-29). The PlayPodcastCommand class constructor takes the podcast URL as a parameter in addition to the receiver instance. The client code can be run from the *document class* of the Flash document.

Example 7-30. Client code for the podcast radio

```
 1  // create radio (receiver)
 2  var radio:Radio = new Radio( );
 3  radio.x = 50;
 4  radio.y = 50;
 5  this.addChild(radio);
 6
 7  // create control buttons (invoker)
 8  var controls:ControlButtons = new ControlButtons( );
 9  controls.setButton(0,"News");
10  controls.setButton(1,"Music");
11  controls.setButton(2,"Technology");
12  controls.setButton(3,"Business");
13  controls.setButton(4,"Sports");
14  controls.x = 50;
15  controls.y = this.stage.stageHeight - 50;
16  this.addChild(controls);
17
18  // attach podcast station commands to invoker buttons
19  var podcastURL_1:String = "http://www.npr.org/rss/podcast.php?id=500005";
20  var podcastURL_2:String = "http://www.npr.org/rss/podcast.php?id=1039";
21  var podcastURL_3:String = "http://www.npr.org/rss/podcast.php?id=1019";
22  var podcastURL_4:String = "http://www.npr.org/rss/podcast.php?id=1095";
23  var podcastURL_5:String = "http://www.npr.org/rss/podcast.php?id=4499275";
24
25  controls.setCommand(0, new PlayPodcastCommand(radio, podcastURL_1));
26  controls.setCommand(1, new PlayPodcastCommand(radio, podcastURL_2));
```

Example 7-30. Client code for the podcast radio (continued)

```
27  controls.setCommand(2, new PlayPodcastCommand(radio, podcastURL_3));
28  controls.setCommand(3, new PlayPodcastCommand(radio, podcastURL_4));
29  controls.setCommand(4, new PlayPodcastCommand(radio, podcastURL_5));
```

Extended Example: Dynamic Command Object Assignment

Remember the classic car radio with the AM and FM stations? Each push button can be programmed with an AM and FM station. What's active depends on the receiver mode. If you choose AM mode (by pressing the AM button), then the push buttons will tune the programmed AM stations. Conversely, they will tune to their FM stations if in FM mode. The buttons are context sensitive. The *Properties panel* in the Flash application is a good example of this context sensitive nature of available commands. The available commands on the *Properties panel* change based on the type of object selected on the stage. Only the commands that are relevant to the selected object are active.

Due to the portability of command objects, we can dynamically assign and replace them at runtime. All the examples we have looked at so far assign commands to invokers at compile time from the client. When we assigned a command to a button, it stayed there for the duration and didn't change. We will extend the podcast radio example application to dynamically assign command objects to the push buttons. Figure 7-6 shows the extended application with two podcast genres: Music and News. It will work very much like the AM and FM mode example described previously. Command objects will be assigned dynamically to buttons 1 through 3. When the Music genre button is pressed, station buttons 1 through 3 will play music podcasts. Similarly, if the News button is pressed, the station buttons will play news podcasts.

A Context Sensitive Invoker

To assign commands dynamically in our extended example, the invoker needs to be mindful of the state of the application. It needs to assign different sets of command objects to the podcast radio station buttons based on the state of the application, or, in this case, the selected podcast genre.

The `DynamicControlButtons` class, shown in Example 7-31, extends the `ControlButtons` class from Example 7-29. It keeps track of the selected genre in the property `currentGenre` (line 7). The two podcast genres are defined by the static constants `NEWS` and `MUSIC` (lines 5-6). It also declares and initializes two arrays (lines 9-10) to hold the command objects assigned to the news and music genres for the three station buttons.

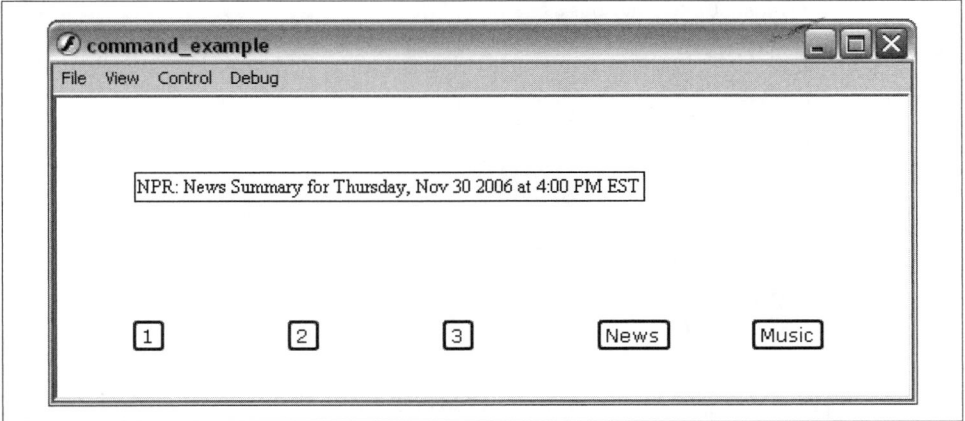

Figure 7-6. Podcast radio with music and news genre buttons

The setGenre( ) method sets the genre by setting the currentGenre property (lines 18-27). The setGenreCommand( ) method (lines 29-38) assigns the passed commands to the two arrays that hold the news and music command objects. After any changes to the state of the application, the updateCommandButtons( ) method is called to dynamically assign the command objects for the chosen genre to the station buttons (positions 1-3 on the commandList array).

Example 7-31. DynamicControlButtons.as

```
1  package
2  {
3      class DynamicControlButtons extends ControlButtons
4      {
5          public static const NEWS:uint = 0;
6          public static const MUSIC:uint = 1;
7          var currentGenre:uint = NEWS;
8
9          var newsPodcastCommands:Array;
10         var musicPodcastCommands:Array;
11
12         public function DynamicControlButtons( )
13         {
14             this.newsPodcastCommands = new Array(3);
15             this.musicPodcastCommands = new Array(3);
16         }
17
18         public function setGenre(genre:uint)
19         {
20             if (genre == NEWS)
21             {
22                 this.currentGenre = NEWS;
23             } else if (genre == MUSIC) {
24                 this.currentGenre = MUSIC;
25             }
```

Example 7-31. DynamicControlButtons.as

```
26              this.updateCommandButtons();
27          }
28
29          public function setGenreCommand(nSlot:int, c:ICommand, genre:uint):void
30          {
31              if (genre == NEWS)
32              {
33                  this.newsPodcastCommands[nSlot] = c;
34              } else if (genre == MUSIC) {
35                  this.musicPodcastCommands[nSlot] = c;
36              }
37              this.updateCommandButtons();
38          }
39
40          private function updateCommandButtons()
41          {
42              for (var i:int = 0; i < 3; i++)
43              {
44                  if (currentGenre == NEWS)
45                  {
46                      this.commandList[i] = this.newsPodcastCommands[i];
47                  } else if (currentGenre == MUSIC) {
48                      this.commandList[i] =  this.musicPodcastCommands[i];
49                  }
50              }
51          }
52      }
53  }
```

Commands to Dynamically Assign Command Objects

To dynamically assign command objects, we need to create two new concrete commands to set the podcast genre to either music or news. This is accomplished by the SetToMusicGenreCommand (Example 7-32) and SetToNewsGenreCommand (Example 7-33) classes.

Example 7-32. SetToMusicGenreCommand.as

```
package
{
    class SetToMusicGenreCommand implements ICommand
    {
        var receiver:DynamicControlButtons;

        public function SetToMusicGenreCommand(
            rec:ControlButtons):void
        {
            this.receiver = rec;
        }

        public function execute():void
```

Example 7-32. SetToMusicGenreCommand.as (continued)

```
        {
            this.receiver.setGenre(
                DynamicControlButtons.MUSIC);
        }
    }
}
```

Example 7-33. SetToNewsGenreCommand.as

```
package
{
    class SetToNewsGenreCommand implements ICommand
    {
        var receiver:DynamicControlButtons;

        public function SetToNewsGenreCommand(
            rec:ControlButtons):void
        {
            this.receiver = rec;
        }

        public function execute():void
        {
            this.receiver.setGenre(DynamicControlButtons.NEWS);
        }
    }
}
```

Note that the receiver for both these commands is of type `DynamicControlButtons`, which is the invoker. Here the invoker is also the receiver for the commands that set the podcast genre.

Dynamic Command Assignment Setup from the Client

The client has to specify command objects for both the music and news genres to the station buttons (the first three buttons), and the commands to change the genre (to the last two buttons). The dynamic assignment of command objects to the station buttons takes place in the invoker. The client essentially programs the buttons on the radio, very much like someone programming actual push buttons on a car radio to specific stations.

The client first creates the *receiver* and adds it to the display list. It then creates the *invoker*, assigns labels to each of the five buttons, and adds it to the display list. Podcast URLs are then assigned to variables (three URLs for each genre). Next, the client does the important job of creating `PlayPodcastCommand` command objects and assigning them to them to the station buttons for each genre. Finally, the client creates and assigns the genre selection command objects to the corresponding buttons on the invoker. Example 7-34 shows the setup.

Example 7-34. Client code for the extended podcast radio

```
// create radio (receiver)
var radio:Radio = new Radio( );
radio.x = 50;
radio.y = 50;
this.addChild(radio);

// create control buttons (invoker)
var controls:DynamicControlButtons = new DynamicControlButtons( );
controls.setButton(0,"1");
controls.setButton(1,"2");
controls.setButton(2,"3");
controls.setButton(3,"News");
controls.setButton(4,"Music");
controls.x = 50;
controls.y = this.stage.stageHeight - 50;
this.addChild(controls);

// podcast URLs
var podcastNewsURL_1:String =
    "http://www.npr.org/rss/podcast.php?id=500005";
var podcastNewsURL_2:String =
    "http://rss.cnn.com/services/podcasting/newscast/rss.xml";
var podcastNewsURL_3:String =
    "http://www.npr.org/rss/podcast.php?id=510053";
var podcastMusicURL_1:String =
    "http://www.npr.org/rss/podcast.php?id=510019";
var podcastMusicURL_2:String =
    "http://www.npr.org/rss/podcast.php?id=510026";
var podcastMusicURL_3:String =
    "http://minnesota.publicradio.org/tools/podcasts/
    new_classical_tracks.xml";

// add station commands to invoker buttons
controls.setGenreCommand(0, new PlayPodcastCommand(radio,
    podcastNewsURL_1), DynamicControlButtons.NEWS);
controls.setGenreCommand(1, new PlayPodcastCommand(radio,
    podcastNewsURL_2), DynamicControlButtons.NEWS);
controls.setGenreCommand(2, new PlayPodcastCommand(radio,
    podcastNewsURL_3), DynamicControlButtons.NEWS);
controls.setGenreCommand(0, new PlayPodcastCommand(radio,
    podcastMusicURL_1), DynamicControlButtons.MUSIC);
controls.setGenreCommand(1, new PlayPodcastCommand(radio,
    podcastMusicURL_2), DynamicControlButtons.MUSIC);
controls.setGenreCommand(2, new PlayPodcastCommand(radio,
    podcastMusicURL_3), DynamicControlButtons.MUSIC);

// add genre selection commands to invoker buttons
controls.setCommand(3, new SetToNewsGenreCommand(controls));
controls.setCommand(4, new SetToMusicGenreCommand(controls));
```

Summary

The command pattern is a very powerful example of encapsulation or information hiding, and shows its utility in many situations common to software design.

In essence, the command pattern embeds behavior in command objects. Commands are executed by calling the execute( ) method in the command object. What classes are delegated to when executing that behavior, and which methods in those classes implement that behavior, are hidden from where the behavior is called. This essentially decouples the code that invokes the behavior from the code that implements the behavior.

This decoupling makes command objects extremely portable, and it is this portability that supports its wide applicability in many situations. A single command object can be shared between several invokers. For example, a single instance of a command object can be used by different code sections in an application. This makes it easy to extend or change application behavior.

One of the most useful characteristics of command objects is that they can be assigned to invokers at runtime. This enables behavior to be changed based on state, a very useful feature in making applications context sensitive.

In addition, the command pattern allows applications to implement some common features required in many applications, such as: command chaining (macro commands), undo, redo, and logging.

CHAPTER 8

Observer Pattern

It is the theory that decides what can be observed.
—Albert Einstein

Every man who observes vigilantly and resolves steadfastly grows unconsciously into genius.
—Edward G. Bulwer-Lytton (Author of the immortal line, "It was a dark and stormy night," written while trying to explain how his Internet connection got knocked out and he missed a deadline.)

The world is full of obvious things which nobody by any chance ever observes.
—Sherlock Holmes (Original reference to syntax errors.)

You can observe a lot just by watching.
—Yogi Berra

What Is the Observer Pattern?

Conceptually, the Observer design pattern is easy to understand. A central point sends information to subscribing instances. This works just like a newspaper or cable television subscription service. When a person subscribes, the service begins, and continues until he unsubscribes.

In applications where a single source of information needs to be broadcast to several different receptors, using a single source in the design makes more sense than having several different sources getting the same information by repeated calls to the data source. For example, in using a web service that sends out stock quotes, setting up your application to receive the information in a single source, and then sending out that information from that source in your application, is more efficient than having each instance calling the information separately from the web service. If your application takes the incoming stock information and displays the information in tabular and different chart forms, having multiple subscriptions to each of the different formatting classes would require separate and repeated calls to the web service.

However, by using a single call to the web service and then broadcasting to the multiple instances, you need far fewer service calls.

In addition to being more efficient, a central data source guarantees that every instance gets the same information. Imagine a change in data from one web service call to the next where a major change occurs. The first instance calls the service and formats the data into a table, and the second instance calls the service to format the data in a bar chat. The data in the chart does not reflect the data in the table, even though it's supposed to. Using an Observer pattern, a single call to the web service *always sends data from the same call* to all subscribers. So the data sent to the table formatting instance and that sent to the charts is guaranteed to be from the same set.

In applications where a high rate of data change occurs, the Observer pattern helps to cut down on the bookkeeping. All data are sent to a central source and then distributed to subscribing instances. For example, in an action game, the score keeps changing as many game conditions rapidly update. When an object in an action game is "destroyed," it no longer needs the information and should not keep gathering in data. Likewise, objects that come into the game or are "resurrected" need to start getting data. This can be a programming nightmare without some kind of system to take in all data changes and then uniformly distribute those changes to the different game elements while taking care of all subscription changes. Here the Observer pattern comes to the rescue by handling all data collection and distribution.

Key Features

The central feature of the Observer pattern is that state change is gathered in one place and sent to all subscribing units. This one-to-many relationship allows developers to create loosely coupled classes and yet maintain information consistency. Figure 8-1 shows the general relationship between the initial data source, the subject class, and the observer classes:

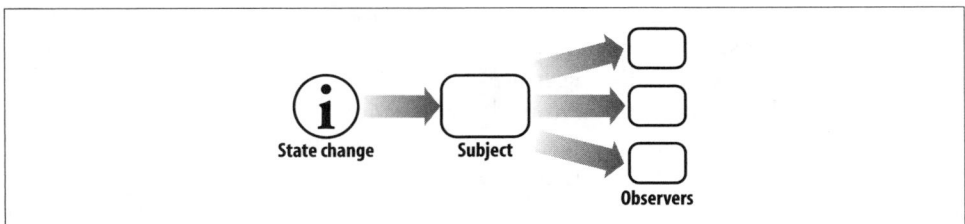

Figure 8-1. Observer information flow

Sending information in this manner to different classes is not only efficient, but also allows for expansion. For example, suppose stock data is subjected to different types of statistical models, each one encapsulated in a class. As new analytical models are introduced, adding a class as part of the application is as easy as creating the class and subscribing it to the subject.

The following key features characterize the Observer pattern:

- Data consistency between loosely coupled but related and interacting objects.
- Data receptors (observers) can subscribe and unsubscribe to data.
- Single source (subject) sends state change information.
- Any number of subscribing observers can subscribe to subject.

To understand the importance of consistency, consider a speech at the United Nations. Suppose the representative from China gives a speech on new trade policies. That information will have to be translated from Chinese to all of the different languages represented at the UN. A good Observer pattern sends the speech information from a single source (subject), to the interpreters (observers), presented in a language that different language users can understand. If each observer got the speech from a different source, the chances of inconsistency increase dramatically, and if inconsistent data were received, the Chinese trade policies could be misconstrued.

The two central objects in the Observer model are the *subject* and *observer*. The subject *notifies* the observer of any state changes. This design relies on *object composition* instead of inheritance as the primary technique for reuse. In this case, the subject delegates operations to the observer. This process is expanded and explained in the section *Key OOP Concepts Used with the Observer Pattern*, later in this chapter.

The Observer Model

The Observer outlined in the class diagram notation shows two key elements: subject and observer. The subject interface provides the method for notifying the observers of state changes. Likewise, the subject holds the methods for subscribing and unsubscribing. The capacity to subscribe objects leaves the door wide open for new objects to be added to the list of objects receiving data. The subject set of methods all delegate to the observer. The observer, by contrast, simply needs a method for updating states. The concrete subject uses the update method of the observer in the notification method implemented from the subject interface. Also, the concrete subject may have both getters and setters for state-related changes. The concrete observer must implement the updating method. However, it may also have methods for subscribing or unsubscribing, most likely the former, leaving the unsubscribing methods up to the concrete object instances or state conditions. Figure 8-2 shows the Observer class diagram:

We can break down the diagram into its four parts—subject, observer, concrete subject and concrete observer. The Subject interface sets up the key connections between itself and the observer by establishing methods that connect and disconnect

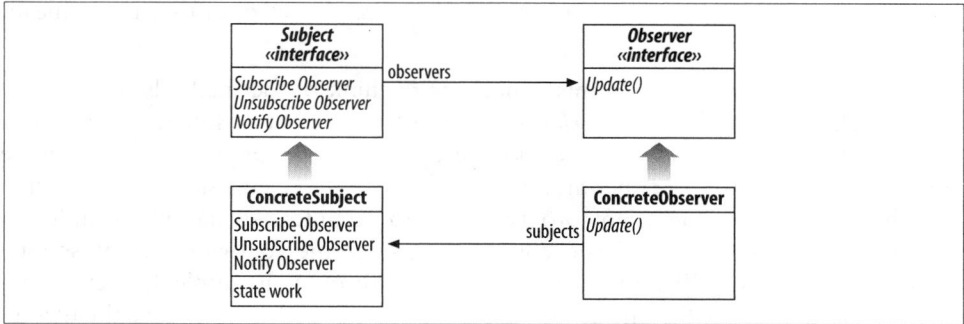

Figure 8-2. Observer pattern class diagram

the observer from the notification process. In fact, *every single* Subject method references the Observer. Likewise, the Observer interface, with its single update( ) method, references the notification process from the subject. The ConcreteSubject provides a property, stateWork, for holding the state about which the observers are notified. It is also responsible for notifying the subscribed observers. Finally, through the update( ) method, the ConcreteObserver keeps a state value consistent with the subject, and, through a state property, stores the current state.

Key OOP Concepts Used with the Observer Pattern

One object-oriented design principle put forth in the original design pattern book by Gamma *et al* is to *favor object composition over class inheritance.* That is, when possible, design your programs using object composition instead of beginning with a superclass and then accomplishing reuse through inheritance. To understand the reason for this dictum, we need to look at *object composition.*

To appreciate the advantage of object composition over inheritance, we need to understand another principle put forth by Gamma, Helm, Johnson and Vlissides:

> Program to an interface, not an implementation.

Let's first look at why programming to an interface is favored over programming to an implementation.

Choose the Interface

In a nutshell, according to Gamma *et al,* programming to an interface is better than programming to an implementation because it reduces implementation dependencies between subsystems. This increases software flexibility. As a result, changes can be made at runtime.

The idea of programming to an interface does not literally mean an ActionScript 3.0 construct interface as opposed to a class. That is, you can program to the interface of an abstract class or an interface instead of a class. What does that really mean, though?

The easiest way to understand this concept is to think of the methods in either an abstract class or interface as *interfaces*. An interface is a set of functions an object implements. Eric and Elisabeth Freeman (*Head First Design Patterns*) suggest that we think of the properties in either an abstract class or interface as *supertypes*. It turns out that the actual practice of programming to an interface has many different approaches, but to see the basic concept, consider the following set of scripts, Example 8-1 through Example 8-6. Example 8-1 through Example 8-4 set up an interface, and Example 8-5 and Example 8-6 implement it. Be sure to save the files all in the same folder.

Example 8-1. SpaceWarrior.as

```
//SpaceWarrior.as
package
{
    interface SpaceWarrior
    {
        function useWeapon( ):void;
    }
}
```

Example 8-2. Alien.as

```
//Alien.as
package
{
    public class Alien implements SpaceWarrior
    {
        function Alien( )
        {
            //Constructor
        }
        public function useWeapon( ):void
        {
            trace("Zaaaapp!!!");
        }
    }
}
```

Example 8-3. Earthling.as

```
//Earthling.as
package
{
    public class Earthling implements SpaceWarrior
    {
        function Earthling( )
        {
            //Constructor
```

Example 8-3. Earthling.as (continued)

```
        }
        public function useWeapon( ):void
        {
            trace("Ka Boom!!!");
        }
    }
}
```

Example 8-4. Main.as

```
//Main.as
package
{
    import flash.display.Sprite;
    public class Main extends Sprite
    {
        public function Main( )
        {
            //Program to implementation
            var alien:Alien=new Alien( );
            alien.useWeapon( );

            //Program to interface
            var spaceWarrior:SpaceWarrior=new Earthling( );
            spaceWarrior.useWeapon( );
        }
    }
}
```

Open a new Flash document file, and, in the Class Document window, type in **Main**. When you test the application, all you're going to see is:

```
Zaaaapp!!!
Ka Boom!!!
```

The first trace( ) output is what's returned when an Alien instance calls the useWeapon( ) method, and the second for the Earthling doing the same thing. To see the difference between programming to an implementation instead of an interface, look at the following lines that are part of the Main.as script:

```
//Program to implementation
var alien:Alien=new Alien( );
alien.useWeapon( );

//Program to interface
var spaceWarrior:SpaceWarrior=new Earthling( );
spaceWarrior.useWeapon( );
```

The first part programs to an implementation because the alien instance is typed as the implementation, Alien. (Alien implements SpaceWarrior interface.) In the second part of the segment, the spaceWarrior instance types as the supertype, SpaceWarrior. However, it is instantiated using the Earthling( ) constructor. As you can see, it works fine. What's more, using the `spaceWarrior` instance, we could redefine it as an `Alien( )` instance, and it'd still work fine. Change the last part to:

```
//Program to interface
var spaceWarrior:SpaceWarrior=new Earthling( );
spaceWarrior.useWeapon( );
spaceWarrior=new Alien( );
spaceWarrior.useWeapon( );
```

Now, the output shows:

```
Zaaaapp!!!
Ka Boom!!!
Zaaaapp!!!
```

As you can see, by programming to the interface, the instances are far more flexible. We don't have to know what's in the function (interface) or what it'll do, we just know that it will do what it's supposed to, depending on the constructor we use.

Object Composition

To see why object composition is favored over class inheritance, we need to see what each does. Previous chapters have used both object composition and inheritance, and so you may have some idea of what each does. Both concepts were introduced in Chapter 1, but because the Observer design pattern clearly illustrates the use of composition, we are reviewing it here again.

Keeping in mind that the comparison between inheritance and object composition relates to building flexible and reusable software elements, we have a base for comparison. So we can restate the principle as:

> For improved flexible and reusable software, favor object composition over class inheritance.

Reusable software developed through inheritance is relatively straightforward. Developers take an existing class and use it again with the particulars created through subclasses. Because the internals of the objects are often visible to the subclasses, the term *white-box reuse* is applied to this implementation.

Object composition, by contrast, achieves new functionality by bringing together existing objects. The composition process can be understood as one class using another class's functionality, whereas inheritance depends on the class having the functionality. So, in composition, one class *uses a* functionality of another class, while in inheritance, a sub class *is-a* class with functionality inherited from another class. Because object composition hides the internal details, the term *black-box reuse* is applied to this kind of development.

Inheritance has some advantages in being simple to create, visible, and relatively simple for making certain types of changes. For example, if you want a change to be applied to all subclasses, a change to the superclass will do the trick. All changes are inherited by the subclasses.

The biggest disadvantage attributed to inheritance is *breaking encapsulation*. This occurs where a subclass is changed because a parent class changes. The change may break certain functionality of the subclass. (Other actions unrelated to inheritance can break encapsulation, but they're not relevant here.) Another disadvantage of inheritance is the inheritance of unwanted features. Subclasses are stuck with the full set of features from the parent class, and, as was seen in Chapter 4, overrides are used to solve this problem. Finally, because inheritance occurs at compile time, you cannot change the implementations from the parent class at runtime. All of these disadvantages reduce flexibility.

One advantage of object composition is the flip side of the main disadvantage of inheritance—maintaining encapsulation. Object composition focuses on what each object in the object set does, and its relationship to other objects. By focusing on clear and limited tasks for each class (object), keeping encapsulation intact is better and simpler. The focus changes from how something works to the relationship between objects, and because each object comes to be dependent on others, object encapsulation and reliability are more important and central.

By having securely encapsulated and focused objects, your number of classes is likely to be larger, and that fact is a disadvantage of object composition. However, these small focused classes also mean small hierarchies, and instead of inheriting and *being* a feature of the object, composition allows one object to *have a* feature of another object.

The Observer design pattern uses object composition instead of inheritance. The two major interfaces and concrete classes are either *subject* or *observer*. Together, these objects are *composed* to create the overall model for the software design.

Minimalist Abstract Observer

To launch an Observer application using the minimum essentials, we need only two interfaces and two classes, reflecting the model in the class diagram (Figure 8-2):

- A subject interface
- An observer interface
- A concrete subject
- A concrete observer

Keeping the overall goal in mind to centrally distribute state information, the constructs boil down to a subscribing method, an unsubscribing method, a notification method for the subject, and an update method for the observer. The key to making this all work right is the use of an array to hold the subscribing observers, and a distribution method for broadcasting the current state.

Subject Interface

All we need for the Subject interface are three methods to take care of the subscription and notification work. Because all of the functions in an interface construct are abstract, we don't have a lot of detail to address. However, we've got to be careful to be sure that all the necessary parts are in place. Example 8-5 shows the script to be saved as Subject.as:

Example 8-5. Subject.as

```
package
{
    //Subject Interface
    public interface Subject
    {
        function subscribeObserver(o:Observer):void;
        function unsubscribeObserver(o:Observer):void;
        function notifyObserver( ):void;
    }
}
```

In the first two functions, you'll see evidence of *composition*. The "o" parameter is an Observer datatype, which is a reference to another interface that'll be built as part of the Observer design pattern. If you look at the diagram in Figure 8-2, you'll see an arrow from the abstract Subject to the abstract Observer. That reference to the Observer datatype is part of the process that uses composition rather than inheritance.

Observer Interface

The Observer interface is deceptively simple. The single update( ) function is actually part of the composition between the Observer and Subject structures. However, we see the composition only when we look at the connection between the concrete observer and subject through the update( ) supertype in the Observer interface. Save the code in Example 8-6 as Observer.as:

Example 8-6. Observer.as

```
package
{
    //Observer Interface
    public interface Observer
    {
        function update(light:String):void;
    }
}
```

To illustrate the Observer design pattern in its minimal form, we've chosen a light that can have an "on" or "off" state. In the abstract interface, though, we simply indicate the data type accepted in the parameter as a string. So the value could be the range of a dimmer. We've got flexibility. The goal in this example is clarity, but the Observer pattern's update( ) function can deal with multiple parameters with any kind of datatype. Later in this chapter, this will be demonstrated.

Concrete Subject

At this stage, we've got to put the interfaces to work. The tasks for the ConcreteSubject class include:

- Establish an array to hold the observers.
- Establish the state property as part of the class—stores the state.
- Set up the details of subscription process tying in the Observer supertype and observers array.
- Work out a process to remove (unsubscribe) elements of the observer array, using an Observer supertype in the parameter.
- Establish a notification process tied to the update( ) method derived from the Observer interface.

The notification process requires some kind of setter. This is where a setter function has a reference to data that changes the state to be broadcast to the observers. In turn, when the state changes (the setter function is called), the notification function kicks in. Save the script in Example 8-7 as ConcreteSubject.as.

Example 8-7. ConcreteSubject.as

```
package
{
    public class ConcreteSubject implements Subject
    {
        private var light:String;
        private var observers:Array;
        function ConcreteSubject ()
        {
            trace ("*|*Concrete Subject*|*");
            observers=new Array();
        }
        public function subscribeObserver (obserNow:Observer):void
        {
            observers.push (obserNow);
        }
        public function unsubscribeObserver (obserNow:Observer):void
        {
            for (var ob:int=0; ob<observers.length; ob++)
            {
                if (observers[ob]==obserNow)
```

Example 8-7. ConcreteSubject.as (continued)

```
                    {
                        observers.splice (ob,1);
                        break;
                    }
                }
            }
        public function notifyObserver ():void
        {
            for (var notify in observers)
            {
                observers[notify].update (light);
                trace ("Observer " + notify + " Light is "+light);
            }
        }
        public function setLight (light:String):void
        {
            this.light=light;
            notifyObserver ();
        }
    }
}
```

In this implementation, you can see that most of the work is done with composition. The constructor has a single construct: instantiating an array. (The trace( ) statements are superfluous and only added so that you can better see the internal workings of the observer structure.) Both the subscribe and unsubscribe functions use composition with an Observer object (supertype) in the parameter. The notify function references the Observer method, update( ). So instead of seeing subclassed elements making up the class, you see composition at work.

When you test the program, you will be programming to an interface rather than an implementation. To make this possible, look at the following line:

```
    public function unsubscribeObserver(obserNow:Observer):void
```

Whatever observer object is placed in the obserNow parameter is typed as a supertype (Observer), not as an implementation type. (In the section "Working the Observer," the programming to an interface process is explored further.)

Concrete Observer

The ConcreteObserver class has a far more focused task than the ConcreteSubject class. It stores the state to be observed to maintain perfect consistency among the subscribing observers. Save the script in Example 8-8 as ConcreteObserver.as.

Example 8-8. ConcreteObserver.as

```
package
{
    //Concrete Observer
```

Example 8-8. ConcreteObserver.as (continued)

```
class ConcreteObserver implements Observer
{
    private var light:String;
    function ConcreteObserver( )
    {
        trace("=Concrete Observer=");
    }
    public function update(light:String):void
    {
        this.light=light;
    }
}
}
```

The update( ) function is tied into the ConcreteSubject class as a parameter. So all instances of the ConcreteObserver are welded to the single source of updating done by the concrete subject's notification function.

Working the Observer

Now we can examine how all the parts work together. In the script that implements the program, we need to create instances of both the ConcreteSubject and ConcreteObserver classes. Then, we will need to subscribe observers to the ConcreteSubject instances. Also, just to be sure that everything's working correctly, we should unsubscribe at least one observer. In order to test the overall functionality, we need to change the state we're observing using the setLight( ) method to different values. Only those observer instances subscribed should be able to see the changes. By first subscribing observers, and then unsubscribing at least one, we should be able to see if everything's working as expected. Example 8-9 implements the Observer design pattern. Save the code as TestSub.as.

Example 8-9. TestSub.as

```
package
{
    import flash.display.Sprite;
    public class TestSub extends Sprite
    {
        public function TestSub( )
        {
            var mySub:ConcreteSubject=new ConcreteSubject( );
            var subObserver:Observer=new ConcreteObserver( );
            var subObserver2:Observer=new ConcreteObserver( );
            var subObserver3:Observer=new ConcreteObserver( );
            mySub.subscribeObserver(subObserver);
            //The subObserver is passed as an instance of Observer
                supertype
            mySub.subscribeObserver(subObserver2);
            mySub.subscribeObserver(subObserver3);
```

Example 8-9. TestSub.as (continued)

```
        mySub.setLight("on");
        mySub.unsubscribeObserver(subObserver);
        mySub.setLight("off");
    }
  }
}
```

Note that this script programs to the interface to instantiate the different observer instances, but must program to the ConcreteSubject directly to implement it. However, we could have typed the observers as ConcreteObserver, and then used the instances as Observer types in the parameters for subscribing. In either case, we would have been following the dictum of programming to the interface.

Open a new Flash document, and, in the Document class window, type in **TestSub,** and then test the application. Your output should appear as the following:

```
*|*Concrete Subject*|*
=Concrete Observer=
=Concrete Observer=
=Concrete Observer=
Observer 0 Light is on
Observer 1 Light is on
Observer 2 Light is on
Observer 0 Light is off
Observer 1 Light is off
```

As you can see, a single instance used the ConcreteSubject constructor and three used the ConcreteObserver constructor, as indicated by the respective trace( ) outputs. The observer state was first set to "on" and, as expected, the three observer instances indicated the correct state. Then, a single observer was unsubscribed, and the state was set to "off." With two observers now, only two indicated the state.

Example: Adding States and Identifying Users

The minimal Observer design pattern example had only a single state. You might think that adding additional states may be complicated, but you'll see that it's very easy. One of the key features about design patterns is that they're flexible, and adding states illustrates this flexibility.

Another issue that can be important in some applications using the Observer pattern is getting to know the observers. In the minimal example in the previous section, the observers were identified by their array index, which changes when observers are removed. However, using a property to identify observers is quite simple as well.

Multiple States

To understand multiple states, just imagine a daily newspaper that has several different sections. For example, an abbreviated list might include the following topic areas that regularly need to be changed:

- News
- Sports
- Stocks
- Entertainment

All these areas can be represented as String data, but for the sake of type variety, we will make Stocks a Number type. In the minimalist example, the initial placement of the state property is in the update( ) parameter. To have additional property states, all we need to do is add more properties. So, in the Observer interface, we'd just need to change the update( ) function to the following:

```
function update(news:String,sports:String,stocks:Number,entertainment:
    String):void;
```

That was easy. As you can see, different data types are not problematic at all.

Next, the concrete subject needs to store the states, and so each state needs a variable declaration that can be used for maintaining the current state. The setter function also needs to deal with each of the four states, and so it too needs to be expanded.

```
public function setType(news:String,sports:String,stocks:Number,
    entertainment:String)
{
    this.news=news;
    this.sports=sports;
    this.stocks=stocks;
    this.entertainment=entertainment;
    notifyObserver( );
}
```

Note that the setType( ) function is structurally identical to the setLight( ) function in the light example. All that's changed is the number of parameters and variables stored.

Finally, in the concrete subject, we need to change the number of parameters in the update( ) function that sends out the state change information:

```
this.observers[notify].update(news,sports,stocks,entertainment);
```

Again, you can see that no structure has changed—just the number of parameters.

Next, in the concrete observer class, all the changes are to the number of variables and nothing in the structure. So, instead of establishing a single variable, four are declared. The key update( ) function is changed to:

```
public function update(news:String,sports:String,stocks:Number,
    entertainment:String):void
{
```

```
    this.news=news;
    this.sports=sports;
    this.stocks=stocks;
    this.entertainment=entertainment;
}
```

Like the other elements in the Observer design pattern, the structure remains the same. The single most complex change in the application is going to be format. The output structure is unchanged, but with four different states, you have to format your output in such a way that all the different states (information categories) are separated from one another and spelled out.

Who Are You?

In some applications, you may want to know who's subscribed to your application. In fact, you may even want to be sure that the same person doesn't accidentally attempt to subscribe more than once, especially where all observers have unique usernames.

So, to get started, we need to begin with the ConcreteObserver class. Using a string variable, we'll add a name to each and every subscriber.

```
//Subscriber's ID
internal var subName:String;

//Constructor Function
function ConcreteObserver(subName:String):void
{
    trace(subName + " has subscribed");
    this.subName=subName;
}
```

By adding a username to the constructor function and connecting that name to the object created, each observer can hold a username. Now, subName is a property of the ConcreteObserver class, and each element of the observers array can use the property to identify itself.

To be sure that no more than a single observer with the same name can subscribe, the ConcreteSubject class's subscription function must be changed. By placing a conditional statement that makes sure that no two observer names are alike—or the same observer doesn't accidentally subscribe twice to the same subject—we can automatically reject a subscription with a duplicate name.

```
//Add variable to check for duplicates
private var duplicate:Boolean;


....(more code)

//Subscribe and Prevent Re-subscription
public function subscribeObserver(obserNow:Observer):void
{
```

```
        duplicate=false;
        for(var ob=0;ob<this.observers.length;ob++)
        {
            if(this.observers[ob]==obserNow)
            {
                duplicate=true;
                trace( this.observers[ob].subName+ " already a subscriber.
                    \n");
            }
        }
        if(! duplicate)
        {
            this.observers.push(obserNow);
        }
    }
```

In some cases, you may not want to limit single subscriptions with a common name.
To allow multiple subscribers with the same name, just don't add the above code
that prevents doing so.

Updated Observer

Now the Observer application has far more functionality. Not only can each
observer be identified by a specific name, no more than a single observer with the
same name will be allowed to subscribe. What's more, four states are now tracked
and sent out if changed. Example 8-10 through Example 8-13 should be saved in the
same folder using the captions for the filenames.

Example 8-10. Subject.as

```
package
{
    //Subject Interface
    public interface Subject
    {
        function subscribeObserver(o:Observer):void;
        function unsubscribeObserver(o:Observer):void;
        function notifyObserver():void;
    }
}
```

Example 8-11. Observer.as

```
package
{
    //Observer Interface
    public interface Observer
    {
    function update(news:String,sports:String,stocks:Number,entertainment:
        String):void;
    }
}
```

Example 8-12. ConcreteSubject.as

```
package
{
    //Concrete Subject
    public class ConcreteSubject implements Subject
    {
        private var news:String;
        private var sports:String;
        private var stocks:Number;
        private var entertainment:String;
        private var observers:Array;

        //Add variable to check for duplicates
        private var duplicate:Boolean;

        //Constructor function
        public function ConcreteSubject ( ):void
        {
            trace ("*|*Concrete Subject*|*");
            observers=new Array( );
        }
        //Subscribe and Prevent Re-subscription
        public function subscribeObserver (obserNow:Observer):void
        {
            var duplicate:Boolean = false;
            for (var ob=0; ob<observers.length; ob++)
            {
                if (observers[ob]==obserNow)
                {
                    duplicate=true;
                    trace (observers[ob].subName+ "
                        is already a subscriber.\n");
                }
            }
            if (! duplicate)
            {
                observers.push (obserNow);
            }
        }
        //Unsubscribe and remove from array
        public function unsubscribeObserver (obserNow:Observer):void
        {
            for (var ob=0; ob<observers.length; ob++)
            {
                if (observers[ob]==obserNow)
                {
                    observers.splice (ob,1);
                }
            }
        }
        //Set up notification and format output
        public function notifyObserver ( ):void
        {
```

Example 8-12. ConcreteSubject.as (continued)

```
            for (var notify in this.observers)
            {
                observers[notify].update (news,sports,
                    stocks,entertainment);
                var nowNews:String=" sees that "+
                    news + " is interesting,";
                var nowSports:String = " and learns that " + sports;
                var nowStocks:String=".\nWhoaa!,
                    the stock market is at " + stocks;
                var nowEntertain:String=" and "+ entertainment +
                    " is showing at the Bijou.";
                trace (observers[notify].subName + nowNews +
                    nowSports + nowStocks + nowEntertain);
            }
        }
        //Add all necessary states
        public function setType (news:String,sports:String,stocks:Number,
            entertainment:String):void
        {
            this.news=news;
            this.sports=sports;
            this.stocks=stocks;
            this.entertainment=entertainment;
            notifyObserver ();
        }
    }
}
```

Example 8-13. ConcreteObserver.as

```
package
{
    //Concrete Observer
    class ConcreteObserver implements Observer
    {
        //Store Additional States
        private var news:String;
        private var sports:String;
        private var stocks:Number;
        private var entertainment:String;

        //Subscriber's ID
        public var subName:String;

        //Constructor Function
        function ConcreteObserver(subName:String):void
        {
            trace(subName + " has subscribed");
            this.subName=subName;
        }
```

Example 8-13. ConcreteObserver.as (continued)

```
    //Add states to update parameter
    public function update(news:String,sports:String,stocks:Number,
        entertainment:String):void
    {
        this.news=news;
        this.sports=sports;
        this.stocks=stocks;
        this.entertainment=entertainment;
    }
}
}
```

Feel free to change the text in the various "headlines" for *The Daily Bugle*.

Playing the Bugle

Now that we've set up an Observer design pattern simulating subscription to a newspaper we've called *The Daily Bugle*, it's time to test the subscription and news distribution process. Our consumer testing class needs to have only a few elements:

- A concrete subject
- Subscribers (concrete observers)
- Daily news (a change of state)
- Unsubscribe (get off the observer list)

This time around, we'll need to name all of our subscribers, and we can expect more information output, but the structure is essentially unchanged. Example 8-14 contains the necessary code that needs to be saved as BugleSubscribe.as.

Example 8-14. BugleSubscribe.as

```
package
{
    //Test Observer Application
    import flash.display.Sprite;
    public class BugleSubscribe extends Sprite
    {
        public function BugleSubscribe( )
        {
            var bigNews:ConcreteSubject=new ConcreteSubject( );
            var larry:ConcreteObserver=new ConcreteObserver("Larry");
            var mo:ConcreteObserver=new ConcreteObserver("Mo");
            var curly:ConcreteObserver=new ConcreteObserver("Curly");
            var shemp:ConcreteObserver=new ConcreteObserver("Shemp");
            bigNews.subscribeObserver(larry);
            bigNews.subscribeObserver(mo);
            bigNews.subscribeObserver(curly);
            bigNews.subscribeObserver(shemp);
```

Example 8-14. BugleSubscribe.as (continued)

```
            //Set State #1
            bigNews.setType("Computer Invented","Home Team Wins",
                3234.54," Mad Duck");

            //Unsubscribe 2 Observers and attempt to re-subscribe
                current subscriber
            trace("\n** Larry and Shemp have unsubscribed **\n");
            bigNews.unsubscribeObserver(larry);
            bigNews.unsubscribeObserver(shemp);

            //Attempt re-subscribe
            bigNews.subscribeObserver(mo);

            //Set State #2
            bigNews.setType("Memory Prices Down","Game Rained Out",
                2987.98," Bad Bug");
        }
    }
}
```

Be sure to save the BugleSubscribe.as in the same folder as the other files in the class. Then, create a new Flash document, and type in **BugleSubscribe** in the Document class window. When you test the application, you should see the following output:

```
*|*Concrete Subject*|*
Larry has subscribed
Mo has subscribed
Curly has subscribed
Shemp has subscribed
Larry sees that Faster Computer Invented is interesting, and learns
    that Home Team Wins.
Whoaa!, the stock market is at 3234.54 and The Mad Duck is showing
    at the Bijou.
Mo sees that Faster Computer Invented is interesting, and learns
    that Home Team Wins.
Whoaa!, the stock market is at 3234.54 and The Mad Duck is showing
    at the Bijou.
Curly sees that Faster Computer Invented is interesting, and learns
    that Home Team Wins.
Whoaa!, the stock market is at 3234.54 and The Mad Duck is showing
    at the Bijou.
Shemp sees that Faster Computer Invented is interesting, and learns
    that Home Team Wins.
Whoaa!, the stock market is at 3234.54 and The Mad Duck is showing
    at the Bijou.

** Larry and Shemp have unsubscribed **

Mo is already a subscriber.

Mo sees that Memory Prices Down is interesting, and learns that Game
    Rained Out.
```

```
Whoaa!, the stock market is at 2987.98 and The Bad Bug is showing
    at the Bijou.
Curly sees that Memory Prices Down is interesting, and learns that Game
    Rained Out.
Whoaa!, the stock market is at 2987.98 and The Bad Bug is showing
    at the Bijou.
```

As each subscription is made, you can see the observer's name and the fact that he has subscribed. You can see that all four subscribers see identically formatted data. The formatting is the same because all the formatting is placed in the ConcreteSubject class. However, that's easy enough to change simply by removing all of the formatting and sending raw data. The Observer design pattern makes sure that whatever information's sent to the subscribing observers is identical as far as the state conditions are concerned, but really doesn't care about the formatting. The data can be taken and reformatted for any purpose by the observers. It just has to be the same data.

Using the unsubscribeObserver method, selected observers are removed from the subscription list using the line:

```
bigNews.unsubscribeObserver(ConcreteObserver instance);
```

As you can see, shemp and larry are unsubscribed between the first and second outputs using this method.

Dynamically Changing States

Up to this point, all the Observer patterns' testing has been done by static assignments of values to the state setters. The purpose was to see how the structure of the pattern works, but for most practical applications using Flash and ActionScript 3.0, we should look at something where the state values are rapidly changing, and new updates have to be sent almost constantly.

To see how rapidly changing data can be sent to a single source, and then dispatched to multiple observers, this next application depicts an action game with three combatants. Two are made up of spaceships with a missile or torpedo and a space station that shoots a beam at the spaceships. There's really nothing much you can do with the game other than fire from the two spaceships and space station, and watch the two spaceships get destroyed, but it serves to illustrate how all of the hits are generated by the action on the stage and broadcast to the different combatants. When a combatant is knocked out of play, he's no longer subscribed and all that is visible is the last message before destruction.

Recording a Space Battle

In setting up this particular Observer application, the Subject and Observer interfaces contain only Number and String parameters in the observer notification and update functions. The subscribe and unsubscribe functions are the same as previous Observer designs in this chapter. Save the classes in Example 8-15 and Example 8-16 by their caption names.

Example 8-15. Subject.as

```
package
{
    //Subject Interface
    public interface Subject
    {
        function subscribeObserver(o:Observer):void;
        function unsubscribeObserver(o:Observer):void;
        function notifyObserver(score:Number,damage:String):void;
    }
}
```

Example 8-16. Observer.as

```
package
{
    //Observer Interface
    public interface Observer
    {
        function update(score:Number,damage:String):void;
    }
}
```

Giving More Work to the Concrete Classes

The two classes representing concrete subjects and observers are changed little from previous examples. The ConcreteSubject class still keeps track of who has subscribed and unsubscribed, and sends out notifications of state changes.

The ConcreteObserver class, though, has taken on another responsibility. When a new ConcreteObserver is created, it makes sense to automatically subscribe her to the notification process. So instead of making it a two-step process, one to instantiate and another to subscribe, the ConcreteObserver now automatically subscribes new instances. To do this, only a single line had to be added to the constructor function:

```
concreteObserver.subscribeObserver(this);
```

The parameter references the instance being instantiated. At any time, the instance can unsubscribe or resubscribe by calling the unsubscribe or subscribe functions. Example 8-17 and Example 8-18 should be saved using the caption names.

Example 8-17. ConcreteSubject.as

```
package
{
    //Concrete Subject
    public class ConcreteSubject implements Subject
    {
        private var score:Number;
        private var damage:String;
        private var duplicate:Boolean;
        private var observers:Array;

        public function ConcreteSubject ()
        {
            observers=new Array();
        }
        //Subscribe observer without duplicates
        public function subscribeObserver (obserNow:Observer):void
        {
            duplicate=false;

            for (var ob=0; ob < observers.length; ob++)
            {
                if (observers[ob] == obserNow)
                {
                    duplicate=true;
                    trace ("Sorry, " + observers[ob].nomDeGuerre +
                        " is already subscribed.");
                }
            }
            if (! duplicate)
            {
                observers.push (obserNow);
            }
        }
        //Unsubscribe observer
        public function unsubscribeObserver (obserNow:Observer):void
        {
            for (var ob=0; ob < this.observers.length; ob++)
            {
                if (observers[ob] == obserNow)
                {
                    trace ("\n***" + this.observers[ob].nomDeGuerre +
                        " has been removed.***\n");
                    observers.splice (ob,1);
                }
            }
        }
        //Notify observers of total score and current damage
        public function notifyObserver (score:Number,damage:String):void
        {
            for (var notify in observers)
            {
                observers[notify].update (score,damage);
```

Example 8-17. ConcreteSubject.as (continued)

```
                }
        }
        //Set the score -- Accumulated score and damage
        public function setScore (score:Number,damage:String):void
        {
            this.score=score;
            this.damage=damage;
            notifyObserver (score,damage);
        }
    }
}
```

Example 8-18. ConcreteObserver.as

```
package
{
    //Concrete Observer
    class ConcreteObserver implements Observer
    {
        public var nomDeGuerre:String;
        private var damage:String;
        private var score:Number;
        private var concreteObserver:Subject;

        function ConcreteObserver(concreteObserver:Subject)
        {
            this.concreteObserver=concreteObserver;
            concreteObserver.subscribeObserver(this);
        }

        //Output to observer
        public function passOn():String
        {
            return "Current score: "+score+"\nCurrent damage: "+ damage;
        }

        //Trap changes in state from subject
        public function update(score:Number,damage:String):void
        {
            this.score=score;
            this.damage=damage;
            passOn();
        }
    }
}
```

Now that all of the basic programs are built, the real work begins. In the following section, you will be building several movie clips to represent two spaceships, their weapons, and a space station with its weapon. Most importantly though, the actions of the different elements will generate state changes processed by the Observer design pattern and sent to subscribing combatants.

Launching the Space Battle

In Example 8-19, you'll find a class that handles a battle in space. However, even before beginning on the ChangleHandler class, you first need to build some movie clips, and to do so, we need to start with a Flash document file. The following steps are just the first to set up the stage.

Setting up the Flash document

1. Open a new Flash document.
2. Set the stage size to 650 × 450, and set the background to gray.
3. Add a star field of your own design using yellow stars and shooting stars. Don't put in too many—just enough to give it an outer-space look and feel.
4. In the Document class window in the Properties inspector, type in **ChangeHandler**.
5. Save the file as AliensAttack.fla in the same folder with the other files for this application.

Building the spaceships

Once you have your Flash document set up, you need to build the spaceship movie clips.

1. Select Insert → New Symbol from the menu bar.

 When you name a movie clip that you'll use as a class, be sure to follow the same naming conventions as you would for any class. The first character should be capitalized and contain no spaces. So be sure to use Earthling rather than earthling, and don't put any spaces or other unacceptable characters in the name.

2. When the New Symbol window opens, type in **Earthling** in the Name window, and select Movie clip as the Behavior. If you see a button named Advanced, click it. It opens up part of the New Symbol window that you need for the next step.
3. Click the Export for ActionScript checkbox in the Linkage group. You should see the Export in first frame checkbox automatically selected. Also, in the Class window, you should see Earthling appear and flash.display.MovieClip in the Base class window. Click OK.
4. You are now in the Symbol edit mode. The center of the movie clip is indicated by the crosshair in the middle of the stage.
5. Using the drawing tools, draw a simple spaceship with the dimensions W=83, H=47. Figure 8-3 shows an example enlarged 400 percent. Click the Scene icon, located at the top left above the stage, when you're finished, and you should see your movie clip in the Library.

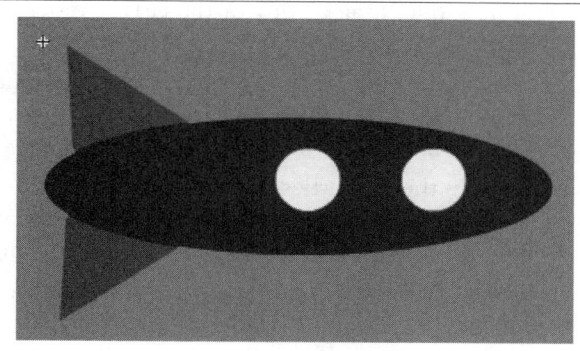

Figure 8-3. Earthling spaceship

6. Repeat Steps 1 through 5 to create a movie clip named Alien. Make a different ship and point it in the opposite direction as the Earthling movie clip spaceship. Once you're finished, you should see both the Alien and Earthling movie clips in the Library panel.

Building the weapons

Originally, we tried building the spaceship and weapon as a single movie clip, but after experimentation, it made more sense to make separate movie clips for better flexibility. The ones provided here are extremely simple, but you can add any kind of enhancement you want—blast trails, sound, and step-down to fire. The following steps show simple ones for seeing how the Observer design pattern state change can be triggered.

1. Select Insert → New Symbol from the menu bar. Name the movie clip bullet, using all lowercase for the name. Select Movie clip as the Behavior, and click OK. You are now in the Symbol editing mode.

2. Draw something that you want to look like the projectile shooting at the Alien. We used a simple oval with a fin on the top for a shark-like missile with the dimensions, W=23, H=7.3. The height includes the fin; so it's a pretty small missile, but proportionate to the Earthling ship. When you're done, click Scene 1 to exit the Symbol editing mode.

3. Select Insert → New Symbol from the menu bar When the New Symbol window opens, type in **Missile** in the Name window, and select Movie clip as the Behavior. If you see a button named Advanced, click it. It opens up part of the New Symbol window that you need for the next step.

4. Click on the Export for ActionScript checkbox in the Linkage group. You should see the Export in first frame checkbox automatically selected. Also, in the Class window, you should see Missile appear and flash.display.MovieClip in the Base class window. Click OK.

5. In the Symbol editing mode, drag a copy of the bullet movie clip to the center position (X=0, Y=0).

6. Click on Frame 20 and press the F5 key to add frames to Frame 20. Now, press F6 to add a keyframe. Select the keyframe in Frame 20, and move the bullet movie clip to X=380, Y=0.

7. Click on Frame 1, and in the Properties panel, select Motion in the Tween menu. You should see an arrow in the Timeline from Frame 1 to Frame 20 with a blue background. When you test it, the bullet MC should move from left to right.

8. Click on Frame 1, and open the Actions panel (Press F9 or Option + F9 on the Mac). Type in **stop( )**.

9. Repeat steps 1 through 8 for the Alien weapon. Make the Alien slug (bullet) look different and use the movie clip name projectile. Use the dimensions W=42, H=11. Instead of the weapon name Missile, use the name Torpedo. The Alien torpedo has to go in the opposite direction of the Earthling missile. So, from the initial position of X=0, Y=0 in the first frame, it should be in X=-423 for the last frame of the tween. Figure 8-4 shows a couple of simple magnified examples of the weapons.

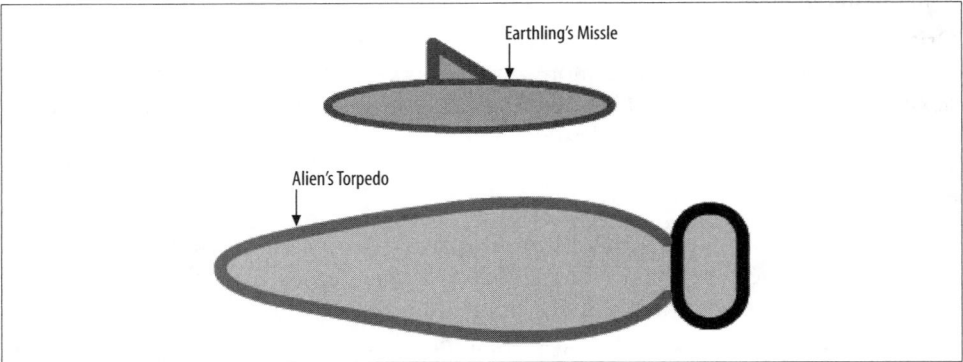

Figure 8-4. Earthling and Alien weapons

Building the Android space station and beam

The Android space station represents an automated space station that fires a double beam at both the Earthling and Alien ships. It's nothing more than a pentagon-shaped object. The v-shaped beam weapon sits on the pentagon movie clip.

1. Select Insert → New Symbol from the menu bar.

2. When the New Symbol window opens, type in **Android** in the Name window, and select Movie clip as the Behavior. If you see a button named Advanced, click it. It opens up part of the New Symbol window that you need for the next step.

3. Click on the Export for ActionScript checkbox in the Linkage group. You should see the Export in first frame checkbox automatically selected. Also, in the Class window, you should see `Android` appear and `flash.display.MovieClip` in the Base class window. Click OK.

4. You are now in the Symbol edit mode. Using the drawing tools, draw a pentagon with the dimension W=57, H=54. Click the Scene icon when you're finished, and you should see your space station movie clip in the Library.

5. Select Insert → New Symbol from the menu bar.

6. When the New Symbol window opens, type in **Beam** in the Name window, and select Movie clip as the Behavior. If you see a button named Advanced, click it. It opens up part of the New Symbol window that you need for the next step.

7. Click on the Export for ActionScript checkbox in the Linkage group. You should see the Export in first frame checkbox automatically selected. Also, in the Class window, you should see `Beam` appear and `flash.display.MovieClip` in the Base class window. Click OK.

8. You are now in the Symbol edit mode. Add two layers to the existing layer. Name the top layer "Actions," the middle layer "Left," and the bottom layer "Right."

9. Click on Frame 20, select the frames for all three layers, and press F5 to add 20 frames to all the layers. Click on the first frame of the Actions layer, and, in the Actions panel, type in **stop( );**.

10. Click on the first frame of the Left layer. Select the Line tool and set the Stroke height in the Properties panel to 6. (The Stroke height sets how wide the line will be.) Select green for the line color. With the base at the X=0, Y=0 position, draw a line at a -45° angle about 12 pixels long. You may have to reposition the base to the center position mark in the Symbol editor.

11. Click on the first frame of the Right layer and repeat step 10, but angle the line to +45°. When finished, you should see a V-shaped drawing with the base of the V at the X=0, Y=0 position.

12. Select the Left layer, click on Frame 20, and press the F6 key to add a keyframe. Select the green line and change the color from green to purple. Set the line dimensions to W=240, H=220 and reposition the base of the line to the center crosshair.

13. Repeat Step 10 with the line in the Right layer, except that the dimensions should be set to W=220, H=240. You should see a large purple "V" when you're finished.

14. Click on the first frame of the Left and Right layers, and select Shape for the tween. Press the Enter/Return key to test the movie. You should see a "beam" shoot out to the left and right, changing from green to purple. Figure 8-5 shows the beam being "fired" at the two ships.

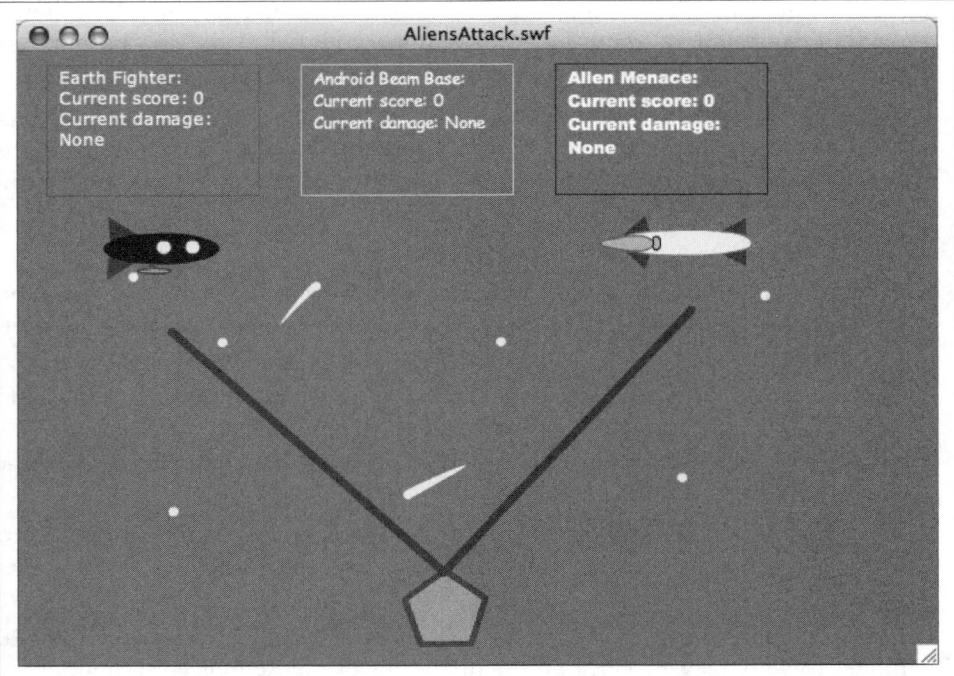

Figure 8-5. Android shooting a beam at the Earthling and Alien ships

You have set up all the classes and objects you'll need for the stage. Check your Library panel to be sure you have the following movie clips:

- Alien
- Android
- Beam
- bullet
- Earthling
- Missile
- projectile
- Torpedo

Those objects beginning with capital letters are classes and those beginning with lowercase letters are objects belonging to one of the classes.

Writing a Change Handler

In creating something to change conditions and send messages to the "Earthling," "Alien," and "Android," you need to use your imagination a bit. If an opponent's projectile or the beam from the Android hits either the Alien or Earthling, its hit total is sent to all subscribers via the Observer design pattern. Each of the windows showing the results represents different languages understood by the combatants. When a combatant is knocked out, it is automatically unsubscribed and no longer receives information, even though it can sustain further hits recorded by the surviving combatants. (The Android is invulnerable, and so can keep firing and receiving information even if all the others are knocked out.)

The ChangeHandler class is divided into several functions. The constructor function instantiates the concrete subjects and concrete observers. Each of the observers is given a name (nomDeGuerre) for keeping track of subscribers who are pushed into a subscriber array (warrior). A second array (battleUpdate) stores the battle names for each combatant placed in the text fields representing each combatant's "damage information center." To simulate the different languages receiving the message from the concrete subject, each combatant has a different font and border color for the text field representing its information display. The createTextWindow( ) and getFont( ) functions handle the viewing objects.

All the objects in the Library panel are placed on the stage along with firing and damage information in a rather large function, getParts( ). These visible objects are coordinated with the instances of the concrete observers.

The setScore( ) method can be invoked by instances of the ConcreteSubject class. Whenever, the setScore( ) method is called, the subscribing observers are notified via the passOn( ) method, which returns the current score through the update( ) method. The killWarrior( ) function invokes the unsubscribeObserver( ) method so that when a spaceship is knocked out of the game, it no longer receives messages.

Example 8-19 is a fairly large class, and you may want to break it down into smaller classes or abstract some of the functions. However, it's designed to show off the ways in which the Observer design pattern can be used in a context where information rapidly changes. Save the script as ChangeHandler.as in the same folder as the other files.

Example 8-19. ChangeHandler.as

```
package
{
    import flash.events.Event;
    import flash.events.MouseEvent;
    import flash.text.TextField;
    import flash.text.TextFormat;
    import flash.display.Sprite;

    public class ChangeHandler extends Sprite
    {
        private var eKiller:uint;
        private var aKiller:uint;
        private var aFlag:Number;
        private var aeFlag:Number;
```

Example 8-19. ChangeHandler.as (continued)

```
    private var eFlag:Number;
    private var lFlag:Number;
    private var outputColor:Number;
    private var battleUpdate:Array=[];
    private var warrior:Array=[];
    private var scoreSetter:ConcreteSubject;
    private var earthling:ConcreteObserver;
    private var alien:ConcreteObserver;
    private var scoreFormat:TextFormat;
    private var missile:Missile;
    private var alienMC:Alien;
    private var torpedo:Torpedo;
    private var androidMC:Android;
    private var beam:Beam;
    private var earthlingMC:Earthling;

    //Main Function
    public function ChangeHandler ()
    {
        scoreSetter=new ConcreteSubject();
        earthling=new ConcreteObserver(scoreSetter);
        warrior.push (earthling);
        earthling.nomDeGuerre="Earth Fighter";

        var android:ConcreteObserver=
            new ConcreteObserver(scoreSetter);
        warrior.push (android);
        android.nomDeGuerre="Android Beam Base";

        alien=new ConcreteObserver(scoreSetter);
        warrior.push (alien);
        alien.nomDeGuerre="Alien Menace";

        var eNm:String=earthling.nomDeGuerre.toLowerCase();
        var anNm:String=android.nomDeGuerre.toLowerCase();
        var alNm:String=alien.nomDeGuerre.toLowerCase();
        battleUpdate=new Array(3);
        scoreSetter.setScore (0,"None");
        createTextWindow ();
        getParts ();
    }
    //Create Output Windows
    private function createTextWindow ():void
    {
        for (var i:int=0; i < battleUpdate.length; i++)
        {
            battleUpdate[i]=new TextField();
            addChild (battleUpdate[i]);
            battleUpdate[i].x=20* 1 + (i * 180);
            battleUpdate[i].y=10;
            battleUpdate[i].width=150;
            battleUpdate[i].height=95;
```

Example 8-19. ChangeHandler.as (continued)

```
                battleUpdate[i].wordWrap=true;
                battleUpdate[i].multiline=true;
                battleUpdate[i].border=true;
                battleUpdate[i].textColor=0xffffee;
                scoreFormat=new TextFormat();
                scoreFormat.leftMargin=7;
                scoreFormat.rightMargin=7;
                getFont (warrior[i].nomDeGuerre);
                battleUpdate[i].borderColor=outputColor;
                battleUpdate[i].defaultTextFormat=scoreFormat;
                battleUpdate[i].text=warrior[i].nomDeGuerre+
                    ":\n"+warrior[i].passOn();
            }
        }
        //Get the font
        private function getFont (creature:String):void
        {
            switch (creature)
            {
                case "Earth Fighter" :
                    outputColor=0xff0000;
                    scoreFormat.font="Verdana";
                    break;

                case "Android Beam Base" :
                    outputColor=0x00ff00;
                    scoreFormat.font="Comic Sans MS";
                    break;

                case "Alien Menace" :
                    outputColor=0x0000ff;
                    scoreFormat.font="Arial Black";
                    break;
            }
        }
        //Get the movie clips from the Library
        private function getParts ():void
        {
            //Earthling
            earthlingMC=new Earthling();
            addChild (earthlingMC);
            earthlingMC.x=60,
            earthlingMC.y=120;
            missile=new Missile();
            addChild (missile);
            missile.x=earthlingMC.x+25;
            missile.y=earthlingMC.y+35;
            earthlingMC.addEventListener (MouseEvent.CLICK,fireMissile);
            earthlingMC.addEventListener
                (Event.ENTER_FRAME,earthlingHit);

            //Android
```

Example 8-19. ChangeHandler.as (continued)

```
        androidMC=new Android( );
        addChild (androidMC);
        androidMC.x=300;
        androidMC.y=380;
        beam=new Beam( );
        addChild (beam);
        beam.x=androidMC.x;
        beam.y=androidMC.y;
        androidMC.addEventListener (MouseEvent.CLICK,fireBeam);
        androidMC.addEventListener (Event.ENTER_FRAME,beamHit);

        //Alien
        alienMC=new Alien( );
        addChild (alienMC);
        torpedo=new Torpedo( );
        addChild (torpedo);
        alienMC.x=420,
        alienMC.y=120;
        torpedo.x=alienMC.x-7;
        torpedo.y=alienMC.y+17;
        alienMC.addEventListener (MouseEvent.CLICK,fireTorpedo);
        alienMC.addEventListener (Event.ENTER_FRAME,alienHit);
    }

    //Earthling fires missle
    private function fireMissile (evt:Event)
    {
        missile.play ();
        eFlag=0;
    }
    //Earthling hits Alien
    private function earthlingHit (evt:Event)
    {
        this.alienMC=alienMC;
        if (missile.hitTestObject(alienMC) && eFlag==0)
        {
            eFlag=1;
            aKiller++;
            scoreSetter.setScore (aKiller,"Alien Hit");
            dataOut ();
            if (aKiller >= 5)
            {
                scoreSetter.setScore (aKiller,"Alien Out");
                alien.nomDeGuerre="Alien Destroyed";
                this.alienMC.rotation=90;
                torpedo.rotation=90;
                killWarrior (alien);
                dataOut ();
            }
        }
    }
    //Android fires beam
```

Example 8-19. ChangeHandler.as (continued)

```
private function fireBeam (evt:Event)
{
    beam.play ();
    aFlag=0;
    aeFlag=0;
}
//Android beam hits Alien or Earthling
private function beamHit (evt:Event)
{
    if (beam.hitTestObject(alienMC) && aFlag==0)
    {
        aFlag=1;
        aKiller++;
        scoreSetter.setScore (aKiller,"BeamHit on Alien");
        dataOut ();
        if (aKiller >= 5)
        {
            scoreSetter.setScore (aKiller,"Alien Out");
            alien.nomDeGuerre="Alien Destroyed";
            this.alienMC.rotation=90;
            torpedo.rotation=90;
            killWarrior (alien);
            dataOut ();
        }
    }
    if (beam.hitTestObject(earthlingMC) && aeFlag==0)
    {
        aeFlag=1;
        eKiller++;
        scoreSetter.setScore (eKiller,"BeamHit on Earthling");
        dataOut ();
        if (eKiller >= 5)
        {
            scoreSetter.setScore (eKiller,"Earthling Out");
            earthling.nomDeGuerre="Earthling Off";
            this.earthlingMC.rotation=90;
            missile.rotation=90;
            killWarrior (earthling);
            dataOut ();
        }
    }
}
//Alien Fires torpedo
private function fireTorpedo (evt:Event)
{
    torpedo.play ();
    lFlag=0;
}
//Alien hits Earthling
private function alienHit (evt:Event)
{
    this.earthlingMC=earthlingMC;
```

Example 8-19. ChangeHandler.as (continued)

```
              if (torpedo.hitTestObject(earthlingMC) && lFlag==0)
              {
                  lFlag=1;
                  eKiller++;
                  scoreSetter.setScore (eKiller,"Earthling Hit");
                  dataOut ( );
                  if (eKiller >= 5)
                  {
                      scoreSetter.setScore (eKiller,"Earthling Out");
                      earthling.nomDeGuerre="Earthling Off";
                      this.earthlingMC.rotation=90;
                      missile.rotation=90;
                      killWarrior (earthling);
                      dataOut ( );
                  }
              }
          }

          //Output Data
          private function dataOut ( )
          {
              for (var i:int = 0; i < battleUpdate.length; i++)
              {
                  battleUpdate[i].text=warrior[i].nomDeGuerre+
                      ":\n"+warrior[i].passOn( );
              }
          }
          //Kill zone
          public function killWarrior (warship:ConcreteObserver)
          {
              scoreSetter.unsubscribeObserver (warship);
          }
      }
}
```

When you test the script, you'll find that when you fire on the Android, only the Earthling's hit can be seen as recorded. That's because both the Alien and Earthling are hit by the same double-beam, and the Alien's hit is recorded and broadcast first, quickly followed by the Earthling's hit. As a result, you can see only the Earthling's beam hit. Figure 8-6 shows the game after the Alien ship has been destroyed, and the Earthling's still sustaining hits from the Android beam, but because the Alien stops receiving messages after it is destroyed, it doesn't show the additional hits on the Earthling.

While this example is not a true game, it does illustrate the great possibilities for sending score information to different subscribers in different formats. Likewise, it illustrates how the Observer design pattern effortlessly handles rapidly changing data through a single subject, and then quickly distributing it to different subscribers.

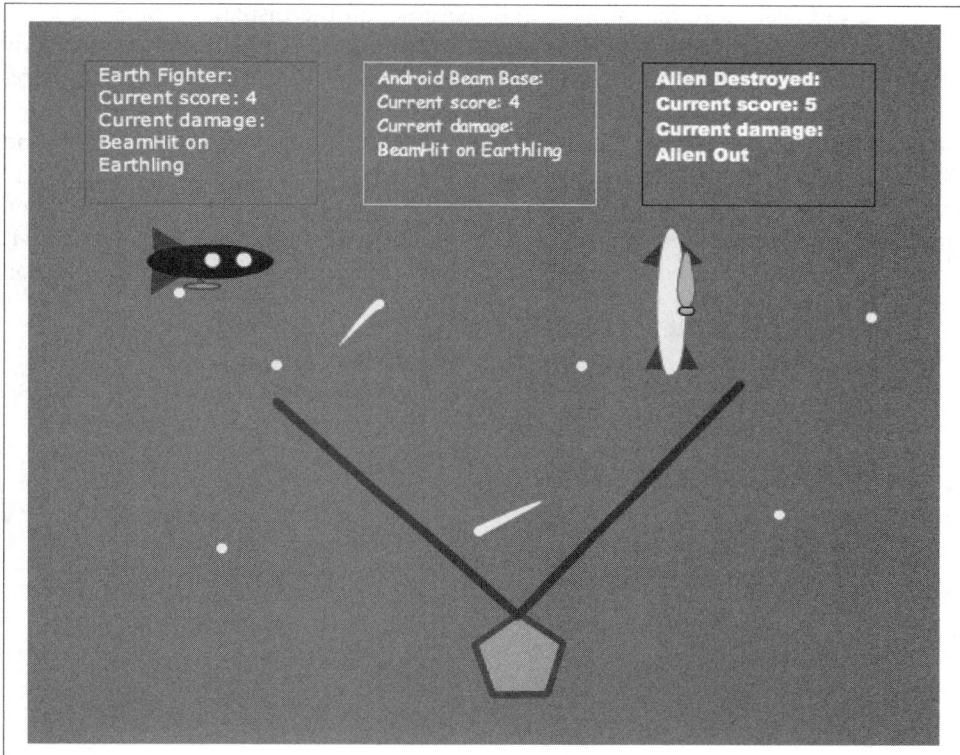

Earth Fighter:
Current score: 4
Current damage:
BeamHit on
Earthling

Android Beam Base:
Current score: 4
Current damage:
BeamHit on Earthling

Alien Destroyed:
Current score: 5
Current damage:
Alien Out

Figure 8-6. Destroyed combatant is unsubscribed

Example: Working with Different Data Displays

The last example showed how quickly changing data could be sent to a central object, and then sent out to subscribers. It also illustrated how subscribers could be dynamically unsubscribed. We showed some minimal output difference in the three combatants' window displays, but the differences were minimal. Now, we'll look at some seriously different output displays and introduce an additional interface.

The Output Designer

In the original design pattern book, the GoF provided a simple diagram for illustrating one use of the Observer pattern. A single source of data was sent to different objects that would display the data in a table, a bar chart, and a pie chart. This seemed like a good way to demonstrate some of Flash 9's and ActionScript 3.0's components and graphic capabilities using the Observer pattern. For our example, let's use a list box component, and then show how to create both a bar chart and line chart with ActionScript.

To make the task more manageable and reusable, all the display outputs are organized into separate classes. We decided that the data would represent quarterly
reports, and so the application is set up to accept four numeric values, each representing quarterly values. Also, to make the whole process of outputting data more
manageable, we have introduced a third interface along with the Subject and
Observer interfaces. This interface is set up so that it returns an array. The array will
contain the four numeric values representing the four quarters. To get started, open
up three ActionScript files, and copy the three files in Example 8-20, Example 8-21,
and Example 8-22 into each of the files. Save the interface files using the caption
names in the same folder.

Example 8-20. Subject.as

```
package
{
    //Subject Interface
    public interface Subject
    {
        function subscribeObserver(o:Observer):void;
        function unsubscribeObserver(o:Observer):void;
        function notifyObserver():void;
    }
}
```

Example 8-21. Observer.as

```
package
{
    //Observer Interface
    public interface Observer
    {
        function update(q1:Number,q2:Number,q3:Number,q4:Number):
            void;
    }
}
```

Example 8-22. DataOut.as

```
package
{
    //Data Output Interface
    public interface DataOut
    {
        function outToDesign():Array;
    }
}
```

Other than the new DataOut interface, the other two are similar to those you've seen
elsewhere in this chapter. The four quarterly numeric values mentioned can be seen
in the Observer interface.

The Concrete Classes and a Double Implementation

Both the concrete subject and observer classes are little changed from previous example. No names are used because the subscribers are data display objects rather than characters or live clients. So, these are actually a bit simpler than the last two examples. Open up two additional ActionScript files, and save Example 8-23 and Example 8-24 using the caption names as filenames.

Example 8-23. ConcreteSubject.as

```
package
{
    //Concrete Subject
    public class ConcreteSubject implements Subject
    {
        private var q1:Number,q2:Number,q3:Number,q4:Number;
        private var observers:Array;
        function ConcreteSubject( ):void
        {
            observers=new Array( );
        }
        public function subscribeObserver(obserNow:Observer):void
        {
            observers.push(obserNow);
        }
        public function unsubscribeObserver(obserNow:Observer):void
        {
            for (var ob=0; ob<observers.length; ob++)
            {
                if (observers[ob]==obserNow)
                {
                    observers.splice(ob,1);
                }
            }
        }
        public function notifyObserver( ):void
        {
            for (var notify in observers)
            {
                observers[notify].update(q1,q2,q3,q4);
            }
        }
        public function setQuarter(q1:Number,q2:Number,
            q3:Number,q4:Number):void
        {
            this.q1=q1;
            this.q2=q2;
            this.q3=q3;
            this.q4=q4;
            notifyObserver( );
        }
    }
}
```

Example 8-24. ConcreteObserver.as

```
package
{
    //Concrete Observer
    class ConcreteObserver implements Observer,DataOut
    {
        private var dataNow:Array;
        private var q1:Number,q2:Number,q3:Number,q4:Number;
        public function ConcreteObserver()
        {
        }
        public function outToDesign():Array
        {
            return dataNow;
        }
        public function update(q1:Number,q2:Number,q3:Number,q4:
            Number):void
        {
            this.q1=q1;
            this.q2=q2;
            this.q3=q3;
            this.q4=q4;
            dataNow=new Array(q1,q2,q3,q4);
            outToDesign();
        }
    }
}
```

In the concrete observer file, you may have noticed that two different interfaces were implemented—Observer and DataOut. The former implements the update() function that calls the outToDesign() function from the DataOut interface. Also, instead of void, the outToDesign() function returns an Array. Note that the array data is stored in the variable dataNow and returned through the outToDesign() method.

The Data Design Classes

The classes invoked for the three different data displays require close attention. Keep in mind that the array for all three classes is the array that returns the value for the four quarters. All three classes use the same array name, listArray, to help you remember that the data are all coming from the same subject. The displays may be different, but the data coming into each object through subscription as an observer is identical.

UIList component

The UIList component needs a copy placed in the Library of the Flash document file (FLA file) that you'll use to launch the application. So, before going on, open a new Flash document file and save it as DoDesign.fla in the same directory as the rest of the files for this application. Once you have your document file open and saved, use the following steps to get it set up for use with some Flash 9 and ActionScript 3.0 components:

1. Open the Components and Library panels from the Window menu, and drag a List component from the Components panel directly into the Library panel. When you do so, you'll see some supporting files and folders appear in the Library as well.

2. Drag a copy of the Button component to the Library panel. You don't need it right away, but you will.

3. In the Properties panel, type **DataDesign** in the Document class window. This will be the main class. You won't need it right away, but once you have all your classes set up, you will.

4. Save the DoDesign.fla file. You won't need it for a while but keep it open as a tab, so you can test your application later.

That's all you have to do with the document file. Open up an ActionScript file, and save the class in Example 8-25 using the caption as the filename:

Example 8-25. QuarterList.as

```
package
{
    //Setup for a List Component to receive array data
    import flash.display.Sprite;
    import fl.controls.List;

    public class QuarterList extends Sprite
    {
        var listArray:Array;

        //Data Displayed in UI List Component
        public function QuarterList(uData:Array)
        {
            listArray=new Array();
            listArray=uData;
            var quarter_list:List=new List();
            quarter_list.addItem({label:"Quarterly Results"});
            for (var quarter in listArray)
            {
                quarter_list.addItem({label:"Q"+(quarter+1)+"="
                    "+listArray[quarter],data:listArray[quarter]});
            }
            quarter_list.rowCount=5;
            quarter_list.width=110;
            addChild(quarter_list);
            quarter_list.x=50;
            quarter_list.y=55;
        }
    }
}
```

In this application, all you're really going to need are the labels that show up indicating the quarterly values. However, in some future application, you may need the actual numeric data, and so the class stores both the label and data. A literal label goes at the top, and so the first label, *Quarterly Results*, is unchanged and serves as a label for the UIList component. Figure 8-7 shows what the list box looks like when it displays data:

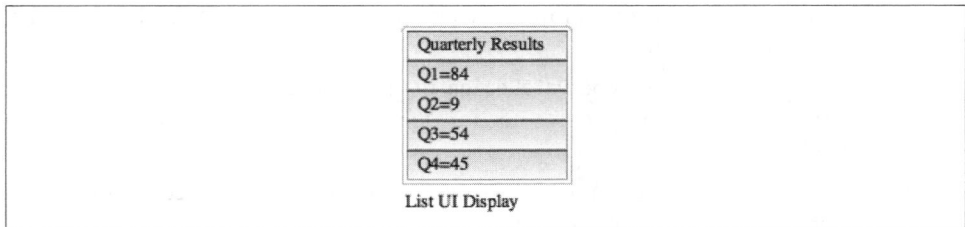

Figure 8-7. Data in list box

As noted, even though you can't see the actual data, it's also stored in the component. In some applications, there may be a need to access the data in the list box.

Bar chart display

Bar charts have an issue that list boxes don't: the relative display of data. A computer screen has a finite number of pixels to display the bars in a bar chart. If your values are relatively small—say between 1 and 100—you have plenty of room to display your charts, but as the values become bigger, you run out of vertical and horizontal screen real estate. Because the quarterly values have to be displayed as relative to one another and not all possible values, the job's somewhat easier. All you have to do is to find the largest value in the group of four in the array. That value can then be treated as a factor representing the largest value in the bar chart. For example, suppose you are using vertical bar charts with a maximum of 200 pixels and you have the following four values:

- 320
- 432
- 121
- 89

The maximum value is 432. That value must be represented by no more than 200 vertical pixels. Using the formula:

```
(currentValue &#247; MaxValue) x maxPixels
```

you can work out what each value should be. As you can see, the highest value would be 200 pixels, and the lesser values in the group would be proportionately smaller:

```
432&#247;432 = 1 x 200 = 200
121&#247;432 =.28 x 200 =56
```

Then, using that converted data, all that's left to do is draw rectangles representing those values. Open a new ActionScript file, and save Example 8-26 using the caption as the filename in the folder with the other files from this application.

Example 8-26. QuarterBar.as

```
package
{
    //Bar chart maker
    import flash.display.Graphics;
    import flash.display.Shape;
    import flash.display.Sprite;

    public class QuarterBar extends Sprite
    {
        private var listArray:Array;
        private var maxVal:Number=0;
        private var b1:Number, b2:Number, b3:Number,b4:Number;
        private var position:uint=160;
        private var maxSize:uint=150;

        //Data Displayed in Bar Chart
        function QuarterBar(cData:Array)
        {
            listArray=new Array( );
            listArray=cData;

            //Set up relative sizes for bars
            for (var max in listArray)
            {
                if (listArray[max] > maxVal)
                {
                    maxVal=listArray[max];
                }
            }
            b1=(listArray[0]/maxVal)*maxSize;
            b2=(listArray[1]/maxVal)*maxSize;
            b3=(listArray[2]/maxVal)*maxSize;
            b4=(listArray[3]/maxVal)*maxSize;

            //Bar Chart
            var bar:Shape=new Shape( );
            bar.graphics.clear( );
            //Draw Chart
            bar.graphics.beginFill(0xdd0000);
            bar.graphics.lineStyle(1,0x000000);
            bar.graphics.drawRect(285,(position-b1),30,b1);
            bar.graphics.drawRect(315,(position-b2),30,b2);
            bar.graphics.drawRect(345,(position-b3),30,b3);
            bar.graphics.drawRect(375,(position-b4),30,b4);
            bar.graphics.endFill( );
```

Example 8-26. QuarterBar.as (continued)

```
        addChild(bar);
    }
}
}
```

Figure 8-8 shows what the bar chart looks like when values have been assigned to it.

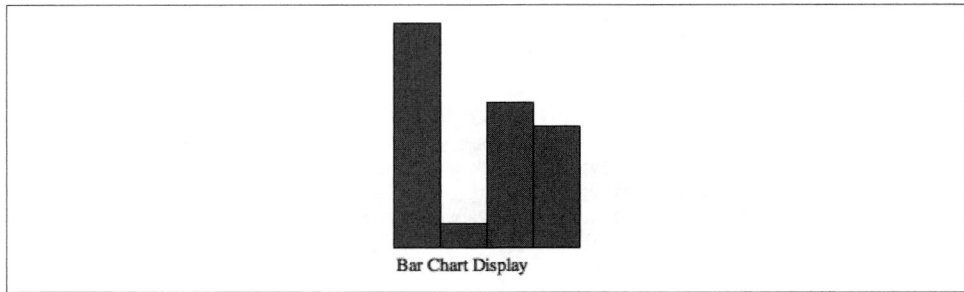

Bar Chart Display

Figure 8-8. Bar chart

Once drawn, a graphic does not automatically clear the stage when a new chart replaces it. The clear( ) method simply clears current memory, but not the stage. To clear the stage, you need to use removeChild( ). That requires an added child. So in the main program, we used a flag to make sure that a graphic element had been added, and then on the next data set, the flag's cleared and the first drawing removed.

The line graph

The line graph has the same issues with having proportionate points for drawing lines as the bar chart has for making rectangles. Fortunately, they're solved in the same way. An added feature in the line graph is some kind of background grid to give some better sense to the lines showing on the screen. The lines, without some kind of grid, just look like disembodied lines floating in space. So in addition to providing a drawing system to draw lines in the right positions, this class includes a background grid. Following the dictum of information designer Edward Tufte, the grid employs the minimum effective difference, so we used a thin light gray line. The line graph uses a wider blue line, so while the grid provides a context for the line graph, it doesn't get in the way. Open up a new ActionScript file and enter the code in Example 8-27, using the caption as the filename.

Example 8-27. QuarterGraph.as

```
package
{
    //Line graph maker
    import flash.display.Graphics;
    import flash.display.Shape;
```

Example 8-27. QuarterGraph.as (continued)

```
import flash.display.Sprite;

public class QuarterGraph extends Sprite
{
    private var listArray:Array;
    private var maxVal:Number=0;
    private var ln1:Number, ln2:Number, ln3:Number,ln4:Number;
    private var position:uint=300;
    private var maxSize:uint=100;

    //Set up relative sizes for lines
    function QuarterGraph (lData:Array)
    {
        listArray=new Array( );
        listArray=lData;

        //Create relative line sizes
        for (var max in listArray)
        {
            if (listArray[max] > maxVal)
            {
                maxVal=listArray[max];
            }
        }
        ln1=(listArray[0]/maxVal)*maxSize;
        ln2=(listArray[1]/maxVal)*maxSize;
        ln3=(listArray[2]/maxVal)*maxSize;
        ln4=(listArray[3]/maxVal)*maxSize;

        //Data Displayed in Line Graph
        var line:Shape=new Shape( );
        //Draw graph outline
        line.graphics.lineStyle (.25,0xcccccc);
        line.graphics.moveTo (50,200);
        line.graphics.lineTo (50,position);
        line.graphics.lineTo (200,position);
        line.graphics.moveTo (100,200);
        line.graphics.lineTo (100,position);
        line.graphics.moveTo (150,200);
        line.graphics.lineTo (150,position);
        line.graphics.moveTo (200,200);
        line.graphics.lineTo (200,position);
        line.graphics.moveTo (50,200);
        line.graphics.lineTo (200,200);
        line.graphics.moveTo (50,250);
        line.graphics.lineTo (200,250);
        line.graphics.moveTo (50,275);
        line.graphics.lineTo (200,275);
        line.graphics.moveTo (50,225);
        line.graphics.lineTo (200,225);
```

Example 8-27. QuarterGraph.as (continued)

```
            //Draw the graph
            line.graphics.lineStyle (2,0x0000cc);
            line.graphics.moveTo (50,(position-ln1));
            line.graphics.lineTo (100,(position-ln2));
            line.graphics.lineTo (150,(position-ln3));
            line.graphics.lineTo (200,(position-ln4));

            addChild (line);
        }
    }
}
```

Figure 8-9 shows the line graph superimposed on the background grid.

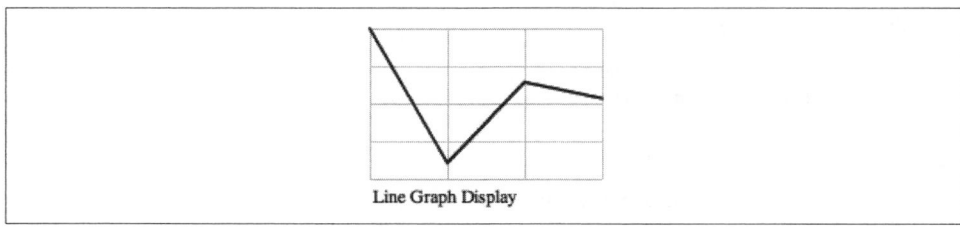

Line Graph Display

Figure 8-9. Line graph

If you ever need to have superimposed line graphs to show change or for comparisons, you can set up the main program *not* to use the removeChild( ) function for redrawing a graph.

Pulling All the Elements Together

With 10 different files, pulling them all together in a main class may seem daunting. However, as you'll see, the task is actually simplified. The classes handle most of the grunt-work, and all you need to do is use them.

The most important feature in the DataDesign class is the data entry in the form of input text fields. As in the space battle example, the different text fields are placed into array elements. However, instead of using the text fields for data display, these text fields are used for data entry. Values entered into the text fields are converted to numbers, and passed to numeric variables. The numeric variables are sent to a concrete subject object, and the setter method establishes them as the current values. In turn, these values are sent out to the concrete observers in an array that's used in displaying the data. Open a new ActionScript file, enter the code in Example 8-28, and save it as the caption name.

Example 8-28. DataDesign.as

```
package
{
    //Main program
    import flash.display.Sprite;
    import fl.controls.Button;
    //Text Fields for Labels
    import flash.text.TextField;
    import flash.text.TextFieldAutoSize;
    import flash.text.TextFieldType;
    //Events
    import flash.events.MouseEvent;
    import flash.events.Event;

    public class DataDesign extends Sprite
    {
        private var dataEntry:Array=[];
        private var quarterGraph:QuarterGraph;
        private var quarterBar:QuarterBar;
        private var quarterList:QuarterList;
        private var dataSub:ConcreteSubject;
        private var listDisplay:ConcreteObserver;
        private var barChart:ConcreteObserver;
        private var lineGraph:ConcreteObserver;
        private var xpos:uint=250;
        private var ypos:uint=250;
        private var dt1:Number,dt2:Number,dt3:Number,dt4:Number;
        private var dataBtn:Button;
        private var barFlag:Boolean=true;

        public function DataDesign ()
        {
            //Set up concrete subjects and observers
            dataSub=new ConcreteSubject();
            listDisplay=new ConcreteObserver();
            barChart=new ConcreteObserver();
            lineGraph=new ConcreteObserver();
            dataSub.subscribeObserver (listDisplay);
            dataSub.subscribeObserver (barChart);
            dataSub.subscribeObserver (lineGraph);

            doText ();
            doDataEntry ();
            doButton ();
            dataBtn.addEventListener (MouseEvent.CLICK,showData);

        }
        //Data Output to Stage
        function showData (ev:Event):void
        {
            if (barFlag)
            {
                barFlag=false;
```

Example 8-28. DataDesign.as (continued)

```
        }
        else
        {
            removeChild (quarterBar);
            removeChild (quarterGraph);
        }
        //doObservers( );
        dt1=Number(dataEntry[0].text);
        dt2=Number(dataEntry[1].text);
        dt3=Number(dataEntry[2].text);
        dt4=Number(dataEntry[3].text);
        doDisplay (dt1,dt2,dt3,dt4);

        //Data Displayed in List UI Component
        quarterList=new QuarterList(listDisplay.outToDesign( ));
        addChild (quarterList);

        //Data Displayed in Bar Chart
        quarterBar=new QuarterBar(barChart.outToDesign( ));
        addChild (quarterBar);

        //Data Displayed in Line Graph
        quarterGraph=new QuarterGraph(lineGraph.outToDesign( ));
        addChild (quarterGraph);
    }
    //Add Text Labels
    private function doText ( ):void
    {
        var ui:TextField=new TextField( );
        var bar:TextField=new TextField( );
        var ln:TextField=new TextField( );
        var dt:TextField=new TextField( );
        ui.autoSize=TextFieldAutoSize.LEFT;
        bar.autoSize=TextFieldAutoSize.LEFT;
        ln.autoSize=TextFieldAutoSize.LEFT;
        addChild(ui),addChild(bar),addChild(ln);
        addChild (dt);
        ui.x=50, bar.x=285,ln.x=50;
        dt.x=xpos;
        ui.y=165, bar.y=165,ln.y=305;
        dt.y=ypos+15;
        ui.text="List UI Display";
        bar.text="Bar Chart Display";
        ln.text="Line Graph Display";
        dt.text="Enter Data";
    }
    //Data value entry function
    private function doDisplay (n1:Number,n2:Number,
        n3:Number,n4:Number):void
    {
        dataSub.setQuarter (n1,n2,n3,n4);
    }
```

Example 8-28. DataDesign.as (continued)

```
//Data Entry
private function doDataEntry ( ):void
{
    for (var de=0; de<4; de++)
    {
        dataEntry[de]=new TextField( );
        dataEntry[de].border=true;
        dataEntry[de].borderColor=0x999999;
        dataEntry[de].background=true;
        dataEntry[de].backgroundColor=0xcccccc;
        dataEntry[de].type=TextFieldType.INPUT;
        dataEntry[de].width=32;
        dataEntry[de].height=14;
        this.addChild (dataEntry[de]);
        dataEntry[de].x=xpos+(40*de);
        dataEntry[de].y=ypos;
    }
}
//Get the Button component
private function doButton ( ):void
{
    dataBtn=new Button( );
    dataBtn.label="Show Data";
    this.addChild (dataBtn);
    dataBtn.x=xpos;
    dataBtn.y=ypos+30;
}
}
}
```

In discussing the chart and graph classes, we noted that unless you removed a current graphic, it would stay on the stage unless removeChild( ) is used to get rid of it. Using the barFlag variable, the class made sure that the chart and graph had been added before trying to remove it. Without using some kind of test flag, it would have encountered an error if it tried to remove before the object was added with addChild( ).

You can probably think of more classes to use to farm out some of the methods. However, in order to better see how all the data went through the input process and was passed to the concrete subject for broadcast out to the different display objects, we allowed this class to grow a bit.

Summary

The real test for a design pattern is its flexibility. As you saw in the examples in this chapter, very little was changed in the Subject or Observer classes. When the task of a design pattern is to distribute state changes to a number of different subscribed observers, you can see that many different kinds of specific applications can use this pattern. Because of this feature, its flexibility, and relative simplicity, the Observer design pattern is seen in many different applications.

Equally important, the Observer shows how to program to an interface and not an implementation. Example 8-1 and Example 8-11 clearly illustrate this process. Each concrete observer is typed as the supertype (interface) Observer. However, also note that in some cases where the Observer pattern is put to work, you can't type an implementation to a supertype, as you may have noted in Example 8-19. This doesn't mean that the example's invalid; it simply shows that in some designs using the Observer, when you attempt to program to the interface, you run into problems because of the characteristics of the interface and its implementation. As a result, such cases require you to create instances by typing them as implementations.

When thinking about where you can use the Observer pattern, consider situations where you have some key states that must be sent to different instances. The most useful implementation is where the exact same information needs to be sent to different data display or interpretations. In this way, the application ensures that the exact same state information is sent without having to generate separate data sources.

Template Method Pattern

If you write a post and put it on a blog, that's a
historical document. If you change your template, then
that entry looks completely different. It's the same
words, but not the same meaning. This all depends on
what historical questions that people will be asking
and we can't know what they will want.

—Josh Greenberg

Well, I did all the pre-production and I did full demos
of all the songs and then I took it into the studio and
played it for all the guys and then we kind of took that
as the template and did the album live very quickly.

—David Sanborn

What Is the Template Method Pattern?

You're going to like this pattern. Essentially the *template method* is an algorithm made up of a sequence of operations that accomplishes some goal. Imagine a general set of steps for getting something done such as going to work. If you take a car, boat, or airplane to work, you're going to be doing certain things that are similar and others that are different. You'll be transporting yourself in a vehicle, guiding it to a particular location, and you always grab a cup of coffee to take with you. So if you make a general template that covers going by car, boat, or airplane, your outline (algorithm) would look something like the following:

1. Prepare transportation.

2. Navigate vehicle.

3. Drink your cup of coffee.

Preparing a car for transportation usually involves little more than making sure it's got enough gas and the tires aren't flat. With a boat, you might want to check to make sure you have the necessary charts on board and that all the life preservers are in good shape. An airplane requires a walk around with a pre-flight checklist of items to inspect. So, you're going to need special instructions for the first item in the outline depending on the vehicle.

 This chapter contains two different types of references to "template method." A reference to the Template Method design pattern will have the first letter of each word capitalized. The template method is also a reference to a method (function), and that reference will use lowercase for both words.

For the second step, navigation in a car requires getting on the road, making all the correct turns, and using the right streets. This can be tricky at times, and the driver may want to check on traffic reports to avoid congestion or road repairs. Depending on the circumstances, a boat trip can be anything from a quick trip across a lake to a complex navigation through shoals, shallows, and currents. Finally, navigating an airplane can be a simple straight flight on a clear day to an IFR (Instrument Flight Rules) flight requiring knowledge of several different navigation instruments in cloudy weather. Like the first step, this too will require specialized instructions.

Finally, you've got the cup of coffee you drink on the way to work. That's pretty much the same no matter what kind of transportation you use. You'd use the same kind of travel container with all three modes of transportation, and you'd have to take care not to spill coffee in your lap. Unlike the first two sets of instructions that differ for each mode of transportation, this last one's going to be the same for all three vehicles.

Making a template for this set of circumstance requires a loosely crafted method for the first two items and a concrete one for the last. Using the Template Method design, each of the three functions would be placed in a method so that the sequence of the steps would be preserved no matter what. The method containing the ordered functions *is the template method*—a method to preserve the sequence. Here's what it would look like in a rough pseudocode:

```
//Within an abstract class

//This the the Template Method
final function templateMethod( )
{
    prepareTransportation( );
    navigatVehicle( );
    drinkCoffee( );
}

//Abstract functions
function prepareTransportation( ):void
{
    //nothing here
}
```

```
function navigateVehicle( ): void
{
    //nothing here
}
//Concrete function
function drinkCoffee( )
{
    trace("Drinking coffee on the way to work ");
}
//End of class
```

The Template Method does not require a concrete function. However, the example illustrates that if you have one that's needed in all instantiations of the template method, it's handy to have.

Key Features

In general, the Template Method design pattern is a flexible algorithm-maker centered around the domain class where the algorithm's defined. The following features characterize the Template Method design pattern:

- Uses inheritance for behavior distribution between classes
- Allows subclasses to provide details for some operations in general algorithm
- Uses inverted control structure—parent class calls operations of a subclass
- Specifies the steps of an algorithm and locks the order of operations in the algorithm
- Allows for optional "hook" operations for extensions at specified points

In the Behavior grouping of design patterns, the GoF specifies only two patterns based on *inheritance* instead of *composition*, and the Template Method is one. Because ActionScript 3.0 doesn't have true abstract classes, you have to remember not to implement the main abstract class. However, you can program to the abstract classes interface (supertype), and not the implementation. This chapter's examples show this.

By allowing the subclasses to fill in some operations in the different parts of the algorithm, the design pattern allows for both the advantages of inheritance and the flexibility of composition. Essentially the Template Method uses inheritance to vary parts of the algorithm. Because the operations allow the subclasses to fill in their details, think of the operations as *placeholders* awaiting details from the subclasses. By selectively overriding the algorithm's (template method's) operations, each subclass can get the functionality it needs.

The inverted control structure is sometimes called the *Hollywood Principle* because the parent classes in effect declare, "*Don't call us, we'll call you,*" to the child classes (subclasses). This makes the general domain as defined in the abstract class the epicenter. The parent class calls the operations of a subclass through the template method. The child classes just give the details to the operations within an algorithm controlled by the parent class.

The template method itself is locked using the `final` attribute. By adding `final` to a function, the function cannot be overridden. At first, this may seem to contradict everything being said about leaving some of the details to the subclasses by overriding the operations. However, you don't lock the abstract functions (operations), only the template method. Figure 9-1 illustrates this arrangement.

```
class AbstractClass
{
        final function templateMethod()
        {
                operationA()                Locked up
                operationB()
                operationC()

        }
---------------------------------------------
        function operationA()
        {}
        function operationB()          Unlocked
        {}
        function operationC()
        {}
}
```

Figure 9-1. Locked Template Method

As you can see in Figure 9-2, the operations that make up the template method are not locked. So the subclasses can override the operations all they need. However, subclasses cannot change the order of the operations that make up the algorithm in the template method itself.

Finally, you can add an optional *hook* operation. On one level, a hook is nothing more than a method that can be overridden in the context of a Template Method design. It also can be seen as a back door where an implementation (subclass) can hook into an algorithm. Because the hook concept is best understood in the context of an example, further discussion will be deferred to later on in the chapter.

The Template Method Model

Upon first encountering the Template Method, most developers are struck by the simplicity of the pattern's design, and then by its utility and clarity. Even though the design as depicted in the class diagram in Figure 9-2 is very simple, it can be used to solve a wide range of problems.

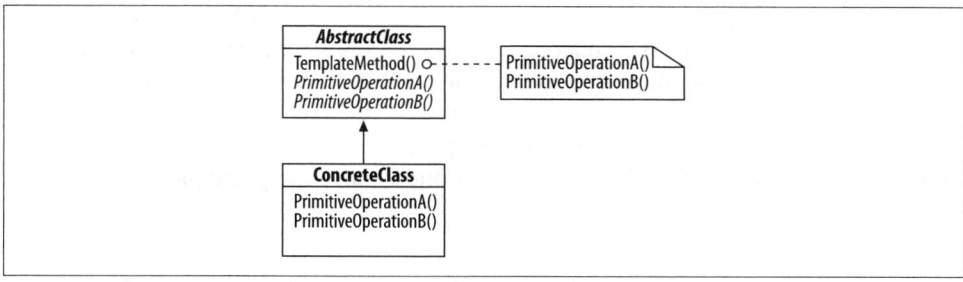

Figure 9-2. Template Method

The Template Method design pattern is simple to understand and apply. However, as you'll see, it has a number of features that make it unique. The real trick to using the Template Method is knowing how to differentiate between the abstract functions that must be overridden, concrete functions used consistently throughout the algorithms that aren't overridden, and those operations that act as hooks and are optionally overridden. Throughout the examples, you'll see more precisely how to do this.

Key OOP Concepts Used with the Template Method

As one of only two design patterns that use inheritance instead of composition in the Behavioral category of design patterns, the Template Method would seem to be a hard sell when it comes to proposing the design pattern as a paragon of good OOP. After all, the second principle put forth by GoF is to *favor composition over inheritance*. Why even bother with a design pattern that seems to favor inheritance over composition? Further, is the *Hollywood Principle* unique to the design patterns using inheritance, or is it a general principle usable in both design patterns using composition as well?

Why Inheritance and Not Composition?

Whenever a design pattern uses inheritance as a key element instead of composition, you need to consider the reason. To understand the reason, you need to fully understand the principle of favoring composition over inheritance as a general principle in good OOP. The principle's established because of certain advantages of composition over inheritance, especially the composition advantage of not breaking encapsulation. However, Gamma, Helm, Johnson and Vlissides (GoF) note that inheritance also has certain advantages. One such advantage is that when using subclasses where *some but not all* operations are overridden, modifying the reused implementation is easier. Because the Template Method design pattern does exactly that—uses some but not all operations that can be overridden to achieve flexibility—it incorporates a key advantage of inheritance over composition.

Further, discussing favoring composition over inheritance, GoF note that reuse by inheritance eases the process of making new components that can be composed with old ones. Hence the dictum that composition should be favored over inheritance needs to be tempered by the knowledge that inheritance and composition actually work together. This is not to say that the principle of favoring composition over inheritance is invalid, but rather you need to understand the principle in the context of its development.

 In the process of learning design patterns and the programming principles surrounding them, do not learn the principles as mantras. Chanting the principles over and over again may help you remember them, but not necessarily understand them. All the principles exist in some context, so be certain to understand the principles' context to use them effectively.

Abstract Functions and Override Flexibility

In previous chapters we've groused about the fact that ActionScript 3.0 doesn't have abstract classes. Well, ActionScript 3.0 doesn't have *abstract functions* either. Rather than rant about that fact, a more important issue is their use. An abstract function is a way of reducing a function to an idea or concept without content. In actual usage, all this involves is naming the function and placing it in the order you want for your main algorithm in the template method, not unlike the functions in an interface. In languages like Java, you can write:

```
abstract myAbstractFunction();
```

and that's it. In ActionScript 3.0, you can accomplish the same thing using:

```
function myAbstractFunction() {}
```

So while you don't have a function that can be designated abstract, you can effectively create all the abstract functions you want, just as you can develop abstract classes, with ActionScript 3.0.

Aside from the fact that ActionScript 3.0 can create functions that act like abstract functions, the more important principle is to understand their use in the context of the Template Method design pattern. Key to all design patterns is the idea of reusability and flexibility. Abstract functions *must be* overridden, and therein is their flexibility. Whenever a function is overridden, it's changed. By setting up abstract functions in the parent class, the subclasses can use them as needed to fill out the particular implementation of the template method algorithm. Reuse is fostered by the fact that as long as the algorithm template is applicable, the developer has flexibility because the abstract functions that make up the template method can be modified to suit the application.

Consider Variation

When selecting a design pattern, developers are advised to *consider what should vary in a design*. Here the emphasis changes from fretting over what causes redesign to considering what you want to change. In the Template Method design pattern, *the template method encapsulates the different parts that go into the main algorithm*. Each abstract operation in the template method varies in the context of the algorithm. Because the function's locked, the sequence of operations doesn't change, but the operations themselves do. Hence, the design pattern principle of *encapsulating what varies* is nicely illustrated in the Template Method design pattern.

The Hollywood Principle

The casting director tells the actors who have tried out for a part, "We'll let you know, but don't call us. We'll call you." The Template Method design pattern mirrors this: the template method itself is in the parent class, and the parent class calls the subclasses. More specifically, the template method can call 1) concrete operations, 2) concrete operations from the main abstract class (where the template method is defined), 3) primitive operations, 4) factory method (see Chapter 2), and 5) hooks. However, these lower level objects cannot call the parent classes.

Because the GoF discuss only the Hollywood Principle in their Template Method chapter, we considered whether this "principle" applies to all design patterns or just certain ones with inverted control structures. If you go back to Chapter 2 and look at the Factory Method, and Chapter 8 on the Observer pattern, you will see the principle at work as well. For example, the inverted control structure in the Observer pattern informs all the relevant state changes to the subscribing objects. The information flows from the top down to the lower level objects.

So, what's the purpose of the principle? What does it do for reusable code? Eric and Elisabeth Freeman summed it up nicely as a way to prevent *dependency rot*. In other words, it reduces the dependencies of higher-level components on lower-level components and all their related dependencies. That's a good thing because your system is clearer to work with and understand. Figure 9-3 illustrates this principle.

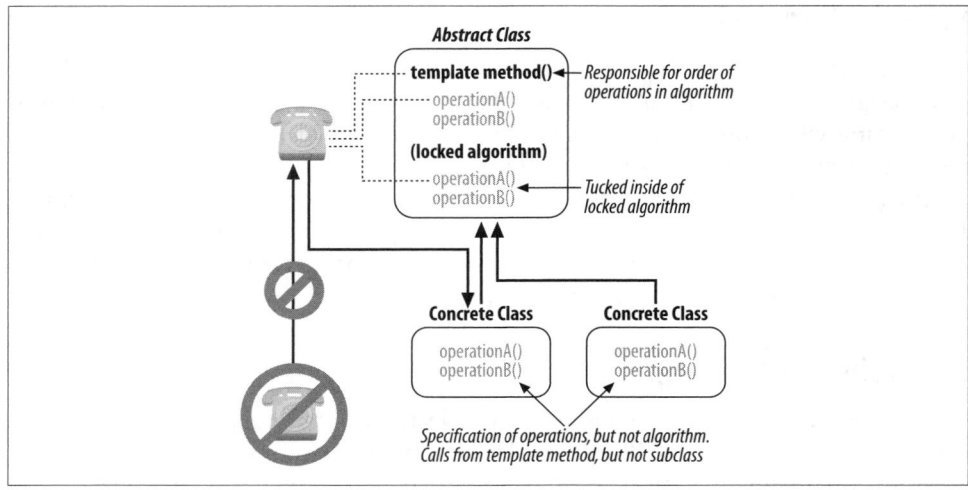

Figure 9-3. Hollywood principle

Minimalist Example: Abstract Template Method

Even though it may not make a lot of sense to use a Template Method design pattern when you have only a single subclass, doing so helps reveal the design pattern's structure. So, in this minimalist example, you should be able to easily see the underlying structure used in the Template Method. We don't need much, just two main classes:

- Abstract class with the algorithm for the template method
- At least one concrete class as a subclass of the abstract class

Look for the operations that will be detailed by the subclasses, and the one operation that will be constant throughout the subclasses.

Bare Bones Template Method

Examples 9-1 and 9-2 show the two classes we need to get started with this simple but useful pattern. Save each class using the caption name as the filename.

Example 9-1. AbstractClass.as

```
package
{
    //Abstract Class
    class AbstractClass
    {
        public final function templateMethod():void
        {
            primitiveA();
            primitiveB();
```

Example 9-1. AbstractClass.as (continued)

```
        fromTemplate( );
    }
    protected function primitiveA( ):void
    {
        //Awaiting instructions
    }
    protected function primitiveB( ):void
    {
        //Awaiting instructions
    }
    private final function fromTemplate( ):void
    {
        trace("Hello everybody!");
    }
};
}
```

Example 9-2. ConcreteClass.as

```
package
{
    //Any concrete class
    public class ConcreteClass extends AbstractClass
    {
        trace("Concrete class");
        override protected function primitiveA( ):void
        {
            trace("Special A");
        }
        override protected function primitiveB( ):void
        {
            trace("Special B");
        }
    }
}
```

Looking at the AbstractClass you can see that the main algorithm is encapsulated in the templateMethod( ) function. The final statement indicates that the method is locked up and cannot be changed by the subclasses. However, all that really means is that the *order* cannot be changed by the subclasses. Both the primitiveA( ) and primitiveB( ) functions, which make up the templateMethod( ), are abstract. They are awaiting the details from the subclasses. So while the templateMethod( ) is locked, the operations that go into it don't have to be, and can be changed by the subclasses.

At the same time, if you want any of the operations that make up the template method to be locked, you can do that as well. The function fromTemplate( ) is locked in the same way as the main template method. As part of the templateMethod( ) function, the fromTemplate( ) operation cannot be changed by an override statement as the two abstract function can. So you can have the best of both worlds. Those operations in the main algorithm that you want to be detailed by the subclasses, you leave abstract, and to those you want to remain constant, you apply the final statement.

In the subclass, ConcreteClass, both abstract methods from the AbstractClass have been overridden. The subclass gives each a different content. However, the third operation that was locked up, fromTemplate( ), is nowhere to be found. That's because it cannot be changed, and because it was inherited from the AbstractClass. There's no need to add anything.

Testing Templates

To test the minimalist example, create a single instance of the concrete class, and then add the template method to the instance. As you saw in the concrete class, the two abstract operations were given details, but nothing else was done. Save Example 9-3 in the same folder as the other two files in the minimalist example using the caption as the filename.

Example 9-3. TestTemplate.as

```
package
{
    import flash.display.Sprite;
    public class TestTemplate extends Sprite
    {
        public function TestTemplate( )
        {
            var testPlate:AbstractClass=new ConcreteClass( );
            testPlate.templateMethod( );
        }
    }
}
```

To test the example, open a new Flash document file, and type in **TestTemplate** in the Document class window in the Properties panel. When you test the application, you should see the following in your Output panel:

```
Concrete class
Special A
Special B
Hello everybody!
```

The output shows that the special details added by the subclass in addition to the invariant method are in the order locked into the template method algorithm. Keeping in mind that the example is to expose the structure of the Template Method, you can see how some of the details are deferred to the subclass (Special A and Special B), how the algorithm's order is preserved, and how any constant (locked) operations are made available.

Employing Flexibility in the Template Method

Now that you have a better idea of how the Template Method design pattern's structure works, let's see how it can be usefully employed. In this next example, you'll see an implementation that uses the same template method for two different concrete classes. Figure 9-4 shows the class diagram:

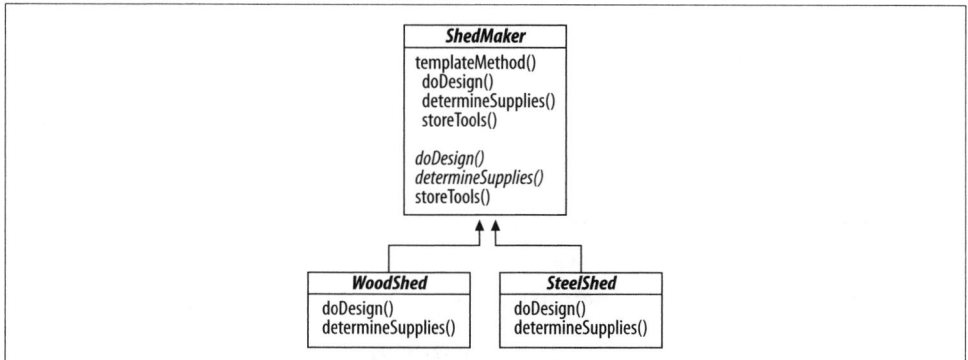

Figure 9-4. Template method with two concrete classes

The main abstract class, ShedMaker, includes three operations in the templateMethod( ) function. Two are abstract and will be overridden by the subclasses where the details will be supplied. The third operation is a final function, not to be overridden, and will be used in all subclasses.

The example looks at what you may need in creating a shed in general, and what different types of sheds may need. The example develops an algorithm that does the following:

- Designs the shed
- Determines which supplies will be required
- Stores tools in the completed shed

All sheds can use these steps, but depending on the kind of shed, the details will vary in certain aspects. In this case, we're supposing that one shed will be made of wood and the other of corrugated steel. Because designing with wood is different than designing for steel, the design operation (doDesign( )) is abstract. Likewise, determining which supplies you need is different as well, and so the determineSupplies( ) function is also abstract. However, no matter what kind of shed is built, storing tools is the same, and so that function is locked so it won't be overridden.

To get started, open three new ActionScript files, and enter the code in Examples 9-4 to 9-6. Use the caption names as the filenames, and save all files in the same directory.

Example 9-4. ShedMaker.as

```
package
{
    //Abstract Class
    class ShedMaker
    {
        public final function templateMethod( ):void
        {
            doDesign( );
            determineSupplies( );
            storeTools( );
        }
        protected function doDesign( ):void
        {
        }
        protected function determineSupplies( ):void
        {
        }
        private final function storeTools( ):void
        {
            trace("Now I can put all my tools away.\n");
        }
    }
}
```

Example 9-5. WoodShed.as

```
package
{
    class WoodShed extends ShedMaker
    {
        trace("WoodShed");
        override protected function doDesign( ):void
        {
            trace("Designing Wood Shed");
        }
        override protected function determineSupplies( ):void
        {
            trace("I'll do it with 1 X 12's for the walls.");
            trace("The rest I'll do with 2 X 4's.");
        }
    }
}
```

Example 9-6. SteelShed.as

```
package
{
    class SteelShed extends ShedMaker
    {
        trace("SteelShed");
        override protected function doDesign( ):void
        {
            trace("Designing Steel Shed");
        }
        override protected function determineSupplies( ):void
        {
            trace("Ok I'll need some corregated sheet metal.")
            trace("Better get some steel fasteners too.");
        }
    }
}
```

In both concrete classes, a trace( ) statement indicates which class is instantiated so that you can see it in the output. More importantly, each of the two concrete classes adds unique details to the two abstract operations, doDesign( ) and determineSupplies( ). Neither includes anything regarding the storeTools( ) function. Because storeTools( ) is invariant in all implementations, there's no reason to include it. It's inherited from the ShedMaker class.

To test it, both concrete classes are instantiated in the same testing class, BuildShed. Example 9-7 shows that the two different instances use the interface data type to instantiate the wood and steel instances. Save the file using the example caption name in the same directory as Examples 9-4 to 9-6.

Example 9-7. BuildShed.as

```
package
{
    import flash.display.Sprite;
    public class BuildShed extends Sprite
    {
        public function BuildShed( )
        {
            //Make a steel shed
            var steel:ShedMaker=new SteelShed( );
            steel.templateMethod( );

            //Make a wood shed
            var wood:ShedMaker=new WoodShed( );
            wood.templateMethod( );
        }
    }
}
```

Both instances employ the templateMethod( ) function, but as you will see when you test the application, the results are very different. Open a new Flash document file, and in the Document class window, type in **BuildShed**. When you test the application, you'll see the following in the Output window:

```
SteelShed
Designing Steel Shed
Ok I'll need some corregated sheet metal.
Better get some steel fasteners too.
Now I can put all my tools away.

WoodShed
Designing Wood Shed
I'll do it with 1 X 12's for the walls.
The rest I'll do with 2 X 4's.
Now I can put all my tools away.
```

In this output, you can see the Template Method at work. In the first instance, you can see that it shows the SteelShed concrete class has been invoked. All the output is uniquely relevant to the steel shed except for the last line before the wood shed output. That last line is the locked up operation from the abstract class, ShedMaker. Then, the WoodShed instance gets an entirely different set of results when it invokes the templateMethod( ), with the exception of the last line.

From this example, we hope you can better see the conceptual structure of the Template Method. All the calls are made from the higher-level ShedMaker class to the lower-level concrete class instances through the templateMethod( ) function. So even though the lower level override functions define the specifics of some of the operations within the template method, the actual call follows the Hollywood Principle and calls downward through the template method.

Selecting and Playing Sound and Video

Considering how Flash handles sound and video, they both share some actions in common. For example, both need to have filenames to play, and both have to somehow have a "play" command. Using the Template Method, we should be able to key in on those two functions of getting a filename and playing, and placing them into an algorithm. However, because of the differences between the two media, we'll leave the details up to the concrete classes. The locked operation that'll be in the main abstract class will be a text header.

Setting Up the Format

The initial abstract class containing an algorithm for a filename selector and play-command operation is pretty simple, because the operations have no content. A third operation that adds a text message to the top of the screen will be locked, and while it's relatively simple, it requires importing a number of packages. Open a new

ActionScript file, copy the contents of Example 9-8, and save it using the caption name for the filename.

Example 9-8. VidAudio.as

```
package
{
    import flash.display.Sprite;
    import flash.text.TextField;
    import flash.text.TextFieldAutoSize;
    import flash.text.TextFormat;

    //Abstract Class
    class VidAudio extends Sprite
    {
        private var mText:TextField;

        //Template method
        public final function mediaProducer ( ):void
        {
            selectMedia ( );
            playNow ( );
            fromMediaDesign ( );
        }
        protected function selectMedia ( ):void
        {
            //Awaiting instructions
        }
        protected function playNow ( ):void
        {
            //Awaiting instructions
        }
        private final function fromMediaDesign ( ):void
        {
            mText=new TextField( );
            mText.autoSize=TextFieldAutoSize.CENTER;
            mText.background=false;
            mText.text="Welcome to Template Media!";
            addChild (mText);
            var pos:Number=mText.length;
            mText.x= 200-(pos/2);
            mText.y=10;
        }
    }
}
```

The template method is named mediaProducer( ), and it orders the three operations, selectMedia( ), playNow( ), and fromMediaDesign( ). In the concrete classes, details are added to the selection and play operations, but the fromMediaDesign( ) function is all set to go, and requires no further details or reference.

Not-So-Concrete Concrete Classes

The next step is to add a couple of concrete classes for selecting between video and audio. First, both need to have some kind of selection, and rather than adding a realistic operation for selecting a video or audio file dynamically, both concrete classes just add a literal. That's pretty simple, but it illustrates the concept of adding necessary details to the operations. Feel free to change the operation to accept dynamic input. The play operations instantiate instances to play whatever names have been placed in the string for the media file. Open up two more ActionScript files and add Example 9-9 and Example 9-10 to the same folder as the abstract classes using the caption names for the filenames.

Example 9-9. Vid.as

```
package
{
    //A concrete class
    //Vid class
    public class Vid extends VidAudio
    {
        private var vidName:String;
        override protected function selectMedia ():void
        {
            vidName="media";
        }
        override protected function playNow ():void
        {
            var playVideo=new PlayVideo(vidName);
            this.addChild (playVideo);
        }
    }
}
```

Example 9-10. Audio.as

```
package
{
    //A concrete class
    //Audio Class
    public class Audio extends VidAudio
    {
        private var tuneName:String;
        override protected function selectMedia ():void
        {
            tuneName="iBlues";
        }
        override protected function playNow ():void
        {
            var playTune:PlayTune=new PlayTune(tuneName);
        }
    }
}
```

The process of actually playing a video or sound file has been farmed out to classes that take care of all the details. So the operation that plays the video or audio is tucked away in another class, and all you need to do in the concrete classes is to instantiate the respective classes and add the instances to a display list.

At this juncture, you need to be aware of the connection between the two operations. The order of the algorithm's operations is still the same; however, both operations are linked by a common private string variable used to store the name of the media. Notice that both concrete classes use the selectMedia( ) and playNow( ) functions, even though they're used in different ways.

The Detail Classes

While the Template Method design pattern allows for details to be added to the operations in the template method itself through the concrete subclasses, both the video and audio operations are a bit more detailed. So rather than shoehorning them into concrete classes, each has its own class. Of course, by doing so, you set up classes that you can very likely use in other applications.

The class built for the video is fairly elaborate, and the one for the sound is quite simple. Open two new ActionScript files and save the code in Example 9-11 and Example 9-12 using the caption names as the filenames. Be sure to save them in the same directory as the others in the application.

Example 9-11. PlayVideo.as

```
package
{
    import flash.display.Sprite;
    import flash.media.Video;
    import flash.events.NetStatusEvent;
    import flash.net.NetConnection;
    import flash.net.NetStream;
    import flash.text.TextField;

    public class PlayVideo extends Sprite
    {
        private var vidNow:Video;
        private var durText:TextField;

        public function PlayVideo(vid:String)
        {
            var nc:NetConnection=new NetConnection( );
            nc.connect(null);
            var ns:NetStream=new NetStream(nc);
            vidNow=new Video( );
            vidNow.attachNetStream(ns);
            vid+=".flv";
            ns.play(vid);
            vidNow.x=((550/2)-(vidNow.width/2));
            vidNow.y=50;
```

Example 9-11. PlayVideo.as (continued)

```
            addChild(vidNow);
            ns.addEventListener(NetStatusEvent.NET_STATUS, stopClear);

            //MetaData check
            var dummy:Object=new Object( );
            ns.client=dummy;
            dummy.onMetaData=getMeta;
        }

        //Clear the video and duration text when video is over
        function stopClear(event:NetStatusEvent):void
        {
            if (event.info.code=="NetStream.Play.Stop")
            {
                vidNow.clear( );
                durText.text="";
            }
        }

        //Show the
        function getMeta(mdata:Object):void
        {
            durText=new TextField( );
            this.addChild(durText);
            durText.text="Duration:"+mdata.duration;
            durText.x=((550/2)-(durText.width/2));
            durText.y=300;
        }
    }
}
```

Example 9-12. PlayTune.as

```
package
{
    import flash.media.Sound;
    import flash.media.SoundChannel;
    import flash.net.URLRequest;

    public class PlayTune
    {
        private var channelNow:SoundChannel;

        public function PlayTune(tuneNow:String)
        {
            tuneNow+=".mp3";
            var playMe:URLRequest=new URLRequest(tuneNow);
            var soundMedia:Sound=new Sound( );
            soundMedia.load(playMe);
            channelNow=soundMedia.play( );
        }
    }
}
```

In setting up the video play, not only did we create a play trigger, we also added functions for cleaning up after the play was complete, and a way to extract duration metadata from the video file being played. That makes the class much handier for use in other applications. In both the video and audio classes, the extension names were added so that all the user needs is a media name without an extension.

Playing the Media

Finally, the application needs a user interface to choose between playing sounds or video. It needs functions to call one of two of the concrete template method classes and some functions to put the interface buttons where they're needed. Open a new ActionScript file and enter Example 9-13 code, saving the file using the caption name. Be sure to save it in the same folder as the other files that make up the application.

Example 9-13. PlayMedia .as

```
package
{
    import flash.display.Sprite;
    import flash.display.DisplayObject;
    import flash.events.MouseEvent;

    public class PlayMedia extends Sprite
    {
        var videoButton:VideoButton;
        var tuneButton:TuneButton;

        public function PlayMedia ():void
        {
            doButton ();
        }
        //Get the buttons out of the library and put them on display
        private function doButton ():void
        {
            tuneButton=new TuneButton();
            videoButton=new VideoButton();
            addChild (tuneButton);
            addChild (videoButton);
            tuneButton.x=((stage.stageWidth/2)-
                (1.5*tuneButton.width)), tuneButton.y=30;
            videoButton.x=((stage.stageWidth/2)+5), videoButton.y=30;
            tuneButton.addEventListener
                (MouseEvent.CLICK,getTune,false,0,true);
            videoButton.addEventListener
                (MouseEvent.CLICK,getVideo,false,0,true);
        }

        //Invoke the template method (mediaProducer) for the video
        private function getVideo (e:MouseEvent):void
        {
            var vidUp:VidAudio=new Vid();
```

Example 9-13. PlayMedia .as (continued)

```
            vidUp.mediaProducer ();
            addChild (vidUp);
        }
        //Invoke the template method (mediaProducer) for the audio
        private function getTune (e:MouseEvent):void
        {
            var tuneUp:VidAudio=new Audio();
            tuneUp.mediaProducer ();
            addChild (tuneUp);
        }
    }
}
```

Most of the work in this application has been done with ActionScript, but a Flash document file will be used to create the buttons for the UI. The following steps show how:

1. Open a new Flash document and save it as PlayMedia.fla in the same folder as the other files in the application.

2. Select Insert → New Symbol from the menu bar.

3. In the New Symbol dialog box, select Button as the type. Type **VideoButton** in the Name window, and click the Export for ActionScript checkbox. Click OK to enter the Symbol editing mode.

4. Select the Rectangle tool, and set the Rectangle Corner Radius to 8. Draw a rectangle with the dimensions W=49 and H=60.

5. Add a second layer while still in the Symbol editing mode. Name the top layer "Text" and the bottom layer "Shape." In the Text layer, add the static text label, "Video." Click OK.

6. Repeat Steps 2 to 5, substituting TuneButton for the button name, and "Tune" for the static text label in Step 5.

7. Your Library panel should show two buttons, one named VideoButton and the other named TuneButton. Each is considered a class, and instances of each are used in the PlayMedia class.

To work with this application, you'll need two additional files; an MP3 file and an FLV file. Rename the MP3 file to iBlues.mp3 and the FLV file to media.flv. Figure 9-5 shows the application running the video.

As you can see by this example, the "details" changed in the algorithm's operations can be extensive. Looking at the two main concrete classes, the methods handling the video are far more extensive than those handling the audio. Not only does it include a mechanism for starting the play, it also has a routine for extracting the metadata from the FLV file, and displaying it on the stage in a text field. In contrast the path taken for sound does not use the display array to add sound children. That's because the sound isn't displayed on the stage, and so no display elements are required.

Figure 9-5. Video and tune player application

Hooking It Up

Controlling subclass extensions is one use for the Template Method. In discussing applicability, the originators of the design pattern concepts (GoF) include what they call a "hook" operation. The hook operation is placed into the template method to allow extensions to the hook in the main algorithm.

For ActionScript 3.0 programmers, hook functions look exactly like the abstract functions. That's because ActionScript 3.0 has no real abstract functions, so we have to keep in mind that the difference between hook operations and abstract ones is that hook operations *can* be overridden, while abstraction operations *must* be overridden. This is where comment lines come in handy, as the following script shows:

```
//Abstract function
function doAbstract():void {}

//Hook function
function doHook():void {}
```

Neither the abstract function nor the hook function has to have any content. However, each is set up differently, and adding content to the hook operation provides a way of setting up default conditions.

When to Hook?

The hook's useful when only part of your algorithm needs to have detailed adjustments made *some of the time* by the subclasses. Because the subclasses are expected to provide detail to a template method's algorithm, you don't need the hook as often as you might expect. A hook is a concrete method, but it can still be overridden just like any abstract method; so it's not a matter of being written in concrete. Given that ActionScript 3.0 doesn't differentiate between abstract and concrete functions, the difference is even more blurred.

One way to approach the use of a hook in a template method is to consider exceptions in an algorithm. For example, if 9 out of 10 times your subclasses will not override the hook operation, it's probably a good idea to use the hook. *The less a hook will be overridden, the more useful it is*. This may seem like a contradiction, but consider that hooks are put into the algorithm because they don't have to be overridden. Most of the time, the subclasses can just implement the template method and be done with it, using the default value provided by your hook. However, when the subclass needs to use the hook to provide an exception to a default value, then it becomes useful.

The Hook as a Lonely Repairman

For years the Maytag Company depicted their repairmen as idle and lonely. The message was that Maytag products were so well manufactured that the repairmen's services were unnecessary. We can look at the hook in the template method in the same light—lonely repairmen who are seldom required.

The hook's use is an exception; so we need to consider a scenario where conditions are usually the same but occasionally change, where we need the hook. One of the great flying areas can be found along the desert border area in Southern California. The weather is typically clear with almost unlimited visibility, allowing pilots to fly under Visual Flight Rules (VFR). Flying down to Baja, Mexico is a beautiful trip, especially along the Sea of Cortez on the eastern side of the Baja peninsula. Consider a pilot who flies tourists down to Punta Bufeo in Baja to visit the sea lion rookery. With just a few exceptions, the pilot can file a VFR flight plan and take off every day. However, every now and then, the weather conditions are less than VFR conditions—cloudy, foggy or extremely hazy. Because the pilot is rated only for VFR conditions, he can't fly under non-VFR or Instrument Flight Conditions (IFR). Using the hook, we'll create a template method to deal with these the situation.

Baja Flight with a Hook

Using our hypothetical Baja pilot, this next application shows how to employ a hook operation in a Template Method design pattern. We're assuming that the pilot flies out of the Calexico airport where the weather's usually sunny and clear. Open four new ActionScript files, and enter the code for Examples 9-14 to 9-17, saving them as the caption name.

Example 9-14. BajaFlight.as

```
package
{
    //Abstract Class
    class BajaFlight
    {
        protected var weatherNow:String;

        public final function templateMethod ():void
        {
            checkAirplane ();
            if (checkWeather()=="Nice and clear")
            {
                fileVFR ();
            }
        }
        protected function fileVFR ():void
        {
            //Awaiting instructions
        }
        protected function checkAirplane ():void
        {
            //Awaiting instructions
        }
        //Hook function
        protected function checkWeather ():String
        {
            weatherNow="Nice and clear";
            return weatherNow;
        }
    }
}
```

The hook function, checkWeather( ), returns a default value of "Nice and clear." The template method algorithm is made up of two operations, checkAirplane( ) and conditionally, fileVFR( ). Both are abstract functions whose details are left to the subclasses for specification. The condition for the fileVFR( ) operation is a string returned by the checkWeather( ) hook method. By setting the default to "Nice and clear," overriding the checkWeather( ) method is usually unnecessary.

Example 9-15. FlightPlan.as

```
package
{
    //Any concrete class
    public class FlightPlan extends BajaFlight
    {
        trace("*^* Clear as a Bell *^*");
        override protected function checkAirplane():void
```

Example 9-15. FlightPlan.as (continued)

```
        {
            trace("Doing the walk around...looking good.");
        }

        override protected function fileVFR():void
        {
            trace("I'm off to Baja on a beautiful day!");
            trace("First I'll file a VFR flightplan\n");
        }
    }
}
```

Because both the checkAirplane() and fileVFR() operations are abstract functions (in intention, at least), they must be overridden. However, the hook method is being treated as a concrete method, so we can optionally override it. In Example 9-15, the hook method checkWeather() is not included in the class. It's inherited from the BajaFlight class and is employed without any changes or need to include it in the class otherwise. However, in Example 9-16, we want to change the value of the checkWeather() hook method, so it is overridden, and "cloudy" is returned instead of the default ("Nice and clear"). The template method only launches the fileVFR() method *if* the return value of checkWeather() is "Nice and clear." As a result, the fileVFR() operation is never launched.

Example 9-16. Cloudy.as

```
package
{
    //Any concrete class
    public class Cloudy extends BajaFlight
    {

        trace ("*^* Cloudy *^*");
        override protected function checkAirplane ():void
        {
            trace ("Doing the walk around...looking good");
        }
        override protected function fileVFR ():void
        {
            trace ("I'm off to Baja on a beautiful day!");
            trace ("First I'll file a VFR flightplan\n");
        }

        //Invoking the hook
        override protected function checkWeather ():String
        {
            weatherNow="Cloudy";
            return weatherNow;
        }
    }
}
```

In Example 9-16, the `fileVFR( )` function shows code that has been overridden, and it contains the exact same content as in the `FlightPlan` class. This was done intentionally to illustrate that it doesn't matter what code you place in the `fileVFR( )` method in this class. Because the hook method has changed the return string that prevents the `fileVFR( )` function from executing, its content is immaterial.

 Unlike Java and other languages where you can create actual abstract functions, in ActionScript 3.0 (following ECMAScript standards) we have to *pretend* that certain methods are abstract. As part of that fiction, the `fileVFR( )` method is overridden in Example 9-16. The method, `fileVFR( )`, could have been completely left out of the `Cloudy` class. It is not going to be launched because the hook method prevents it. By changing the hook return value to something other than "Nice and clear," the `fileVFR( )` method won't launch. So the only reason that the `fileVFR( )` method is included in the class at all is to help understand it as an abstract method that must be overridden by every class that subclasses the main abstract class, `BajaFlight`.

By learning design patterns from examples where abstract functions do exist, you'll find it easier if you have "abstract" functions of your own in your ActionScript 3.0 applications. Also, in certain design patterns such as the Template Method, the hook methods are differentiated from the abstract methods because all abstract methods must be overridden, while hook methods need to be overridden only when they're changed by a subclass.

Finally, we're all set to test the application. Ideally, we would have received data from a weather service that we could use to indicate whether or not the conditions were favorable for VFR flight. Instead, the `TestFlight` class in Example 9-17 simply creates instances of both the `FlightPlan` and `Cloudy` classes.

Example 9-17. TestFlight.as

```
package
{
    import flash.display.Sprite;
    public class TestFlight extends Sprite
    {
        public function TestFlight( )
        {
            var takeOff:BajaFlight=new FlightPlan( );
            takeOff.templateMethod( );

            var grounded:BajaFlight=new Cloudy( );
            grounded.templateMethod( );
        }
    }
}
```

Open a new Flash document, and type **TestFlight** into the document class window. You should see the following results:

```
*^* Clear as a Bell *^*
Doing the walk around...looking good.
I'm off to Baja on a beautiful day!
First I'll file a VFR flightplan

*^* Cloudy *^*
Doing the walk around...looking good
```

In the first part, you can see that both of the algorithm's operations successfully output the checkAirplane( ) and fileVFR( ) method results. However, in the Cloudy instance, only the checkAirplane( ) method invokes. This is as expected because in the Cloudy class, the checkWeather( ) hook method returned something other than "Nice and clear," thereby canceling the fileVFR( ) operation.

Summary

The Template Method design pattern shows how to distribute behavior among subclasses. It leaves much of the detail work to the subclasses, but at the same time it can control the order of the algorithm making up the template method. It stands as a good example of controlling dependencies and use of the inverted control structure.

As such, the Template Method has many uses where both control and flexibility are required while minimizing dependency. It is a widely used pattern, and in many abstract classes you can find some a template method at work to some degree. It's truly a general pattern because it offers both algorithm control and subclass flexibility in implementing the class methods.

The Template Method in ActionScript 3.0 is quite useful even though the language lacks abstract functions and classes. By treating the default internal functions with no content as though they are abstract operations, it's possible to use template methods that are virtually identical to languages that feature both abstract classes and functions.

Finally, hook methods offer further flexibility without really disrupting the main algorithm's flow. These methods can act like "back doors" to the main algorithm. All the operations in the template methods stay in the same order, but they can be changed in terms of what they do, or if they're omitted in the invocation of the template method. It's little wonder that the Template Method, with its strong structure and flexible implementation, is so widely used.

CHAPTER 10

State Pattern

A State without the means of some change is without
the means of its conservation.
—Edmund Burke
All modern revolutions have ended in a reinforcement
of the power of the State.
—Albert Camus

Design Pattern to Create a State Machine

The State design pattern focuses on the different states in an application, transitions between states, and the different behaviors within a state. Looking at a simple light switch application, we can see two states, On and Off. In the Off state, the light is not illuminated, and in the On state, the light illuminates. Further, the light switch transitions from the Off state to the On state using a method that changes the application's state—flipping the switch. Likewise, it transitions from On to Off with a different transition and method. An interface holds the transitions, and each state implements the transitions as methods unique to the state. Each method is implemented differently depending on the context of its use. So, a method, illuminateLight( ), for example, would do one thing in the Off state and something entirely different in the On state, even though illuminateLight( ) method is part of both states.

Key Features

The following key features characterize the State design pattern:

- States exist internally as part of an object.
- Objects change in certain ways when states change. Objects may appear to change classes, but they're changing behavior that is part of the class.
- Each state's behavior depends on the current state of other states in the object.

One application where the state pattern's popular is device simulation. Devices that change an object's state are subject to change as the states change. The volume knob on a radio changes the sound's volume state. More complex simulated devices include a music sound mixer board where simulated sliders change different states to affect the overall object (sound mixer) and the resulting sound. A Flash video player has several states to manage: play, record, append, pause and stop. Each state in the video player behaves according to the state of the other states as well as its own state.

The State Model

To understand and appreciate the value of the State design pattern, we need to understand something about *State Machines*. A State Machine is the general model of states you would be using in an application with the State design pattern. So if a video player application is designed around key states, the application would be the state machine. We can also refer to state engines that run the state machines. (Think of your automobile's blueprints as a state machine, and the actual car as the state engine.) The programming we use to move from one state to another is the state engine. The state engine data structure defines mechanisms for handling messages and managing contexts.

Rather than beginning with the usual diagrams associated with design patterns, we're going to start with a *statechart*. At its most basic level, a statechart is an illustration of an application's states and transitions, and as such is a model for the state machine and engine. Taking a simple video player application, we can see the Play and Stop states. When the application first runs, the application enters the Stop state and can only transition to the Play state. Figure 10-1 shows a statechart depicting this condition.

 The illustration is computer-drawn. The idea when sketching statecharts is to start with a rough idea, and then refine the idea with sketches. You'll find that the process goes quicker using hand sketches with a pencil and scratch paper instead of a drawing program.

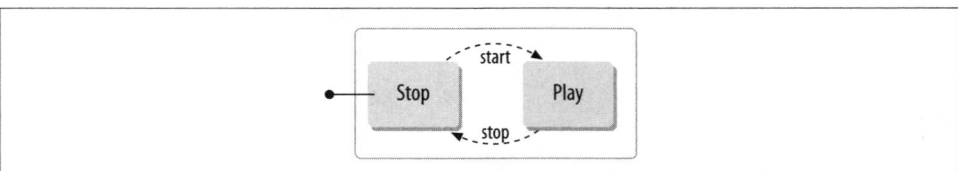

Figure 10-1. Simple statechart showing states

The line going from a black dot to the Stop state shows the Application-Not-Running state, but we'll assume that the starting point is with the application running in the Stop state. This could be illustrated in a hierarchical state with Application

Running and Application-Not-Running states, or we could place the whole hierarchy into Computer-On and Computer-Off states, but that's not too useful because we're not coding to those states.

Before going on to discuss getting from one state to another, let's consider what each state can actually do. In the Stop state, I can only initiate the Play state. That is, in the Stop state, I can't stop because I'm already stopped. By the same token, if I'm in the Play state, the only thing I can do is transition to the Stop state.

Transitions

The transitions in a state machine are the actions to change states. In Figure 10-1, the line from Stop to Play might be a startPlay( ) method of some sort. From the Play to Stop state, it might be a stopPlay( ) method. As more states are added, you might find that you can't transition directly from one state to another, but rather you have to go through a series of states to get where you want to go. As we'll see later, if you're in the Stop state, you can't go directly to the Pause state. You first have to go to the Play state, and then, once in the Play state, go to the Pause state.

Triggers

To initiate a transition, you need some kind of trigger. A trigger is any event that initiates a transition from one state to another. Usually, we think of some kind of user action such as a mouse movement or button click, but in simulations certain states can be triggered by ongoing conditions such as running out of fuel, draining a battery or a collision with an object. Likewise, triggers are subject to contexts and should only work in the appropriate contexts to initiate a state. So, while you might use a Play button to initiate the Play state from the Stop state, it shouldn't trigger a Play state from the Play state.

Triggers are often placed along with the transitions on the statecharts. This helps to identify the trigger events and the transitions they trigger. Figure 10-2 shows the statechart updated to include both the triggers and transitions they initiate.

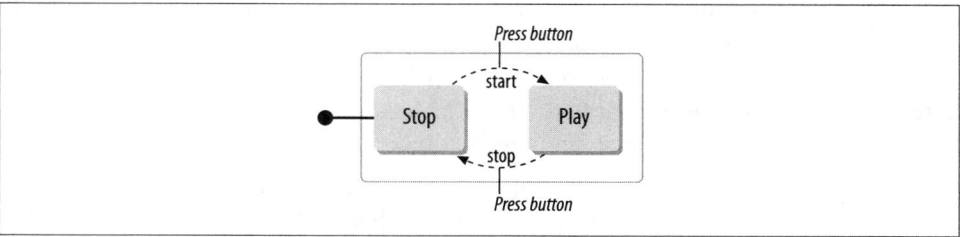

Figure 10-2. Statechart with states, transitions, and triggers

If you're interested in more information about using state engines, statecharts, and the more general aspects of working with Flash and states, see *Flash Mx for Interac-*

tive Simulation by Jonathan Kaye and David Castillo (Thomson, 2003). While going back a few generations of Flash, the book is timeless in its concepts and shows some very smooth device simulations.

State design structure

As one of the design patterns described in *Design Patterns: Elements of Reusable Object-Oriented Software* by the Gang of Four, the value of the State design was recognized beyond the boundaries of those who were primarily interested in state machines. Closely resembling the Strategy pattern, the State pattern is used when an application's behavior depends on changing states at runtime, or has complex conditional statements that branch depending on a current state. When the internal states change, an object alters its behavior when designed using the State pattern. Figure 10-3 shows the general structure in the class diagram of the State pattern.

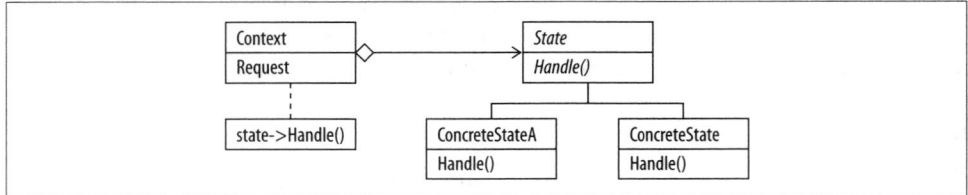

Figure 10-3. State design pattern

Key OOP Concepts Used with the State Pattern

While polymorphism is a fundamental OOP concept, it doesn't help very much if its use and purpose are not understood. It's just one of the many basic concepts in object-oriented programming that's used to point to different implementations of objects in multiple forms. One feature you'll see in the State design pattern is that the polymorphism is pretty obvious. This will help you better understand how polymorphism can be useful in OO programs.

Looking at the State interface in Example 10-1, you can see the different methods that become core behaviors for different states. Each state is its own class. However, as you look at each class, you can see that the behaviors of the same methods take on different forms—polymorphism hard at work. Just look at each of the state classes, and there you see all of the same methods but in different forms.

Perhaps most significant is the ability of each state to take care of knowing itself. For instance, in the following examples, you will see that both the Stop and Play states (classes) have a startPlay( ) method. However, each acts differently in its context. Moving from a Stop state initiates playing the video. If the same method, startPlay( ), is fired while the play is in progress, it does nothing. Doing nothing is important sometimes. Let's say that someone is looking at a video and, for whatever reason, presses the Play Button. In a typical video player application, the player will start over again. In that application, the startPlay( ) method is as dumb as a box of rocks. However, because polymorphism allows multiple forms of the same method, it allows us to provide the application with multiple forms that know what to do in different contexts. So in the Play state, the method knows it's already playing, and so it does nothing. A user can pound on the Play Button all he wants, and the video just keeps on playing. He can press the Stop Button, and the video will stop, just like it's supposed to do.

To better appreciate polymorphism, you will see that as more states are added to the application, there's more to keep track of. With more methods, we absolutely, positively *do not* want to modify the wrong thing. Without polymorphism, we run the risk of having the same method do something we definitely do not want it to do. Thus, if you don't want your application to start playing video all over again every time the startPlay( ) method is invoked, using the State design pattern, you can structure the application to only start at the beginning when the originating state is the Stop state. Likewise, you can structure the startPlay( ) to begin playing all over again from the Play state—you write the code, and so you control how the methods behave.

When you read the next chapter on the Strategy design pattern, you may have a major case of *déjà vu*. The juxtaposition of these two chapters is no accident. Once you complete the example applications in each chapter, you should definitely get a different feel for each, even though the structures look very similar. The State design pattern has its focus on the states and well-defined transitions. This is one reason we use statecharts—they help clarify and simplify the architectural work in focusing on the different states and how they transition from one to another. The transitions in the State design can be controlled by the states themselves or by the context class. Also, because the State design creates a class for each state (behavior environment), you tend to generate more classes with the State design than with the Strategy design. Determining which behavior to use is delegated to the State classes, while the Strategy pattern encapsulates a family of algorithms and allows them to vary independent of the client within the structure that uses them.

Minimalist Abstract State Pattern

Using the State design pattern, all the behaviors (methods) for a single state are placed into single objects (concrete states), and all transition behaviors for the application (state machine) are placed into a single interface. Each state object implements the interface in a fashion appropriate for the state. Because of this structure, no conditional statements are required to branch differentially depending on the current state. Rather than writing complex conditional statements, the individual state objects define how the methods are to behave for that state.

For example, with a two-state machine (Play and Stop), the following pseudocode could direct the state behavior to start playing the video, depending on the state machine's current state.

```
function doPlay( ):void {
    if(state == Play)
    {
        trace("You're already playing.");
    }
    else if (state == Stop)
    {
        trace("Go to the Play state.");
    }
}
```

With a couple of states that's not too difficult. However, as you add states, things get more complicated and you find a sea of conditional statements that have to all work in sync. The alternative is to set up "contextual" behavior using a State pattern. For example, the following code in Example 10-1 has two different objects with different implementations of behaviors from an interface:

Example 10-1. State.as

```
//Interface
interface State
{
    function startPlay( ):void;
    function stopPlay( ):void;
}
//Play State object
class PlayState implements State
{
    public function startPlay( ):void
    {
        trace("You're already playing");
    }
    public function stopPlay( ):void
    {
        trace("Go to the Stop state.");
    }
}
//Stop State object
class StopState implements State
{
    public function startPlay( ):void
    {
        trace("Go to the Play state.");
    }
    public function stopPlay( ):void
    {
        trace("You're already stopped");
    }
}
```

As you can see, the behaviors (methods) have different implementations in the different states. When you add more states, all you need to do is add their transitional behaviors to the interface and create a new concrete state (class) that implements the behaviors. Each new behavior needs to be added to the existing state classes.

Managing All Those States: Hardworking Context Class

To manage the states and their transitions, you need some kind of management object—the state engine for your state machine. In Figure 10-3 the box labeled "Context" is the abstraction of the state engine. The context manages the different states that make up the state machine and contain the different states. Figure 10-4 shows a more concrete representation of what needs to be transformed:

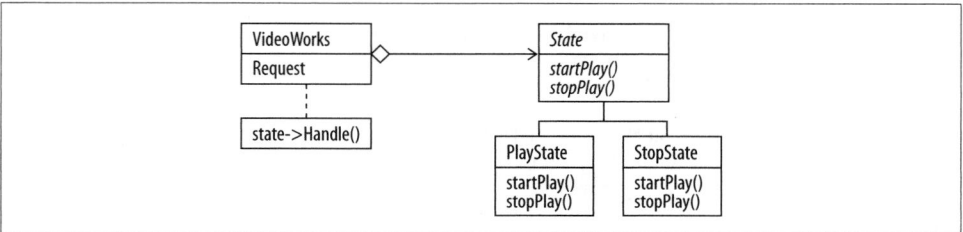

Figure 10-4. State Design Pattern applied to video

Creating a context class

Looking at our example of creating a simple video player, we need a context that will serve to get and set the different states. So, the next phase will be to look at a class (object) that does just that. This context class should be saved as `VideoWorks.as`. First, take a look at the class in Example 10-2, and then we'll see what's going on:

Example 10-2. VideoWorks.as

```
1  package
2  {
3      //Context class
4      class VideoWorks
5      {
6          var playState:State;
7          var stopState:State;
8          var state:State;
9          public function VideoWorks()
10         {
11             trace("Video Player is On");
12             playState = new PlayState(this);
13             stopState = new StopState(this);
14             state=stopState;
15         }
16         public function startPlay():void
17         {
```

Example 10-2. VideoWorks.as (continued)

```
18              state.startPlay( );
19          }
20          public function stopPlay( ):void
21          {
22              state.stopPlay( );
23          }
24          public function setState(state:State):void
25          {
26              trace("A new state is set");
27              this.state=state;
28          }
29          public function getState( ):State
30          {
31              return state;
32          }
33          public function getPlayState( ):State
34          {
35              return this.playState;
36          }
37          public function getStopState( ):State
38          {
39              return this.stopState;
40          }
41      }
42  }
43
```

Initially, in lines 6-8, the script instantiates three State objects—one of each of the two we designed (PlayState and StopState), and one (state) that acts as a variable to hold the current state. Because the state machine begins in the Stop state, the state variable is assigned the Stop state. (This works just like the light switch before you change it from the **off** state to the **on** state.)

Next, the two behaviors from the State interface are specified in terms of the current state's context (lines 16-23). We're going to have to add some code to the two state classes for it to work with the context class, but for now, think of what will happen in the two different states when those behaviors are executed. For example, in the Play state, the startPlay( ) method doesn't do anything, but in the Stop state, it switches to the Play state.

Finally, add the getter and setter methods (lines 24-40). We need a total of six methods—a set and get function for each of the three state instances. The setters return nothing and the getters return a State object.

Completing and testing the abstract state machine

To get everything working, we need to revise the state classes to include the reference to the context—VideoWorks. Save Example 10-3 as StopState.as.

Example 10-3. StopState.as

```
 1  package
 2  {
 3      //Stop State;
 4      class StopState implements State
 5      {
 6          var videoWorks:VideoWorks;
 7          public function StopState(videoWorks:VideoWorks)
 8          {
 9              trace("--Stop State--");
10              this.videoWorks=videoWorks;
11          }
12          public function startPlay():void
13          {
14              trace("Begin playing");
15              videoWorks.setState(videoWorks.getPlayState());
16          }
17          public function stopPlay():void
18          {
19              trace("You're already stopped");
20          }
21      }
22  }
```

By adding a VideoWorks instance, we have a way to access the getter and setter methods in each state. Line 15 invokes the VideoWorks instance to change the state to the Play state.

Next, we'll do the same thing with the Play state shown in Example 10-4. Save the following as PlayState.as.

Example 10-4. PlayState.as

```
 1  package
 2  {
 3      //Play State
 4      class PlayState implements State
 5      {
 6          var videoWorks:VideoWorks;
 7          public function PlayState(videoWorks:VideoWorks)
 8          {
 9              trace("--Play State--");
10              this.videoWorks=videoWorks;
11          }
12          public function startPlay():void
13          {
14              trace("You're already playing");
15          }
16          public function stopPlay():void
17          {
18              trace("Stop playing.");
19              videoWorks.setState(videoWorks.getStopState());
20          }
21      }
22  }
```

To complete the state machine, we need to create the actual interface, and because the machine has only two states and two behaviors, this is a simple matter. Returning to the original statechart, you can see only two transitions—one to start the play and one to stop the play. So, all we'll need are two functions for abstractions of those two transitions. Save the script in Example 10-5 as State.as:

Example 10-5. State.as

```
1  package
2  {
3      //State Machine Interface
4      interface State
5      {
6          function startPlay( ):void;
7          function stopPlay( ):void;
8      }
9  }
```

The transition behaviors are in lines 6 and 7. Later, we'll be adding more transitional behaviors as the project grows, but the actual machine is complete. Finally, we need to create an FLA file with ActionScript that will execute the state machine.

To both test the abstract application and show features of the State design pattern, the test should invoke the VideoWorks class and the two states of Play and Stop using the primary transitions (methods)—startPlay( ) and stopPlay( ). In fact, it should call both states twice. From the Stop state (default initial state), the application should be transitioned to the Play state. Then, it should do it a second time to make sure that the state recognizes the new context. The same should be done to transition back to the Stop state. Save Example 10-6 as TestState.as in the same folder as the other files:

Example 10-6. TestState.as

```
1  package
2  {
3      //Test states
4      import flash.display.Sprite;
5      public class TestState extends Sprite
6      {
7          public function TestState( ):void
8          {
9              var test:VideoWorks = new VideoWorks( );
10             test.startPlay( );
11             test.startPlay( );
12             test.stopPlay( );
13             test.stopPlay( );
14         }
15     }
16 }
```

Because the application at this stage only provides traces, you will need to use the Flash Test (Control → Test or Control → Test Project) to see the output. Open a new Flash document, and, in the Document class window, type in **TestState**. The following should appear in the Output window:

```
Video Player is On
--Play State--
--Stop State--
Begin playing
A new state is set
You're already playing
Stop playing.
A new state is set
You're already stopped
```

Both the VideoWorks class and the PlayState and StopState classes include a trace statement to indicate their instantiation, and appear as soon as you test the script. Because the initial state is Stop, it changes states to the Play state when the first startPlay( ) method is invoked. Also, because you're changing states, a trace statement from the VideoWorks class indicates a state change. However, when the second startPlay( ) method is invoked a second time, the same method in a different context recognizes that it's already in the Play state and simply indicates that you're already playing. When you press the Stop button, you move to the Stop state, setting a new state, but on the second press, the same function in this new context recognizes that you're already in the Stop state, and indicates that fact.

Video Player Concrete State Application

All that you've seen so far has been the output as trace( ) statements to help understand how a State design pattern and State machine works. To add something useful, we need to include a reference to both a NetStream object and a string for referencing an FLV file. However, we need a string reference only for playing the video, because we can stop it simply by closing the NetStream instance. The following four scripts set up the state machine to actually play and stop a video. All of the trace statements have been left in place.

With the implementation of an application that actually plays a video, we'll need to import the necessary parts. Because the NetStream class is used in the interface and the two states, each of those files will need to import the class. However, while the VideoWorks class uses both the Play and Stop classes, it does not have to import the NetStream( ) class. This is because it's already imported in the Play and Stop classes.

The following five listings, Example 10-7 through Example 10-11, should be entered into an ActionScript file and saved with the captions as the filenames. Save all the files in the same folder.

Example 10-7. State.as

```
package
{
    //State Interface #1
    import flash.net.NetStream;
    interface State
    {
        function startPlay(ns:NetStream,flv:String):void;
        function stopPlay(ns:NetStream):void;
    }
}
```

In the following StopState class shown in Example 10-8, you will note that the startPlay( ) method has been implemented to actually play the selected FLV file. That transition to the Play state is not to start playing the video, but rather to set the state where the video is playing.

Example 10-8. StopState.as

```
package
{
    //Stop State #2
    import flash.net.NetStream;

    class StopState implements State
    {
        private var videoWorks:VideoWorks;
        public function StopState(videoWorks:VideoWorks)
        {
            trace("--Stop State--");
            this.videoWorks=videoWorks;
        }
        public function startPlay(ns:NetStream,flv:String):void
        {
            ns.play(flv);
            trace("Begin playing");
            videoWorks.setState(videoWorks.getPlayState( ));
        }
        public function stopPlay(ns:NetStream):void
        {
            trace("You're already stopped");
        }
    }
}
```

Note that in the PlayState class shown in Example 10-9, the startPlay( ) method wisely does nothing other than issue a statement to remind the user that the video is already playing. In the test mode, the message appears in the Output window, but when the user's working with it, no message is issued. The feedback issues from the playing video.

Example 10-9. PlayState.as

```
package
{
    //Play State #3
    import flash.net.NetStream;

    class PlayState implements State
    {
        private var videoWorks:VideoWorks;
        public function PlayState(videoWorks:VideoWorks)
        {
            trace("--Play State--");
            this.videoWorks=videoWorks;
        }
        public function startPlay(ns:NetStream,flv:String):void
        {
            trace("You're already playing");
        }
        public function stopPlay(ns:NetStream):void
        {
            ns.close();
            trace("Stop playing.");
            videoWorks.setState(videoWorks.getStopState());
        }
    }
}
```

Next, the context class shown in Example 10-10 for this design pattern pulls it all together. Note that there is no import of the NetStream object. However, the listing clearly shows that the NetSteam object is one of the parameters of both the startPlay( ) and stopPlay( ) function parameters. If you look closely, you'll see that both the functions to start and stop play are instances of the PlayState and StopState classes, which did import the necessary NetStream class.

Example 10-10. VideoWorks.as

```
package
{
    import flash.net.NetStream;
    //Context Class #4
    class VideoWorks
    {
        private var playState:State;
        private var stopState:State;
        private var state:State;
        public function VideoWorks()
        {
            trace("Video Player is on");
            playState = new PlayState(this);
            stopState = new StopState(this);
            state=stopState;
        }
```

Example 10-10. VideoWorks.as (continued)

```
        public function startPlay(ns:NetStream,flv:String):void
        {
            state.startPlay(ns,flv);
        }
        public function stopPlay(ns:NetStream):void
        {
            state.stopPlay(ns);
        }
        public function setState(state:State):void
        {
            trace("A new state is set");
            this.state=state;
        }
        public function getState():State
        {
            return state;
        }
        public function getPlayState():State
        {
            return this.playState;
        }
        public function getStopState():State
        {
            return this.stopState;
        }
    }
}
```

In addition to the classes that make up the State design pattern, you will need a copy of the NetBtn and BtnState classes shown in Example 10-11 and Example 10-12. In fact, in all the examples in this chapter, the NetBtn.as and BtnState.as files will be required in the same folder as the other files. In subsequent listings, we didn't include the listing for the class because they're all identical. (That means once you've entered it, you don't have to do anything else with it.) So keep the files handy, and make sure that they're included in the folders with your other classes.

Example 10-11. NetBtn.as

```
package
{
    //Button for transition triggers
    import flash.display.Sprite;
    import flash.display.SimpleButton;
    import flash.display.Shape;
    import flash.text.TextFormat;
    import flash.text.TextField;
    import flash.text.TextFieldAutoSize;
    public class NetBtn extends SimpleButton
    {
        public function NetBtn (txt:String)
```

Example 10-11. NetBtn.as (continued)

```
        {
            upState = new BtnState(0xfab383, 0x9e0039,txt);
            downState = new BtnState(0xffffff,0x9e0039, txt);
            overState= new BtnState (0x9e0039,0xfab383,txt);
            hitTestState=upState;
        }
    }
}
```

Example 10-12. BtnState.as

```
package
{
    //States for transition buttons
    import flash.display.Sprite;
    import flash.display.Shape;
    import flash.text.TextFormat;
    import flash.text.TextField;
    import flash.text.TextFieldAutoSize;
    class BtnState extends Sprite
    {
        public var btnLabel:TextField;
        public function BtnState (color:uint,color2:uint,btnLabelText:String)
        {
            btnLabel=new TextField  ;
            btnLabel.text=btnLabelText;
            btnLabel.x=5;
            btnLabel.autoSize=TextFieldAutoSize.LEFT;
            var format:TextFormat=new TextFormat("Verdana");
            format.size=12;
            btnLabel.setTextFormat (format);
            var btnWidth:Number=btnLabel.textWidth + 10;
            var bkground:Shape=new Shape;
            bkground.graphics.beginFill (color);
            bkground.graphics.lineStyle (2,color2);
            bkground.graphics.drawRect (0,0,btnWidth,18);
            addChild (bkground);
            addChild (btnLabel);
        }
    }
}
```

To test the application, you'll need an FLV file named test.flv. You can convert an existing video file (e.g. *avi, mov*) or use any *flv* file on hand. Place the file in the same folder as the application. Finally, you'll need a script to test the application, so open a new ActionScript file, enter the following listing in Example 10-13, and save it as *TestVid.as*:

Example 10-13. TestVid.as

```
package
{
    //Implement FMS2 App and Test State Machine #7
    import flash.display.Sprite;
    import flash.net.NetConnection;
    import flash.net.NetStream;
    import flash.media.Video;
    import flash.text.TextField;
    import flash.text.TextFieldType;
    import flash.events.MouseEvent;
    import flash.events.NetStatusEvent;

    public class TestVid extends Sprite
    {
        private var nc:NetConnection=new NetConnection();
        private var ns:NetStream;
        private var vid:Video=new Video(320,240);
        private var vidTest:VideoWorks;
        private var playBtn:NetBtn;
        private var stopBtn:NetBtn;
        private var flv:String;
        private var flv_txt:TextField;
        private var dummy:Object;

        public function TestVid ()
        {
            nc.connect (null);
            ns=new NetStream(nc);
            addChild (vid);
            vid.x=(stage.stageWidth/2)-(vid.width/2);
            vid.y=(stage.stageHeight/2)-(vid.height/2);

            //Instantiate State Machine
            vidTest=new VideoWorks();

            //Play and Stop Buttons
            playBtn=new NetBtn("Play");
            addChild (playBtn);
            playBtn.x=(stage.stageWidth/2)-50;
            playBtn.y=350;
            stopBtn=new NetBtn("Stop");
            addChild (stopBtn);
            stopBtn.x=(stage.stageWidth/2)+50;
            stopBtn.y=350;

            //Add Event Listeners
            playBtn.addEventListener (MouseEvent.CLICK,doPlay);
            stopBtn.addEventListener (MouseEvent.CLICK,doStop);

            //Add the text field
            flv_txt= new TextField();
            flv_txt.border=true;
```

Example 10-13. TestVid.as (continued)

```
        flv_txt.borderColor=0x9e0039;
        flv_txt.background=true;
        flv_txt.backgroundColor=0xfab383;
        flv_txt.type=TextFieldType.INPUT;
        flv_txt.x=(stage.stageWidth/2)-45;
        flv_txt.y=10;
        flv_txt.width=90;
        flv_txt.height=16;
        addChild (flv_txt);

        //This prevents a MetaData error being thrown
        dummy=new Object( );
        ns.client=dummy;
        dummy.onMetaData=getMeta;

        //NetStream
        ns.addEventListener (NetStatusEvent.NET_STATUS, flvCheck);
    }
    //MetaData
    private function getMeta (mdata:Object):void
    {
        trace (mdata.duration);
    }
    //Handle flv
    private function flvCheck (event:NetStatusEvent):void
    {
        switch (event.info.code)
        {
            case "NetStream.Play.Stop" :
                vidTest.stopPlay (ns);
                vid.clear ( );
                break;
            case "NetStream.Play.StreamNotFound" :
                vidTest.stopPlay (ns);
                flv_txt.text="File not found";
                break;
        }
    }
    //Start play
    private function doPlay (e:MouseEvent):void
    {
        if (flv_txt.text != "" && flv_txt.text !=
            "Provide file name")
        {
            flv_txt.textColor=0x000000;
            flv=flv_txt.text + ".flv";
            vidTest.startPlay (ns,flv);
            vid.attachNetStream (ns);
        }
        else
        {
            flv_txt.textColor=0xcc0000;
```

Example 10-13. TestVid.as (continued)

```
                flv_txt.text="Provide file name";
        }
    }
    //Stop play
    private function doStop (e:MouseEvent):void
    {
        vidTest.stopPlay (ns);
        vid.clear ();
    }
    }
}
```

Open a new Flash document file, and in the center of the stage, draw a rectangle (W=320, H=240) with a 6-point stroke, the color value 9E0039, and the fill color FAB383. Use the Align panel to make sure that the rectangle is perfectly centered because it serves as a backdrop for the video that will be placed on top of it. In the Document class window, type in **TestVid**, and test the application.

The UI is simple and related to the transitions—Stop and Start (playing video).You can see the relationship between the video playing and the related trace statement showing what happens when you press the button. For example, if you press Start and the video is running, nothing new occurs because in the Play state, the startPlay( ) function does nothing other than offering a trace statement to the effect that you're already playing.

Expanding the State Design: Adding States

A fundamental feature of virtually all design patterns is their ability to expand and accept change. The kind of change you're expecting in an application determines, to some extent, the type of design pattern you select. In this particular application, we're adding states.

Adding the Pause State to the Statechart

The first state to be added to the state machine is a Pause state. This state only exists inside the Play state, and you cannot get to the Pause state directly from the Stop state. To get to the Pause state, you must first be in the Play state, and then you can turn the Pause state on and off. To correctly depict this new state, we need to use a hierarchical state diagram. Figure 10-5 shows a statechart with the necessary hierarchy.

The hierarchy in Figure 10-5 is a simple one. The first level is the Play and Stop states, and then, within the Play state are the Pause and No Pause states.

Because the pause function is a toggle between the Play and Pause states, the No Pause state is exactly the same as the Play state. So, rather than creating Pause Start

---

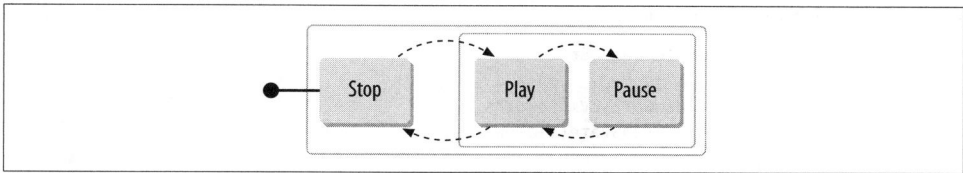

Figure 10-5. Hierarchical statechart

and Pause Stop functions, a "Do Pause" behavior will be established to act differently in different states. In a Pause state, the Do Pause behavior returns to the default Play state and in the Play state, it goes to the Pause state.

Adding New Behaviors

The first step is to add a new behavior (method) to the current ones in the State.as file. This behavior is a state transition from playing to pause and back to playing. To begin, the first element to add is the pause behavior to the set of states. This is fairly simple because it too has a NetStream parameter, so changes can be made without further imports:

```
function doPause(ns:NetStream):void;
```

The first step is to change the State.as by adding the new function as shown in Example 10-14 line 9:

Example 10-14. State.as

```
1 package
2 {
3      //State Interface #1
4      import flash.net.NetStream;
5      interface State
6      {
7          function startPlay(ns:NetStream,flv:String):void;
8          function stopPlay(ns:NetStream):void;
9          function doPause(ns:NetStream):void;
10     }
11 }
```

One of the requirements for an interface is that all implementations of the interface include all the interface methods. The next step will be to add the method to the Stop and Play states as in Example 10-15:

Example 10-15. StopState.as

```
1 package
2 {
3      //Stop State #2
4      import flash.net.NetStream;
5
```

Example 10-15. StopState.as (continued)

```
6      class StopState implements State
7      {
8          private var videoWorks:VideoWorks;
9          public function StopState(videoWorks:VideoWorks)
10         {
11             trace("--Stop State--");
12             this.videoWorks=videoWorks;
13         }
14         public function startPlay(ns:NetStream,flv:String):void
15         {
16             ns.play(flv);
17             trace("Begin playing");
18             videoWorks.setState(videoWorks.getPlayState( ));
19         }
20         public function stopPlay(ns:NetStream):void
21         {
22             trace("You're already stopped");
23         }
24         public function doPause(ns:NetStream):void
25         {
26             trace("Cannot go to Stop from Pause.");
27         }
28     }
29 }
```

The doPause( ) method is added to the StopState.as file as shown in line 24, but it makes no sense to set the Pause state from the Stop state because then nothing is playing to pause. So all that's added is a trace( ) statement on line 26 that indicates that such a transition is not possible.

Working with the Play state is an entirely different proposition. Essentially, the Pause state is a subset of the Play state. In fact, when using a toggle pause, you can think of the play as "play without pause" and "play with pause." With ActionScript 3.0, another option is to use the new NetStream.pause( ) and NetStream.resume( ) methods. Had we done that, two, instead of one, additional states would be required. For now, though, just change the PlayState.as file as shown in Example 10-16, in lines 24–29:

Example 10-16. PlayState.as

```
1 package
2 {
3     //Play State #3
4     import flash.net.NetStream;
5
6     class PlayState implements State
7     {
8         private var videoWorks:VideoWorks;
9         public function PlayState(videoWorks:VideoWorks)
10        {
```

Example 10-16. PlayState.as (continued)

```
11              trace("--Play State--");
12              this.videoWorks=videoWorks;
13          }
14      public function startPlay(ns:NetStream,flv:String):void
15      {
16              trace("You're already playing");
17      }
18      public function stopPlay(ns:NetStream):void
19      {
20              ns.close();
21              trace("Stop playing.");
22              videoWorks.setState(videoWorks.getStopState());
23      }
24      public function doPause(ns:NetStream):void
25      {
26              ns.togglePause();
27              trace("Begin pause.");
28              videoWorks.setState(videoWorks.getPauseState());
29      }
30   }
31 }
```

Next, the new PauseState class implements the State interface. The doPause( ) function in the Pause state uses the exact same ns.togglePause( ) used in the PlayState class as shown in Example 10-17. However, instead of getting the PauseState, it gets the PlayState. The interesting feature of a toggle method is that very different functions may use the same class method.

Example 10-17. PauseState.as

```
1 package
2 {
3      //Pause State #4
4      import flash.net.NetStream;
5
6      class PauseState implements State
7      {
8          var videoWorks:VideoWorks;
9          public function PauseState(videoWorks:VideoWorks)
10         {
11              trace("--Pause State--");
12              this.videoWorks=videoWorks;
13         }
14         public function startPlay(ns:NetStream,flv:String):void
15         {
16              trace("You have to go to unpause");
17         }
18         public function stopPlay(ns:NetStream):void
19         {
20              trace("Don't go to Stop from Pause");
21         }
```

Example 10-17. PauseState.as

```
22          public function doPause(ns:NetStream):void
23          {
24              ns.togglePause();
25              trace("Quit pausing.");
26              videoWorks.setState(videoWorks.getPlayState());
27          }
28      }
29  }
```

As with the individual state classes, you also need to add a PauseState instance to the VideoWorks class as shown in Example 10-18. Remember that this class contains all the setters and getters, and you certainly need that to invoke the pause behavior for the application. This is easy to do because all it takes is a single variable for the PauseState instance, a doPause( ) function, and then adding the pause getter.

Example 10-18. VideoWorks.as

```
package
{
    //Context Class #5
    import flash.net.NetStream;

    class VideoWorks
    {
        private var playState:State;
        private var stopState:State;
        private var pauseState:State;
        private var state:State;
        public function VideoWorks()
        {
            trace("Video Player is on");
            playState = new PlayState(this);
            stopState = new StopState(this);
            pauseState = new PauseState(this);
            state=stopState;
        }
        public function startPlay(ns:NetStream,flv:String):void
        {
            state.startPlay(ns,flv);
        }
        public function stopPlay(ns:NetStream):void
        {
            state.stopPlay(ns);
        }
        public function doPause(ns:NetStream):void
        {
            state.doPause(ns);
        }
        public function setState(state:State):void
        {
            trace("A new state is set");
```

Example 10-18. VideoWorks.as (continued)

```
            this.state=state;
        }
        public function getState( ):State
        {
            return state;
        }
        public function getPlayState( ):State
        {
            return this.playState;
        }
        public function getStopState( ):State
        {
            return this.stopState;
        }
        public function getPauseState( ):State
        {
            return this.pauseState;
        }
    }
}
```

To test the additional pause class, all you need to do in the test class is add another button instance. With three buttons, a little more positioning thought has to go into it, but expanding the State design pattern is very easy. All the changes for adding the additional button are on lines 45-48 and 53. So just edit the *TestVid.as* file as shown in Example 10-19, and save it as *TestPause.as*.

Example 10-19. TestPause.as

```
1  package
2  {
3      //Implement FMS2 App and Test State Machine #6
4      import flash.display.Sprite;
5      import flash.net.NetConnection;
6      import flash.net.NetStream;
7      import flash.media.Video;
8      import flash.text.TextField;
9      import flash.text.TextFieldType;
10     import flash.events.MouseEvent;
11     import flash.events.NetStatusEvent;
12
13     public class TestPause extends Sprite
14     {
15         private var nc:NetConnection=new NetConnection( );
16         private var ns:NetStream;
17         private var vid:Video=new Video(320,240);
18         private var vidTest:VideoWorks;
19         private var playBtn:NetBtn;
20         private var stopBtn:NetBtn;
21         private var flv:String;
```

Example 10-19. TestPause.as (continued)

```
22          private var flv_txt:TextField;
23          private var dummy:Object;
24
25          public function TestPause ()
26          {
27              nc.connect (null);
28              ns=new NetStream(nc);
29              addChild (vid);
30              vid.x=stage.stageWidth / 2 - vid.width / 2;
31              vid.y=stage.stageHeight / 2 - vid.height / 2;
32
33              //Instantiate State Machine
34              vidTest=new VideoWorks   ;
35
36              //Play, Stop and Pause Buttons
37              playBtn=new NetBtn("Play");
38              addChild (playBtn);
39              playBtn.x=stage.stageWidth / 2 - 100 + playBtn.width / 2;
40              playBtn.y=350;
41              stopBtn=new NetBtn("Stop");
42              addChild (stopBtn);
43              stopBtn.x=stage.stageWidth / 2 - stopBtn.width / 2;
44              stopBtn.y=350;
45              var pauseBtn:NetBtn=new NetBtn("Pause");
46              addChild (pauseBtn);
47              pauseBtn.x=(stage.stageWidth / 2 + 100) - pauseBtn.width;
48              pauseBtn.y=350;
49
50              //Add Event Listeners
51              playBtn.addEventListener (MouseEvent.CLICK,doPlay);
52              stopBtn.addEventListener (MouseEvent.CLICK,doStop);
53              pauseBtn.addEventListener (MouseEvent.CLICK,pauseNow);
54
55              //Add the text field
56              flv_txt=new TextField   ;
57              flv_txt.border=true;
58              flv_txt.borderColor=0x9e0039;
59              flv_txt.background=true;
60              flv_txt.backgroundColor=0xfab383;
61              flv_txt.type=TextFieldType.INPUT;
62              flv_txt.x=stage.stageWidth / 2 - 45;
63              flv_txt.y=10;
64              flv_txt.width=90;
65              flv_txt.height=16;
66              addChild (flv_txt);
67
68              //This prevents a MetaData error being thrown
69              dummy=new Object   ;
70              ns.client=dummy;
71              dummy.onMetaData=getMeta;
72
73              //NetStream
74              ns.addEventListener (NetStatusEvent.NET_STATUS,flvCheck);
```

Example 10-19. TestPause.as (continued)

```
75          }
76          //MetaData
77          private function getMeta (mdata:Object):void
78          {
79              trace (mdata.duration);
80          }
81          //Handle flv
82          private function flvCheck (event:NetStatusEvent):void
83          {
84              switch (event.info.code)
85              {
86                  case "NetStream.Play.Stop" :
87                      vidTest.stopPlay (ns);
88                      vid.clear ();
89                      break;
90                  case "NetStream.Play.StreamNotFound" :
91                      vidTest.stopPlay (ns);
92                      flv_txt.text="File not found";
93                      break;
94              }
95          }
96          //Start play
97          private function doPlay (e:MouseEvent):void
98          {
99              if (flv_txt.text != "" && flv_txt.text !=
100             "Provide file name")
101             {
102                 flv_txt.textColor=0x000000;
103                 flv=flv_txt.text + ".flv";
104                 vidTest.startPlay (ns,flv);
105                 vid.attachNetStream (ns);
106             }
107             else
108             {
109                 flv_txt.textColor=0xcc0000;
110                 flv_txt.text="Provide file name";
111             }
112         }
113         //Stop play
114         private function doStop (e:MouseEvent):void
115         {
116             vidTest.stopPlay (ns);
117             vid.clear ();
118         }
119         //Pause play
120         function pauseNow (e:MouseEvent):void
121         {
122             vidTest.doPause (ns);
123         }
124     }
125 }
126
```

Figure 10-6 shows what your video player should look like.

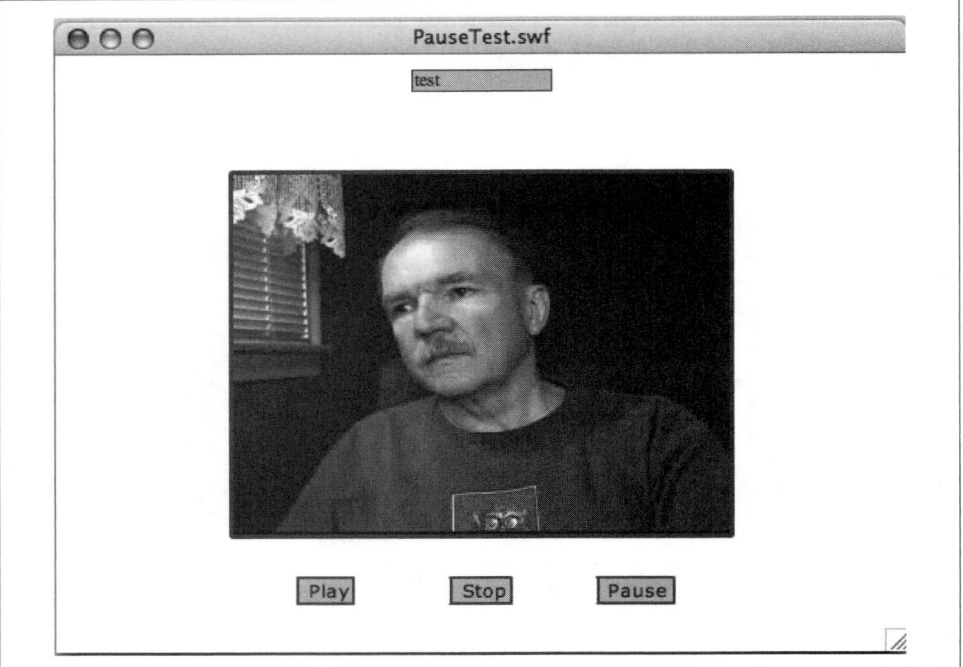

Figure 10-6. Player with added Pause button

Adding More States and Streaming Capabilities

Now that the structure can support a simple FLV playback system, the next step will be to add two additional states and see if the state machine can be adapted to a Flash Media Server application. Keeping the focus on the design pattern, only two new states will be added—Record and Append.

Changing from a Flash application to a Flash Media Server 2 (FMS2) application requires key changes in the FLA script to include a connection to the server, and adding Camera and Microphone objects. Otherwise, you'll find that adding the additional states of Record and Append are relatively simple.

Setting Up Your ActionScript 3.0 Script for FMS2

Adding states is relatively easy, as you've seen. However, when you add Flash Media Server 2, you need to take care of a few matters to make sure that your application works correctly. Because AS 3.0 and Client-Side ActionScript (CSAS) used in FMS2 are a bit different, you need to import the `net.ObjectEncoding` class. By doing so,

ActionScript 3.0 and CSAS can work together. The ActionScript 3.0 default Action Message Format (AMF) is AMF3, but FMS2 needs AMF0. So, you need to change the ObjectEncoding class to AMF0 using the line,

```
NetConnection.defaultObjectEncoding=flash.net.ObjectEncoding.AMF0;
```

This line needs to be in your implementation of the State design pattern, but not in the classes that make up the pattern. (See Example 10-27)

You will see in the StopState class we made for this application (Example 10-21) we need to have a key difference in the way that the NetStream.play( ) method is employed. By adding a second parameter to the method, it's effectively changed into a CSAS method. However, because the flash.net.ObjectEncoding has been imported, the two different versions of ActionScript can work together.

Flash Media Server 2 is an open socket media server available from Adobe. You can download the Developer's Version free from

http://www.adobe.com/products/flashmediaserver/

You will need to set it up in a Windows or Linux server environment, or just on your own computer with Windows OS. On a Macintosh, you'll need to be in the Windows mode to set it up.

Once installed on your system, just add a folder named flvstate in the applications folder of the Flash Media Server. Once that's done, you don't need to do anything else with the server other than make sure that it's running when you use the FMS application. (You'll need to follow the FMS2 documentation for the setup.)

The Adaptable States

The first task when working with state machine models is to update the model. Figure 10-7 shows the addition of two new states—Append and Record. The original three states are pretty much the same as before. Note that the Stop state is the central one for all transitions except for the Play-Pause toggle. To change from any state except Pause, the transition must first go to the Stop state.

As noted at the outset, statecharts make it easy to see required program changes. By adding two more states, Append and Record, all the other states and contexts need to be changed as well. However, you don't have to change a huge number of conditional statements. The testing application also needs changes, but because that code is more a user of the state machine than an actual part of the state machine, it will be handled separately. The following scripts, Examples 10-20 through 10-26, add all the necessary changes for the state machine:

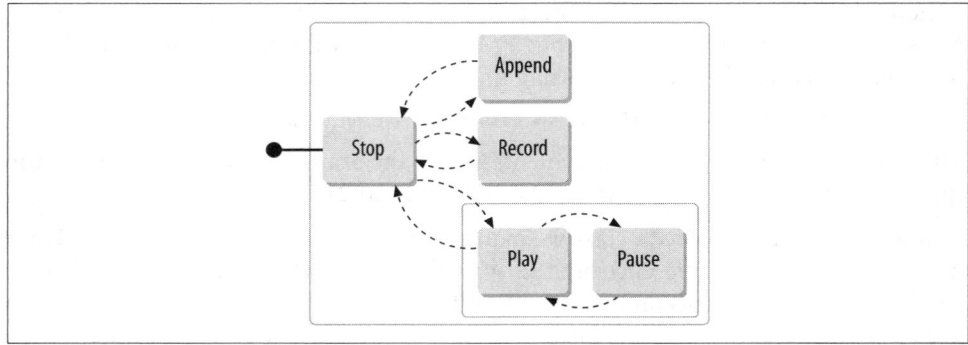

Figure 10-7. Statechart with five states

Example 10-20. State.as

```
 1  package
 2  {
 3      //State Interface #1
 4      import flash.net.NetStream;
 5      interface State
 6      {
 7          function startPlay(ns:NetStream, flv:String):void;
 8          function startRecord(ns:NetStream, flv:String):void;
 9          function startAppend(ns:NetStream, flv:String):void;
10          function stopAll(ns:NetStream):void;
11          function doPause(ns:NetStream):void;
12      }
13  }
```

Note that instead of naming the method for stopping the video play, it's been changed to stopAll( ) in line 10. The reason for this is that in the different states, stopping means something different. It can mean stop recording and appending in addition to stop playing the video. So the change focuses on the fact that it's not just to do one thing. It's another instance where polymorphism is coming in handy.

Next, the StopState class has one NetStream method that's part of an older Action-Script, Client-Side ActionScript (CSAS) from Flash Media Server 2. In ActionScript 3. 0, the NetStream.play( ) method expects only a single argument—a string for the FLV file's URL. However, in CSAS, you can add a second parameter to specify what type of stream to play. In order for AS 3.0 to work with classes from prior versions of ActionScript that serialize objects, the application will have to import the ObjectEncoding class. However, if that's done, AS 3.0 can fully integrate these other objects and their parameters. Line 20 shows this second argument added to the NetStream.play( ) method.

Example 10-21. StopState.as

```
1  package
2  {
3      //Stop State #2
4      import flash.net.NetStream;
5
6      class StopState implements State
7      {
8          var videoWorks:VideoWorks;
9          public function StopState(videoWorks:VideoWorks)
10         {
11             trace("--Stop State--");
12             this.videoWorks=videoWorks;
13         }
14         public function startPlay(ns:NetStream,flv:String):void
15         {
16             //Note: the second paramater - 0 - specifies an FLV file
17             //the NetStream method is from Client-Side
18             //ActionScript but works with AS 3.0
19             //because ObjectEncoding is imported.
20             ns.play(flv,0);
21             trace("Begin playing");
22             videoWorks.setState(videoWorks.getPlayState());
23         }
24         public function startRecord(ns:NetStream,flv:String):void
25         {
26             ns.publish(flv,"record");
27             trace("Begin recording");
28             videoWorks.setState(videoWorks.getRecordState());
29         }
30         public function startAppend(ns:NetStream,flv:String):void
31         {
32             ns.publish(flv,"append");
33             trace("Begin appending");
34             videoWorks.setState(videoWorks.getAppendState());
35         }
36         public function stopAll(ns:NetStream):void
37         {
38             trace("You're already stopped");
39         }
40         public function doPause(ns:NetStream):void
41         {
42             trace("Must be playing to pause.");
43         }
44     }
45 }
46
```

It may seem ironic that the state with the most active implementations of the video is called "stop." However, only from the StopState should transitions be made to Append and Record states. The PlayState shown in Example 10-22 can be transitioned to from both the Stop state and the Pause state.

Example 10-22. PlayState.as

```
 1 package
 2 {
 3     //Play State #3
 4     import flash.net.NetStream;
 5
 6     class PlayState implements State
 7     {
 8         var videoWorks:VideoWorks;
 9         public function PlayState(videoWorks:VideoWorks)
10         {
11             trace("--Play State--");
12             this.videoWorks=videoWorks;
13         }
14         public function startPlay(ns:NetStream,flv:String):void
15         {
16             trace("You're already playing");
17         }
18         public function stopAll(ns:NetStream):void
19         {
20             ns.close();
21             trace("Stop playing.");
22             videoWorks.setState(videoWorks.getStopState());
23         }
24         public function startRecord(ns:NetStream,flv:String):void
25         {
26             trace("You have to stop first.");
27         }
28         public function startAppend(ns:NetStream,flv:String):void
29         {
30             trace("You have to stop first.");
31         }
32         public function doPause(ns:NetStream):void
33         {
34             ns.togglePause();
35             trace("Start pausing.");
36             videoWorks.setState(videoWorks.getPauseState());
37         }
38     }
39 }
40
```

The Play state is little changed from previous versions. While playing a video, the structure won't allow direct transitioning to either recording or appending a video. It would be possible to do so, but you'd run the risk over overwriting a video you're watching with one you want to record. So, from the Play state, the only possible transitions are to the Stop and Pause states. The Pause state is shown in Example 10-23.

Example 10-23. PauseState.as

```
1  package
2  {
3      //Pause State #4
4      import flash.net.NetStream;
5
6      class PauseState implements State
7      {
8          var videoWorks:VideoWorks;
9          public function PauseState(videoWorks:VideoWorks)
10         {
11             trace("--Pause State--");
12             this.videoWorks=videoWorks;
13         }
14         public function startPlay(ns:NetStream,flv:String):void
15         {
16             trace("You have to go to unpause");
17         }
18         public function stopAll(ns:NetStream):void
19         {
20             trace("Don't go to Stop from Pause");
21         }
22         public function startRecord(ns:NetStream,flv:String):void
23         {
24             trace("You have to stop first.");
25         }
26         public function startAppend(ns:NetStream,flv:String):void
27         {
28             trace("You have to stop first.");
29         }
30         public function doPause(ns:NetStream):void
31         {
32             ns.togglePause( );
33             trace("Quit pausing.");
34             videoWorks.setState(videoWorks.getPlayState( ));
35         }
36     }
37
38 }
```

Like the Play state, little is changed with the Pause state shown in Example 10-23, because it only toggles between playing and not playing, and can't pause a recording.

The RecordState class is a whole new state. If you look closely, it's very close to the PlayState class, with the exception that it can't transition to the Pause state. Remember that while in the Record state, the only option is to stop recording, and that is how the stopAll( ) method is implemented in the RecordState class in Example 10-24. Save the new state with the caption name as the filename. Be sure to save it in the same folder as the other files.

Example 10-24. RecordState.as

```
1  package
2  {
3      //Record State #5
4      import flash.net.NetStream;
5
6      class RecordState implements State
7      {
8          var videoWorks:VideoWorks;
9          public function RecordState(videoWorks:VideoWorks)
10         {
11             trace("--Record State--");
12             this.videoWorks=videoWorks;
13         }
14         public function startPlay(ns:NetStream,flv:String):void
15         {
16             trace("You have to stop first.");
17         }
18         public function stopAll(ns:NetStream):void
19         {
20             ns.close( );
21             trace("Stop recording.");
22             videoWorks.setState(videoWorks.getStopState( ));
23         }
24         public function startRecord(ns:NetStream,flv:String):void
25         {
26             trace("You're already recording");
27         }
28         public function startAppend(ns:NetStream,flv:String):void
29         {
30             trace("You have to stop first.");
31         }
32         public function doPause(ns:NetStream):void
33         {
34             trace("Must be playing to pause.");
35         }
36     }
37  }
```

The AppendState shown in Example 10-25 is the other new class. It's virtually identical to the RecordState class in its makeup. However, because the processes of recording and appending are very similar, this should come as no surprise. Save this class in the same folder as the others for this application with the caption as the filename.

Example 10-25. AppendState.as

```
1  package
2  {
3      //Append State #6
4      import flash.net.NetStream;
5
6
7      class AppendState implements State
```

Example 10-25. AppendState.as (continued)

```
8        {
9            var videoWorks:VideoWorks;
10           public function AppendState(videoWorks:VideoWorks)
11           {
12               trace("--Append State--");
13               this.videoWorks=videoWorks;
14           }
15           public function startPlay(ns:NetStream,flv:String):void
16           {
17               trace("You have to stop first.");
18           }
19           public function stopAll(ns:NetStream):void
20           {
21               ns.close();
22               trace("Stop appending.");
23               videoWorks.setState(videoWorks.getStopState());
24           }
25           public function startRecord(ns:NetStream,flv:String):void
26           {
27               trace("You have to stop first.");
28           }
29           public function startAppend(ns:NetStream,flv:String):void
30           {
31               trace("You're already appending");
32           }
33           public function doPause(ns:NetStream):void
34           {
35               trace("Must be playing to pause.");
36           }
37       }
38   }
```

Other than adding instances of the new states, nothing is too different from the previous versions in the VideoWorks class shown in Example 10-26. This is a case where little change shows the strength of the State design structure. Not only has the application been expanded to include two additional classes for record and append, it's also changed from a simple Flash Player using progressive download to play a video to a Flash Media Server 2 streaming media application.

Example 10-26. VideoWorks.as

```
1   package
2   {
3       //Context Class #7
4       import flash.net.NetStream;
5       public class VideoWorks
6       {
7           var playState:State;
8           var stopState:State;
9           var recordState:State;
10          var appendState:State;
```

Example 10-26. VideoWorks.as (continued)

```
11          var pauseState:State;
12          var state:State;
13          public function VideoWorks ()
14          {
15              trace ("Video Player is on");
16              playState = new PlayState(this);
17              stopState = new StopState(this);
18              recordState = new RecordState(this);
19              appendState = new AppendState(this);
20              pauseState=new PauseState(this);
21              state=stopState;
22          }
23          public function startPlay (ns:NetStream,flv:String):void
24          {
25              state.startPlay (ns,flv);
26          }
27          public function startRecord (ns:NetStream,flv:String):void
28          {
29              state.startRecord (ns,flv);
30          }
31          public function startAppend (ns:NetStream,flv:String):void
32          {
33              state.startAppend (ns,flv);
34          }
35          public function stopAll (ns:NetStream):void
36          {
37              state.stopAll (ns);
38          }
39          public function doPause (ns:NetStream):void
40          {
41              state.doPause (ns);
42          }
43          public function setState (state:State):void
44          {
45              trace ("A new state is set");
46              this.state=state;
47          }
48          public function getState ():State
49          {
50              return state;
51          }
52          public function getPlayState ():State
53          {
54              return this.playState;
55          }
56          public function getRecordState ():State
57          {
58              return this.recordState;
59          }
60          public function getAppendState ():State
61          {
62              return this.appendState;
```

Example 10-26. VideoWorks.as (continued)

```
63          }
64          public function getPauseState ():State
65          {
66              return this.pauseState;
67          }
68          public function getStopState ():State
69          {
70              return this.stopState;
71          }
72      }
73  }
```

The test module, Example 10-27, that follows in the TestFMS.as class is a bit more
robust than the previous testing classes used. (In fact it would have probably been a
good idea to break it down into its own class set, but we're focusing on using it to
demonstrate the State design pattern, and so a humbler test class emerged.) Be sure
to place a copy of the NetBtn.as and BtnState.as files in the folder where you're saving the rest of your files for this application.

Example 10-27. TestFMS.as

```
1  package
2  {
3      //Test Module #8
4      import flash.display.Sprite;
5      import flash.net.NetConnection;
6      import flash.net.NetStream;
7      import flash.net.ObjectEncoding;
8      import flash.media.Video;
9      import flash.media.Camera;
10     import flash.media.Microphone;
11     import flash.text.TextField;
12     import flash.text.TextFieldType;
13     import flash.events.MouseEvent;
14     import flash.events.NetStatusEvent;
15
16     public class TestVidFMS extends Sprite
17     {
18         private var nc:NetConnection;
19         private var ns:NetStream;
20         private var dummy:Object;
21         private var flv_txt:TextField;
22         private var cam:Camera;
23         private var mic:Microphone;
24         private var stateVid:VideoWorks;
25         private var playCheck:Boolean;
26         private var pauseCheck:Boolean;
27         private var playBtn:NetBtn;
28         private var stopBtn:NetBtn;
29         private var pauseBtn:NetBtn;
30         private var recordBtn:NetBtn;
```

Example 10-27. TestFMS.as (continued)

```
31          private var appendBtn:NetBtn;
32
33          public function TestVidFMS ( )
34          {
35              //*************
36              //Add the text field
37              //***********
38              flv_txt= new TextField( );
39              flv_txt.border=true;
40              flv_txt.background=true;
41              flv_txt.backgroundColor=0xfab383;
42              flv_txt.type=TextFieldType.INPUT;
43              flv_txt.x=(550/2)-45;
44              flv_txt.y=15;
45              flv_txt.width=90;
46              flv_txt.height=18;
47              addChild (flv_txt);
48              //FMS State Machine
49              NetConnection.defaultObjectEncoding = flash.net.ObjectEncoding.AMF0;
50              nc = new NetConnection( );
51              nc.objectEncoding = flash.net.ObjectEncoding.AMF0;
52              nc.addEventListener (NetStatusEvent.NET_STATUS,checkHookupStatus);
53              //Use your own domain/IP address on RTMP
54              nc.connect ("rtmp://192.168.0.11/flvstate/flv");
55              //OR set up a local connection
56              //nc.connect("rtmp:/flvstate/flv");
57              //nc.connect(null);
58
59              //Camera & Microphone Settings
60              cam = Camera.getCamera( );
61              cam.setMode (320,240,15);
62              cam.setKeyFrameInterval (30);
63              cam.setQuality (0,80);
64              mic = Microphone.getMicrophone( );
65              mic.rate=11;
66
67              //Add video object
68              vid=new Video(320,240);
69
70              addChild (vid);
71              vid.x=(550/2)-(320/2);
72              vid.y=40;
73              setLocal ( );
74
75              //Instantiate State Machine
76              stateVid=new VideoWorks;
77
78              //Play, Stop, Record, Append and Pause Buttons
79              playBtn=new NetBtn("Play");
80              addChild (playBtn);
81              playBtn.x=(550/2)-(320/2);
82              playBtn.y=300;
```

Example 10-27. TestFMS.as (continued)

```
83                  var playCheck:Boolean=false;
84
85                  recordBtn=new NetBtn("Record");
86                  addChild (recordBtn);
87                  recordBtn.x=(550/2)+((320/2)-60);
88                  recordBtn.y=300;
89
90                  appendBtn=new NetBtn("Append");
91                  addChild (appendBtn);
92                  appendBtn.x=(550/2)+((320/2)-60);
93                  appendBtn.y=330;
94
95                  stopBtn=new NetBtn("Stop");
96                  addChild (stopBtn);
97                  stopBtn.x=(550/2)-25;
98                  stopBtn.y=300;
99
100                 pauseBtn=new NetBtn("Pause");
101                 addChild (pauseBtn);
102                 pauseBtn.x=(550/2)-(320/2);
103                 pauseBtn.y=330;
104                 pauseCheck=true;
105
106                 //Add Event Listeners
107                 playBtn.addEventListener (MouseEvent.CLICK,doPlay);
108                 stopBtn.addEventListener (MouseEvent.CLICK,doStop);
109                 recordBtn.addEventListener (MouseEvent.CLICK,doRecord);
110                 appendBtn.addEventListener (MouseEvent.CLICK,doAppend);
111                 pauseBtn.addEventListener (MouseEvent.CLICK,doPause);
112
113             }
114         //Add Control Functions
115         function setNet ( )
116         {
117             vid.attachNetStream (ns);
118         }
119         function setLocal ( )
120         {
121             vid.attachCamera (cam);
122         }
123         var flv:String;
124         function doPlay (e:MouseEvent):void
125         {
126             if (flv_txt.text != "" && flv_txt.text != "Provide file name")
127             {
128                 setNet ( );
129                 flv_txt.textColor=0x000000;
130                 flv=flv_txt.text;
131                 stateVid.startPlay (ns,flv);
132                 if (! playCheck)
133                 {
134                     playCheck=true;
```

Example 10-27. TestFMS.as (continued)

```
135                }
136            }
137            else
138            {
139                flv_txt.textColor=0xcc0000;
140                flv_txt.text="Provide file name";
141            }
142        }
143        function doRecord (e:MouseEvent):void
144        {
145            if (flv_txt.text != "" && flv_txt.text != "Provide file name")
146
147            {
148                ns.attachAudio (mic);
149                ns.attachCamera (cam);
150                flv_txt.textColor=0x000000;
151                flv=flv_txt.text;
152                stateVid.startRecord (ns,flv);
153                if (! playCheck)
154                {
155                    playCheck=true;
156                }
157            }
158            else
159            {
160                flv_txt.textColor=0xcc0000;
161                flv_txt.text="Provide file name";
162            }
163        }
164        function doAppend (e:MouseEvent):void
165        {
166            if (flv_txt.text != "" && flv_txt.text != "Provide file name")
167            {
168                ns.attachAudio (mic);
169                ns.attachCamera (cam);
170                flv_txt.textColor=0x000000;
171                flv=flv_txt.text;
172                stateVid.startAppend (ns,flv);
173                if (! playCheck)
174                {
175                    playCheck=true;
176                }
177            }
178            else
179            {
180                flv_txt.textColor=0xcc0000;
181                flv_txt.text="Provide file name";
182            }
183        }
184        function doPause (e:MouseEvent):void
185        {
186            if (pauseCheck)
```

Example 10-27. TestFMS.as (continued)

```
187              {
188                  pauseCheck=false;
189                  if (playCheck)
190                  {
191                      stopBtn.visible=false;
192                  }
193                  stateVid.doPause (ns);
194              }
195              else
196              {
197                  pauseCheck=true;
198                  stopBtn.visible=true;
199                  stateVid.doPause (ns);
200
201              }
202          }
203          function doStop (e:MouseEvent):void
204          {
205              playCheck=false;
206              stateVid.stopAll (ns);
207              vid.clear ();
208              setLocal ();
209          }
210          //Check connection, instantiate stream,
211          //and set up metadata event handler
212          function checkHookupStatus (event:NetStatusEvent):void
213          {
214              if (event.info.code == "NetConnection.Connect.Success")
215              {
216                  ns = new NetStream(nc);
217                  dummy=new Object( );
218                  ns.client=dummy;
219                  dummy.onMetaData=getMeta;
220                  ns.addEventListener (NetStatusEvent.NET_STATUS,flvCheck);
221              }
222          }
223          //MetaData
224          function getMeta (mdata:Object):void
225          {
226              trace (mdata.duration);
227          }
228          //Handle flv
229          private function flvCheck (event:NetStatusEvent):void
230          {
231              switch (event.info.code)
232              {
233                  case "NetStream.Play.Stop" :
234                      stateVid.stopAll(ns);
235                      setLocal( );
236                      break;
237                  case "NetStream.Play.StreamNotFound" :
238                      stateVid.stopAll(ns);
```

Example 10-27. TestFMS.as (continued)

```
239                    flv_txt.text="File not found";
240                    setLocal();
241                    break;
242             }
243         }
244     }
245 }
```

The most important setup in testing this application is making sure you have the right Real-Time Messaging Protocol (RTMP) configuration. If you're testing the application on your system using it as a Flash Media Server platform, you can just comment out line 54 and remove the comment slashes from line 56. That will work where your application is on the same server as your SWF file. Otherwise, adjust line 38 to point to your FMS location.

Figure 10-8 shows what your application will look like once it's running correctly. As you can see, it's not much different on the outside because all you see are two additional buttons. However, its functionality has increased significantly with the ability to record and append video.

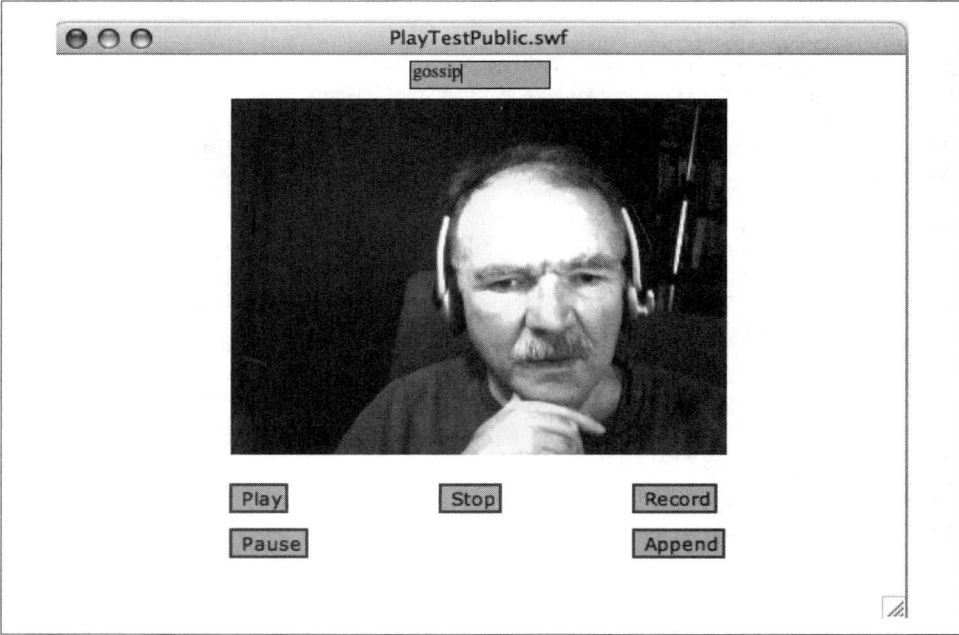

Figure 10-8. Recording video

Summary

We're used to thinking in noun-verb pairs, and so designs using the verb element of a pair may take a bit of getting used to. You can think of a state as a "state of action" such as a video playing or recording. However, you can also think of a state as a "state of rest" or "inactivity." Likewise, transitions between states have a verb-centric character to them.

The focus of the State design pattern has always been on what is done rather than the characteristics of the objects. Additionally, statecharts are an incredibly easy and effective way to design applications. It begins with the part that is often left to the end of a project—making all of the connections between the different elements. Once the statecharts are complete, casting the project in State design patterns terms is equally easy because the structure of the class is so simply organized. Each state will have its own class, and the classes are made up of the different transitions defined in the state interface. All that's left is the context class to pull it all together. So if your project involves different actions that need to be organized and coordinated, consider a state machine using the State design pattern.

CHAPTER 11

Strategy Pattern

Enact strategy broadly, correctly and openly. Then you will come to think of things in a wide sense and, taking the void as the Way, you will see the Way as void.

—Miyamoto Musashi (16th-17th Century Japanese developer of Sword Method Design Pattern [Kenjutsu] and guy who reminds us that in ActionScript 3.0, the void statement is all lowercase.)

All men can see these tactics whereby I conquer, but what none can see is the strategy out of which victory is evolved.

—Sun Tzu

However beautiful the strategy, you should occasionally look at the results.

—Winston Churchill (Remark made after finishing up a "Hello world" application using the Strategy pattern.)

What is the Strategy Pattern?

The Strategy design pattern is sometimes used to illustrate good OOP practices rather than offered as a design pattern that has focused applications. In one article [Agerbo and Cornils, 98], the authors set up a number of guidelines for judging design patterns. One guideline posits that a *design pattern should not be an inherent object-oriented way of thinking*. Then they proceed to reject the Strategy design pattern because it seems to be nothing but a collection of fundamental OOP principles!

Whether the Strategy pattern is a true design pattern or just a template for how to go about OOP programming, it has lots to offer. Because the class model looks identical to the State design pattern, we need to spend some time distinguishing the Strategy from the State pattern to show not only how each is unique, but to suggest focal applications each may have.

Key Features

When looking at the key features of the Strategy pattern, you'll benefit from comparing them with the key features of the State pattern in the previous chapter (Chapter 10). The comparison will not only help you understand the difference between the State and Strategy patterns, it'll also help you better understand each pattern in its own right.

The following key features are used in concert to create the Strategy design pattern, but you will find the same elements when looking at good practices for just about any object-oriented programming:

- Define and encapsulate a family of algorithms.
- Make encapsulated algorithms interchangeable.
- Allow algorithms to change independently from the clients that use it.

Before going back to Chapter 10 and looking at the list of features in the State pattern, take a look at the next section, "The Strategy Model." Then make the comparison. Right off the bat you'll see that the key features of the State and Strategy differ, but by comparing the models as well, you'll see the differences more clearly.

Because the features of the Strategy pattern are so fundamental to good OOP, we're going to save a more detailed discussion of them for the section, "Key OOP Concepts used with the Strategy Pattern." As you'll see, all the features are discussed as applicable to the more general principles of programming with OO languages such as ActionScript 3.0.

The Strategy Model

When you look at the class diagram for the Strategy design pattern, you may be struck by a sense of déjà vu. In Figure 10-3 in Chapter 10, the labels look different, but the State design looks very similar. Fear not. They're very different in intent and implementation. So in looking at Figure 11-1, keep the Strategy design pattern key features in mind.

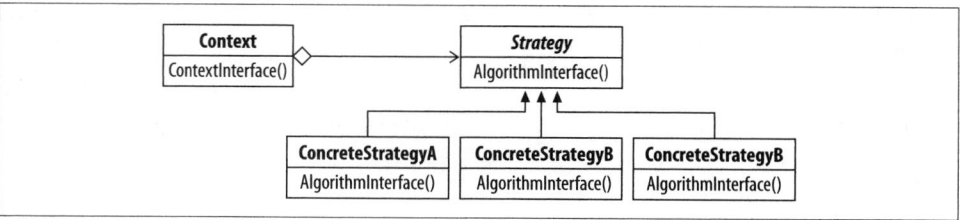

Figure 11-1. Strategy design pattern class diagram

Looking at the Context class in the Strategy class diagram, you can see that the Strategy interface is an aggregate of the Context class. Because of this aggregation, we can say that the Context class (aggregator) *owns* the Strategy interface (aggregate), just as in the State design pattern. (See Figure 10-3 in Chapter 10.) As you will see in the examples, the Context class aggregates the Strategy operations. Because aggregation is so fundamental to many of the design patterns and an integral part of OOP, look for its actual use in the examples. The Strategy design pattern is one of the best sources of clear examples showing aggregation at work.

Key OOP Concepts Used with the Strategy Pattern

David Geary (JavaWorld.com, 04/26/02) points out that the Strategy pattern embodies several of the OOP principles put forth by Gamma, Helm, Johnson and Vlissides. One of those principles is:

> Encapsulate the concept that varies

Eric and Elisabeth Freeman (*Head First Design Patterns*, O'Reilly 2004) make the same point in discussing the Strategy pattern, and we're not ones to break tradition and miss an important connection between a design pattern and an OOP concept.

Encapsulating Variation

In Chapter 10, you saw that with the State design pattern, the states varied in the video player, and so the State object encapsulated the state-dependent behavior, such as playing and stopping the video. With the Strategy pattern, the Strategy object encapsulates algorithms. What both these design patterns have in common is that the elements that change are encapsulated. (As a hint of what is encapsulated, look at the name of the class. In both the State and Strategy classes, the encapsulating object is the name of the class—check the class diagrams.)

More important is why GoF suggests encapsulating those concepts that vary. Essentially, if you encapsulate those parts that vary, then, when you change the application, you'll have fewer surprises. Encapsulated concepts allow the objects in object-oriented programming to act like objects. Rather than being sticky-glued to and dependent on other elements in a single program, encapsulated objects can act in concert with any new element added to the application, because they can vary independent of other objects.

To better see what it means to encapsulate what varies, consider a script from an example in this chapter with and without encapsulation. This involves clowns and what they do in clown venues.

Unencapsulated version (pseudocode)

```
class Clown {
    function juggle( ) {
    //juggle code
    }
```

```
    function balloonAnimals( ) {
    //balloon animal code
    }
  }

  class Bojo extends Clown {
    //Bojo unique
  }

  class Koka extends Clown {
    //Koka unique
  }
```

All the algorithms for juggling and making balloon animals are placed in the Clown class. They're passed on to the specific subclasses via inheritance. That works fine as long as all the clowns can perform all the tricks. But what happens if one of the clowns doesn't know how to make balloon animals or juggle? Or what about a new act being added? What will happen then?

So now, let's encapsulate the algorithms in a Strategy object.

Encapsulated algorithms (pseudocode)

```
  interface ClownTricks {
    function someTrick( ): void;
  }
  class Juggle implements ClownTricks {
    function someTrick( ): void {
    //Juggling algorithm
    }
  }
  class BalloonAnimals implements ClownTricks {
    function someTrick( ): void {
    //Making balloon animal algorithm
    }
  }
```

Now, using the Clown class as an aggregator, the program can delegate requests for the different algorithms to the concrete Clown subclasses. If new tricks are introduced, just implement them from the ClownTricks interface and use them as delegates to the Clown subclasses that want to use them. (The actual application using these concepts begins with Example 11-6.)

The encapsulated algorithms aren't going to be very useful unless some object can employ them. This is where delegation comes in, as you'll see in the next section.

Using Delegation and Delegates

The Strategy design pattern is a perfect example of delegation. In delegation, two objects are involved in handling a single request. One of the objects receives the request and then delegates operations to a *delegate*. This is exactly what transpires between the context classes and the strategy classes. The context classes are made up of a class and its subclasses. The context classes delegate actions to the strategy classes, made up of strategy interfaces and implementations of those interfaces. So the context classes delegate to the strategy classes.

The delegation process begins in the main context class. It includes reference variables to the strategy interfaces. Methods in the context class do the actual delegation. The concrete context classes inherit the instance variables from the context class, and use those variables to specify which behaviors they want from the concrete strategies. Figure 11-2 shows a visual depiction of delegation.

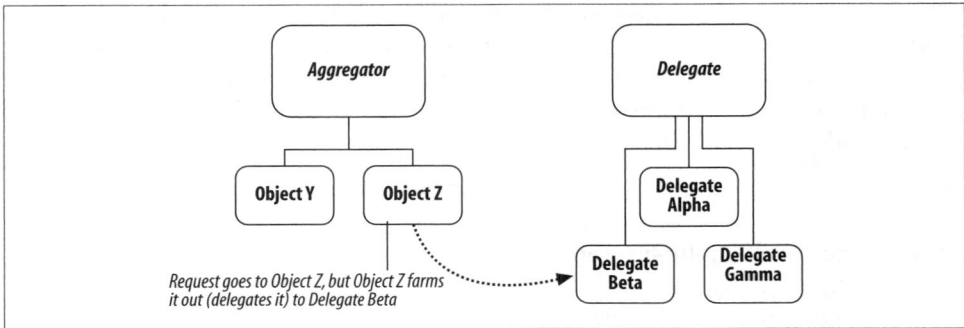

Figure 11-2. Delegation

If an instance of a class, which has a reference to a delegate that is called, is called, the delegate invokes the called method containing the encapsulated algorithm. So instead of inheriting the operation, the object can be said to *have a* method that handles a call.

Minimalist Abstract State Pattern

This first example cuts to the bare bones of a Strategy design pattern to reveal the structure of the design pattern. Each part is analyzed in terms of what it does for the overall pattern. This example should help make the structure clearer.

You need to see the Strategy design pattern in a context where several different objects delegate behaviors to different delegates. (The second example provides this richer applicability.) In this minimalist example, you need to look at the points of delegation and how it all works. In Figure 11-3, following the listing, you will be able to see what looks like a web of intrigue. Not to worry; the illustration just shows the delegation work going on between the objects in the application.

Using Delegation with the Context

The Context class shown in Example 11-1 is an aggregator—it owns the Strategy object. So in every Context class where Strategy patterns are found, you will find a reference to the strategy class—in this example a variable taking the lowercase name of the Strategy interface. (Example 11-1 to Example 11-5 make up the first application.)

Example 11-1. Context.as

```
package
{
    class Context
    {
        protected var strategy:Strategy;

        public function doStrategy():void
        {
            strategy.think();
        }
    }
}
```

The Context class is pretty simple. One reason is that all the methods it needs are delegates implemented from the Strategy interface. Let's now look at such an interface.

Adding a Strategy

In a Strategy design pattern, you're likely to see more than one interface, depending on the different types of methods required. Example 11-2 shows a single method in the interface.

Example 11-2. Strategy.as

```
package
{
    interface Strategy
    {
        function think():void;
    }
}
```

This represents the first step in encapsulating a behavior. The subsequent concrete Strategy implementations add detail.

Details of the Strategy

Next, in Example 11-3, a concrete strategy adds a method, think( ), which does something. In this case, it just sends out a trace message.

Example 11-3. ConcreteStrategy.as

```
package
{
    class ConcreteStrategy implements Strategy
    {
        public function think():void
        {
            trace("Great thoughts now...");
        }
    }
}
```

More Delegation in a Concrete Context

In a concrete context class as in Example 11-4, you can see that the work is delegated to a concrete strategy class.

Example 11-4. ConcreteContext.as

```
package
{
    class ConcreteContext extends Context
    {
        public function ConcreteContext()
        {
            strategy = new ConcreteStrategy();
        }
    }
}
```

Pulling All the Parts Together

Finally, to test the Strategy design pattern, Example 11-5's script creates an instance of the concrete context, but types the instance as a Context data type—an example of programming to the interface and not the implementation.

Example 11-5. TestStrategy.as

```
package
{
    import flash.display.Sprite;

    public class TestStrategy extends Sprite
    {
        public function TestStrategy()
        {
            var thinker:Context= new ConcreteContext();
            thinker.doStrategy();
        }
    }
}
```

Now that you have an abstract Strategy design pattern where you can see the arrangement of the different parts, an illustration where you can see all of the connections, delegation and interactions in a single view will give you an overview of the process. Figure 11-3 shows the connections between the different parts, all in one view.

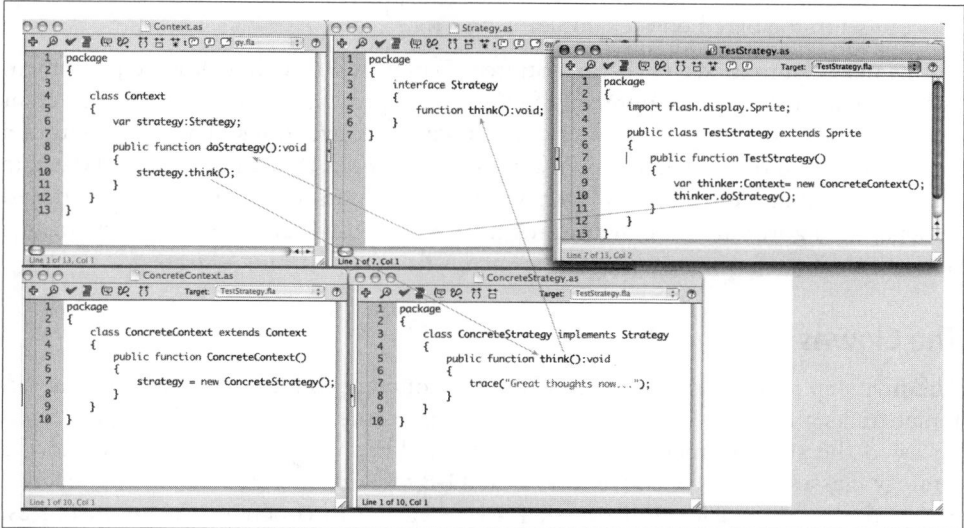

Figure 11-3. Delegation connections

In Figure 11-3, note how the call:

```
thinker.doStrategy();
```

is delegated. The thinker instance in the TestStrategy class is typed as a Context type and instantiated as a ConcreteContext object. The doStrategy() method is created in the Context class, and so that would be the first place to look, as the arrow from doStrategy() in the TestStrategy class to the doStrategy() in the Context class shows.

However, in the Context class the doStrategy() method has delegated the details to the think() method, so we need to look elsewhere. In the ConcreteStrategy class, you can see the details of the think() method. Because the ConcreteContext strategy is instantiated in the thinker instance, it actually did the work, but since ConcreteContext is a subclass of Context, the delegation is structured in the Context class.

Finally, we can trace the delegation framework back to the Strategy interface. Because the origin of the think() method is in the Strategy class, we can see how it is a delegate of the Context class.

Adding More Concrete Strategies and Concrete Contexts

The purpose of the minimalist example is to expose a design pattern's structure. However, with the Strategy pattern, a more robust example may actually do a better job of showing the pattern's features, because it places the pattern in a more practical context in the bare bones example.

In this next example, we envision a Strategy pattern used with a clown employment agency. The agency has a number of clowns it represents. Clients call for different clown venues—circuses, birthday parties, political conventions. They want either a particular clown or particular clown acts (skits) or tricks they can perform. To create a flexible program for the clown agency, each of the skits and tricks has been created in separate algorithms. The algorithms are encapsulated, and the clown characters delegate their performance skills to the encapsulated algorithms—strategies.

The Clowns

The first step is to create a context class and concrete contexts that will use the different tricks and skits. Example 11-6 is the main context class establishing the references to the strategy methods. The trick and skit operations are delegated to the strategy classes. Then Examples 11-7 and 11-8 create two concrete clowns. Each is assigned a different trick and skit that are delegated to concrete strategy instances. To get started, open three ActionScript files and enter the code in Examples 11-6 to 11-8, saving each with the caption name provided. (Examples 11-6 through 11-16 make up the entire application.)

Example 11-6. Clown.as

```
package
{

    class Clown
    {
        protected var tricks:Tricks;
        protected var skits:Skits;

        public function doTrick():void
        {
            tricks.trick();
        }

        public function doSkit():void
        {
```

Example 11-6. Clown.as (continued)

```
            skits.skit();
        }
    }
}
```

Example 11-7. Koka.as

```
package
{
    class Koka extends Clown
    {
        public function Koka()
        {
            tricks = new Disappear();
            skits = new Chase();
        }
    }
}
```

Example 11-8. Bojo.as

```
package
{
    class Bojo extends Clown
    {
        public function Bojo()
        {
            tricks = new BaloonAnimals();
            skits = new FallDown();
        }
    }
}
```

Notice that each clown can perform only a single trick and a single skit. We'll have to reconsider how to set up our strategies, or see if we can find a way to dynamically add features later. For now, though, the clowns can choose only a single trick or skit.

The Trick Interface and Implementations

All the algorithms for doing tricks are encapsulated in the concrete strategy subclasses. The Tricks interface (Example 11-9) provides the abstract method, and the subclasses add detail to the operations. A total of three trick algorithms (Examples 11-10, 11-11, and 11-12) are implemented.

Example 11-9. Tricks.as

```
package
{
```

Example 11-9. Tricks.as (continued)

```
interface Tricks
{
    function trick( ):void;
}
}
```

Example 11-10. BalloonAnimals.as

```
package
{
    //Make Balloon Animals
    public class BalloonAnimals implements Tricks
    {
        public function trick( ):void
        {
            trace("See! It's a doggy! No, it's not an elephant!!\n")
        }
    }
}
```

Example 11-11. Disappear.as

```
package
{
    //Make Something Disappear
    public class Disappear implements Tricks
    {
        public function trick( ):void
        {
            trace("Now you see it! Presto! It's gone!\n")
        }
    }
}
```

Example 11-12. Juggle.as

```
package
{
    //Juggle Balls
    public class Juggle implements Tricks
    {

        public function trick( ):void
        {
            trace("Look at me juggle! Whoops!\n")
        }
    }
}
```

By using a general concept like "tricks," we're limiting the range of what the clowns can do. The way the Strategy pattern's set up, each clown can have only a single trick. We could implement an "All Tricks" class, but that's too broad at the opposite extreme in that it would require a clown to do everything, even if he could only do two of the tricks.

The Skits Interface and Implementations

The Skits interface (Example 11-13) and its implemented classes (Examples 11-14 and 11-15) are set up exactly the same as the Tricks class and its implementations. It also has the same limitations.

Example 11-13. Skits.as

```
package
{
    //Skits Interface
    interface Skits
    {
        function skit():void;
    }
}
```

Example 11-14. FallDown.as

```
package
{
    //Falls down a ladder
    public class FallDown implements Skits
    {
        public function skit():void
        {
            trace("I'm climbing up this ladder!")
            trace("Where's my banana peel?")
            trace("Whoaaaa! I'm falling!!")
            trace("Thanks for finding my banana peel!\n")
        }
    }
}
```

Example 11-15. Chase.as

```
package
{
    //Clowns chase each other
    public class Chase implements Skits
    {
        public function skit():void
        {
            trace("Here I come! I'm going to get you!")
            trace("Nah! Nah! Can't catch me!\n")
        }
    }
}
```

Even though we've discussed some possible shortcomings in this design, it still shows how the strategies are built in the implementations of the Tricks and Skits classes. The final step is to see how to launch the program.

Here Come the Clowns!

For this example, the ClownCollege class (Example 11-16) instantiates two different clowns. Both clowns are typed as Clown types following the dictum of programming to the interface instead of the implementations; however, each instantiates through a Clown subclass. Each is given a trick and skit, and it's ready to run. Save Example 11-16 using the caption name as the filename.

Example 11-16. ClownCollege.as

```
package
{
    import flash.display.Sprite;

    public class ClownCollege extends Sprite
    {
        public function ClownCollege()
        {
            var joker:Clown=new Koka();
            joker.doTrick();
            joker.doSkit();

            var gagGrrrl:Clown=new Bojo();
            gagGrrrl.doTrick();
            gagGrrrl.doSkit();
        }
    }
}
```

Once you're finished saving Examples 11-6 through 11-16, open a new Flash document and save it as ClownCollege.fla. In the Document class window, type in **ClownCollege** and test the application. You should see the following in the Output window:

```
* =>Koka<= *
Now you see it! Presto! It's gone!

Here I come! I'm going to get you!
Nah! Nah! Can't catch me!

* =>Bojo<= *
See! It's a doggy! No, it's not that!!

I'm climbing up this ladder!
Where's my banana peel?
Whoaaaa! I'm falling!!
Thanks for finding my banana peel!
```

The output represents the algorithms set up in the strategy classes. All are delegated from the Clown context class and implemented in the concrete clown classes.

Additional Clown Functionality

As noted in the initial clown application using the Strategy design pattern, the structure allowed very little flexibility and no way to dynamically change a concrete context to accept another strategy. So what happens if we add another clown who can do more than one trick but not all the tricks?

Fortunately, we have a simple solution. By adding setters to the context class, Clown, it will be possible to dynamically add strategies to the concrete context classes—the clowns. Example 11-17 revises the original Clown class by adding the setters (shown in bold).

Example 11-17. Clown.as

```
package
{
    class Clown
    {
        protected var tricks:Tricks;
        protected var skits:Skits;

        public function doTrick():void
        {
            tricks.trick();
        }

        public function doSkit():void
        {
            skits.skit();
        }

        public function setTrick(addTrick:Tricks):void
        {
            tricks=addTrick;
        }

        public function setSkit(addSkit:Tricks):void
        {
            tricks=addSkit;
        }
    }
}
```

Adding a new clown

The application is already structured to easily accept a new concrete context class. So all we have to do is to add a subclass, and include the concrete strategies to be delegated. Example 11-18 does just that. Save the file using the caption as the filename.

Example 11-18. Bubbles.as

```
package
{
    class Bubbles extends Clown
    {
        trace("* =>Bubbles<= *");
        public function Bubbles()
        {
            tricks=new Juggle();
            skits = new FallDown();
        }
    }
}
```

Adding a new trick

Just as adding a new concrete context class in a Strategy pattern is easy, so too is adding a new concrete strategy. Save Example 11-19 using the caption name as the filename. The new script is indistinguishable from any of the other concrete strategies except for the name of the class and the content in the trick method.

Example 11-19. BubblePants.as

```
package
{
    class BubblePants implements Tricks
    {
        public function trick():void
        {
            trace("Woo woo woo! Bubbles are coming out of my pants!\n");
        }
    }
}
```

Revising clown college

To see both how easy it is to add new elements to the application and to dynamically add new strategies to a concrete context class, the ClownCollege class is revised (bold text). First, the new concrete clown class, Bubbles, is instantiated and the two existing delegation methods launch the operations to display the skit and tricks. Then, the clown instance uses the new setTrick() method to add the new trick to its repertoire. Finally, the doTrick() method is launched a second time to display the new trick. Save Example 11-20 using the caption name for the filename.

Example 11-20. ClownCollege.as

```
package
{
    import flash.display.Sprite;

    public class ClownCollege extends Sprite
```

Example 11-20. ClownCollege.as (continued)

```
{
    public function ClownCollege( )
    {
        var joker:Clown=new Koka( );
        joker.doTrick( );
        joker.doSkit( );

        var gagGrrrl:Clown=new Bojo( );
        gagGrrrl.doTrick( );
        gagGrrrl.doSkit( );

        var gurgle:Clown=new Bubbles( );
        gurgle.doSkit( );
        gurgle.doTrick( );
        gurgle.setTrick(new BubblePants( ));
        gurgle.doTrick( );
    }
}
}
```

Nothing will change for the first two clowns. However, the new clown instance should do something different, but what? In looking at the code, the initial skit and trick involve falling off the ladder and juggling. That is unchanged, and so the new clown's initial displays should be no different than anything you've seen so far.

However, after the doTrick( ) method is invoked, the instance, gurgle, is given a new trick. Then, when the doTrick( ) launches a second time for the gurgle instance, a different trick display is shown. The bold output in the following output shows the results of the added materials:

```
* =>Koka<= *
Now you see it! Presto! It's gone!

Here I come! I'm going to get you!
Nah! Nah! Can't catch me!

* =>Bojo<= *
See! It's a doggy! No, it's not that!!

I'm climbing up this ladder!
Where's my banana peel?
Whoaaaa! I'm falling!!
Thanks for finding my banana peel!

* =>Bubbles<= *
I'm climbing up this ladder!
Where's my banana peel?
Whoaaaa! I'm falling!!
Thanks for finding my banana peel!

Look at me juggle! Whoops!

Woo woo woo! Bubbles are coming out of my pants!
```

Simply by adding setters to the context class, the application has been given a dynamic way to change which strategy the concrete context class delegates.

Tricks and Skits Reorganization: Clown Planning

Before going on to the next example, we need to consider how the strategy sub-classes were organized for the task at hand. Keep in mind that no matter how sophisticated or cool your application is, good planning will make it better.

The more components in your system, the more *granularity* your application is said to have. Granularity affords more flexibility, and that's a good thing. However, greater granularity also leads to a greater number of classes, often adding housekeeping headaches.

To optimize your application, especially one using the Strategy design pattern where you can have a large number of both concrete contexts and strategies, you need to plan. Taking a closer look at the clown example, we can see where our planning was incomplete.

Starting with the trick strategies, the structure allows for only a single trick per clown. So, we might want to reorganize the strategies from what we have to something like that shown in Table 11-1.

Table 11-1. Strategies

Juggle Tricks	Balloon Tricks	Magic Tricks
Balls	Animal shapes	Card tricks
Rings	Human shapes	Escape tricks
Flaming Torches	Politicians	Disappearing children
Any objects	Any shapes	Any magic

Now, instead of a single trick interface, it has three. Additionally, a general algorithm covering any tricks in the category is covered as well (any object, any shapes and any magic). To cover contingencies, the context class retains its ability to dynamically add a strategy to an instance of a concrete context object. The skit strategies can be reorganized as well, and new strategies can be added as the application grows and changes.

Working with String Strategies

The best aspect of the Strategy design pattern is its ability to allow change and adaptation. The design pattern is a virtual poster child for composition, where change and flexibility are handled with aplomb. Also, it's a great tool for working with algorithms large and small.

With any application, you're likely to encounter recurring algorithms. For this application, we decided to include some little algorithms that we use with different applications that have to be rebuilt every time we create an application that uses them. However, we don't want to make them into classes where the main objective is to inherit the functionality. Rather, we want to use them in composition so that we have more flexibility, and use their functionality only where we need them.

For our example, we've taken two simple types of string and sorting issues that seem to come up in a lot of different applications. First, we built some simple strategies for checking strings. The first strategy is designed to see if the @ symbol is placed in an email address, and if it's not in the first or last position in a string. The second strategy is a password-checking algorithm that knocks all entries to lowercase, and then sees if they match the correct password.

Our second strategy interface is for demonstrating different sorting possibilities using the Array class and sort( ) method. By changing the sort parameters, you will be able to see which constants to use with different types of sorts and see the outcomes. Figure 11-4 shows all of the connections between the classes.

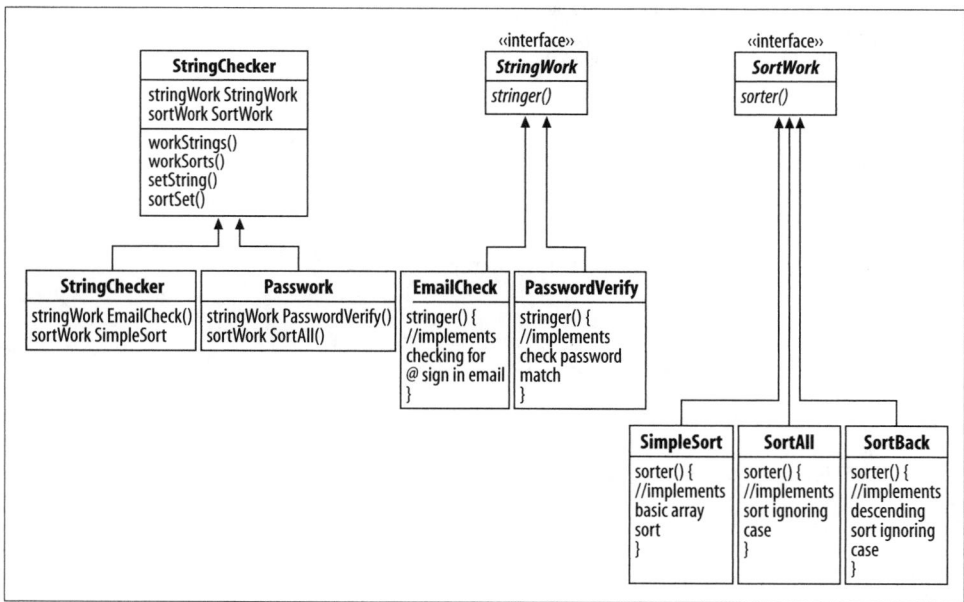

Figure 11-4. Applying the Strategy pattern

The code in Examples 11-21 through 11-33 makes up the ActionScript files that constitute this next application. The application also requires a single Flash document file with the Document class name TestStringStrategy.

Contexts for String Strategies

You can think of the context classes as the *clients* for the strategies. They use the different strategies. Often, you will hear that a client *has-a* behavior. Whenever a client class delegates to a delegate class, such as the strategy classes in Figure 11-4, it *has-a* behavior generated by the strategy class. In this application, the context classes represent the client classes for the strategy classes.

Like all context classes, the StringChecker class in Example 11-21 sets a reference to the two strategy interfaces, StringWork and SortWork. In addition, it has functions, workStrings( ) and workSorts( ) that constitute the methods used to delegate work to the strategies.

Example 11-21. StringChecker.as

```
package
{
    //Context class
    class StringChecker
    {
        protected var stringWork:StringWork;
        protected var sortWork:SortWork;
        public function StringChecker():void
        {
        }

        public function workStrings(s:String):String
        {
            return stringWork.stringer(s);
        }
        public function workSorts(a:Array):Array
        {
            return sortWork.sorter(a);
        }
        public function setString(sw:StringWork):void
        {
            stringWork=sw;
        }
        public function setSort(sow:SortWork):void
        {
            sortWork=sow;
        }
    }
}
```

In addition to having reference properties and methods, the context class includes setter operations, setString( ) and setSort( ), to dynamically set strategies to instances of the context classes.

Next, in Examples 11-22 and 11-23, two concrete context classes extend the primary context class. Note that they inherit the references to the strategies, stringWork( ) and sortWork( ). These references are then used to specify exactly which of the concrete strategies each will be using.

Example 11-22. Checker.as

```
package
{
    //Concrete Context
    class Checker extends StringChecker
    {
        public function Checker( )
        {
            stringWork = new EmailCheck( );
            sortWork = new SimpleSort( );
        }
    }
}
```

Example 11-23. Passwork.as

```
package
{
    //Concrete Context
    class Passwork extends StringChecker
    {
        public function Passwork( )
        {
            stringWork = new PasswordVerify( );
            sortWork = new SortAll( );
        }
    }
}
```

Keep in mind that both of these classes inherit the methods of the main context class, StringChecker, and when you test instances of these classes, you will be using the workStrings( ) and workSorts( ) methods.

String Strategies

The classes associated with the strategies are quite simple by comparison to the client classes in the Strategy design pattern. The interfaces specify the methods, and then each of the concrete strategy classes implements them, supplying the details in the form of algorithms. However, in this example (Examples 11-24 and 11-25), both methods in the interfaces require parameters and expect returns.

Example 11-24. StringWork.as

```
package
{
    //Strategy
    interface StringWork
    {
        function stringer(s:String):String;
    }
}
```

Example 11-25. SortWork.as

```
package
{
    //Strategy
    interface SortWork
    {
        function sorter(a:Array):Array;
    }
}
```

Even with the added parameter and the return datatype, the interfaces are very simple. They get more interesting in their implementation.

Checking strategies

The first two concrete strategies (Examples 11-26 and 11-27) create algorithms using String methods. Each adds an algorithm requiring work with strings. Neither is especially sophisticated, but both are handy for certain applications that require checking strings.

Example 11-26. EmailCheck.as

```
package
{
    //Concrete Strategy
    class EmailCheck implements StringWork
    {
        public function stringer(s:String):String
        {
            var atPlace:int=s.indexOf("@");
            if (atPlace != -1 && atPlace !=0 && atPlace != (s.length-1))
            {
                return "Email address verified";
            } else
            {
                return "Email does not verify.\nMissing or
                    misplaced @ sign";
            }
        }
    }
}
```

Example 11-27. PasswordVerify.as

```
package
{
    //Concrete Strategy
    class PasswordVerify implements StringWork
    {
        public function stringer(s:String):String
        {
            var pwv:String=s;
            pwv=pwv.toLocaleLowerCase( );
            if (pwv == "sandlight")
            {
                return "Welcome to Sandlight";
            } else
            {
                return "Your password is incorrect.
                    Please enter again.";
            }
        }
    }
}
```

Instead of using simple string comparisons, you could use regular expressions. Far more sophisticated substring searches and comparisons are possible using RegExp data types and algorithms.

Sort strategies

The algorithms used for the sorting strategies (Examples 11-28, 11-29, and 11-30) are much simpler than the simple string algorithms used in the two StringWork implantations. All three of the algorithms use a single Array method—sort( ). However, by changing the parameters, you actually have three different kinds of sorts.

Example 11-28. SimpleSort.as

```
package
{
    //Concrete Strategy
    class SimpleSort implements SortWork
    {
        public function sorter(a:Array):Array
        {
            a.sort( );
            return a;


        }
    }
}
```

Example 11-29. SortAll.as

```
package
{
    //Concrete Strategy
    class SortAll implements SortWork
    {
        public function sorter(a:Array):Array
        {
            a.sort(Array.CASEINSENSITIVE);
            return a;


        }
    }
}
```

Example 11-30. SortBack.as

```
package
{
    //Concrete Strategy
    class SortBack implements SortWork
    {
        public function sorter(a:Array):Array
        {
            a.sort(Array.CASEINSENSITIVE | Array.DESCENDING);
            return a;

        }
    }
}
```

As you can see, you can do quite a bit with a single method. To add more options to sorting, add some implementations using the `Array.sortOn()` method and multi-dimension arrays.

Support Classes

Two support classes help keep the main test application clear, and make good use of the whole idea of a class structural arrangement. The ShowText class (Example 11-31) organizes a dynamic text field, and TextShow (Example 11-32) provides the format.

Example 11-31. ShowText.as

```
package
{
    import flash.text.TextField;
    import flash.text.TextFieldType;

    class ShowText extends TextField
    {
        public function ShowText():void
```

Example 11-31. ShowText.as (continued)

```
        {
            this.type=TextFieldType.DYNAMIC;
            this.multiline=true;
            this.wordWrap=true;
            this.border=true;
            this.borderColor=0xcccccc;
        }
    }
}
```

Example 11-32. TextShow.as

```
package
{
    import flash.text.TextFormat;

    class TextShow extends TextFormat
    {
        function TextShow( ):void
        {
            this.font="Verdana";
            this.color=0xcc0000;
            this.size=11;
            this.leading=3;
            this.leftMargin=11;
            this.rightMargin=6;
        }
    }
}
```

Feel free to change any of the support classes' features to meet your own tastes.

String Strategy Test

The test of the applied Strategy design pattern uses two objects (Example 11-33). The first object instantiates the concrete context class, Checker, and the second uses Passwork.

Example 11-33. TestStringStrategy.as

```
package
{
    import flash.display.Sprite;

    public class TestStringStrategy extends Sprite
    {
        private var showText:ShowText;
        private var showText2:ShowText;
        private var textShow:TextShow;

        public function TestStringStrategy( ):void
```

Example 11-33. TestStringStrategy.as (continued)

```
    {
        doText( );

        //Stringer -- Uses Checker concrete context
        var stringer:StringChecker= new Checker( );
        showText.text="Stringer\n\n"+stringer.workStrings
            ("Bill@office.net");
        var friends:Array=new Array("John","Carl","aYo","Delia");
        showText.appendText("\n"+stringer.workSorts(friends));
        stringer.setString(new PasswordVerify( ));
        showText.appendText("\n"+stringer.workStrings("Sandlight"));

        //Passer -- Uses Passwork concrete context
        var passer:StringChecker= new Passwork( );
        showText2.text="Passer\n\n"+passer.workStrings("Rumple");
        showText2.appendText("\n"+passer.workSorts(friends));
        passer.setSort(new SortBack( ));
        showText2.appendText("\n"+passer.workSorts(friends));
        passer.setString(new EmailCheck);
        showText2.appendText
            ("\n"+passer.workStrings("@passGuy.com"));
    }
    private function doText( ):void
    {
        showText=new ShowText( );
        showText2=new ShowText( );
        textShow=new TextShow( );
        showText.defaultTextFormat = textShow;
        showText2.defaultTextFormat = textShow;
        addChild(showText),addChild(showText2);
        showText.x=50, showText2.x=270;
        showText.y=100, showText2.y=100;
        showText.width=200,showText2.width=200;
        showText.height=150,showText2.height=150;
    }
  }
}
```

Keep in mind that the call to the concrete class methods, workStrings and workSorts, are calls that are delegated to the strategy classes. After opening a new Flash document file and placing TextStringStrate in the Document class window, test the application. Figure 11-5 shows what you can expect to see.

Also, note that after the dynamic changes were reset using setString( ) and setSort( ), the output changes. Even though adding the setter is optional for a true Strategy design pattern, setters add a whole other level of flexibility and should not be overlooked.

```
Stringer

Email address verified
Carl,Delia,John,aYo
Welcome to Sandlight
```
```
Passer

Your password is incorrect.
Please enter again.
aYo,Carl,Delia,John
John,Delia,Carl,aYo
Email does not verify.
Missing or misplaced @ sign
```

Figure 11-5. Output from TestStringStrategy

Summary

After examining some applications using the Strategy design pattern, you can see the scope of possibilities for it as a design pattern. It's certainly a showcase for good OOP practices. Perhaps most obvious is how it uses composition instead of inheritance to develop and use the algorithms. However, it still uses the basic OOP feature of *inheritance* in its concrete context classes.

Furthermore, you can clearly see *polymorphism* in the variety of ways the different strategies are implemented. Each of the interfaces demonstrates *abstraction* along with the main context class. All the strategies *encapsulate* an algorithm, and each serves as a delegate to another class. So there you have it, the four basic elements of good OOP:

- Inheritance
- Polymorphism
- Abstraction
- Encapsulation

As we saw in this chapter in the section on the key OOP practices, the Strategy design pattern demonstrates several other good OOP practices in addition to the basics.

So, while we believe that the Strategy design pattern certainly demonstrates fundamental OOP practices, it's still a distinct design pattern. Ironically, this fact is most obvious when you compare it to the State design pattern—the pattern it's often accused of duplicating. The State pattern encapsulates states and state contexts, and the Strategy pattern encapsulates algorithms. Both have different intents but these intentions are masked by the almost identical class diagrams. Only when you understand and use each one do the differences manifest themselves. As these differences become clear, you can see the actual use of the State and Strategy patterns as solutions to different kinds of problems. Since the definition of design patterns is that of design solution to recurring problems, we can see that the Strategy design pattern clearly meets this fundamental criterion.

PART V

Multiple Patterns

A multiple personality is in a certain sense normal.
—George Herbert Mead (Describing what is normal for
programmers who attempt to use multiple design
patterns.)

*Language can be abstracted, language can be used as
a very beautiful code in poetry, the nuances and the
multiple meanings of things, it has a music to it. It has
so many things in it. It is also reduced from prose and
therefore can be both mathematical, or very, very
abstract.*
—Jim Jarmusch

For every disciplined effort there is a multiple reward.
—Jim Rohn

*One is sorry one could not have taken both branches
of the road. But we were not allotted multiple selves.*
—Gore Vidal (Describing the process in mutually
exclusive radio buttons.)

Using More Than One Pattern

The two chapters in this last part present two designs that implement more than a
single design pattern. First, we examine the Model View Controller (MVC). The
MVC uses the Observer pattern (Chapter 8) in the Model to hold the data, the View
entity uses the Composite pattern (Chapter 6) for representation of the model state,
and the Controller makes use of the Strategy pattern (Chapter 11) for the user interaction. Our implementation of the MVC in ActionScript 3.0 reflects the design patterns suggested by the Gang of Four. Other options are possible in the MVC, such as
including Factory and Decorator design patterns.

The second multiple design pattern is an implementation of the Symmetric Proxy pattern. The Symmetric Proxy uses a Template Method pattern (Chapter 9) and the Proxy pattern, a pattern not covered in the book. We used Flash Media Server 2 for delivering the moves into a proxy method residing in a player class instead of a separate class for the proxy and real player. However, the Symmetric Proxy, like all good designs, is resilient enough to accept these changes without losing its own basic structure or function.

Chapter 12, *Model-View-Controller Pattern*

Chapter 13, *Symmetric Proxy Pattern*

Model-View-Controller Pattern

*According to the standard model billions of years ago
some little quantum fluctuation, perhaps a slightly
lower density of matter, maybe right where we're
sitting right now, caused our galaxy to start collapsing
around here.*

—Seth Lloyd

*We view things not only from different sides, but with
different eyes; we have no wish to find them alike.*

—Blaise Pascal

*The primary symptom of a controller is denial, that is
I can't see its symptoms in myself.*

—Keith Miller

What Is the Model-View-Controller (MVC) Pattern?

The Model-View-Controller (MVC) is a compound pattern, or multiple patterns working together to create complex applications. The MVC pattern is most commonly used to create interfaces for software applications, and, as the name implies, consists of three elements.

Model
> Contains the application data and logic to manage the state of the application

View
> Presents the user interface and the state of the application onscreen

Controller
> Handles user input to change the state of the application

The power of the MVC pattern can be directly attributed to the separation of the three elements without overlap in each of their responsibilities. Let's look at each element's responsibilities.

Model

The model is responsible for managing the state of the application. The application logic in the model performs two important tasks: it responds to requests for information about the state of the application, and takes action on requests to change the state.

View

A view is the external face of the application. Users interact with the application through the view. An application can contain multiple views that can be both inputs and outputs. For example, in the case of a portable digital music player such as an iPod, the screen is a view. In addition, the buttons that control song playback are views as well. The screen shows the name of the current song, song duration, album art, and so on, that communicate the current state of the device. Views don't necessarily have to be visual. In the case of a digital music player, the sound that comes through the headphones represents a view as well. For example, clicking a button may provide some auditory feedback in the form of the click sound. Changing the volume is reflected in the audio output as well. The auditory feedback corresponds to the state of the application.

Controller

Although the term controller implies an interface that controls an application, in an MVC pattern, the controller does not contain any user interface elements. As pointed out previously, user interface elements that provide input belong to the *view* component. The controller determines how views respond to user input.

For example, our digital music player has *volume up* and *volume down* buttons in a *view*. The sound volume of the device is a state variable. The model will hold this variable with the necessary application logic to change it. If the sound volume range is 0 to 10, the controller determines how much the volume should go up or down with a single click on the volume up and down buttons. The controller can tell the model to raise the volume by 0.5 or 1.0, or any value, programmatically. In this sense, controllers are specific implementations that determine how the application responds to user input.

Although each element in the MVC triad has separate and unique responsibilities, they don't function in isolation. In fact, in order to be an MVC pattern, each element needs to communicate with one or more elements. That is what we'll look at next.

Communication Between the MVC Elements

Each element in the MVC pattern communicates with each other in very specific ways. Communication is necessitated by a sequence of events that are generally triggered by a user interacting with the application. The sequence of events is represented as follows:

1. User interacts with a user interface element (e.g. clicks on a button in a view).
2. The view sends the click event to the controller to decide how to handle it.
3. The controller changes the model based on how it decides to handle the button click.
4. The model informs the view that the state of the model has now changed.
5. The view reads state information from the model and updates itself.

Figure 12-1 shows the graphical representation of the channels of communication between MVC elements. The arrows' directions show the direction of communication.

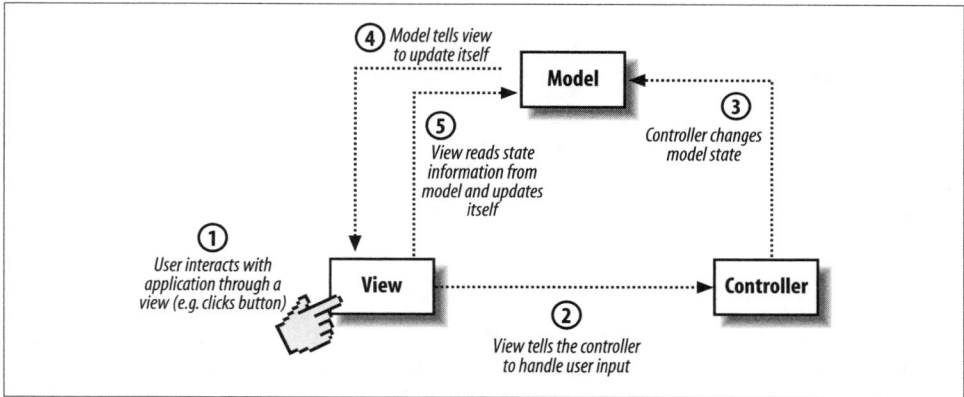

Figure 12-1. Direction of communication between MVC elements

This is a very simple model of how MVC elements communicate. In some cases the controller can directly tell the view to make changes as well. This is the case only when the changes in the view necessitated by user action don't require a change in the model itself, but simply a change in visuals. For example, think about the process whereby a user selects a song to play in our portable digital music player. The user selects songs from a list using buttons that scroll the list. The view would tell the controller that the scroll up or scroll down button has been clicked, but the controller won't inform the model of this. It'll directly tell the view to scroll the list of songs in the appropriate direction. This user action doesn't represent a change in the model. However, when the user actually selects a song from the list to play, the controller will change the model to reflect this change in the currently selected song.

Furthermore, changes in the model are not always initiated by user interaction. The model can update itself based on certain events. For example, think of a stock ticker application. The model would hold the current prices of certain stocks. However, stock prices change, and the model could set a timer to periodically update the stock prices from a web service. Then, whenever the model updated its stock prices, it would inform the view that its state has changed.

Another feature of the MVC is that each model can have more than one view associated with it. For example, in our portable music player, the volume setting of the device can be viewed on the display screen using a level indicator. In addition, sound level is represented in the level of the sound output from the headphones as well. Both the display and auditory feedback from the headphones represent views of the device state.

Take a look at Figure 12-1 and make note of the arrows' directions. This shows who initiates communication between elements. In order for an MVC element to communicate with another element, it needs to know about and hold a reference to that element.

Think of the model, view, and controller as three separate classes. Let's look at which classes need to have references to which other classes.

Model
> Needs to have a reference to *views*

View
> Needs references to both the *model* and *controller*

Controller
> Needs a reference to the *model*

We started off by saying that the MVC is a compound pattern that consists of several patterns. You may be wondering where the embedded patterns are. It is precisely at this point that they can be introduced. The primary advantage of using the MVC pattern is the loose coupling it allows us to implement between the three elements. It lets us bind multiple views to the same model, and swap out models and controllers without breaking other elements. But some element in the MVC triad needs to hold references to other elements, and there's a whole lot of talking going on between them. How can we call this loose coupling? This is where the observer, strategy, and composite patterns help us out.

Embedded Patterns in the MVC

We pointed out that a model can be associated with several views. In the MVC, the model needs to inform all associated views that a change has taken place. It also needs to do this without knowing specific details about the views, or how many views need to be changed. This is a recurring problem best solved by implementing an *observer pattern* (see Chapter 8).

Each model can have multiple views associated with it. Views can also be complex, with multiple windows or panels that contain other user interface elements. For example, user interface elements such as buttons, text fields, lists, sliders, etc. can be grouped together in a tabbed panel that in turn will be part of a window with other tabbed panels. Each button or group of buttons can be a view. So can a collection of text fields. It would be very useful to treat a panel or window that contains collections of simple views the same way as we would treat any other view. This is where the *composite pattern* will save us a lot of effort (see Chapter 6). Why would a composite pattern implementation be useful in this context? If views can be nested, as they would be if they were implemented in a composite pattern, the update process would be simpler. Update events would automatically cascade down to child views. Creating complex views would be easier without having to worry about sending update events to each nested view.

Views confine themselves solely to the external representation of the model state. They delegate user interface events to a controller. Therefore, the controller is essentially an algorithm of how to handle user input in a particular view. This delegation encapsulates the implementation of how a particular user interface element behaves in terms of modifying the model. We can easily substitute a different controller for the same view to get different behavior. This is a perfect context to implement a *strategy pattern*.

We will look at how each of these patterns is implemented in an MVC by developing a minimalist example.

Minimalist Example of an MVC Pattern

This simple example keeps track of the last key pressed. When a new key is pressed, it changes the model and informs the view to update itself. The view uses the Flash output panel to print the *character code* of the key that's pressed. The character code is the numeric value of that key in the current character set. This example is meant to clarify how the observer, strategy, and composite patterns are integrated within the MVC.

Model as a Concrete Subject in an Observer Pattern

The relationship between the model and view is that of subject and observer (see Chapter 8). The model has to implement the subject interface that's part of the observer pattern. Fortuitously, ActionScript 3.0 has built in classes that do this already, using the ActionScript event model to notify observers of changes.

The EventDispatcher class in ActionScript 3.0

The EventDispatcher class implements the IEventDispatcher interface. Among other methods, the IEventDispatcher interface defines the following methods required of the subject in an observer pattern. (See AS3 documentation for a detailed explanation of all method parameters.)

```
addEventListener(type:String,
    listener:Function,
    useCapture:Boolean = false,
    priority:int = 0,
    useWeakReference:Boolean = false):void

removeEventListener(type:String,
    listener:Function,
    useCapture:Boolean = false):void

dispatchEvent(event:Event):Boolean
```

For the model to serve as a concrete subject in an observer pattern, it needs to implement the IEventDispatcher interface. However, the easiest way for a user-defined class to gain event dispatching capabilities is to extend the EventDispatcher class.

Observers register listener methods to receive event notifications from EventDispatcher objects through the addEventListener( ) method.

The model

Our model holds the character code of the last key pressed in a property. It needs to implement *setter* and *getter* methods to enable the view and controller to access and modify it. Let's first define an interface for our model (Example 12-1).

Example 12-1. IModel.as

```
package
{
    import flash.events.*;

    public interface IModel extends IEventDispatcher
    {
        function setKey(key:uint):void
        function getKey( ):uint
    }
}
```

The IModel interface shown in Example 12-1 extends the IEventDispatcher interface and defines two methods to get and set the character code of the last key pressed. Because the IModel interface extends IEventDispatcher, any class implementing it has to implement all the methods defined in both interfaces. The Model class shown in Example 12-2 implements the IModel interface.

Example 12-2. Model.as

```
package
{
    import flash.events.*;

    public class Model extends EventDispatcher implements IModel
    {
```

Example 12-2. Model.as (continued)

```
        private var lastKeyPressed:uint = 0;

        public function setKey(key:uint):void
        {
            this.lastKeyPressed = key;
            dispatchEvent(new Event(Event.CHANGE)); // dispatch event
        }

        public function getKey():uint
        {
            return lastKeyPressed;
        }
    }
}
```

The Model class extends the EventDispatcher class that already implements the IEventDispatcher interface. Note the dispatchEvent() function call within the setKey() method. This sends a CHANGE event to all registered observers when the value of lastKeyPressed is changed within the setKey() method.

Controller as a Concrete Strategy in a Strategy Pattern

The relationship between the controller and view is that of strategy and context in a strategy pattern. Each controller will be a concrete strategy implementing a required behavior defined in a strategy interface.

The controller

For our minimalist example, the behavior required of the controller is to handle a key press event. IKeyboardInputHandler is the strategy interface (Example 12-3), and defines a single method called keyPressHandler().

Example 12-3. IKeyboardInputHandler.as

```
package
{
    import flash.events.*;

    public interface IKeyboardInputHandler
    {
        function keyPressHandler(event:KeyboardEvent):void
    }
}
```

The concrete controller is the Controller class (Example 12-4) that implements the IKeyboardInputHandler interface.

Example 12-4. Controller.as

```
package
{
    import flash.events.*;

    public class Controller implements IKeyboardInputHandler
    {
        private var model:IModel;

        public function Controller(aModel:IModel)
        {
            this.model = aModel;
        }

        public function keyPressHandler(event:KeyboardEvent):void
        {
            model.setKey(event.charCode); // change model
        }
    }
}
```

Note that the controller has a constructor that takes an instance of the model as a parameter. This is necessary as the controller initiates communication with the model as shown in Figure 12-1. Therefore, it needs to hold a reference to the model.

The keyPressHandler( ) method takes the user interface event (a KeyboardEvent in this case) as a parameter and decides how to handle it. In this example, it simply sets the last key pressed in the model to the character code of the key pressed.

View as a Concrete Observer in an Observer Pattern and Context in a Strategy Pattern

The view is arguably the most complex element in the MVC pattern. It plays an integral part in both the observer and strategy pattern implementations that form the basis of its relationship with the model and controller. The View class shown in Example 12-5 implements the view for the minimalist example.

Example 12-5. View.as

```
1  package
2  {
3      import flash.events.*;
4      import flash.display.*;
5
6      public class View
7      {
8          private var model:IModel;
9          private var controller:IKeyboardInputHandler;
10
```

Example 12-5. View.as (continued)

```
11          public function View(aModel:IModel, oController:
                            IKeyboardInputHandler,target:Stage)
12          {
13              this.model = aModel;
14              this.controller = oController;
15
16              // register to receive notifications from the model
17              model.addEventListener(Event.CHANGE, this.update);
18
19              // register to receive key press notifications from the stage
20              target.addEventListener(KeyboardEvent.KEY_DOWN,
21
22          }
23
24          private function update(event:Event):void
25          {
26              // get data from model and update view
27              trace(model.getKey());
28          }
29
30          private function onKeyPress(event:KeyboardEvent):void
31          {
32              // delegate to the controller (strategy) to handle it
33              controller.keyPressHandler(event);
34          }
35      }
36  }
```

The view needs to hold references to both the model and controller as it initiates communication with them as shown in Figure 12-1. Both the model and controller instances are passed to the view in its constructor. Also, the view in our example needs a reference to the stage to register itself to receive key press events.

In addition to drawing the user interface, the View class does a couple of important tasks. It registers with the model to receive update events, and delegates to the controller to handle user input. In our example, the view does not have an external visual representation on the stage, but displays the model state in the output panel. It needs to receive key press events, and registers the method called onKeyPress() to receive KEY_DOWN events from the stage (line 20). The second task is to register a listener method called update() to receive a CHANGE event from the model (line 16). On notification of a change, the update() method reads the character code for the last key pressed from the model and prints it to the output panel using the trace function.

Building the MVC Triad

We have looked at the individual implementations of the three elements that make up the MVC pattern. However, there has to be a client that initializes each element and builds the MVC model. There's no real building involved – all that needs to be done is to instantiate the model, view, and controller classes. Example 12-6 shows the Flash document class that instantiates the MVC elements.

Example 12-6. Main.as (document class for minimalist example)

```
package
{
    import flash.display.*;
    import flash.events.*;

    /**
     *    Main Class
     *    @ purpose:        Document class for movie
     */
    public class Main extends Sprite
    {
        public function Main( )
        {
            var model:IModel = new Model( );
            var controller:IKeyboardInputHandler = new Controller(model);
            var view:View = new View(model, controller, this.stage);
        }
    }
}
```

After the model, controller, and view are instantiated, they'll communicate with each other and work. Clicking a key on the keyboard will result in the key code for that key being printed in the output panel.

 You have to disable keyboard shortcuts to test for key presses. Otherwise the Flash user interface intercepts certain key press events that match keyboard shortcuts. To disable keyboard shortcuts select Disable Keyboard Shortcuts from the Control menu when your Flash movie is playing.

Note that the model instance is passed to the controller. Similarly, the model and controller instances are passed to the view as well. We can easily substitute different models and controllers on the condition that they implement the IModel and IKeyboardInputHandler interfaces. Additional view elements can also be added without disruption due to the subject-observer relationship between the model and view. The model doesn't know about views as it's the responsibility of the view to register itself to receive update notifications from the model. This is the beauty of the MVC pattern; the model, view, and controller are separate, loosely coupled elements that allow for flexibility in their use.

Nested Views as Leaves and Nodes of a Composite Pattern

You may remember that the view is arguably the most complex element in the MVC triad because it participates in both the observer and strategy pattern implementations in the MVC. Our view elements are going to get more complex as they can implement a third pattern, the composite (see Chapter 6 for examples of the composite pattern). Implementing views as elements of a composite pattern only makes sense for complex nested user interfaces that contain multiple views. Nested views bring several advantages to updating the user interface, as updates can cascade down the composite view tree structure. Also, composite views can create and remove child views based on application state and user mode. A good example of a complex user interface is the *Properties inspector* panel in the Flash authoring environment. The *Properties inspector* is context sensitive, and adds or removes user interface elements based on the object selected on the stage.

Component and composite views

The first step is to create the component and composite classes for the view. These classes should behave as abstract classes and should be subclassed and not instantiated, as shown in Example 12-7.

Example 12-7. ComponentView.as

```
package
{
    import flash.errors.IllegalOperationError;
    import flash.events.Event;
    import flash.display.Sprite;

    // ABSTRACT Class (should be subclassed and not instantiated)
    public class ComponentView extends Sprite {
    {
        protected var model:Object;
        protected var controller:Object;

        public function ComponentView(aModel:Object, aController:Object = null)

        {
            this.model = aModel;
            this.controller = aController;
        }

        public function add(c:ComponentView):void
        {
            throw new IllegalOperationError("add operation not supported");
        }

        public function remove(c:ComponentView):void
        {
            throw new IllegalOperationError("remove operation not supported");
        }

        public function getChild(n:int):ComponentView
        {
            throw new IllegalOperationError("getChild operation not supported");
```

Example 12-7. ComponentView.as (continued)

```
            return null;
        }

        // ABSTRACT Method (must be overridden in a subclass)
        public function update(event:Event = null):void {}
    }
}
```

The `ComponentView` class shown in Example 12-7 defines the abstract interface for component views. This is similar to the classic component class introduced in Chapter 6, with a few key differences. The `ComponentView` class keeps references to the model and view, and includes a constructor. Not all views handle user input, and a component view can be constructed by just passing a model instance. Therefore, the `aController` parameter has a default value of `null` in the constructor. Also note that the `ComponentView` class extends the `Sprite` class. This makes sense as most views draw a user interface on the stage. We can use the properties and methods implemented in the built-in `Sprite` class to draw and add objects to the display list.

The `update( )` method should behave as an abstract method. Leaf views that subclass `ComponentView` must override and implement the `update( )` method to update their user interface. This method is the listener function that intercepts update notifications from the model. For this reason, a parameter of type `Event` is passed to it. This parameter also has a default value of `null`, allowing `update( )` to be called without passing an event parameter. This is useful when initially drawing the user interface in its default state, and our subsequent examples illustrate it.

The `CompositeView` class extends `ComponentView` and overrides the methods that deal with handing child views. In Example 12-8, we will implement only the `add( )` method for simplicity.

Example 12-8. CompositeView.as

```
package {

    import flash.events.Event;

    // ABSTRACT Class (should be subclassed and not instantiated)
    public class CompositeView extends ComponentView
    {
        private var aChildren:Array;

        public function CompositeView(aModel:Object,aController:Object = null)
        {
            super(aModel, aController);
            this.aChildren = new Array( );
        }

        override public function add(c:ComponentView):void
        {
```

Example 12-8. CompositeView.as (continued)

```
        aChildren.push(c);
    }

    override public function update(event:Event = null):void
    {
        for each (var c:ComponentView in aChildren)
        {
            c.update(event);
        }
    }
  }
}
```

Note the overridden update( ) function in the CompositeView class shown in Example 12-8. It calls the update method in all its children. Therefore, calling the update( ) function in the root node of the composite view structure will cascade down and traverse the component tree updating all views. Let's subclass CompositeView and ComponentView classes and create a nested view structure to see how this works.

Creating nested views

To illustrate nested views, we will create a composite view node and two child component views as shown in Figure 12-2.

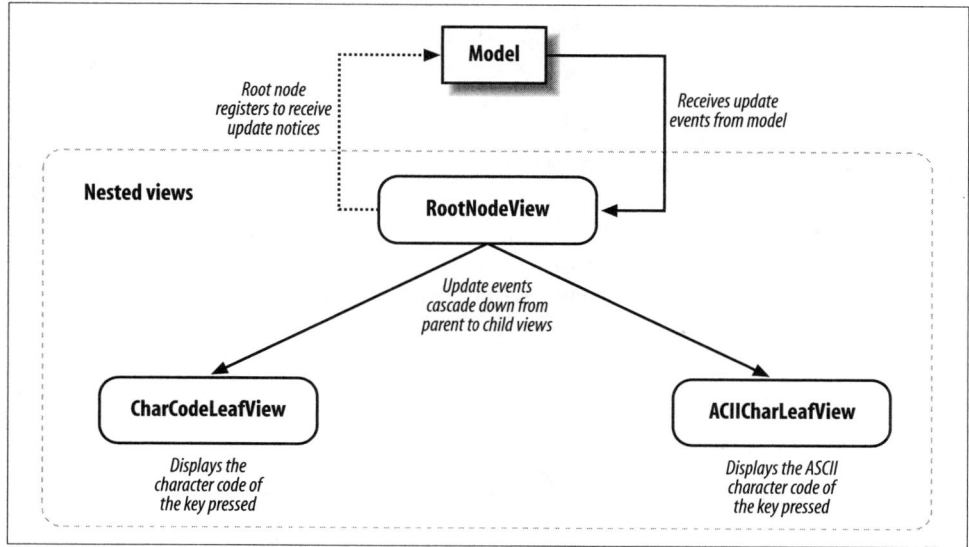

Figure 12-2. Nested view structure in minimalist example

We will first create a composite view called RootNodeView. This composite view will receive keyboard input events from the stage. This view will also register to receive update notices from the model. The RootNodeView composite view will have two child component views called CharCodeLeafView and AsciiCharLeafView. The CharCodeLeafView will trace the *character code* for the last key pressed. Similarly, the AsciiCharLeafView will trace the *ASCII character* corresponding to the character code. Let's create the composite view first, as shown in Example 12-9.

Example 12-9. RootNodeView.as

```
package
{
    import flash.events.*;
    import flash.display.*;

    public class RootNodeView extends CompositeView
    {
        public function RootNodeView (aModel:IModel,

        {
            super(aModel, aController);

            // register to receive key press notifications form the stage
            target.addEventListener(KeyboardEvent.KEY_DOWN,

        }

        private function onKeyPress(event:KeyboardEvent):void
        {
            // delegate to the controller (strategy) to handle it
            (controller as IKeyboardInputHandler).keyPressHandler(event);
        }
    }
}
```

The RootNodeView class shown in Example 12-9 subclasses the CompositeView class (Example 12-8). It does not draw a user interface; it simply listens for key press events and delegates to the controller to handle them. Note the super statement in the constructor. This is required to call the constructor in the superclass. We can now create the two component views (Examples 12-10 and 12-11).

Example 12-10. CharCodeLeafView.as

```
package
{
    import flash.events.Event;

    public class CharCodeLeafView extends ComponentView
    {
        public function CharCodeLeafView(aModel:IModel, aController:Object = null)
        {
            super(aModel, aController);
        }
```

Example 12-10. CharCodeLeafView.as (continued)

```
        override public function update(event:Event = null):void
        {
            // get data from model and update view
            trace(model.getKey());
        }
    }
}
```

Example 12-11. AsciiCharLeafView.as

```
package
{
    import flash.events.Event;

    public class AsciiCharLeafView extends ComponentView
    {
        public function AsciiCharLeafView(aModel:IModel,aController:Object = null)
        {
            super(aModel, aController);
        }

        override public function update(event:Event = null):void
        {
            // get data from model and update view
            trace(String.fromCharCode(model.getKey()));
        }
    }
}
```

Both component view classes `CharCodeLeafView` (Example 12-10) and `AsciiCharLeafView` (Example 12-11) subclass the `ComponentView` class (Example 12-8). Note that they don't receive any input from the user interface. These two views can therefore be instantiated without passing a controller object to the constructor. The controller will default to `null` in this case.

Now all that's left to do is build the MVC triad with the nested view. We'll allow the client to build the nested view and register the root node with the model to receive update events.

Building the Nested View Structure

Building nested view structures is identical to developing composite structures using the composite pattern. We have to visualize the view as a tree (an upside-down tree) and use the `add()` method in the composite view to add child views.

```
var model:IModel = new Model();
var controller:IKeyboardInputHandler = new Controller(model);
```

```
// composite view
var rootView:CompositeView = new RootNodeView(model,controller, this.stage);

// add child leaf views
rootView.add(new CharCodeLeafView(model));
rootView.add(new AsciiCharLeafView(model));

// register view to receive notifications from the model
model.addEventListener(Event.CHANGE, rootView.update);
```

Note that only the root view registers with the model to receive update events. Because the root view is a composite view, the event cascades down to each of its child nodes. Now whenever a key is pressed, one child node will trace the character code and the other will trace the ASCII character of the corresponding key. Even though the nested view structure in our minimalist example was simple, this structure can work well for nested views with many components.

In our minimalist example, the client built the nested view structure. However, the build statements for the nested view could have been embedded in the RootNodeView class, further encapsulating implementation. Now the root view can dynamically add and remove child views based on application state and user mode. This allows the user interface element of an application to gain some very powerful capabilities.

Key Features of the MVC Pattern

The primary usefulness of the MVC pattern is the flexibility it affords when creating applications that have user interfaces. The pattern separates the model, view, and controller elements and leverages the observer, strategy, and composite patterns to decouple them.

- MVC consists of three elements called the model, view, and controller that separate the responsibilities of an application with a graphical user interface.
- The relationship between models and views is that of a concrete subject and a concrete observer in an observer pattern.
- The relationship between views and controllers is that of a context and concrete strategy in a strategy pattern.
- Multiple views can register with the model.
- Views can be nested using the composite pattern to create complex user interfaces that streamline the update process.

Key OOP Concepts in the MVC Pattern

The key concept in the MVC pattern is *loose coupling*. Loose coupling reduces the dependencies between the separate elements in the MVC pattern. For example, the subject-observer relationship between the model and view enables the model to function independently of how its state is displayed in the user interface. It's the responsibility of the view to register for updates and update the user interface elements. The model can function independently, blissfully unaware of the number and type of views. Similarly, nested views can be added without disruption. Update events will trickle down to all nested views as long as the root node is registered with the model to receive updates. This makes the MVC pattern highly extensible.

In addition, each element in the MVC adheres to the single responsibility principle. Each element has a well-defined role. The model manages state, the view represents state, and the controller handles user input. This allows each element to be swapped out without affecting other elements. If we need a different behavior for a particular user interface element in a view, we simply substitute a different controller for it. This makes the MVC pattern very customizable, allowing reuse.

Example: Weather Maps

The National Oceanic and Atmospheric Administration (NOAA), a division of the U.S. Department of Commerce, runs a *Geostationary Satellite Server* on the Web (*http://www.goes.noaa.gov*). The site publishes satellite images of the United States, including Puerto Rico, Alaska, and Hawaii. We will use these images (they're in the public domain and free to use) to develop a simple weather map application leveraging the MVC pattern. For this example we will use the built-in user interface components provided in Flash CS3 to develop view elements.

For the first iteration of our application shown in Figure 12-3, we'll allow the user to choose the map region (East Coast, West Coast, Puerto Rico, Alaska, and Hawaii) using a combo box (a drop-down list that displays the currently chosen item). The application will then load the latest visible satellite image of the corresponding region.

This example illustrates the use of built-in components in Flash CS3 to implement the user interface elements in each view. It also shows the usefulness of nested views for screen layout and automatic view updates. Let's create the model element of our example application.

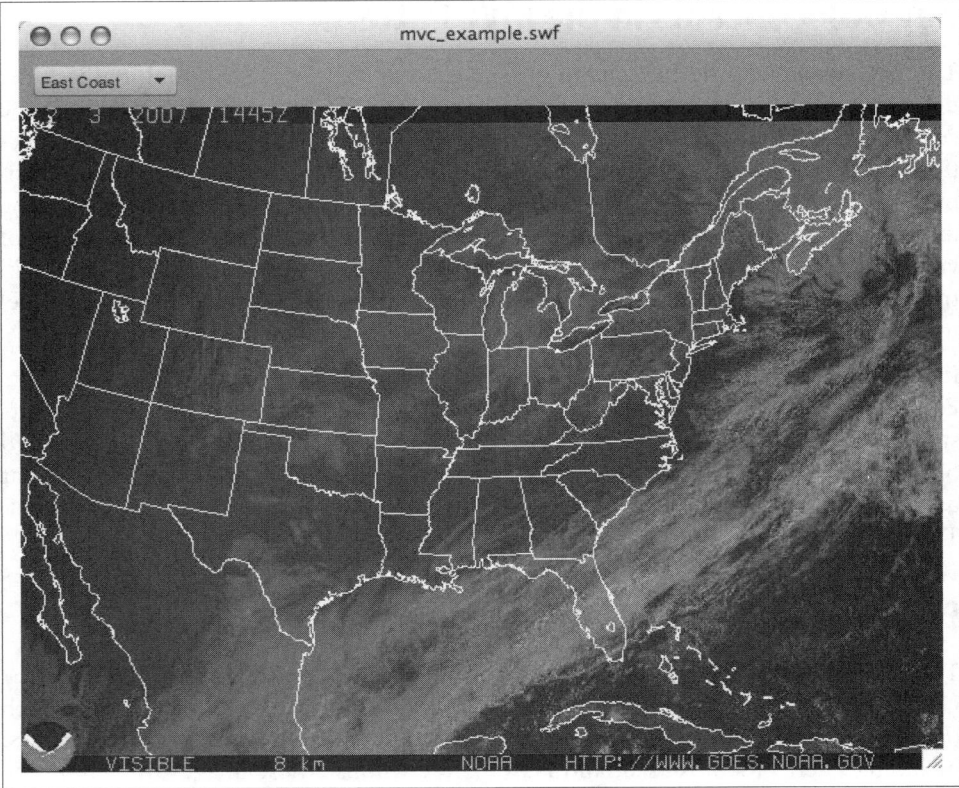

Figure 12-3. Weather map example application showing a visible map of the East Coast

The Model

The model element of the MVC pattern contains the application data and state including the logic to manage data and state. The application state is the region the user has chosen to display. The region can be one of five, corresponding to the regional maps available from the web site. The data is the URLs of the satellite images corresponding to each region.

The application logic should allow users to manage the state of the application. Users should be able to set the current region. The view element that draws the combo box needs to get the list of available regions and the currently selected region. In addition, the view that displays the satellite image needs to access the URL of the currently selected region. Let's develop a model interface (Example 12-12) based on these requirements.

Example 12-12. IModel.as (Model interface for the weather map example)

```
package
{
    import flash.events.*;

    public interface IModel extends IEventDispatcher
    {
        function getRegionList( ):Array
        function getRegion( ):uint
        function setRegion(index:uint):void
        function getMapURL( ):String
    }
}
```

The next step is to implement the IModel interface and develop the model (Example 12-13).

Example 12-13. Model.as (Model for the weather map example)

```
package {

    import flash.events.*;

    public class Model extends EventDispatcher implements IModel
    {

        protected var aRegions:Array;
        protected var chosenRegion:uint;

        protected var aImageURLs:Array;

        public function Model( )
        {
            this.aRegions = new Array(
                    "East Coast",
                    "West Coast",
                    "Puerto Rico",
                    "Alaska",
                    "Hawaii");
            this.aImageURLs = new Array(
                    "http://www.goes.noaa.gov/GIFS/ECVS.JPG",
                    "http://www.goes.noaa.gov/GIFS/WCVS.JPG",
                    "http://www.goes.noaa.gov/GIFS/PRVS.JPG",
                    "http://www.goes.noaa.gov/GIFS/ALVS.JPG",
                    "http://www.goes.noaa.gov/GIFS/HAVS.JPG");
            this.chosenRegion = 0;
        }

        public function getRegionList( ):Array
        {
            return aRegions;
        }
```

Example 12-13. Model.as (Model for the weather map example) (continued)

```
    public function getRegion():uint
    {
        return this.chosenRegion;
    }

    public function setRegion(index:uint):void
    {
        this.chosenRegion = index;
        this.update();
    }

    public function getMapURL():String
    {
        return this.aImageURLs[chosenRegion];
    }

    protected function update():void
    {
        dispatchEvent(new Event(Event.CHANGE)); // dispatch event
    }
    }
}
```

Note the update( ) method in the Model class shown in Example 12-13. It dispatches a CHANGE event to registered observers. The update( ) method is called whenever the application state changes.

As a developer, you may be tempted to store the region list in the view for simplicity. However, this greatly reduces flexibility and reuse. Adding another region, for example, would require changes to both the view and the model. It's always a good practice to adhere to the delineated responsibilities of the three MVC elements. Application data should be accessible only through the model.

The Controller

The combo box view is the only interface element in the application that users can control. The interface for the corresponding controller is shown in Example 12-14.

Example 12-14. ICompInputHandler.as

```
package
{
    public interface ICompInputHandler
    {
        function compChangeHandler(index:uint):void
    }
}
```

The implementation is show in Example 12-15.

Example 12-15. Controller.as (Controller for the weather map example)

```
package
{
    public class Controller implements ICompInputHandler
    {

        private var model:Object;

        public function Controller(aModel:IModel)
        {
            this.model = aModel;
        }

        public function compChangeHandler(index:uint):void {
            (model as IModel).setRegion(index); // update model
        }
    }
}
```

The Views

The weather map application consists of two views. The first is a user interface element that contains a combo box to select a region to display. The second view displays the corresponding regional satellite image.

We will use the built-in ComboBox and UILoader components in Flash CS3 to implement the user interface elements in each view. Components are movie clips with parameters that allow you to modify their appearance and behavior. They allow developers to build Flash applications with consistent behavior and appearance without creating custom user interface elements such as buttons and sliders. For the weather map application, we need to drag the ComboBox and UILoader components from the *Components panel* to the *Library panel* in our Flash document. The Components and Library panels can be accessed from the Windows menu in Flash CS3. Note that we don't want to place the component on the stage. We'll add the components to the stage at runtime using ActionScript. The ComboBox component uses several additional assets as well. Your library panel will look like Figure 12-4 after the ComboBox and UILoader components are dragged into it.

We can now develop the combo box and map views for the application. The combo box view will be a composite view containing the map view as one of its children.

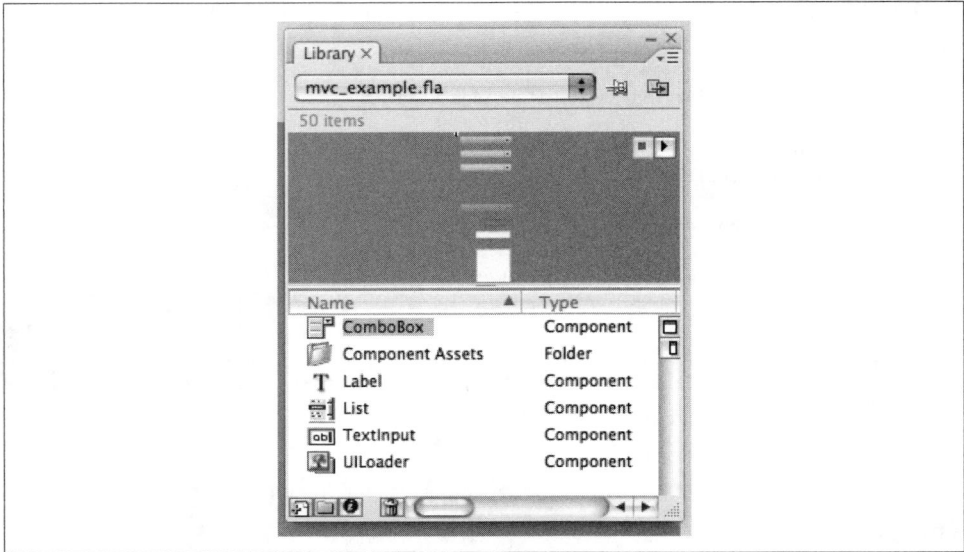

Figure 12-4. Library panel with ComboBox and UILoader components

Combo box view

The CBView class (Example 12-16) subclasses CompositeView (Example 12-8) and draws the ComboBox component.

Example 12-16. CBView.as

```
1  package
2  {
3      import flash.events.Event;
4      import fl.controls.ComboBox;
5
6      public class CBView extends CompositeView
7      {
8
9          private var cb:ComboBox;
10
11         public function CBView(aModel:IModel,aController:ICompInputHandler= null)
12     {
13             super(aModel, aController);
14
15             // get region names from model
16             var aRegions:Array = (model as IModel).getRegionList( );
17
18             // draw combo box using region names
19             cb = new ComboBox( );
20             for (var i:uint = 0; i < aRegions.length; i++)
21             {
22                 cb.addItem( { label: aRegions[i], data:i } );
23             }
```

Example 12-16. CBView.as

```
24                 update( );
25                 addChild(cb);
26
27                 // register to recieve changes to combo box
28                 cb.addEventListener(Event.CHANGE, this.changeHandler);
29             }
30
31         override public function update(event:Event = null):void
32         {
33             // get data from model and update view
34             cb.selectedIndex = (model as IModel).getRegion( );
35             super.update(event);
36         }
37
38         private function changeHandler(event:Event):void
39         {
40             // delegate to the controller (strategy) to handle
41
42             (controller as ICompInputHandler).compChangeHandler
                     (ComboBox(event.target).selectedItem.data);
43         }
44     }
45 }
```

The CBView class (Example 12-16) gets the list of region names from the model (line 16) and adds them to the component. Line 24 calls the update( ) method without any parameters. The update( ) method reads the currently selected region from the model and updates the combo box. It then adds the combo box to the display list (line 25) and registers the changeHandler( ) function to receive change events from the combo box component (line 28). Note that because this is a composite view, the overridden update( ) function needs to call its superclass (line 35) to ensure that updates trickle down to its children as well.

Map view

The MapView class (Example 12-17) subclasses ComponentView (Example 12-7) and draws the UILoader component.

Example 12-17. MapView.as

```
1  package
2  {
3      import flash.events.Event;
4      import fl.containers.UILoader;
5
6      public class MapView extends ComponentView
7      {
8          private var uiLoader:UILoader;
9
10         public function MapView(aModel:IModel, aController:Object = null)
```

Example 12-17. MapView.as

```
11        {
12              super(aModel, aController);
13
14              uiLoader = new UILoader();
15              uiLoader.scaleContent = false;
16              update();
17              addChild(uiLoader);
18        }
19
20        override public function update(event:Event = null):void
21        {
22              // get data from model and update view
23              uiLoader.source = (model as IModel).getMapURL();
24        }
25    }
26 }
```

The MapView class (Example 12-17) loads and displays the satellite image, and doesn't otherwise interact with the user. As in the combo box view, the update( ) method is called without any parameters from the constructor (line 16) to load the image for the default region. Assigning a URL of an image to the source parameter in the UILoader component loads the corresponding image. Unlike the combo box, map view is a component view that cannot have any children. Therefore, the overridden update( ) method does not have to call its superclass method.

Building the MVC Triad

The last task is to instantiate the model and controller, and construct the composite view structure by adding the map view as a child of the combo box view. The following statements should be executed from the document class of the Flash document.

```
var model:IModel = new Model();
var controller:ICompInputHandler= new Controller(model);

// composite view
var view:CompositeView = new CBView(model, controller);
view.x =  view.y = 10;
addChild(view);

// adding a child view
var map:ComponentView = new MapView(model);
view.add(map);
map.x = 0
map.y = 40;
addChild(map);

// register to view to recieve notifications from the model
model.addEventListener(Event.CHANGE, view.update);
```

Note that only the combo box view that's at the root of the composite view structure has registered with the model to receive update events. These will trickle down from the combo box view to its child map view.

The views extend the Sprite class. Therefore, the client has the flexibility to place them on the stage that fits the required application layout.

Setting the Model to Self-Update

Changes in the model are not always initiated by user interaction. You may have noticed a time stamp on the satellite images (in GMT). The time stamp tells us that the satellite images are updated about every 15 minutes. We can easily add a self-update timer to our model to dispatch an event every 15 minutes that tells the map view to reload the updated image. We should add the following statements to the end of the Model class constructor in Example 12-13 (make sure to import the flash.utils.Timer class first).

```
var updateTimer:Timer = new Timer(1000 * 60 * 15);
updateTimer.addEventListener("timer", timerHandler);
updateTimer.start();
```

The following listener method should be added to the Model class in Example 12-13. The listener method timerHandler() is set to listen for a new TimerEvent to be dispatched every 15 minutes. The timerHandler() calls the update() method to dispatch an update event to registered observers.

```
public function timerHandler(event:TimerEvent):void {
    this.update();
}
```

Extended Example: Infrared Weather Maps

To illustrate how the MVC pattern allows for flexible expansion and reuse of its model, view, and controller elements, we will extend our weather maps example. You may have noticed that there are three types of satellite image maps on the *Geostationary Satellite Server* web site (*http://www.goes.noaa.gov*). What if we want to give the user the option of choosing whether to view a visible or infrared image? What changes would be required to extend our weather maps application to view infrared satellite images?

To begin with, we'll need to add another view such as a radio button group to choose the type of satellite image (visible or infrared as shown in Figure 12-5).

We will need to create a new controller to handle the user input to the new view element. Our model will also need to hold more data, as we need to integrate five additional image URLs, one for each region as an infrared image. The application logic in the model will also need to be updated to handle the new data. Can we add all these new features without changing existing code? Can we leverage the flexibility and reuse of the MVC pattern without breaking anything?

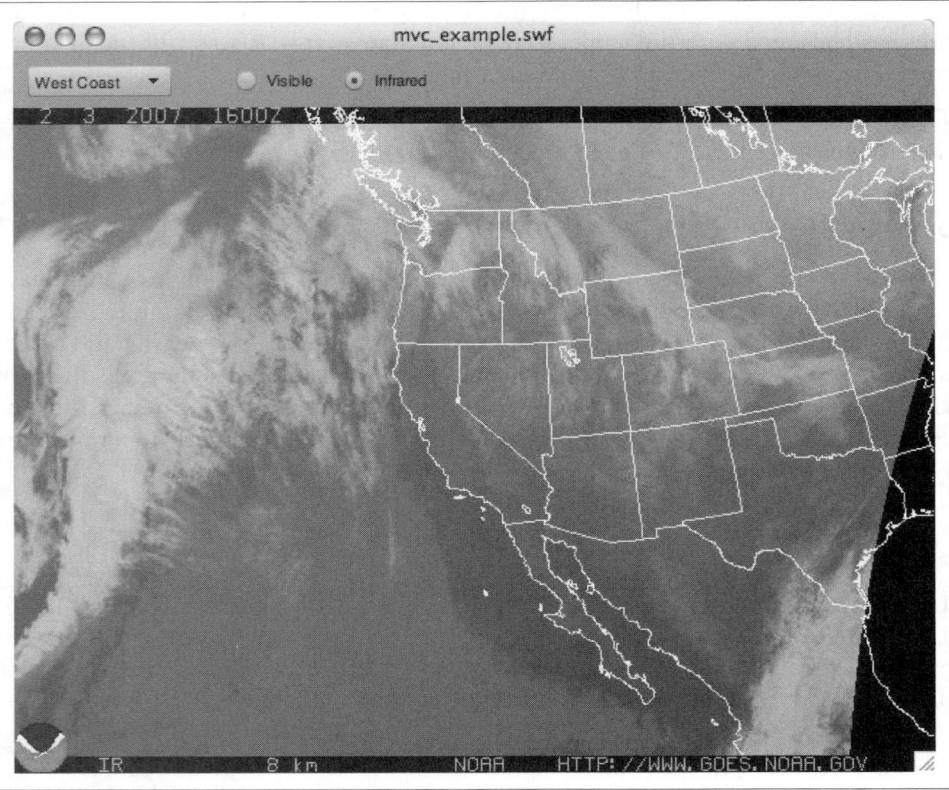

Figure 12-5. Extended example showing an infrared map of the West Coast

Let's look at the changes needed to update the model.

Adding a New Model

Instead of modifying the current weather maps model (Example 12-13), we will extend it to incorporate the new data and additional state information. We need to add another property to indicate the chosen map type, either a visible map or an infrared one. In addition, we need to update the application logic to work with the new data. Example 12-18 shows a new interface for the model that defines the methods required for the new features.

Example 12-18. INewModel.as

```
package
{
    import flash.events.*;

    public interface INewModel extends IModel
```

Example 12-18. INewModel.as (continued)

```
    {
        function getMapTypeList( ):Array
        function getMapType( ):uint
        function setMapType(index:uint):void
    }
}
```

Interface INewModel extends the IModel interface (Example 12-12) and defines the methods required to get the list of image types as an array, including get and set methods for the currently selected map type (visible or infrared). Example 12-19 shows the NewModel class that extends the previous Model class to implement the new INewModel interface.

Example 12-19. NewModel.as

```
package {

    public class NewModel extends Model implements INewModel {

        protected var aMapTypes:Array;
        protected var chosenMapType:uint;

        protected var aIRImageURLs:Array;

        public function NewModel( ) {
            this.aIRImageURLs = new Array(
                    "http://www.goes.noaa.gov/GIFS/ECIR.JPG",
                    "http://www.goes.noaa.gov/GIFS/WCIR.JPG",
                    "http://www.goes.noaa.gov/GIFS/PRIR.JPG",
                    "http://www.goes.noaa.gov/GIFS/ALIR.JPG",
                    "http://www.goes.noaa.gov/GIFS/HAIR.JPG");
            this.aMapTypes = new Array(
                    "Visible",
                    "Infrared");
            this.chosenMapType = 0;
        }

        public function getMapTypeList( ):Array {
            return aMapTypes;
        }

        public function getMapType( ):uint {
            return this.chosenMapType;
        }

        public function setMapType(index:uint):void {
            this.chosenMapType = index;
            this.update( );
        }
```

Example 12-19. NewModel.as (continued)

```
    override public function getMapURL():String {
        switch(chosenMapType) {
            case 1:
                return this.aIRImageURLs[chosenRegion];
                break;
            default:
                return this.aImageURLs[chosenRegion];
                break;
        }
    }
  }
}
```

The getMapURL( ) method was overridden, as the returned image URL now depends on the currently chosen map type. Note that we didn't modify any existing code, but extended the existing model class Model to implement the new interface requirements.

Adding a New Controller

A new controller (Example 12-20) is necessary to handle the input to the map type selector view. We can implement the same ICompInputHandler interface (Example 12-14) for the new controller.

Example 12-20. MapTypeController.as

```
package
{
    public class MapTypeController implements ICompInputHandler {

        private var model:Object;

        public function MapTypeController(oModel:INewModel)
        {
            this.model = oModel;
        }

        public function compChangeHandler(index:uint):void
        {
            (model as INewModel).setMapType(index); // update model
        }
    }
}
```

Adding a New View

We will add a new view (Example 12-21) that consists of two grouped radio buttons that allow the user to select from either visible or infrared map images. The view will use the built-in RadioButtton component in Flash CS3. Make sure the radio button component is dragged from the Components panel into the Library panel in the Flash document.

Example 12-21. RBView.as

```
package
{
    import flash.events.*;
    import fl.controls.RadioButton;
    import fl.controls.RadioButtonGroup;

    public class RBView extends ComponentView
    {
        private var rbList:Array = new Array( );
        private var rbGrp:RadioButtonGroup;

        public function RBView(aModel:INewModel,aController:ICompInputHandler)
        {
            super(aModel, aController);
            // get region names from model
            var aMapTypes:Array = model.getMapTypeList( );
            // develop radio buttons using map type names
            rbGrp = new RadioButtonGroup("Map Type");
            for (var i:uint = 0; i < aMapTypes.length; i++)
            {
                var rb:RadioButton = new RadioButton( );
                rb.label = aMapTypes[i];
                rb.value = i;
                rb.group = rbGrp;
                rb.x = i * 75;
                addChild(rb);
                rbList.push(rb);
            }
            update( ); // select default buttton
            // register to recieve changes to radio button group
            rbGrp.addEventListener(MouseEvent.CLICK, this.changeHandler);
        }

        override public function update(event:Event = null):void
        {
            // get data from model and update view
            var index:uint = (model as INewModel).getMapType( );
            rbList[index].selected = true;
            super.update(event);
        }

        private function changeHandler(event:Event):void
        {
            // delegate to the controller (strategy) to handle map type change
            controller.compChangeHandler(event.target.selection.value);
        }
    }
}
```

The RBView class (Example 12-21) subclasses ComponentView (Example 12-7) and draws the radio buttons. The RadioButtton component must be used in a group of at least two RadioButtton instances. Only one member of the group can be selected at any given time. As in previous view implementations, the update( ) method is called without parameters from the constructor immediately after drawing the components. This ensures that the UI component displays the default selection specified in the model. We can now instantiate the MVC elements and develop the composite view.

Building the MVC Triad

The nested view structure of our extended weather map application is shown in Figure 12-6.

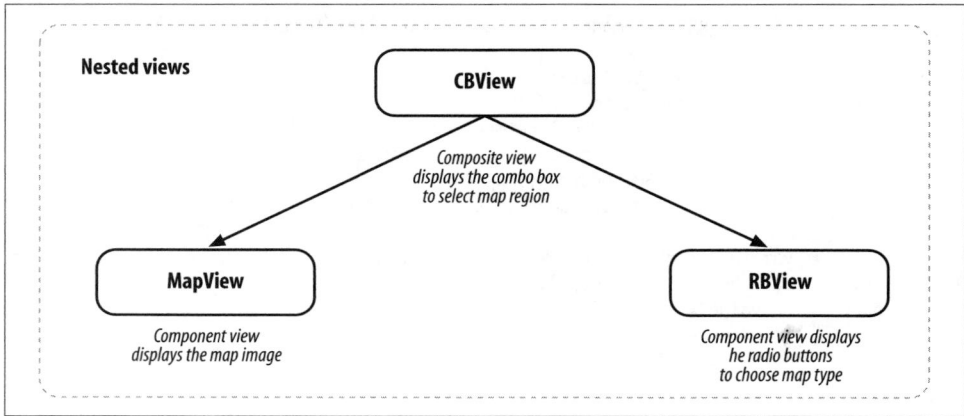

Figure 12-6. Nested view structure for extended weather map example

The following statements should be executed from the document class of the Flash document. Only the root node CBView object (see Figure 12-6) will register with the model to receive update events. Update events will trickle down to the child nodes because of the composite pattern implementation.

```
var model:INewModel = new NewModel(); // new model
var controller:ICompInputHandler = new Controller(model);

// region select combo box view
var view:CompositeView = new CBView(model, controller);
view.x =  view.y = 10;
addChild(view);

// add map view as child
var map:ComponentView = new MapView(model);
view.add(map);
map.x = 0
map.y = 40;
addChild(map);

// controller to handle map type input
var mapTypeController:ICompInputHandler = new MapTypeController(model);
```

```
// add map type select radio button group view as child
var mapTypeView:ComponentView = new RBView(model, mapTypeController);
view.add(mapTypeView);
mapTypeView.x =  150;
mapTypeView.y = 10;
addChild(mapTypeView);

// register root view to recieve notifications from the model
model.addEventListener(Event.CHANGE, view.update);
```

To extend our original weather map application, we added a new view, a new controller and a new model. However, at no point did we modify or change existing code. What the pundits say about the MVC pattern is indeed borne out in this extended example. All the elements in the MVC are loosely coupled, allowing us to add or swap out any element without changing existing elements. In addition, implementing nested views using the composite pattern allows us to reconfigure the screen layout and the view update process from the client without making changes to individual views.

Example: Cars

In this example, we will develop a simple car using the MVC pattern that can be controlled from the keyboard. The emphasis will be on developing custom views using ActionScript as opposed to using built-in components. We will also see how simply changing the controller can turn a car that responds to keyboard input into one that chases another car. Casual game developers will find this example useful for game design. Figure 12-7 shows the final iteration of the example application.

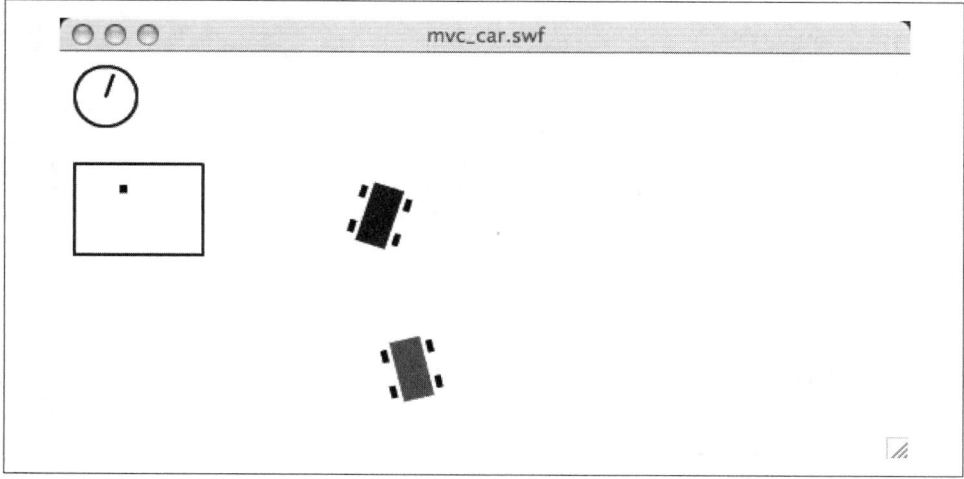

Figure 12-7. Car example showing views and chase car

The Model

Let's first develop the interface for our car model. We should be able to set its location on the stage and steer it by simply changing its rotation angle. We will also declare methods to set its color. Example 12-22 shows the ICar interface.

Example 12-22. ICar.as

```
package
{
    import flash.geom.Point;
    import flash.events.IEventDispatcher;

    public interface ICar extends IEventDispatcher {
    {
        function setLoc(pt:Point):void;
        function getLoc():Point;
        function setColor(color:uint):void;
        function getColor():uint;
        function addToRotationAngle(nAngle:int):void;
        function getRotation():int;
    }
}
```

The CarModel class shown in Example 12-23 implements the ICar interface. The car will move at a constant speed in the forward direction. Note that the model updates the car position using a timer.

Example 12-23. CarModel.as

```
package
{
    import flash.events.*;
    import flash.geom.*;
    import flash.utils.Timer;

    public class CarModel extends EventDispatcher implements ICar
    {
        protected var nSpeed:Number; // holds speed of car in pixels/frame
        protected var nRotation:Number; // car rotation in Degrees
        protected var ptLoc:Point; // current location
        protected var carColor:uint; // car color

        public function CarModel()
        {
            nSpeed = 3;
            nRotation = 0;
            ptLoc = new Point(0, 0); // default loc is 0,0
            carColor = 0x000000; // default color is black

            // set timer to update car position every 1/20 second
            var carMoveTimer:Timer = new Timer(1000 / 20);
            carMoveTimer.addEventListener("timer", doMoveCar);
```

Example 12-23. CarModel.as (continued)

```
            carMoveTimer.start( );
        }

        public function setLoc(pt:Point):void
        {
            ptLoc = pt;
        }

        public function getLoc( ):Point
        {
            return ptLoc;
        }

        public function setColor(color:uint):void
        {
            this.carColor = color;
        }

        public function getColor( ):uint
        {
            return carColor;
        }

        public function getRotation( ):int
        {
            return nRotation;
        }

        // Add this to car rotation angle (in Degrees)
        public function addToRotationAngle(nAngle:int):void
        {
            nRotation += nAngle;
        }

        // move the car
        private function doMoveCar(event:TimerEvent):void
        {
            var newLocOffset:Point = Point.polar(nSpeed, nRotation * Math.PI / 180);
            ptLoc.x += newLocOffset.x; // move by the x offset
            ptLoc.y += newLocOffset.y; // move by the y offset
            this.update( );
        }

        protected function update( ):void
        {
            dispatchEvent(new Event(Event.CHANGE)); // dispatch event
        }
    }
}
```

The Controller

The controller responds to keyboard input, and updates the model to turn the car by rotating it. Example 12-24 shows the `IKeyboardInputHandler` interface for the controller.

Example 12-24. IKeyboardInputHandler.as

```
package
{
    import flash.events.*;

    public interface IKeyboardInputHandler
    {
        function keyPressHandler(event:KeyboardEvent):void
    }
}
```

The `RHController` class shown in Example 12-25 implements the `IKeyboardInputHandler` interface. It responds to keyboard events and decides how much the car should turn, based on left or right arrow key presses. This is a good example of a controller deciding in what ways and by how much it responds to user input. In this example, each left or right arrow press rotates the car 8 degrees clockwise or counterclockwise.

Example 12-25. RHController.as

```
package
{
    import flash.events.*;
    import flash.ui.*;

    public class RHController implements IKeyboardInputHandler
    {
        private var model:ICar;

        public function RHController(aModel:ICar)
        {
            this.model = aModel;
        }

        public function keyPressHandler(event:KeyboardEvent):void
        {
            switch (event.keyCode)
            {
                case Keyboard.LEFT :
                    model.addToRotationAngle(-8);
                    break;
                case Keyboard.RIGHT :
                    model.addToRotationAngle(8);
                    break;
```

Example 12-25. RHController.as (continued)

```
            }
        }
    }
}
```

The Views

We will implement two nested views: one for keyboard input and another that will draw and update the car on stage. The KeyboardInputView class shown in Example 12-26 is a composite view. It registers with the stage to receive key press events, and delegates to the controller to handle them.

Example 12-26. KeyboardInputView.as

```
package
{
    import flash.events.*;
    import flash.display.*;

    public class KeyboardInputView extends CompositeView
    {
        public function KeyboardInputView(aModel:ICar,
                                aController:IKeyboardInputHandler, target:Stage)
        {
            super(aModel, aController);
            target.addEventListener(KeyboardEvent.KEY_DOWN, onKeyPress);
        }

        protected function onKeyPress(event:KeyboardEvent):void
        {
            (controller as IKeyboardInputHandler).keyPressHandler(event);
        }
    }
}
```

The CarView class shown in Example 12-27 is a component view. It draws the car using its assigned color. In the update( ) method, it reads the current state of the car from the model and sets its location and rotation. The interesting aspect of this view is that its position changes. Views don't necessarily have to be classic user interface elements like buttons, image placeholders, etc. They can be any customized representation of model state.

Example 12-27. CarView.as

```
package {
    import flash.geom.*;
    import flash.events.*;

    public class CarView extends ComponentView {
```

Example 12-27. CarView.as (continued)

```
        public function CarView(aModel:ICar, aController:Object = null) {

            super(aModel, aController);

            // draw car body
            graphics.beginFill(model.getColor());
            graphics.drawRect(-20, -10, 40, 20);
            graphics.endFill();
            // draw tires
            drawTire(-12, -15);
            drawTire(12, -15);
            drawTire(-12, 15);
            drawTire(12, 15);

            // update car
            this.update();
        }

        private function drawTire(xLoc:int, yLoc:int) {
            graphics.beginFill(0x000000); // black color
            graphics.drawRect(xLoc - 4, yLoc - 2, 8, 4);
            graphics.endFill();
        }

        override public function update(event:Event = null):void {
            // get data from model and update view
            var ptLoc:Point = (model as ICar).getLoc();
            this.x = ptLoc.x;
            this.y = ptLoc.y;
            this.rotation = (model as ICar).getRotation();
        }
    }
}
```

Building the Car

As in our previous examples, building the MVC triad is straightforward. We develop a nested view for the car with the KeyboardInputView class object as the root node, with a CarView object added as a child. The client code shown in Example 12-28 will instantiate the MVC components and develop the nested view structure.

Example 12-28. Main.as (document class for car example)

```
1  package {
2
3      import flash.display.*;
4      import flash.events.*;
5      import flash.geom.*;
6
7      /**
8       *    Main Class
```

Example 12-28. Main.as (document class for car example) (continued)

```
9     *    @ purpose:          Document class for movie
10    */
11    public class Main extends Sprite {
12
13        public function Main( ) {
14
15            var carModel:ICar = new CarModel( );
16            carModel.setLoc(new Point(200,200));
17            carModel.setColor(0x0000FF); // blue
18
19            var carController:IKeyboardInputHandler = new RHController(carModel);
20
21            // keyboard input view (composite)
22            var kbInputView:CompositeView = new KeyboardInputView
23
24
25            // car view (component)
26            var car:ComponentView = new CarView(carModel);
27            kbInputView.add(car); // add car view to keyboard input
28
29            addChild(car);
30
31            // register keyboard input view to recieve
32
33            carModel.addEventListener(Event.CHANGE, kbInputView.update);
34
35        }
36    }
37 }
```

The car should now move on the stage and turn based on left- and right-arrow key presses. Note that there are no boundary checks for the car, and it can keep going right off the stage. We will now add some custom views to the car that show its direction and location on the stage.

Custom Views

To illustrate the ease by which custom views can be created and added to an MVC model, we will create two additional views. The first will be a circular gauge with a hand showing the current direction of motion for the car. The other view will show the position of the car relative to stage boundaries, somewhat like the display screen of a global positioning system (GPS).

Direction Gauge View

Example 12-29 shows the `DirectionGaugeView` class. This is a component view that shows the direction of motion of the car using a circular gauge with a hand like a clock. The gauge hand is a sprite whose rotation is set to the same value as the car rotation.

Example 12-29. DirectionGaugeView.as

```
package
{
    import flash.geom.*;
    import flash.events.*;
    import flash.display.*;

    public class DirectionGaugeView extends ComponentView
    {

        private var guageHand:Sprite;

        public function DirectionGaugeView(aModel:Object, aController:Object = null)
        {
            super(aModel, aController);

            // draw circle for guage
            graphics.lineStyle(2, (model as ICar).getColor( ));
            graphics.drawCircle(10, 10, 20);

            // draw guage hand as sprite
            guageHand = new Sprite( );
            guageHand.graphics.lineStyle(2, 0x000000);
            guageHand.graphics.moveTo(0,0);
            guageHand.graphics.lineTo(15,0);
            guageHand.x = guageHand.y = 10;
            this.addChild(guageHand);
        }

        override public function update(event:Event = null):void
        {
            this.guageHand.rotation = (model as ICar).getRotation( );
        }
    }
}
```

GPS View

The `GPSView` class shown in Example 12-30 draws a rectangle in proportion to the stage, and displays the location of the car relative to stage boundaries.

Example 12-30. GPSView.as

```
package
{
    import flash.geom.*;
    import flash.events.*;
    import flash.display.*;

    public class GPSView extends ComponentView
    {
        private var carPos:Sprite;
        private static const SF:Number = 0.15; // scale factor

        public function GPSView(aModel:ICar, target:Stage)
        {
            super(aModel);

            // draw rectangle in proportion to stage
            graphics.lineStyle(2, (model as ICar).getColor());
            graphics.drawRect(0, 0, target.stageWidth * SF, target.stageHeight * SF);

            // draw guage hand as sprite
            carPos = new Sprite();
            carPos.graphics.beginFill(0x000000); // black color
            carPos.graphics.drawRect(-2, -2, 5, 5);
            carPos.graphics.endFill();
            this.addChild(carPos);
        }

        override public function update(event:Event = null):void
        {
            var pt:Point = (model as ICar).getLoc();
            this.carPos.x = pt.x * SF;
            this.carPos.y = pt.y * SF;
        }
    }
}
```

Adding the Custom Views

Adding the custom views to the nested view structure is easy, without worrying about registering for update events. We can simply add the two composite views as child nodes to the root node of the view structure. The following code inserted at line 23 to Example 12-28 will accomplish this.

```
// direction gauge view (component)
var dash:ComponentView = new DirectionGaugeView(carModel);
kbInputView.add(dash); // add car view to keyboard input
                       // view as child component
dash.x = dash.y = 20;
addChild(dash);

// GPS view (component)
var gps:ComponentView = new GPSView(carModel, this.stage);
```

```
kbInputView.add(gps); // add gps view to keyboard input
                      // view as child component
gps.x = 10;
gps.y = 75;
addChild(gps);
```

Adding a Chase Car

How difficult would it be to add a chase car that chases the car controlled by the keyboard? The chase car will need to automatically steer itself to catch up with the user controlled car. We will use a simple chase algorithm for the chase car. If the lead car is to the left of the chaser, the chase car will turn slightly to the left. If the lead car is to the right, then the chase car will turn to the right.

The only additional element we need is a new controller. Example 12-31 shows the IChaseHandler interface that defines a chase algorithm based on timer events. It also declares a method to set the chase target, which is of type ICar.

Example 12-31. IChaseHandler.as

```
package
{
    import flash.events.*;

    public interface IChaseHandler
    {
        function chaseHandler(event:TimerEvent):void
        function setChaseTarget(car:ICar):void
    }
}
```

The ChaseController class shown in Example 12-32 implements the IChaseHandler interface. It sets a timer to call the chaseHander( ) listener method every 1/20 of a second to tell the model how much to change the rotation angle of the chase car. It's a good idea to set the timer to the same frequency as the movie frame rate. Another issue of note is the turn radius of the chase controller. It is half that of the user controlled car (see Example 12-25). The chase car can only turn 4 degrees at a time compared to 8 degrees for the user-controlled car. Therefore the user-controlled car should be able to evade the chaser by making some tight turns.

Example 12-32. ChaseController.as

```
package
{
    import flash.events.*;
    import flash.geom.*;
    import flash.utils.Timer;

    public class ChaseController implements IChaseHandler
    {
```

Example 12-32. ChaseController.as (continued)

```
    private var model:ICar;
    private var target:ICar;

    public function ChaseController(aModel:ICar)
    {
        this.model = aModel;

        // set timer to call chase controller every 1/20 second
        var timer:Timer = new Timer(1000 / 20);
        timer.addEventListener("timer", chaseHandler);
        timer.start();
    }

    public function chaseHandler(event:TimerEvent):void
    {
        var myLoc:Point = model.getLoc();
        var targetLoc:Point = target.getLoc();
        var myRotationAngle:Number = model.getRotation();
        var angleToTarget:Number = Math.atan2(targetLoc.y - myLoc.y,
                                targetLoc.x - myLoc.x) * 180 / Math.PI;

        if ((myRotationAngle % 360) < angleToTarget)
        {
            model.addToRotationAngle(4);
        } else {
            model.addToRotationAngle(-4);
        }
    }

    public function setChaseTarget(car:ICar):void
    {
        target = car;
    }
    }
}
```

The controller sets the chase algorithm; the utility of using the strategy pattern here should be clear. We can simply substitute another controller with a more sophisticated chase algorithm without requiring any changes to the other elements of the MVC pattern. The following code will add the chase car to the example.

```
// ** chase car **
var chaseCarModel:ICar = new CarModel();
chaseCarModel.setLoc(new Point(100,100));
chaseCarModel.setColor(0xFF0000); // red

var chaseCarController:IChaseHandler = new ChaseController(chaseCarModel);
chaseCarController.setChaseTarget(ICar(carModel));

// chase car view (component)
var chaseCarView:ComponentView = new

addChild(chaseCarView);
```

```
// register chase car to receive notifications from the model
chaseCarModel.addEventListener(Event.CHANGE, chaseCarView.update);
```

Note that the chase car consists of a new MVC triad separate from the lead car. It has its own model, views, and controllers. We reuse the same CarModel and CarView classes, but change the behavior of the chase car by swapping out the controller. Combining new or subclassed model, view, and controller components makes applications designed using the MVC pattern infinitely extensible.

Summary

The Model-View-Controller (MVC) pattern is commonly used to create software applications that contain user interfaces. The power of the MVC pattern can be attributed to the separation of responsibilities among the three elements that make up the pattern. The *Model* contains the application data and logic to manage the state of the application. The *View* presents the user interface and the state of the application onscreen. The *Controller* handles user input to change the state of the application.

The MVC pattern can integrate the observer, strategy, and composite patterns to manage the dependencies both within and between its elements. The relationship between the model and view is that of *concrete subject* and *concrete observer* in an observer pattern. The relationship between the view and controller is that of *context* and *concrete strategy* in a strategy pattern. Views in an MVC pattern can have multiple nested views. The relationship between nested views can be in the form of *components* and *composite* nodes in a composite pattern.

Most importantly, the MVC pattern provides a clear framework for design. The separation of responsibilities among the model, view, and controller elements allows easy substitution of elements without disruptions to the overall application. This lets us easily expand applications based on the MVC pattern to meet changing requirements.

CHAPTER 13

Symmetric Proxy Pattern

Now an allegory is but a translation of abstract notions into a picture-language, which is itself nothing but an abstraction from objects of the senses; the principal being more worthless even than its phantom proxy, both alike unsubstantial, and the former shapeless to boot. On the other hand, a symbol is characterized by a translucence of the special in the individual, or of the general in the special, or of the universal in the general; above all though the translucence of the eternal through and in the temporal. It always partakes of the reality which it renders intelligible; and while it enunciates the whole, abides itself as a living part in that unity of which it is the representative.

—Samuel Taylor Coleridge

There is no country in the world where machinery is so lovely as in America. It was not until I had seen the water-works at Chicago that I realised the wonders of machinery; the rise and fall of the steel rods, the Symmetric motion of the great wheels is the most beautiful rhythmic thing I have ever seen.

—Oscar Wilde

Computers that are commercially available are symmetric or non-handed but it is possible that some existing software and algorithms are left- or right-handed.

—Philip Emeagwali

Simultaneous Game Moves and Outcomes

One of the more interesting problems for programmers is dealing with interaction over the Internet. This is especially true in the case of games where the developer must work out how two or more players can interact in the context of a set of rules that describe the game. This process gets more challenging when the players are making simultaneous (parallel) moves, and both players won't know the outcome of a turn until both have completed their moves.

One such game is *Rock, Paper, Scissors* (RPS). In this game, two players simultaneously throw hand signals for a rock (fist), paper (a flat hand) or scissors (a horizontal V-sign with the index and middle fingers). Rock defeats scissors, scissors defeat paper, and paper defeats rock. (See *http://www.worldrps.com* for details). With such clear, simple, and universal rules, the game is an ideal way to discover design patterns that accommodate the role of parallel Internet interaction.

As a point of reference, the concept of the Symmetric Proxy design pattern grew out of a paper, a Pattern for Distributing Turn-Based Games, by James Heliotis and Axel Schreiner, both of Rochester Institute of Technology, and a presentation based on that paper at the 2006 OOPSLA conference in Portland, Oregon by Axel Schreiner.

 Just about any background work in design patterns will sooner or later lead you to OOPSLA. The acronym stands for Object-Oriented Programming, Systems, Languages & Applications. It's an annual conference that focuses on different OOP topics, mixing in both academic and practical materials. In 1991, the first part of the Design Pattern catalog was presented at an OOPSLA conference, and ever since, design patterns have played a role at OOPSLA conferences. The European sister conference is ECOOP (European Conference on Object-Oriented Programming).

What we developed for this book is based on both the paper and conference presentation, but the example for this book took on a life of its own, and we in no way hold Drs. Heliotis or Schreiner responsible for what has been developed here. In part, this is because we're using ActionScript 3.0 and Flash Media Server 2, and in part because we deviated from the specifics. Nevertheless, we've strived to keep the original concepts and reasoning intact. They deserve credit for what we did right, but we take responsibility for anything gone wrong.

The Player

At the very base of the idea of a symmetric proxy is the concept of a player interface containing methods for playing a game, *any* game, not just RPS, that can be conducted over the Internet. Our list is slightly different from that presented by Heliotis and Schreiner, but the core concepts are borrowed from their work.

- Make a move (makeMove). Each player needs a method for translating user input through a user interface (UI).

- Indicate that a local player has made a move (localMove). Once a move has been made, a game requires that the state (local player has moved) be recorded. It also prevents the same user from making another move until the next turn.

- Indicate that a remote player has made a move (onProxyMove). Records the move of the remote player, and prevents a further move by the remote player until the next turn.

- Send the local player move to the remote player (doMove). The move will be picked up by the opponent's onProxyMove method.

- Conclude the turn after both players have moved (takeTurn). Once both players have moved, the moves are turned over to the Referee to determine who's won and reset the values for the next turn.

- Prevents play until both players are connected (numConnect). This method has the dual function of letting players know of each other's presence, and prevents a move if only one player's present.

By first working out the basics of a move and a turn, we've laid the basis for turn-based games. The next step is putting the moves into a game context.

The Referee

In order to keep everything fair and fun, we need a referee. The class diagram for the referee in relationship to the player can be seen in Figure 13-1:

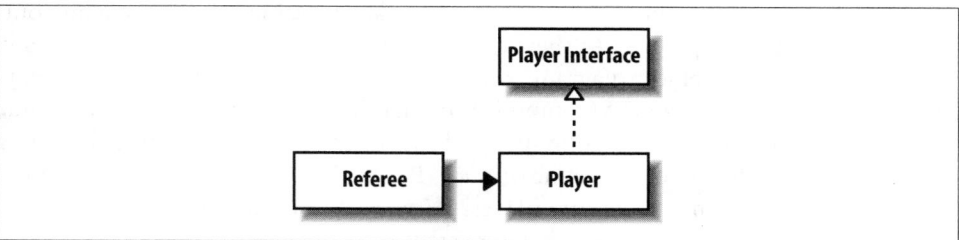

Figure 13-1. Referee and Player class diagram

Essentially, the referee will be a class containing the rules of the game encased in a template method. As a design pattern, the methods need to be fairly general, in case we want to reuse the same Referee class for another game. Using a template method, we can order the operations in the methods to launch in sequence, but we want flexibility for other games. So, we begin with a list of operations for the referee that applies to all games:

- Evaluate the moves and determine who won. All games need a set of winning conditions and the ability to determine which player won, which lost or whether they tied.

- Display the results of the game. Once the results have been calculated, they must be communicated to all players.

- Reset the game variables to the beginning conditions. Because the players have been keeping track of who has moved, which moves were selected, and which player was declared the winner, all the variables keeping track of these different states have to be cleared.

Each operation will be cast as a method and then arranged into an order that constitutes the template method. Following the Hollywood Principle (see Chapter 9), the Referee instance will make calls on the Player objects.

Now that we have a referee, we need to look at the relationship between the players and the referee. Figure 13-2 is an object diagram for a two-player game with a referee:

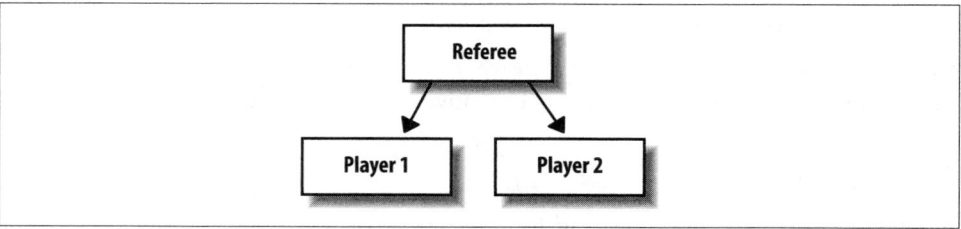

Figure 13-2. Referee and players

Just like a non-virtual game, the single referee makes decisions about the game outcome for two or more players. At this point, the game is immaterial—it could be any game. Looking at the object diagram, it's not difficult to imagine two or more players interacting on a single host (computer). In fact, if the goal were to create a game where one of the players is the computer and the other's a user interacting through a UI, our job would be done. In a game of *Rock, Paper, Scissors*, a random move generator could easily be one of the two players. However, because we want to play the game over the Internet, we have a few more steps.

The Internet, Proxies, and Players

As soon as we introduce remote players over the Internet, everything changes. Each player makes a move, that move is sent over the Internet, and the referee decides the outcome, displays it, and then cleans everything up. With serial turn taking, the problem may not be as daunting because after each move, both players can see the other's move. The referee can wait until the first win condition is met and then send messages to all players. However, this can get messy because you have to decide where the referee's going to reside. The referee could be placed on the host with the first player to start. The second player would be referenced through a proxy.

Another solution would be to place the referee on its own server, and, while workable, this requires that the moves travel over the Internet twice. Also, depending on the server, the basic game design may have to be changed to accommodate what the referee looks like.

Even though both of the solutions are workable, they may lack the flexibility and reusability desired in good design patterns. We need to look further.

The Symmetric Proxy Pattern

The Symmetric Proxy pattern is as much a discovery as an invention. Heliotis and Schreiner found that they could establish instances of two player objects arranged as peers over the Internet. Each side has both a proxy and a "real" player. Likewise, the referees on each side have the same information. Whatever move a player makes is treated the same by each of the referees. The referee object has no idea where a move comes from—it's clueless, as Heliotis and Schreiner note. All that the referee has to do is to call the players when the game is over and let them know the outcome. The referees are perfectly synchronized because they're reacting to the same state information, without caring whether the information is local or from a proxy; as a result, when the game-over conditions are met, both inform the players in exactly the same way, resetting all variables, and preparing for the next game.

Figure 13-3 shows the object diagram of the Symmetric Proxy Pattern:

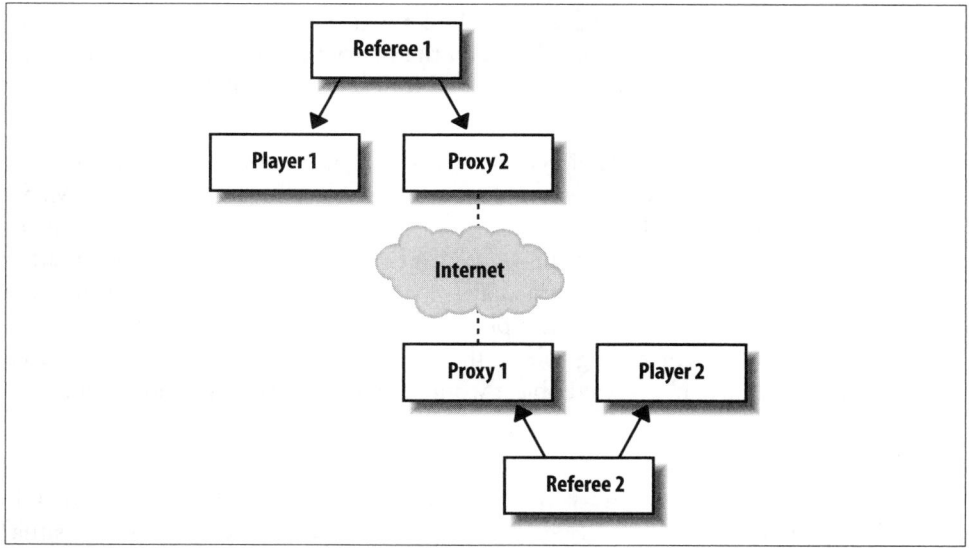

Figure 13-3. Symmetric Proxy object diagram

Keeping in mind that Figure 13-3 is an object diagram and not a class diagram, we can clearly see that the Symmetric Proxy pattern has each player's proxy in the opposition's camp, so to speak. The referees are treating each side of the Symmetric Proxy as a complete game. The referee simply takes the moves, evaluates them as being from one side or the other, and makes game decisions as though only a single host is in use. In other words, the proxies are treated as the computer playing the live player, or two live players taking turns on the same keyboard.

Key Features

Most of the key features of the Symmetric Proxy pattern have been described, but there are a few more. In this section we'll summarize:

- A player interface that includes move-taking, move display, and outcome methods
- A referee class based on a Template Method for determining game outcome
- Synchronizing cell between the UI and player
- Mirrored referee, proxy and player objects

Having discussed the player interface and referee concepts, we are left with two key elements to discuss before going on to look at key OOP concepts in this design pattern. First, we need to take a closer look at the synchronizing cell, and where the cell goes in the overall scheme of things. Second, we need to look more closely at the concept of a proxy object.

The cell

Heliotis and Schreiner refer to the cell in their design as a monitored single-element queue placed between the player object and the graphical elements. In most cases, the graphical elements would be the UI. In looking at the sequence diagram for parallel turn taking, the cells are placed between the proxy players, one for each player. For simultaneous turns, two cells are used; one for each player making a move at the same time.

Looking at the code used by Heliotis and Schreiner, an alternative implementation came to mind in the form of a remote shared object available through Flash Media Server 2 (FMS2). The shared object could act as the synchronizing mechanism, ensuring that both sides had the same information at the same time. As soon as either player entered a move, it would immediately be available to the proxy object as a move. The "cell" itself would be in the player in a function waiting for both sides to move. In effect, the synchronizing role of the cell has been taken over by the shared object. Setting the move in a shared object would fall to a FMS2 server-side script.

The proxy

Because using FMS2 takes care of the synchronizing problems and is immediately available to connected clients through a client-side method, we end up with a situation where we have to ask whether we really need a separate object for the proxies. Instead of creating four player objects, would it be possible to create two? Each player object, based on a common interface, would contain both the real player and the proxy player. This is an androgynous variation of the Symmetric Proxy design pattern, but conceptually, it's virtually identical. Figure 13-4 shows an object diagram of this variation.

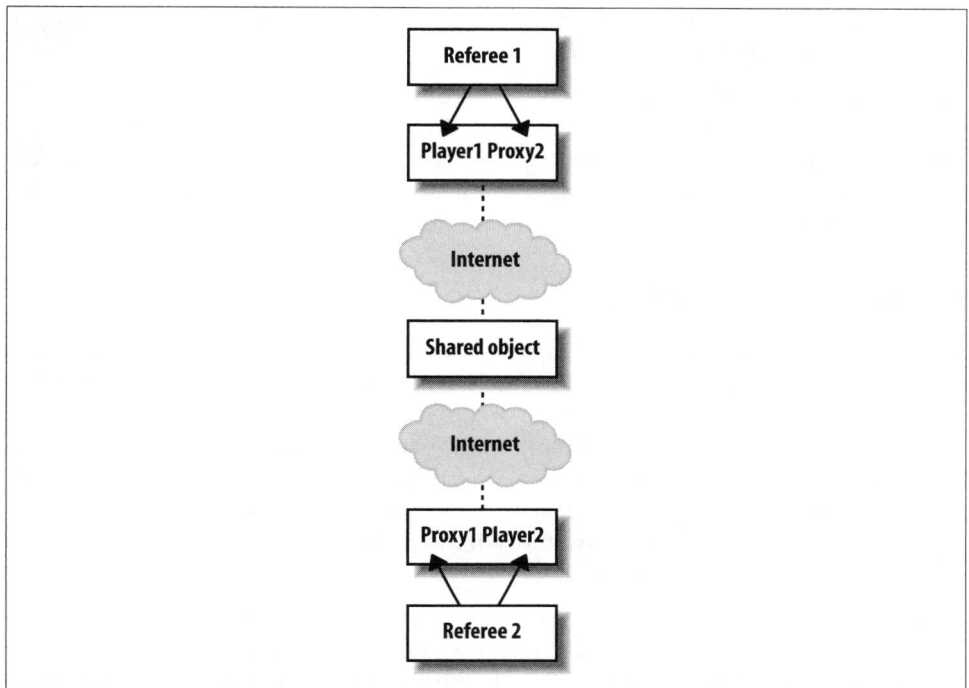

Figure 13-4. Androgynous variation of Symmetric Proxy

The only real difference between Figure 13-4 and Figure 13-3 is that the proxy and players are placed into single objects and the details of the Internet are spelled out a bit more in the latter. The same model could be used another way to send the proxy's move such as PHP, ColdFusion, or any other mechanism for sending information over the Internet. (Axel Schreiner commented that you could use smoke signals—the method of sending information over the network is immaterial.)

The one thing we don't particularly like about the androgynous variation on the Symmetric Proxy is the loss of granularity in the model. By placing the proxy move method in the same object as the real player, we collapse the real and proxy in a way that may not be easily adaptable to other games. At this point, though, no clear disadvantage is apparent. Both players are perfectly symmetrical, and the variation maintains the role of the referee.

Key OOP Concepts Used with the Symmetric Proxy

For a compound design, all the OOP concepts we have discussed for the different design patterns collected in a single compound design apply. So, to avoid repeating the same key concepts discussed in the chapters where the compounding elements were reviewed, we'd like to focus on a more general key OOP concept for the Symmetric Proxy design pattern—*flexibility*.

Because the Symmetric Proxy design focuses on interaction over the Internet, we need to look at two different kinds of flexibility. First, we need to look at communication flexibility. That is, can the model be used with different communication technologies over the Internet? Second, we must consider game flexibility. To what extent can different games be employed with the design?

Communication Flexibility

The first question to address is whether or not any trans-Internet communication can work with the Symmetric Proxy pattern. Because of its ease of use and built-in features like remote shared objects, using an application such as Flash Media Server 2 has a built-in disadvantage as a communication testing and development platform for a general communication design pattern. The server-side script automatically informs all players of the current game state in the form of one or both players having moved. Once both players have moved, the referee determines who has won and resets the game for another round.

In the original model of the Symmetric Proxy and the Androgynous variation, as long as the proxy player makes the same move as the original player, whether FMS, another open socket technology, or middleware such as PHP, C#, Perl, ColdFusion, or VB.NET, is not important. The move for the proxy is the only state that really needs to be sent over the Internet. The proxy plays the move, and the referee takes care of deciding whether the proxy or its player opponent wins, displaying the outcome and resetting the variables for a new game. So any communication system that can send the player's state to its proxy is acceptable, meeting the criteria of communication flexibility.

Game Flexibility

In the implementation you will see in this chapter, the referee's not quite as active as the one envisioned by Heliotis and Schreiner. The primary difference is that the referee only inspects the moves after both moves have been made in a game. Because each round in a game of *RPS* is a complete game, each game is over as soon as both players have moved. At this point, the referee kicks in with its template method, decides who won, displays the outcome, and resets the values to the start states.

One way of reducing the referee's work is in the UI. Players can only enter one of three different moves displayed on the buttons. The real player blocks any attempt to make any other move, such as one where the player has not made a move selection. In a more complex game with a wider selection of moves, either more responsibilities would be delegated to the referee or the UI would take care of allowing a wider but still limited move set.

With a single template method, and three methods that make up the template method within an abstract class, the Referee class has both flexibility and utility. In the example application in this chapter, the implementation of the Referee class subclasses RPS. The RPS class provides the specific details for the *RPS* game. The measure of flexibility is whether a different game could be subclassed from the Referee class to create a whole different game.

Of the three functions that make up the template method, flexibility is most important in the function that determines who won or if the play results in a tie. The following shows that function in the Referee class:

```
function doWinner(p1Move:String,p2Move:String):String
{
    return winner;
}
```

Because the method resides in an abstract class, we can expect it to be overridden for different games. It takes the move of players 1 and 2, having no idea whether the move is by the proxy or not, and returns a string with the winner or a tie result. Because it is abstract in a literal sense, it simply waits until one of the two moves results in a win or tie condition. With the *RPS* game, this is relatively easy because each round of moves is a complete game.

However, what about games like *Tic Tac Toe*? It's a game of several different rounds and a wider range of outcomes. Because the doWinner method includes parameters for both players, all moves can be calculated. Each move can be described in terms of the 3-by-3 matrix as C1R1 to C3R3 (Column#/Row#). Once either player has met the win conditions or the play has reached a point where neither can win (a draw), the entire template method can launch.

Alternatively, each move can be delegated to a Referee class, including a Referee subclass. This alternative is the original intention of Heliotis and Schreiner, and the flexibility of the Symmetric Proxy design allows either alternative. In games with more than two players, teams, or some other combination of individual players or teams, only a few changes in the doWinner method parameters could set it up for more complex alternatives.

The key to game flexibility in the Symmetric Proxy class lies in the ability to override the methods in the original template method in the Referee class. Creating multiplayer games beyond two players is quite easy as long as each has a "home" referee, immediately sends all moves to all players and/or referees, but does not have to make adjustments to the basic design pattern.

The Player Interface

The player interface is the starting point for creating a Symmetric Proxy design pattern. The player interface contains six methods. As with all interfaces, it contains the abstract methods and their parameters. Example 13-1 shows the ISymPlayer interface.

Example 13-1. ISymPlayer.as

```
package
{
    //Symetrical Proxy Interface
    import flash.events.Event;

    interface ISymPlayer
    {
        function numConnect(cl:uint):void;
        function makeMove(event:Event):void;
        function doMove(s:String):void;
        function localMove(locMove:String):void;
        function onProxyMove(proxMove:String):void;
        function takeTurn( ):void;
    }
}
```

At this point, we'll provide a quick overview of what each method does. In order to get a mental image of what occurs, the functions are placed in the approximate order of their launch, except for the last one, which is part of the housekeeping chore of making sure that two players are connected to FMS prior to any move by either side.

1. First, the numConnect( ) method checks to see how many clients are connected, and, if two are connected, it allows moves to be made by both players.

2. The players select a move by pressing one of the three possible move buttons (Rock, Paper, or Scissors). Once a player selects a move, he presses a move button that fires the makeMove( ) method.

3. The makeMove( ) function fires both the doMove( ) and localMove( ) methods.

4. The doMove( ) operation calls the server to pass on the move to its proxy.

5. The localMove( ) method first stores the move in a variable, and then sets a Boolean indicating the fact that the player has moved.

6. Next, the onProxyMove( ) function responds to the server call of a shared object and acts like the localMove( ) method, except it's on the player's proxy.

7. When either the localMove( ) or onProxyMove( ) indicates that both players have moved, the takeTurn( ) method acts to force a call from the Referee to determine the winner and reset the values for a new game.

Some variation in the implementation of these methods determines whether moves can be taken simultaneously or serially.

The Referee

Because the Referee class is abstract, it's relatively small. The methods are fairly general with the idea that they can be overridden; however, they must be purposely developed. Further, because they'll be placed in a template method, they have to be developed with an eye to the order in which they'll be placed. We'll begin with a look at the Referee class to get an overview and then look at the methods for the class. Example 13-2 shows the Referee class.

Example 13-2. Referee.as

```
package
{
    //Abstract Class
    public class Referee
    {
        //Move
        private var p1Move:String;//Player 1's move
        private var p2Move:String;//Player 2's move
        private var winner:String;//Value for winner
        private var outcome:String;//Describe winnder
        private var displayWindow:DynamicText;
        private var movecheck:Array;//Array to keep track of moves

        //Template Method
        final function moveComplete(p1Move:String,p2Move:String,
            displayWindow:DynamicText,movecheck:Array):void
        {
            outcome=doWinner(p1Move,p2Move);
            displayResults(displayWindow,outcome);
            resetGame(movecheck);
        }

        //Abstract methods

        protected function doWinner(p1Move:String,p2Move:String):String
        {
            return winner;
        }
        function displayResults(displayWindow:DynamicText,
            outcome:String):void
        {
            displayWindow.setMove(outcome);
        }
        protected function resetGame(movecheck:Array):void
        {
            for (var r:uint =0; r< movecheck.length; r++)
            {
                movecheck[r]=false;
            }
        }
    }
}
```

The comment at the top of the class indicating that the class is an abstract one is simply a comment. It stands as a reminder that ActionScript 3.0 has no real abstract classes, and we need to remind ourselves to use overrides where needed. Likewise, the comment line (//Abstract methods) indicating abstract methods is a similar reminder that the abstract methods are not real abstract methods, because they're not supported in ActionScript 3.0.

Methods

Of the three methods in the Referee class, the first needs to be very flexible because it will return the winner of the game. The real implementation of the method will lie in any subclass that describes a game. The doWinner method is most likely to be part of a subclass specifying the rules of the game.

```
function doWinner(p1Move:String,p2Move:String):String
{
    return winner;
}
```

It includes parameters for moves by both players. In the context of *RPS*, where the game has only a single move by each player, the moves represent the endgame conditions. In other games, though, the Referee may need to call for moves every round to accumulate information about win conditions.

The next method is designed to display outcomes, requesting both a reference to a text field and a string.

```
function displayResults(displayWindow:DynamicText,outcome:String):void
{
    displayWindow.setMove(outcome);
}
```

In the context of *RPS* and most games, this method has two different roles. On one hand, as part of the template method, it displays who has won. However, it can also be used to display information independent of the template method. Keeping in mind that moves in *RPS* are simultaneous, neither player can see the other player's move until both have made their moves. So this method can also be used to display other information such as the opponent's move any time it's appropriate to do so.

The third method in the Referee class is to reset all of the values to the start conditions—setting up the chess pieces in their original positions, so to speak. This method has a housekeeping character, but it's essential if you're going to play the game more than once without reloading it.

```
function resetGame(movecheck:Array):void
{
    for (var r:uint =0; r< movecheck.length; r++)
    {
        movecheck[r]=false;
    }
}
```

By keeping track of the moves in an array, resetting a game is made both easier and more flexible. With only two moves, the function could be written to reset two

Boolean variables to false. (The false state means that the move *has not* been made.) Because the method uses an array, it doesn't care how many moves have to be reset. It's far more flexible and reusable than using non-array variables.

Template Method

The final method is constructed from the three methods that currently exist in the Referee class. As a template method, it is locked using the final statement. As a reminder, the final statement disallows any overrides of the method; however, the methods *that make up* the template method can be overridden, and we generally expect that at least some methods in the template method will be.

```
final function moveComplete(p1Move,p2Move,displayWindow,movecheck):void
{
    outcome=doWinner(p1Move,p2Move);
    displayResults(displayWindow,outcome);
    resetGame(movecheck);
}
```

In this particular template method, the first method passes the game outcome, a String variable. This variable is then used as a parameter in the second method to display the outcome to a specified output object. Finally, the template method resets the game to the start state. Simplified, the template does the following:

1. Determines who won or if it's a tie, and places that information in a variable.
2. Displays the game outcome.
3. Resets the game to play again.

By invoking the Referee, all the information is neatly packaged and ready to resolve the game outcome, display the results, and reset the game.

RPS Subclass

The Referee class is set up to be subclassed and its methods overridden so that developers can reuse the design pattern for more than a single type of game. Example 13-3 shows the Referee subclass, RPS, designed to determine the outcome of a *Rock, Paper, Scissors* game.

Example 13-3. RPS.as

```
package
{
    //Rock, Paper, Scissors
    public class RPS extends Referee
    {
        private var winner:uint;
        private var gameOver:Array;
        private var winNow:String;
        //
```

Example 13-3. RPS.as (continued)

```
override protected function doWinner(p1Move:String,
    p2Move:String):String
{
    if (p1Move=="rock")
    {
        switch (p2Move)
        {
            case "rock" :
                winner=2;
                break;

            case "paper" :
                winner=1;
                break;

            default :
                winner=0;
        }
    }
    else if (p1Move=="paper")
    {
        switch (p2Move)
        {
            case "rock" :
                winner=0;
                break;

            case "paper" :
                winner=2;
                break;

            default :
                winner=1;
        }
    }
    else
    {
        switch (p2Move)
        {
            case "rock" :
                winner=1;
                break;

            case "paper" :
                winner=0;
                break;

            default :
                winner=2;
        }
    }
```

Example 13-3. RPS.as (continued)

```
            gameOver=new Array("p1 Wins!","p2 Wins!","Tie!");
            winNow=gameOver[winner];
            return winNow;
        }
    }
}
```

The RPS class overrides the doWinner method developed in the Referee class. The other two methods in the Referee class are usable without any changes. A single algorithm determines which side has won or if a tie occurred, and then transfers the information into an array element that is then stored in a String variable and returned.

> If you're wondering whether it would be easier simply to make the winner variable a string and return it, you're absolutely right. However, we liked the idea of being able to have a single array in one place where you could add your own "smack" or "trash talk" to be displayed. So instead of simply displaying, "p1 Wins!" you could have something like, "The Mighty Player 1 Conquers All!" Of course you can be more creative than that.

When employing the RPS class, we will observe the dictum to program to the interface and not the implementation. So, in typing any instance where we would use the *RPS* class, we will type it as Referee and instantiate it as RPS. (Look for this instantiation of the RPS class in the SymPlayer1 and SymPlayer2 classes.)

Information Shared Over the Internet

At this point we need to take a little detour to discuss the techniques we used to send data over the Internet for proxy work. As noted earlier in this chapter, we have chosen to use Flash Media Server 2 to pass the move information from a player to its proxy over the Internet. In order to see the relationships involved, we will show the purely FMS2 server-side script and those portions of the player/proxy class that use it.

To begin, Example 13-4 shows the *proxygame.asc* file (all lowercase). It is written in ActionScript 1.0 because, at the time of this writing, all the code written for the server-side could only be written in Server Side Communication ActionScript (SSCA). The client-side counterpart is all ActionScript 3.0. This file sits in the server-side location of the FMS2 host server. Generally, the host for the SWF files containing the compiled application and the server-side *.asc* file are on the same host, but not always. The connection to the server is through an RTMP protocol that's part of the client-side script.

Example 13-4. proxygame.asc

```
application.onAppStart=function( )
{
    trace(this.name + " is reloaded");
    this.ss_so = SharedObject.get("proxmove",false);
    this.dup1=false;
    this.dup2=false;
};
//-----------------------
application.onConnect=function(currentClient,username)
{

    currentClient.name=username;
    if(currentClient.moveNow==null)
    {
        currentClient.moveNow="ready";
    }

    var cl=application.clients.length;

    //Check username and see if there are no
        duplications or more than two players
    if(((username == "player1" && !this.dup1) || (
        username == "player2" && !this.dup2)) && cl<=1)
    {
     this.acceptConnection(currentClient);
     this.ss_so.setProperty(currentClient.name,username);
        if(username=="player1")
        {
            this.dup1=true;
        }
        else
        {
            this.dup2=true;
        }

    }
    else
    {
     this.rejectConnection(currentClient);
     trace("Connection rejected");
    }

    currentClient.makeMove=function(moveit)
    {
        application.ss_so.setProperty(currentClient.moveNow,moveit)
        someMove=application.ss_so.getProperty(currentClient.moveNow);
        playerNow=application.ss_so.getProperty(currentClient.name);
        someMove+="~"+playerNow;
        application.ss_so.send("onProxyMove",someMove);
    };

    currentClient.checkPlayNum=function( )
```

Example 13-4. proxygame.asc (continued)

```
    {
        var c2=application.clients.length;
        application.ss_so.send("numConnect",c2);
    }
};

//-----------------------
application.onDisconnect = function(currentClient)
{
    dupeName=currentClient.name;
    if(dupeName=="player1")
        {
            this.dup1=false;
        }
        else
        {
            this.dup2=false;
        }
    trace("disconnect: "+currentClient.name);
    this.ss_so.setProperty(currentClient.name,null);
    c2=application.clients.length;
    application.ss_so.send("numConnect",c2);
};
```

The program is broken down into three main parts. The first part launches only when the application first starts (application.onAppStart). Either player can initially launch the server-side script, and, once launched, it won't launch again until both players have quit the application, and it's not launched again until about 20 minutes after the last player has quit.

 You may be wondering if the comment about ActionScript being version 1.0 when everything else in this book is written in ActionScript 3.0 is a typographical error. No, there's no typo. The subset of Action-Script build for FMS2 changed little from the original Server Side Communication ActionScript (SSCA) released with Flash Communication Server (FCS). When FMS2 was released, ActionScript 2.0 was part of the Flash package, but couldn't be used for server-side coding. So, while SSCA is slightly different from standard ActionScript in any format, it's also a different version.

The second part of the script launches during the time the application is being used by either player beginning with the attempt to connect to the application (application.onConnect). It generates a default value ("ready") for the moveNow variable, and checks to see if the correct names are used, and the number of players connected. The function to assign a move to the shared object (currentClient. makeMove) serves to record both the move and which player made the move. A string separated by a tilde (~) character is then sent to all players (application.ss_so. send). The tilde is used to identify the line of demarcation between the player and the player's move. The client-side script checks which player is making the move and assigns the move to the proxy player. The rest of the connection function deals with housekeeping.

The third part (application.onDisconnect) takes care of further housekeeping by resetting the Boolean variables. It also lets the player know the number of players currently connected. When working with applications over the Internet, letting remotely connected players know whether anyone's connected is an essential ingredient.

Player-Proxy Classes

The main implementation of the ISymPlayer is in two classes, each representing one of two players. The classes are virtually identical except for identifying themselves as either "player1" or "player2" to the media server. Also, each contains a proxy for its opponent, giving it the androgynous character described previously in this chapter.

Example 13-5 shows the script for the entire class. It can be broken down into six parts:

1. Imports the necessary name spaces and classes.
2. Establishes variables required for the different methods.
3. Contains the Constructor function. This includes all the necessary connection statements, calls to the text field and button functions, and event listeners for the four buttons.
4. Implements the six methods from the interface in the order in which they appear in the interface. This is the core of the class.
5. Checks to see if connection has been made and if so, turns on the connection light and sets up the client-side shared object. Also, this function establishes the shared object and connects the shared object through the NetConnection instance (nc). Finally, it calls the server-side script function checkPlayNum( ). This call is a "bounce" in that it triggers the server-side function that sends the number of connected users right back to the client-side function numConnect( ). ·
6. Sets up the text fields and buttons.

By placing Example 13-4 and Example 13-5 side by side, you can better see the interaction between the client-side class and the server-side application. (The .asc files are not actually classes, but they have much in common with a class.) Wherever you see nc. call("functionName",p1,p2) in the SymPlayer1 class, it's a reference to a function in the server-side script. Likewise, in the server-side script, any application.ss_so. send("functionName",p1) is a reference to a function in the SymPlayer1 or SymPlayer2 classes.

Example 13-5. SymPlayer1.as

```
package
{
    //Symmetric Player 1/Proxy 2

    import flash.net.NetConnection;
    import flash.net.ObjectEncoding;
    import flash.display.Sprite;
    import flash.display.MovieClip;
    import flash.events.Event;
    import flash.events.NetStatusEvent;
    import flash.net.SharedObject;
    import flash.events.MouseEvent;

    public class SymPlayer1 extends Sprite implements ISymPlayer
    {
        private var nc:NetConnection;
        private var rtmpNow:String;
        private var playerNow:String;
        private var cs_so:SharedObject;
        private var playerText:DynamicText;
        private var showText:DynamicText;
        private var oppText:DynamicText;
        private var moveText:DynamicText;
        private var rockBtn:MoveButton;
        private var paperBtn:MoveButton;
        private var scissorsBtn:MoveButton;
        private var moveBtn:MoveButton;
        private var connect:Connect;
        private var moveVal:String;
        private var p1move:String="ready";
        private var p2move:String="ready";
        private var rps:Referee;
        private var winner:uint;
        private var monitor:Array=new Array(false,false,false);
        private var cl:uint;
        private var mcheck:Boolean=false;
        private var connected:String;

        public function SymPlayer1()
        {
            NetConnection.defaultObjectEncoding =
                flash.net.ObjectEncoding.AMF0;
            SharedObject.defaultObjectEncoding =
                flash.net.ObjectEncoding.AMF0;
            setDynamic();
            setButton();
            rockBtn.addEventListener(MouseEvent.CLICK, makeMove);
            paperBtn.addEventListener(MouseEvent.CLICK, makeMove);
            scissorsBtn.addEventListener(MouseEvent.CLICK, makeMove);
            moveBtn.addEventListener(MouseEvent.CLICK, makeMove);
            //rtmpNow="rtmp://192.168.0.11/proxygame/";
            rtmpNow="rtmp://mojo.iit.hartford.edu/proxygame/";
```

Example 13-5. SymPlayer1.as (continued)

```
        //rtmpNow="rtmp:/proxygame/";
        nc = new NetConnection();
        nc.connect(rtmpNow,"player1");
        nc.addEventListener(NetStatusEvent.NET_STATUS,
            checkHookupStatus);
    }
    //
    //makeMove Make Move
    //
    public function makeMove(event:Event):void
    {
        moveVal=event.currentTarget.name;
        if (!monitor[0] && mcheck)
        {
            switch (moveVal)
            {
                case "scissors" :
                    showText.setMove("scissors");
                    moveText.setMove("scissors");
                    break;

                case "rock" :
                    showText.setMove("rock");
                    moveText.setMove("rock");
                    break;

                case "paper" :
                    showText.setMove("paper");
                    moveText.setMove("paper");
                    break;

                case "move" :
                    var m:String=showText.getMove();
                    if (m != "ready" && m != "Error!")
                    {
                        //Proxy 1 move
                        doMove(m);
                        //Player 1 move
                        localMove(m);
                    }
                    else
                    {
                        showText.setMove("Error!");
                    }
            }
        }
    }
    //
    //localMove Player Move
    //
    public function localMove(locMove:String):void
    {
```

Example 13-5. SymPlayer1.as (continued)

```
        playerText.setMove("player1");
        if (!monitor[0])
        {
            p1move=locMove;
            monitor[0]=true;
        }
        //Check to see if both have moved
        monitor[2]=(monitor[0] && monitor[1]);
        if (monitor[2])
        {
            takeTurn( );
        }
    }
    //
    //onProxyMove: Info from server
    //
    public function onProxyMove(proxMove:String):void
    {
        playerNow=proxMove.substring(proxMove.indexOf("~")+1);
        proxMove=proxMove.substring(0, proxMove.indexOf("~"));
        if (playerNow=="player2" && !monitor[1])
        {
            playerText.setMove(playerNow);
            p2move=proxMove;
            monitor[1]=true;
        }
        //Check to see if both have moved
        monitor[2]=(monitor[0] && monitor[1]);
        if (monitor[2])
        {
            takeTurn( );
        }
    }
    //
    //doMove: Call server
    //
    public function doMove(m:String):void
    {
        nc.call("makeMove",null,m);
    }
    //
    //takeTurn Complete the turn
    //
    public function takeTurn( ):void
    {
        rps=new RPS( );
        rps.moveComplete(p1move,p2move,playerText,monitor);
        rps.displayResults(oppText,p2move);
        showText.setMove("ready");
    }
    //Get number connected
    public function numConnect(cl:uint):void
```

Example 13-5. SymPlayer1.as (continued)

```
        {
            if (cl==2)
            {
                mcheck=true;
            }
            else
            {
                mcheck=false;
            }
            connected=String(cl+ " connected");
            playerText.setMove(connected);
        }
        //
        //Connect Check and Set Up Shared Objects
        //
        public function checkHookupStatus(event:NetStatusEvent):void
        {
            if (event.info.code == "NetConnection.Connect.Success")
            {
                connect.gotoAndStop(2);
                cs_so=SharedObject.getRemote("proxmove",nc.uri,false);
                cs_so.client=this;
                cs_so.connect(nc);
                nc.call("checkPlayNum",null,null);
            }
        }
        //Text
        public function setDynamic( ):void
        {
            playerText=new DynamicText( );
            addChild(playerText);
            playerText.x=180;
            playerText.y=50;

            showText=new DynamicText( );
            addChild(showText);
            showText.x=260;
            showText.y=50;
            showText.setMove("ready");

            moveText=new DynamicText( );
            addChild(moveText);
            moveText.x=180;
            moveText.y=140;

            oppText=new DynamicText( );
            addChild(oppText);
            oppText.x=100;
            oppText.y=140;
            oppText.setMove("opponent");
        }
        //Button
```

Example 13-5. SymPlayer1.as (continued)

```
    public function setButton():void
    {
        moveBtn=new MoveButton("Make Move",0xcccccc);
        moveBtn.name="move";
        addChild(moveBtn);
        moveBtn.x=100;
        moveBtn.y=50;

        rockBtn=new MoveButton("Rock",0xcccccc);
        rockBtn.name="rock";
        addChild(rockBtn);
        rockBtn.x=100;
        rockBtn.y=80;

        paperBtn=new MoveButton("Paper",0xcccccc);
        paperBtn.name="paper";
        addChild(paperBtn);
        paperBtn.x=150;
        paperBtn.y=80;

        scissorsBtn=new MoveButton("Scissors",0xcccccc);
        scissorsBtn.name="scissors";
        addChild(scissorsBtn);
        scissorsBtn.x=200;
        scissorsBtn.y=80;

        connect=new Connect();
        addChild(connect);
        connect.x=175;
        connect.y=250;
    }
  }
}
```

All the text fields and buttons are user classes and they need to be built prior to testing the class. In the section "Supporting Classes and Document Files" later in the chapter, you will find the necessary classes for including the buttons and dynamic text fields.

Move Making

While the player class may seem fairly long and unwieldy, its key elements are quite simple. Everything is focused on making one of three moves—rock, paper, or scissors. Each move is nothing more than a string.

Event to move

The first step is encapsulated in the makeMove() function that's launched by a button event. Using the name of the button (not the label), an algorithm finds which of the three moves has been selected, or if the Move button is clicked. To simplify matters, all name properties are lowercase while the label properties begin with an uppercase letter. (e.g., Rock=label, rock=name). The Move button is included to let the user change her mind after selecting one of the three moves. By clicking the Move button, the player commits to the selected move by launching two methods, doMove( ) and localMove( ).

Dual moves

The function to actually make a move once its been selected by clicking the Move button sends the move to the proxy using doMove( ), and stores it locally in a variable with localMove( ). This is the heart of the Symmetric Proxy. The symmetry lies in the fact that all moves are sent to both the local and proxy players.

The local move checks to be sure that the local player has not moved yet, and then checks to see if the other side has moved. If the other side has moved, then the information about the moves is turned over to the Referee to determine and display the outcome.

Now the doMove( ) is really nothing more than a call to the server-side script. It passes the move to the server and does no more.

Proxy move

The onProxyMove( ) method is the mirror image of the localMove( ). Because the method is fired no matter which player moves, the algorithm in the method first filters out the local move by splitting the string returned from the server into a move and a player name. It looks at the player name, and if it's the local's name, it ignores it and the move associated with it. (The move is handled by the localMove( ) method.) However, once the filtering has been completed, the algorithm is essentially the same as the local move operation. It *does* display the fact that the opponent has moved by displaying the name of the player but *not* the move. In this way, the application maintains the simultaneous nature of the play.

Referee object

The end game conditions are delegated to the Referee object. In this case, the Referee object is the RPS subclass contained within the takeTurn( ) method. By passing the moves, output text field, and name of the array used to keep track of who took a turn to the RPS object's moveComplete( ) template method, everything can be neatly wrapped up. The single line,

```
rps.moveComplete(p1move,p2move,playerText,monitor);
```

takes advantage of the template method in the Referee class and launches the operations that make up the template method—doWinner( ), displayResults( ), and resetGame( ).

In addition to using the Referee to show the winner and tidy ready the game for a new round, one of the methods, displayResults( ), is used to show each player the other's move. So, in addition to the using the template method, it uses one of the methods that make up the template method separately.

Player 2 Changes

The second player class also implements the ISymPlayer interface, but it's slightly different, and a few parameter values have changed. All you need to do is make a few changes in SymPlayer1. Begin by saving the SymPlayer1.as file as SymPlayer2.as, and then make the changes in bold in the following segments:

```
    public class SymPlayer2 extends Sprite implements ISymPlayer
....
    public function SymPlayer2( )
....
        //
        //makeMove: Make Move
        //
        public function makeMove(event:Event):void
        ....
            moveVal=event.currentTarget.name;
            if (!monitor[1] && mcheck)
            ....
                    var m:String=showText.getMove( );
                    if (m != "ready" && m != "Error!")
                    {
                        //Proxy 2 move
                        doMove(m);
                        //Player 2 move
                        localMove(m);
                    }
                    ....

        //
        //localMove Player Move
        //
        public function localMove(locMove:String):void
        {
            playerText.setMove("player2");
            if (!monitor[1])
            {
                p2move=locMove;
                monitor[1]=true;
            }
        }
....
        //
        //onProxyMove: Info from server
        //
        public function onProxyMove(proxMove:String):void
        {
            playerNow=proxMove.substring(proxMove.indexOf("~")+1);
```

```
                    proxMove=proxMove.substring(0, proxMove.indexOf("~"));
                    if (playerNow=="player1" && !monitor[0])
                    {
                        playerText.setMove(playerNow);
                        p1move=proxMove;
                        monitor[0]=true;
      ....
    public function takeTurn( ):void
            {
                rps=new RPS( );
                rps.moveComplete(p1move,p2move,playerText,monitor);
                rps.displayResults(oppText,p2move);
                showText.setMove("ready");
            }
      ....
```

Simply change a few 1s to 2s and some 0s to 1s in the key methods in the SymPlayer1 class, and you're good to go.

Classes and Document Files Support

As big as the two player class implementations are, they would be much bigger if not for the work done by the supporting classes that create the buttons and dynamic text fields.

Dynamic Output Text Fields

Because all the data input is done with button entries, the text fields for displaying data is all typed as DYNAMIC. Example 13-6 shows the class for the text fields.

Example 13-6. DynamicText.as

```
package
{
    import flash.text.TextField;
    import flash.text.TextFieldType;
    import flash.text.TextFormat;
    import flash.display.Sprite;

    public class DynamicText extends Sprite
    {
        private var gameInfo:TextField;
        private var gameFormat:TextFormat;

        public function DynamicText( ):void
        {
            gameInfo=new TextField( );
            addChild(gameInfo);
            gameInfo.border=false;
            gameInfo.background=true;
            gameInfo.type=TextFieldType.DYNAMIC;
```

Example 13-6. DynamicText.as (continued)

```
                gameInfo.width=70;
                gameInfo.height=20;
                gameFormat=new TextFormat( );
                gameFormat.color=0xcc0000;
                gameFormat.font="Verdana";
                gameFormat.size=10;
                gameInfo.defaultTextFormat=gameFormat;
        }
        public function setMove(pMove:String)
        {
                gameInfo.text=pMove;
        }
        public function getMove( ):String
        {
                return gameInfo.text;
        }
    }
}
```

The getter/setter functions make it far easier to access and display the available moves. At the same time, the text fields act as temporary storage of values that can be placed into variables or parameters.

Button Controls

The class for buttons is made up of Sprite, TextField and TextFieldType classes. Example 13-7 shows the script for the class.

Example 13-7. MoveButton.as

```
package
{
    import flash.text.TextField;
    import flash.text.TextFieldType;
    import flash.display.Sprite;

    public class MoveButton extends Sprite
    {
        private var mvBtn:Sprite;
        private var id:String;

        public function MoveButton(mover:String,btncolor:int)
        {
            mvBtn=new Sprite( );
            this.id=id;
            addChild(mvBtn);
            mvBtn.buttonMode=true;
            mvBtn.useHandCursor=true;
            mvBtn.graphics.beginFill(btncolor);
            mvBtn.graphics.drawRoundRect(0,0,(mover.length*8),20,5,5);
            var mvLbl:TextField=new TextField( );
```

Example 13-7. MoveButton.as (continued)

```
        mvBtn.addChild(mvLbl);
        mvLbl.text=mover;
        mvLbl.selectable=false;
    }
  }
}
```

The combined sprite and text provide a bit more information than just using a SimpleButton class would. Because we wanted the information in the text to be the information sent as moves, and the interactive aspects to be displayed in the dynamic text field rather than changes in the button's appearance, the choice was not a difficult one. Also, we experimented with different colors for the buttons, decided to let the designer pass his own color scheme, and so included a color parameter (btncolor).

The Flash File and Connection Movie Clip

The final aspects of the application include static text placed directly on the stage and a movie clip created to serve as a connection light. Figure 13-5 shows the static text placement in the right portion on the stage, and what the application looks like when running on the left.

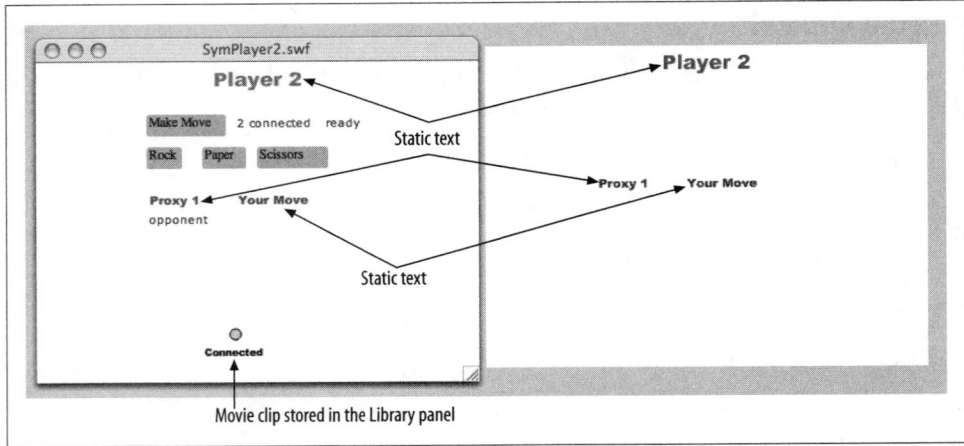

Figure 13-5. Stage and SWF file views

The following steps show how to create the last part of the application:

1. Open a new Flash File (ActionScript 3.0). Add a layer. Name the top layer "Connect" and the bottom layer "Text."

2. In the Document class window, type in **SymPlayer1**. Then save the file as *SymPlayer1.fla*.

3. Click the Text layer to select it. Using the Text Tool, select Static Text, and set the font to Arial Black, size to18 points and color #666666. Type in **Player 1** and position it at X=158, Y=1.

4. Still using the Text Tool, change the size to 11, and first type in **Proxy 2** and position it at X=100, Y=120. Then type in **Your Move** and position it at X=180, Y=120. Lock the Text layer.

5. Click on the Connect layer to select it. Using the Oval Tool, select a red fill color and black stroke color. Set the stroke width to .25. Draw a W=10, H=10 circle.

6. Select the circle and press the F8 key to open the Convert to Symbol dialog box. In the Name window, type in **Connect**, and select Movie clip as the Type. If you see the Advanced button, click it to open the Linkage and Source views. Click the Export for ActionScript Linkage checkbox. You should now see "Connect" in the Class window and flash.display.MovieClip in the Base class window. Click OK.

7. Click in Frame 1 and open the Actions panel (Press F9 Windows, Option + F9 Macintosh). Type in **stop( )** in the Actions panel. Close the Actions panel.

8. Click Frame 2 and press F6 to add a second keyframe. Change the fill color in the second frame from red to green. Click the Scene1 icon to exit the Symbol edit mode.

9. You should see the movie clip on the stage. Delete it from the stage. Open your Library panel (Window → Library from the menu bar or Ctrl+L Windows or Command+L Macintosh). You should see the movie clip with the name Connect in the Library. Be sure that it's spelled exactly that way, with an uppercase "C." This is the class name you use in your SymPlayer1 and SymPlayer2 classes.

10. Select File → Publish to generate SWF and HTML files.

This application is designed to have two different players accessed from two different Flash files. To create the second file, use the following steps.

1. Open *SymPlayer1.fla*, and, using File → Save As, save the file as *SymPlayer2.fla*.

2. Change the Document class to *SymPlayer2*.

3. Change the static text from "Player 1" to "Player 2," and "Proxy 2" to "Proxy 1." Save the file.

4. Select File → Publish to generate SWF and HTML files.

That's it. Place both HTML and SWF files on a web server, one player selects Player 1 and the other Player 2, and you're good to go. You might want to set up a little HTML file that allows the user to choose either Player 1 or Player 2, and then links to the players through the HTML file. If one is in use, indicated by a red connect button, then the user can just switch back and use the other.

Summary

The Symmetrical Proxy design pattern represents the kinds of experiments with design patterns envisioned by Gamma and his associates when they wrote *Design Patterns: Elements of Reusable Object-Oriented Software*. James Heliotis and Axel Schreiner's key insight is that two sides of a game over the Internet can be played on a client using symmetrical referees and each side pitting a local player against the proxy of an opponent. This is not an isolated solution to any single game, but rather any games played over a network.

Our particular implementation of the design pattern used Flash Media Server 2 to send the moves of each side to the other, and it's doubtful whether Heliotis or Schreiner had a clue about FMS2. Therein lies the strength of the design pattern. Design patterns should represent general solutions to problems and not specific implementations of a solution. Because of the flexibility of the Symmetrical Proxy pattern, we were able to apply it using the Internet communication program of our choosing, rather than one specified by the original designers.

By building in a proxy method into the interface and its implementations in the two players, we were able to make changes to the general design that did not violate its flexibility. This "androgynous" feature may have reduced the granularity of the design and slightly enlarged the size of the main classes, but it remained within both the structure and the spirit of the design pattern. Design patterns are general solutions, and as long as the patterns meet the key criteria of flexibility and reusability while maintaining good OOP practices, they can be implemented in an unlimited number of ways.

Index

We'd like to hear your suggestions for improving our indexes. Send email to *index@oreilly.com*.

About the Authors

Dr. William B. Sanders is a Professor of Multimedia Web Design and Development at the University of Hartford. He teaches courses in Flash, ActionScript, Flash Media Server, PHP, C#, SQL, and XHTML, among other Internet languages. He has published 44 computer and computer-related books, written software ranging from Basic to Flash Media Server ActionScript and served as a consultant for different computer software companies.

Dr. Chadima Cumaranatunge is an Assistant Professor of Multimedia Web Design and Development at the University of Hartford. He teaches an introduction to the IIT major, covering Flash and some ActionScript, a gaming course using Flash and ActionScript, as well as educational technology courses in the Education, Nursing, and Health Professions Colleges. He recently received a grant to teach an experimental course in robotics.

Colophon

The animal on the cover of *ActionScript Design Patterns 3.0* is a rosy feather starfish (*Antedon bifida*). This unique sea creature grips the ocean floor with strong claw-like protuberances and uses five pairs of feathery arms to move around and trap food. They vary in color and can be red, pink, orange or yellow, and are sometimes mottled or banded. They are found at all depths, and often congregate in large numbers.

The cover image is from *Cassell's Natural History*. The cover font is Adobe ITC Garamond. The text font is Linotype Birka; the heading font is Adobe Myriad Condensed; and the code font is LucasFont's TheSans Mono Condensed.

Better than e-books

Buy *ActionScript 3.0 Design Patterns,* and access
the digital edition FREE on Safari for 45 days.

Go to www.oreilly.com/go/safarienabled
and type in coupon code ARVTIVH

Search
thousands of
top tech books

Download
whole chapters

Cut and Paste
code examples

Find
answers fast

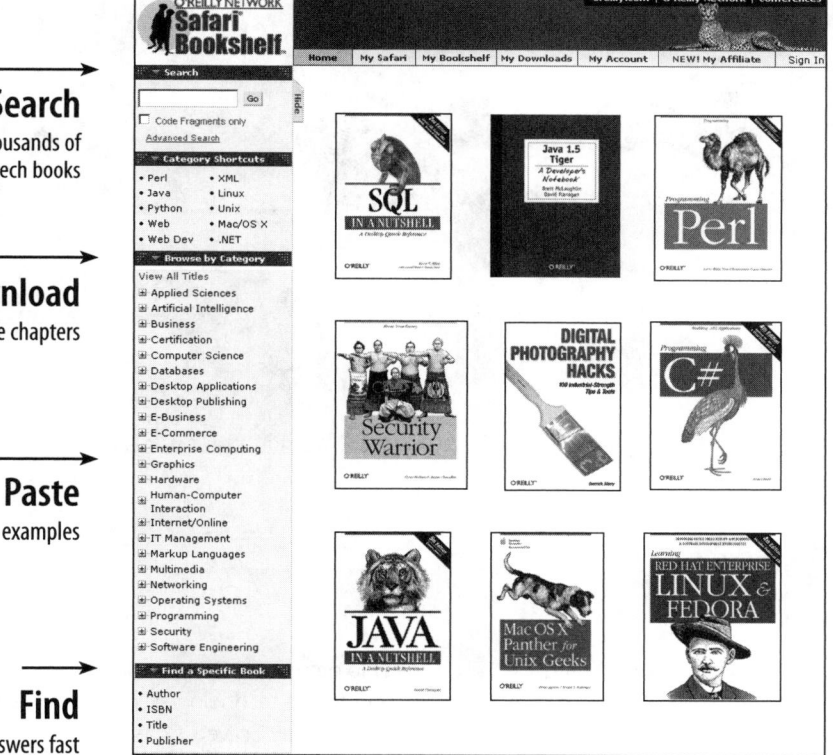

Search Safari! The premier electronic reference
library for programmers and IT professionals.

The Authoritative Resource